From Chattel Slaves
to Wage Slaves

This is a rare pictorial representation by a worker of the labour extraction process. It is a wood-cut copied from an original caricature by a Chinese immigrant in British Guiana presented to John Edward Jenkins who attended the 1870 Commission on the Treatment of Immigrants. Jenkins' explanation is that to the left a free Coolie drives his cattle, to the bottom right a rural constable seizes a Chinese immigrant attempting to flee the work gang to convey him to the lock up. The house is a manager's house and at the foot of the steps the Chinese to the right and the Indians to the left with their arms bound represent an emblem of indentureship. A Chinaman and a Coolie stand on either side of the steps: 'from whose breasts two drivers are drawing blood with a knife, the life fluid being caught by boys in the swizzle glasses of the colony. A boy is carrying the glasses up the steps to the attorney and the manager, who sit on the left of the verandah, and who are obviously fattening at the expense of the bound people below them. A fat wife and children look out through the windows. Behind through a break in the wall are represented the happy and healthy owners in England; to the right under the tree, through a gap in the fence, are aged Chinese, weeping over their unfortunate relatives. In the right hand corner is the pay table with the overseers discussing and arranging stoppages of wages. The smoking chimney and the horse eating his provender seem to be intended to contrast with the scene in front' – *The Coolie, his Rights and Wrongs*, John Edward Jenkins (London, 1871), pp. 10, 12.

From Chattel Slaves to Wage Slaves

The Dynamics of Labour Bargaining in the Americas

Edited by
MARY TURNER

Ian Randle
KINGSTON
Indiana University Press
BLOOMINGTON AND INDIANAPOLIS
James Currey
LONDON

Published by
James Currey Ltd
54b Thornhill Square, Islington
London N1 1BE

Ian Randle Publishers Ltd
206 Old Hope Road
Kingston 6

Indiana University Press
601 North Morton Street
Bloomington, Indiana 47404

First published 1995

1 2 3 4 5 99 98 97 96 95

British Library Cataloguing in Publication Data
From Chattel Slaves to Wage Slaves:
Dynamics of Labour Bargaining in the Americas
I. Turner, Mary
331.89097

ISBN 0-85255-712-4 (Paper)
0-85255-713-2 (Cloth)

Library of Congress Cataloging-in-Publication Data
From chattel slaves to wage slaves : the dynamics of labour bargaining
in the Americas / edited by Mary Turner.
p.   cm.
This book incorporates findings from a conference held under the
auspices of London University's Institutes of Commonwealth and Latin
American Studies in May 1991.
Includes index.
ISBN 0-253-32972-8 (alk. paper). — ISBN 0-253-21001-1 (pbk.
alk. paper)
1. Slaves—Emancipation—America—History.   2. Slaves—America—
Social conditions.   3. Labor movement—America—History.
I. Turner, Mary. date
HT1050.F76 1995
331.89′097—dc20   95-14397

Typeset in 11/12pt Baskerville by Colset Pte Ltd, Singapore
Printed by Villiers Publications, London N3

Contents

II *Counteracting Freedom*

Contract & Coercion

III Achieving Rights for Labour

Confrontation & Collective Bargaining

Illustrations

With thanks for permission to reprint from: The British Library (9475614, 9478987, 8154bbb.36, A.107), Trade Union Congress Library and the University of the West Indies, St Augustine Trinidad Library.

Preface

This book incorporates findings from a conference held under the auspices of London University's Institutes of Commonwealth and Latin American Studies in May 1991. Some 40 scholars met to discuss the terms on which slave, contract, full and part time wage work was extracted in the Americas and Africa and the methods workers used to secure and improve living standards. The chapters which follow relate exclusively to the Caribbean and mainland America; a separate volume, *The Wages of Slavery*, (London 1993) edited by Michael Twaddle, co-organizer of the conference incorporates other contributions.

Professor Shula Marks, Director of the Institute of Commonwealth Studies, and the staff generously provided logistical as well as intellectual support. I am grateful to my colleague at Dalhousie, Dr Michael Earle for expediting the editorial process, to Sharon Earle for express typing and to David Blake at ICS for processing the manuscript. I wish to thank the Social Science and Research Council of Canada, the British Academy for conference funding and the Isobel Thornley Bequest for a grant toward publication.

A book of this sort is a co-operative effort and I wish to thank the authors and my co-worker Michael Twaddle, whose expertise and enthusiasm made him from the early days of conference organization to publication an invaluable partner in the enterprise.

Contributors

O. Nigel Bolland is Professor of Sociology at Colgate University and his publications include *Colonialism and Resistance in Belize: Essays in Historical Sociology* (Mona, 1988) and *On the March: Labour Rebellions in the British Caribbean, 1934-39* (Kingston and London, 1995).

Rosemary Brana-Shute teaches history at the University of Charleston and is the author of numerous studies of slave society and gender issues in Suriname.

Michael J. Gonzales directs the Center for Latino and Latin American Studies at Northern Illinois University. His publications on labour history in Peru include *Plantation Agriculture and Social Control in Northern Peru, 1875-1933*, (Austin, Texas, 1985).

Kusha Haraksingh teaches history at the University of the West Indies in Trinidad and is the author of numerous studies on labour and plantation management in nineteenth- and twentieth-century Trinidad.

Gad Heuman teaches at Warwick University in the Department of History and the Centre for Caribbean Studies. He is co-editor of *Slavery and Abolition: a Journal of Comparative Studies* and author of *'The Killing Time': the Morant Bay Rebellion in Jamaica*, (London and Knoxville 1994).

Howard D. Johnson teaches in the Department of Black American Studies, in the University of Delaware. His publications include *The Bahamas in Slavery and Freedom*, (London, 1991).

Contributors

Lucia Lamounier is head of the Economics Department at the Sao Paulo State University, Araraquara, Brazil and the author of *Da escrivadão ao trabalho livre. A lei de loçao de 1879* (Sao Paulo, 1988).

Michael Mullin teaches history at California State University, Sacramento and in 1992 the University of Illinois Press published *Africa in America: Slave Acculturation in the American South and the British Caribbean, 1736–1831*.

Glen Richards teaches history at the University of the West Indies in Jamaica where he researches Caribbean labour history and the role of Caribbean immigrants in the United States trade union movement.

Richard B. Sheridan is Professor of Economics at the University of Kansas and Fellow of the Royal Historical Society. In 1988 Cambridge University Press published his *Doctors and Slaves: a Medical and Demographic History of Slavery in the British West Indies, 1680–1834*.

Dale W. Tomich teaches sociology at New York State University, Binghamton and is the author of *Slavery in the Circuit of Sugar. Martinique in the World Economy, 1830–1848* (Baltimore and London, 1990).

Mary Turner is Visiting Fellow at the Institute of Commonwealth Studies, London University, Professor of History at Dalhousie University, Nova Scotia and is the author of *Slaves and Missionaries: the Disintegration of Jamaican Slave Society 1784–1834* (Urbana, London, 1982).

Lorena S. Walsh is a researcher with the Colonial Williamsburg Foundation, has published widely on material culture and living standards and is co-author of *Robert Cole's World: Agriculture and Society in Early Maryland* (Chapel Hill, 1991).

Betty Wood, a Fellow of Girton College, teaches history at Cambridge University. Her publications include *Women's Work, Men's Work: the informal slave economies of Low-country Georgia 1750–1830* (Athens, 1995).

Introduction

MARY TURNER

The demarcation between slave and legally free labour has been etched into the history of the Americas by the political upheavals that characterized the destruction of property rights in persons. Revolution, war, prolonged popular agitation as well as legal and diplomatic struggles made slave labour illegal. Workers purchased as parcels of hereditable labour were gradually, over the course of the nineteenth century, replaced by workers who owned their person and sold their labour power, a change in legal status emotively designated freedom.

This time-honoured divide is probed here in a series of studies by scholars who were invited to explore the proposition (set out in Chapter 1) that all categories of worker – slave, serf, contract and wage – faced fundamentally the same problem: all were forced to spend their lives expending labour over and above what was required for their own subsistence. Improvement in work conditions for all these workers meant improving their rewards for labour extracted, and cutting down the coercive powers of their owners or employers. The question to be addressed was, did these fundamental similarities in the nature of exploitation indicate similarities in their methods of struggle? While contributors each wrote as experts in different forms of labour, it was anticipated that their findings, taken in juxtaposition, would elucidate key common features in methods of labour extraction and in methods of resistance.

Their findings, incorporated in this book demonstrate that all categories of worker in the Americas practised forms of collective labour bargaining customarily associated with industrial wage labourers. Procedures which

1

included collective withdrawal of labour and appeals for mediation were established by slave workers and developed with varying degrees of success by their heirs and successors.

Labour bargaining by slave workers, dealt with in the first part of this volume, is of particular interest. It throws new light on the dynamics which sustained and elaborated the system to serve the increasingly complex needs of expanding capitalist economies. More importantly, it elucidates a new strand of slave worker resistance, traditionally categorized as accommodation and rebellion, which reveals a slave working population conscious of the value of its labour and determined to win the best returns for it. Placed in relation to the bargaining powers available to contract and wage workers, slave labour bargaining also enables us to assess concretely in terms of specific work-place conditions the legal and political changes associated with free status. The power workers command to secure, or improve, their customary living standard, illuminates from the standpoint of the majority of people ongoing discussions about the meaning of freedom and the re-thinking of democracy.

These chapters deal with the mid-eighteenth to mid-twentieth century and focus primarily on the Caribbean where export-oriented plantation agriculture remained throughout the period a significant sector of the economy and continuities and changes in the bargaining process emerge with great clarity. The balance of the investigation provides illuminating comparative data from continental America, north and south. Labour bargaining was generated by the slave workers' need to secure their subsistence. The extraction of slave labour necessarily involved one fundamental informal contract term: the exchange of work for subsistence. Subsistence together with clothing and, in some cases, medical attention, comprised the slave workers' basic wages in kind. At issue between workers and owners was the question – how much "wages" for how much work?

The owners substantively dictated the answer to this question by physical punishment at the work-place backed up when necessary by the use of military force. Only the workers' capacity for violent retaliation, repeatedly demonstrated in property destruction, murder and where they dominated the society demographically as in the Caribbean and Bahia, by large-scale rebellions, established *de facto* a bottom line to exploitation levels; it also put a certain premium, even, on methods of resolving work-place conflicts short of retaliatory violence.

For much of the period under review the slave work-force was replaced and expanded by purchase. Subsistence standards could consequently be minimized to provide simply for the reproduction of labour rather than, as was customary, for the reproduction of both labour and the labour force. Reduced overall labour costs offset the capital cost of slave purchase, but the owners' relentless pursuit of economy in this regard could subject the slave population as a whole, as in eighteenth-century Jamaica for example, to regular hunger cycles. Workers' lives were sacrificed for the want, as one manager put it, of the odd slice of pork (Chapters 1 and 2). While keeping wages in kind as low as possible for the slave population as a whole, the owners recognized the need for reward differentials to reflect the skills and responsibilities required in the division of labour dictated by plantation production – headmen, drivers and artisans – and for their own comfort and safety – housekeepers and domestics. Reward differentials applied the principle of divide and rule to the slave working population; more significantly, the practice gave oblique recognition to the fact that the plantations were embedded in societies characterized by wage labour. Slave-owners were maintaining an apartheid system which legally designated Africans and their progeny as a cheaper form of labour. But the juxtaposition at the work-place and outside it of slave and wage workers established for the slaves the parameters for improvements in their terms of work and for their owners and managers the parameters for concessions which did not destroy their property rights in chattel workers.

Labour bargaining within this general framework was generated, as these studies show, by the slaves' need to secure and where possible to maximize their wages in kind. Their efforts to do so constituted a political struggle to establish the procedures necessary to express grievances and secure their resolution: to establish a customary right to the labour bargaining process. This node of customary right contributed to regulating conditions at the work-place and was an essential component in the network of claims to customary rights outside it.

To supply the slaves' wages in kind the owners either provided protein rations (salt fish or meat) and a plot of ground on the estate backlands to grow staples, or supplied them with protein and staple rations to be supplemented from garden plots. The provision ground system offloaded onto the slaves themselves responsibility for fuelling the labour used on the estates: it subjected them like peasants to the natural hazards of drought and hurricane and made subsistence production contingent on the demand for estate work. In the best of circumstances, as in the Georgia rice lands where the slaves' right to Sunday for their grounds was customarily acknowledged (Chapter 4), it subjected the slaves to a seven-day working week. Jamaican sugar estate workers, who comprised some 70 per cent of the total work-force, regularly worked in addition an industrial-style relay system round the clock seven days a week during the six-month crop period. Their survival at times depended on being sent, or taking themselves off, to forage at risk of brutal flogging, hanging and shooting (Chapters 2 and 3). Improvement in wages in kind meant acquiring both regular allowances and time for the provision grounds.

The ration-allotment system shortened the slaves' working week,[1] but increased the owners' command of subsistence levels. In the Chesapeake a wealth of evidence (Chapter 5) establishes that owners supplied a weekly staple ration of locally produced maize (16 pints for adults and 8 pints for old people and children) together with one half to two pounds of salt meat or fish supplemented in some cases by fresh beef, molasses, milk and salt as well as the slaves' garden-grown vegetables. These supplies were intended to provide seven days' subsistence, so the produce of Sunday hunting and fishing was supplementary.

Chesapeake wages in kind had been set just below the quantities customary for the indentured servants that slave labourers were first introduced to supplement; yet the diet afforded no more than marginal subsistence – a judgement confirmed by the owners themselves who increased meat and liquor rations to improve productivity at harvest (Chapter 5). Wages in kind on mainland rice and cotton plantations and on Caribbean sugar estates did not always reach even Chesapeake standards. The legal minimum in the Leeward Islands fixed in 1798 was only 9 pints per adult and this was said to be an increase of one third on local practice; in the ration-allotment parish of Vere, Jamaica, one estate in 1818 supplied as little as 8 pints.[2]

The weapons slave workers commanded to secure their subsistence, or to modify their contract terms in any way were limited. They could beg for favours; proffer or supply on demand additional services in the hope of reward; make verbal protests; withdraw their labour – covertly by malingering, working slowly and inefficiently or overtly by flight or strike; and commit sabotage, destroy or steal estate property. These methods were used within the work-place both individually and collectively. All forms of labour withdrawal and sabotage risked flogging and/or imprisonment on the estate, or as a result of formal procedures. This put a premium on deferential gestures, offers of willing and obedient service and oblique or indirectly addressed verbal articulation of grievances. The outright challenge of flight or strike was moderated by invoking an authority higher than the overseer to mediate the conflict – the owner, his attorney, a neighbouring planter, even, in some cases, the magistrates. The specific utility of these weapons, as the evidence here indicates, depended on circumstances specific to each slave society and even each work-place. Loud and persistent verbal complaints sparked by the slightest modification in rations had a resonance for resident owners in post-revolutionary Chesapeake quite lacking for managers in Jamaica (Chapters 2 and 5). Overall and increasing shortages of prime hands opened the way in post-slave-trade Jamaica to informal contract terms impossible in conditions of labour plenty (Chapter 1). The important point, however, is that whatever the circumstances, slave workers were willing, in a context where they 'took flog' for routine infractions of work discipline, to put their bodies on the line to assert the value of their labour (Chapters 1, 2 and 5).

The workers best placed to labour bargain were the confidential slaves. The owners' demands for special services opened the way to claims for special rewards and privileges conceded to individuals which were transformed, in some cases, into customary rights for the whole population. The evidence here suggests that confidential slaves played an important role in securing the legal (in Jamaica 1725, and Savannah, Georgia 1774) or customary (Chesapeake) right to slave participation in the commercial economy as traders. Trade maximized the value of food production from gardens and grounds, by hunting and fishing and complemented wages in kind. It was a distinct modification of the slaves' basic contract term which conceded to the slaves ownership of their own produce, the cash they earned from its sale, limited freedom of movement outside the plantation and the right to travel to market.

Participation in the commercial economy as a privilege for individual slaves reflected both the slaves' needs and their owners' interests. Trading activity was actively aided and abetted by owners and managers eager to use the slaves' talents as traders on their own behalf (Chapters 3 and 5) and promoted the emergence of slave hucksters, many of them women, as a new privileged stratum. The impetus for the slaves in general to follow the example set by the confidential slaves, reflecting both their needs and their African experience as peasants and traders, proved impossible to resist for owners in Lowcountry Georgia, despite man-traps and patrols, and difficult, for owners in the Chesapeake, to restrain (Chapters 4 and 5).

The leverage enjoyed by confidential slaves to establish individual contract terms and maximize profits from their grounds and trade ramified and elaborated the stratification of the work-force dictated by the division of labour. The wide divergences in subsistence levels which resulted are neatly illustrated on one mid-eighteenth-century Jamaican estate where the housekeeper's range of extra services (sex, sewing and money-lending) won her trading privileges, shares in a horse-breeding business and a house worth £100 while the field slaves were periodically sent to forage for subsistence (Chapter 3).

Individual deals made by confidential slaves together with popular participation in the commercial economy created a context in which managers and slaves were continuously enmeshed in exchanging goods and cash for services. Slaves used every opportunity to claim extra rewards for extra service; resident slaves, for example, commonly required in Jamaica to train new African forced immigrant workers, claimed in return the right to use them on their own provision grounds – a relationship which also served in some cases to establish kinship ties. This practice in due course was extended to absorb layers of single, elderly and feckless slaves who formed a pool of 'poorer sort' available to work the grounds of the 'better' sort and be paid in kind (Chapters 1 and 3). The divergent view of the Jamaican slaves' terms of work presented in the following pages (Chapters 2 and 3) can be reconciled by recognizing that privileges were won by the confidential slaves (some 12.5 per cent of the sugar estate population) who were in a position to maximize both land-holdings and trading profits.

Confidential and skilled slave workers also claimed and won in the closed labour market of the work-place outright cash payments for their regular work in the form of seasonal, or even weekly bonuses which served in the last resort as protection money against sabotage in the production process. They also won payments in goods, leisure, or cash for extra services in terms of hours spent on the job, or tasks fulfilled. Such payments indicate the slaves had some success in establishing customary work norms, but the evidence here, selected from the extensive literature on the use of cash rewards (Chapter 6), demonstrates more certainly the owners' use of cash incentives to stimulate overwork and achieve new levels of labour extraction. Slave workers also sold their labour part-time in the open market. In Jamaica this was a privilege largely confined to estate-based artisans in the dead season and urban domestics; but in Lowcountry Georgia and the Chesapeake where a pool of Sunday workers relieved labour shortages, slaves could hire themselves out on Sundays for day or casual work in town, or to planters of their own choosing as an alternative to maximizing their subsistence from the sale of produce.

Regular exchange of slave labour for cash, the substitution of cash payments for wages in kind were not instituted as a result of labour bargaining. Slave-owners used it at their own convenience with their own slaves – in up-country South Carolina for example[3] – or took advantage of the open labour market to invest slave property in it, either in gangs hired directly to other slave-owners, or as individuals who worked on hire and paid them rent (or in the slaves' terms, 'wages') (Chapter 8) for the privilege of earning their subsistence in cash. Profit margins were good enough for owners to apprentice young slaves to increase their value as investments (Chapters 5 and 6). Slaves on individual hire were directly involved in negotiating their work conditions, but on terms which made their labour cheaper than wage workers' and exposed them to discipline by fines and withheld wages. To pay cash for slave labour gave employers a second lash to their whip. Their compensation was the daily enjoyment of street freedoms and the status derived from payment in wage workers' currency. Slaves on gang hire, or slaves hired individually, but working in gangs – on Cuban sugar estates for example – had varied opportunities for collective bargaining and further research may establish its overall influence. Cash-rewarded slaves necessarily remained a minor feature of a labour system predicated on sustaining the value of slave property as such.

The influence of individual labour bargaining was put to its severest test usually by domestic slaves who attempted to negotiate manumission. Manumission procedures established by law or custom provided a narrow meshed vent for slave ambitions for free legal status for themselves and their families and for owners who were concerned to bestow it on their slave children or to restructure and rationalize their work-force by offloading women and children (Chapter 5). Slaves taking this initiative found it difficult to acquire the purchase price, and that a negotiation which started with their owner often involved legal procedures intended to curtail access to free status. In the United States legal avenues to self-purchase were closed off in the decades 1830–60; in Suriname increasingly complex manumission laws (1788–1832) added legal expenses, tax and a large cash security as a bond against any future charge on the municipality to the purchase price (Chapter 7). Extraordinary efforts were required of slaves to negotiate with their owners, secure prospective employers among the free black and coloured population, as well as accumulate cash. By the 1830s pressures were reduced by the fact that the majority of manumitters were free coloureds and blacks of modest means often assisting their relatives; even so, less than 1 per cent of urban slave workers, mostly female, mulatto and domestic, were successful (Chapter 7).

The negotiation between slave and owner was clearly the crucial factor here and this seems to have been the case elsewhere; in Brazil, where manumission terms were determined (until 1871) by custom not law, the number and category of slaves manumitted followed the same pattern. And in Cuba, where the right to self-purchase was guaranteed by law, approximately the same proportion of the slave population was so much as engaged in the process in 1871 and more began than completed it (Chapter 9).[4] The inference is that in the last resort property rights in slave persons were almost non-negotiable.

Individual bargaining affirmed the particular value of a particular labour group and collective labour bargaining affirmed the value of labour as such. The slaves united to withdraw their labour and turn it into a bargaining tool capable of defending or expanding established customary rights and of setting limits to the use of physical coercion. Withdrawal of labour might be timed to threaten or actually disrupt harvest or be accompanied by theft or crop destruction; arson strategically applied could prove an effective bargaining tool even when used simply to express grievance and posit a threat of further action.[5]

The strike actions cited here, prompted in some cases by women workers, were occasioned either by what the slaves judged to be excessive and unjust use of force to intensify labour extraction – 'flogging it out of them' – or by the denial of allowances. The procedure was to stop work, in some cases withdrawing from the estate and appoint a delegation to appeal over the head of the overseer to the nearest higher authority: the resident owner, itinerant attorney, neighbouring owner or even the magistrates. The statement of grievance was accompanied by a proposed solution; in one case slaves specified the price in cash and kind of Sunday day work (Chapter 4). More commonly, they wanted the overseer dismissed. Slaves also at times publicized their grievances by leaving their estate in an organized band to parade through the countryside and put unresolved problems – in recorded cases, the denial of allowances – to the magistrates. Such a high-profile operation, appealing over the head of management to a public officer, was easily construed as a threat to law and order and alerted fears of rebellion. Punishment could range from the execution of leaders to public flogging in the market place to discourage emulation.[6] The magistrates' response to public protest underlines the significance of the work-place practices slave workers established. They arrived naked and rightless and hammered out procedures to assert the value of their labour and give it political weight. It was a distinct political achievement.

Crucial to this development were the confidential slaves, the headmen and drivers who mediated between the demands of the owners and managers and the workers they organized and punished. They acted in part out of necessity since their functions as agents of management could be fulfilled only with the co-operation of the work-force. They were the sounding board for work-place grievances and had to decide when best to unite with their fellows to confront management, or when it was worthwhile to lend their authority to spontaneous acts of protest. At such moments of crisis they could play off the workers' long-term value as resident workers against employees with large responsibilities, small salaries and low status hired by the year. Overseers had every incentive to arrive at informal deals with headmen and drivers about the slaves' terms of work, as careful resident owners appreciated.

Complex local as well as overall political and economic circumstances determined the outcome of labour bargaining procedures. Chesapeake slave demands were restrained by vigilant owners, regular food supplies and the all-pervasive threat of removal to the expanding plantation frontier which decimated the eastern slave population in the early nineteenth century. In Jamaica, by contrast, conditions for labour bargaining improved with the abolition of the slave trade, particularly on the sugar estates where the proportion of effective workers was reduced to some 40 per cent of the population by 1832. Slave worker demands consequently intensified: sugar estate slaves won time for their grounds in excess of the time allowed by law, pressed for task work and for the use of hired jobbing gangs. Women slaves, offered incentives to reproduce, took the reduced workload and extra rations by simply claiming to be pregnant. Maximum gains required both determined leadership and complaisant managers, a combination which enabled the slaves on one sugar estate to establish a form of workers' control by forcing an end to sugar production in favour of pen-keeping – a utility which facilitated their activities as petty producers and traders (Chapters 1 and 2).

Two factors stand out as crucial to success: leadership and labour shortage. The scale of the work unit, the demographic dominance of the work-force and the weakness of state power were also important. This rule-of-thumb equation was subject to variation, however, under the impact, for example, of revolutionary change (Chapter 5).

The customs established at the work-place assisted claims to other nodes of customary rights outside the work-place. One such cluster of claims concerned the maintenance of family ties, manifested in stubborn resistance to being sold, to demands for sexual services and in efforts to promote job changes (Chapters 1, 2 and 5). Another such cluster related to religious rights. Slave workers kept a tenacious hold, usually illegally and in secret, on their command of supernatural powers derived from ancestral spirits, the deities associated with Africa's traditional religions and Islam and significant numbers claimed access to Christianity. In some cases they stated their claim simply by voting with their feet – in colonial and post-revolutionary Georgia, for example, where a society-wide nonconformist religious revival allowed the formation of Black Baptist churches. Slave converts became active in local politics as a result, participating in Sabbatarian campaigns to deny their fellows access to Sunday market (Chapter 4). In Jamaica, by contrast, where nonconformist missionaries excited suspicion as agents of Wilberforce, slave claims proved more contentious and individuals were severely punished 'for righteousness sake'. While the sheer number of Jamaican slave converts precluded systematic persecution, only their conscious and purposive pursuit of religious rights and support from the free coloured and black population secured their claim to public worship and an active role in church organization.[7] The right to public worship, however obtained, comprised a new element of self-possession and civil status.

The evidence here indicates the modifications that labour bargaining made in the slaves' informal contract terms at the work-place and outside it; further research may show that the nodes of customary rights they established also influenced both legal concessions – in the Jamaican Slave Codes 1798–1831 for example – and regressions such as Georgia's Sabbatarian regulations.

Strike action, with its attendant threat of reduced crops and destruction of property, was a high-risk operation, particularly for the leaders who, as men with status and property, had more to lose than the average field-hand. While some managers took no reprisals, others demoted leaders or had them punished with imprisonment and flogging. The price paid for collective labour bargaining proclaimed its political purpose: to challenge the totalitarianism of property rights in persons and set limits to the use of the whip. It was their will and capacity to defy and endure the terror of the whip which made it possible for slave workers to establish customary rights and claim elements of self-possession.

Yet the most substantial changes effected in the terms for slave workers as a whole in any of the societies under review were determined less by labour bargaining than by economic conditions beyond the control of owners and slaves. The collapse in the early nineteenth century of the cotton plantation export economy in the Bahamas made the slave work-force to a large extent surplus to plantation needs and forced a reversal of established economic priorities: subsistence production and trade substantially replaced export crop agriculture. Slaves with provision grounds became labour tenants, working half-time on their own land, or sharecroppers claiming up to two-thirds of the produce for themselves. Where plantations survived,

slaves worked on tasks and often assumed full responsibility for their subsistence. Surplus slaves went to Nassau and sold themselves to new owners,
or engaged themselves in the well established system of self-rent, self-hire
and 'worked out on wages' to subsist their owners who commuted the labour
services due to them into cash payments (Chapter 8)

Even more striking is the fact that by 1832 the Solicitor-General was
prepared to rule that slaves on self-rent, self-hire could not be punished by
flogging for failure to pay their owners' wages; it was a non-fulfilment of
an agreement and not a crime. This gave official recognition to the substitution of contract terms for physical coercion and Bahamian slaves acquired
de facto a new civil right which encouraged some to stop paying their owners
'wages'. Contemporary observers indulged the idea that emancipation by
slow degrees was a real possibility, particularly since an increasing number
of slaves were able to purchase manumission.

The slave population was re-stratified into labour tenants and sharecroppers who subsisted themselves and traded, and workers with only their
labour to hire; this group was subdivided between skilled slaves, earning
up to ten times the rate of the unskilled and paying 15 per cent of earnings
to their owners, and the unskilled competing in an overcrowded labour
market with one another as well as with wage workers and paying as much
as 50 per cent of their earnings to their owner.

Release from the confines of the plantation also removed the framework for collective labour bargaining. New organizational forms among
skilled slaves appeared in some urban contexts (notably Rio de Janeiro)
where skilled slaves on hire in periods of labour shortage organized brotherhoods based on skills or nationality to secure the best possible rate for
the job. No such manifestation appears in the Bahamas. Nor did skilled
and unskilled collectively challenge their owners' right to rent payments –
the price of self-subsistence. The re-formation of the slave labour system
in the Bahamas while opening up the possibility of gradual emancipation
also affords a glimpse of the system which replaced slavery: with the
property interest of the ruling class concentrated in land and the workers,
relieved of chattel status, scrambling to sell their labour for subsistence.

The development by slave agricultural workers of labour bargaining
procedures customarily associated with industrial wage workers throws into
relief the extent to which the organization of capitalist agriculture, both on
large-scale plantations characteristic of Jamaica and the smaller-scale enterprises of the Chesapeake, pre-figured and paralleled capitalist industrial
organization. Production in both cases imposed divisions of labour which
stratified the work-force and subjected substantial segments to supervised
collective gang labour. In both cases men, women and children were utilized
as workers and labour supplies were expanded and replenished at some
stages of growth by owners and employers tapping reserve armies of
labour – from Africa, or adjacent rural reserves.

Parallels in the organization of production are reinforced by parallels in the terms of work: the number of hours of labour a day, of days in the working week and the minimum subsistence rates. The similarities emerge most forcefully on the sugar estates: agro-industrial units whose acreage and work-force density were determined by available cane milling and sugar boiling technology. The crop season turned the estates for six months of the year into a factory, the mill fed directly from the fields by one section of the work-force and the boiling house fuelled and manned by another. Within this framework technological change affected work routines, and the slave sugar workers, like wage factory workers, had to keep abreast of innovations – a demand which affected to differing degrees commercial farming in general (Chapter 5). At the same time the methods of labour extraction used to maximize sugar production pioneered methods which characterized manufacturing, in particular the relay or shift work system which kept both sugar and cotton mills (breakdowns apart) turning continuously.

In the context created by these parallels in the organization of capitalist agriculture and industry, the generation of collective bargaining procedures can be seen as a natural, possibly inevitable development.

This conclusion touches directly the long-standing and ongoing debate on the characterization of slave workers in the Americas, a debate which has made the terms proto-peasant and proto-proletarian common currency in the literature.[8]

All the evidence here indicates that slave workers were an immanent form of proletariat. They differed from wage workers in important ways: their labour was purchased by the person, in bulk, an investment in futures of labour supply. Slave labour was marketable only in strictly limited and well defined conditions which did not impinge in any way on their owners' property rights. The owners, like employers, were directly or indirectly the slave workers' main source of subsistence: food rations, allotments and provision grounds were all supplied by the owners. The fact that some slave workers were not supplied with staple food, but with land to work to supply the food is an interesting variant of the food supply system which does not alter its fundamental characteristic, that the owners supplied and controlled the workers' means of subsistence. Slave workers with provision grounds were slaves working on land allotted to them to supply the food to reproduce the labour they would use on the estate. In so far as they functioned as peasants-on-Sunday, their primary purpose was to support the slave labour extraction system, not to make a 'peasant breach' in it. The distinguishing feature of the provision ground subsistence system was that it dictated a seven-day working week, a fact which may have fuelled slave support for Sabbatarianism as a method of making their owners as Christians acknowledge that their labourers were 'worthy of their hire' in the shape of seven days' supplied subsistence for six days' work, or self-subsistence for five days' work. There were compensatory aspects of the provision ground system: greater variety of diet, some freedom of movement and trade, but they all derived from putting in compulsory overtime (by Biblical standards) in order to eat.

Evidence from the Caribbean suggests that the slaves identified free status with wages. When hopes and aspirations were at their peak in Jamaica in 1831, the rebels wanted wages and free status, not land and free status. And their tactics did not include land occupations. A working life consumed by unpaid agricultural labour on the estates, sustained only by the uncertainties of Sunday small-holding cultivation, had evidently made the idea of regular, adequate cash wages a cause worth fighting for. Wages together with small-holdings appeared to guarantee a better life in material terms and a clear change in social status. They were driven from the estates post-emancipation by low wages, high rents, competition from cut-rate contract workers and the discovery that to become an estate-based wage earner was to remain, in social terms, a slave. They turned to the land for want of a different option.

The concept of the 'peasant breach' has recently been re-formulated and made the gateway to a slave economy, one of two overlapping economies, 'one organised by and for the masters; the other by and for slaves'.[9] This is not what the evidence here (or, I would argue, in the collection cited) demonstrates. The slaves' Sunday activities contributed to the economy primarily by reproducing the labour used for commercial agriculture and also contributed to the growth of the internal economic infrastructure necessary for the survival and growth of the colonial and post-colonial economies. Provision ground cultivation contributed to overall economic growth, but the best most slaves got out of it was to win cash rewards for their labour one day a week.

The stratification of the slave labour force allowed a layer to emerge which could be considered a form of slave labour aristocracy who did better than average, who managed in popular parlance 'to save a few bob', set themselves up (like Thistlewood's housekeeper) lending money and/or banking it, or have a few goods to pass on to their heirs; but there was little enough to show for a lifetime's expenditure of their life force and none of it gave them more than, at best, a toe-nail hold on the ownership of the means of production.

The endless inventiveness of the human race ensured, nevertheless, that the slave workers' narrow, uncertain and hard won returns became the foundation for a social, cultural and political superstructure out of all proportion to its material base. But the superstructure does not alter the fact that there was only one economy and the slaves contributed to it seven days a week.

Slave worker labour bargaining, as the evidence throughout this section indicates, was a high-risk, high-profile operation usually directed to securing immediate practical modification of the terms of labour extraction, not to overturning the slave system.

The Jamaican slaves, however, demonstrated its potential as a revolutionary strategy in December 1831 when, on the brink of crop season they transformed their experience of local work-place actions into a general strike. Their large scale withdrawal of labour combined with massive destruction – valued at £1 million – of crops and property, and military action, aimed to secure free legal status and wages for their work. Their effort, while not in itself successful, had a significant impact in England, itself in the process of political transformation, and contributed to determining the timing of British slave emancipation (Chapter 1).

The development of labour bargaining, within the slave labour system, throws into fresh relief the fear, which gripped both employers and policy makers threatened by the shift from chattel to wage labour, that emancipation would change the balance of power between capital and labour. These fears were to an extent confirmed by the reaction of workers in the British Caribbean to the terms the British government defined for the first large-scale emancipation by legal process in 1834. This scheme required the workers to buy themselves free legal status by serving out a period of labour debt – a process cosmetically labelled Apprenticeship. These terms constituted, *de facto*, the workers' first official state-wide collective contract and it proved contentious. In St Kitts, for example, frustrated by the denial of wages for their work, they put down their hoes declaring, 'Me free, no bind, no work' and retreated to the mountains. It required the military to force them back to the plantations (Chapter 13). The extent of slave resistance and the practical difficulties encountered by the officials sent out to administer it, combined with abolitionist opposition to the scheme in England, terminated the contract prematurely in 1838.[10] At full emancipation, workers in territories with an overall shortage of labour and with land waiting to be cultivated found their bargaining position further enhanced.

To counteract the workers' bargaining power employers used two basic strategies; they endeavoured to recapture resident workers as cheap wage labour for plantation work by curtailing, where necessary, their access to land, to make them dependent on wage work; or they tapped into and developed reserves of immigrant contract workers to replace or supplement resident wage workers. Both methods, replacement and recapture, relied to differing degrees on laws and law enforcement mechanisms symptomatic of the increasing power of developing nineteenth-century colonial and post-colonial states.

The contract worker trade is touched on only peripherally in the following pages; it had, however, a number of features worth commenting on. The trade supplied a special category of bound labour in a global labour market increasingly dominated from the mid-1840s not by African slaves, but by Europeans moving in family units, some of whom were recruited as contract workers (Chapter 9). The non-European trade was world-wide in scope, extending throughout Asia into the Pacific Islands, Africa and Central

America and comparable in scale to the last 50 years of the African slave trade.[11]

Recruits for the Americas came primarily from India and China driven by bad harvests, landlessness and war, lured by cash advances and the prospect of wage levels unobtainable at home. As a Brahmin-turned-Trinidadian contract worker commented, 'For the belly's sake one plays many parts'.[12] The trade was initiated on a commercially viable scale by employers in British Guiana where outright labour shortages in relation to the land suitable for cane production made the workers' bargaining position particularly strong. They were alerted by merchant houses in British India engaged in the Indian Ocean contract trade of plentiful supplies at a cost not half that of a slave.[13] The British government, despite a decade of abolitionist opposition eventually gave its full support and until 1917, when the Indian trade was terminated, presided over the largest single supply of contract workers. The legal contract trade from India was complemented by illegal trading in China and supplemented from Europe and the Yucatan.

Contract work revived, in a remodelled nineteenth-century form, the indentured servitude used to bind immigrant European wage workers to their American-based employers from the seventeenth to the late eighteenth century. Contract workers, like indentured servants, bound themselves to supply labour for a fixed period, counted in years, on specified terms and at a fixed rate. They emancipated their employers from the need to pay labour the market rate in conditions of labour shortage and secured its regular supply. The reversion to an earlier form of bound labour in an era of wage work in response, primarily, to the labour requirements of export agriculture, parallels the recourse to chattel slavery in the sixteenth century which facilitated its inception.

There was a significant difference, however, between seventeenth-century and nineteenth-century indentures: the lure to seventeenth-century recruitment was that a period of labour extraction exchanged for subsistence would earn 'freedom dues' in the form of land for settlement. Workers were often cheated or priced out of their expectations (as in Barbados), or fobbed off with inferior land (as in Virginia), but the lure of recruitment was freedom from wage work. Nineteenth-century contract workers were lured with the promise of wages; a contract worker was not a potential settler. The only potential for a change of status written into his contract was to become a non-contracted wage worker, or in some cases (discussed below), to return home: conditions which were, of course, in line with the policy of controlling access to land.

The contract promised to eliminate labour bargaining by legally binding worker and employer to specified terms. The contract itself embodied, notionally, the bargain freely struck by negotiation between the employer or his agent and the worker. The workers found it primarily an employers' instrument used to claw back or maintain the economic and political power of slave ownership.

The second part of the volume focuses on the labour bargaining position of Asian and European contract workers. It affords some interesting comparisons and contrasts between the terms and conditions of Asian contract workers imported pre-emancipation to Cuba and post-emancipation to Trinidad and Peru for sugar and cotton cultivation and Europeans imported to pre- and post-emancipation Sao Paulo for coffee cultivation. In all these cases contract workers comprised initially a minority which attained significant proportions in Trinidad and Sao Paulo. In Trinidad Indian contract and post-contract workers comprised 25 per cent of the population by 1870; in Sao Paulo European contract workers essentially replaced slave labour on the coffee plantations by 1887.[14] Inserted into societies where class divisions ramified by ethnic differences were intense, their vulnerability to exploitation and intimidation by their employers was enhanced by their limited numbers while the ethnic distinctiveness of Asian workers from Blacks and Indians facilitated for employers the tactics of divide and rule.

Their contract terms were strikingly similar. In the first place their wage rates were significantly lower than, and in fact undercut, the wage rates for resident workers. Wages in kind supplemented cash wages in Cuba and Peru; cash wages in Cuba for both European and Chinese were only 15–25 per cent of the wages for unskilled labour, although many Chinese were employed in skilled occupations in the increasingly industrialized sugar works (Chapter 9). In Peru, rations and wages were held at levels the workers defined as 'insufficient for people' and even after the contract trade ended in 1874 could be as much as 60 per cent below the standard for wage workers.[15] European contract workers in Sao Paulo were sharecroppers with provision grounds to work for food production and trade. Cash earnings from sharecropping proved contingent on the good faith of the employer. In Trinidad, where contract workers depended on cash earnings, pay rates were officially established by the Immigration Ordinances as equal with rates for resident workers (1870) and a minimum rate of 25 cents a task was laid down (1872). The employers' techniques for evasion, however, were comprehensive.[16]

Wage levels for contract workers were intended to sustain individuals, not families. Only Europeans and Japanese were recruited in family units and even in their case children were expected to be self-sufficient as soon as possible. Immigrant Chinese on contract were almost exclusively male and it was not until 1868, 20 years after the Indian trade got under way that the British Government imposed an official 40 per cent quota of females to males – a rate just half the proportion of women customary among non-contract emigrants in the British Empire.[17] Male workers were housed economically in one-room, barrack-style housing which continued in use after families were established. Workers were contracted at these rates of pay for periods of 3–8 years: Europeans and Japanese in the 3–5 year range: Chinese and Indians in the 5–8 year range.

The methods of coercion used to enforce labour extraction were broadly similar, but not identical. Contract workers imported largely at the expense of employers tended to be regarded, like slaves, as their personal property and disciplined accordingly. In Cuba, where the Chinese worked beside slaves and slaves on hire, they worked like them under armed overseers, needed a pass to leave the plantations and were flogged, fined, imprisoned and subjected to a punishment particular to nineteenth – as well as seventeenth-century contract workers – an extension of the contract to compensate the employer for any days lost on the job, including time in jail. In post-emancipation Peru where Chinese contract workers were the mainstay of the country's important sugar and cotton plantation sector the same methods were used. The Japanese workers imported through the agency of an immigration company at the end of the nineteenth century also found themselves flogged, imprisoned and defrauded of wages. The plantation remained a country to itself and employers did not change their slave-handling habits (Chapter 10). In Trinidad, where Indian contract workers were imported as part of a state subsidized and supervised immigration scheme the contract was enforced (as throughout the British Caribbean) for both contract and wage workers by laws and law-enforcement agencies which treated all forms of contract breaking – including absenteeism and malingering – as criminal offences to be punished by fines and prison sentences which, under the Immigration Ordinances automatically extended the period of service, indirectly by debt or directly by time to be served. Recent analysis indicates that some 30 per cent of the indentured labour force were before the courts for labour offences every year in this period and no less than 20 per cent were convicted.[18] The legal apparatus for labour coercion also developed in Sao Paulo once state-aided European immigration was organized in 1871 (Chapter 9).

Contract workers were also exposed, however, to a wide range of techniques intended to perpetuate their contract status. The employers, having secured a new supply of bound labour at minimal subsistence cost aimed to keep it. Cuban employers did not scruple to extend contracts indefinitely by simply refusing to supply the certificate which confirmed it had been completed.[19] The government formalized and standardized this practice in 1860 by requiring all workers with unexpired contracts to recontract themselves, or return home at their own expense. These practices were reinforced by the more subtle, but no less effective constraints of class and race which limited employment opportunities and ensured that the majority of ex-contract Chinese remained plantation workers.

Trinidad contract workers were (as we have seen) coralled partly by due legal process, but were also lured into recontracting themselves for a further five years by the idea of a 'free' passage home.[20] The technique applied informally and universally, however, was debt servitude. European recruits to Cuba and Sao Paulo arrived burdened with the debt incurred from their share of transport costs, calculated in Sao Paulo to take minimally four years to pay off and on which interest charges were added after only two years.

They were not allowed to leave the property until the debt was paid (Chapter 9). Minimal wages, however, inevitably generated indebted workers and employers exploited the fact by providing credit at company stores (Peru and Trinidad), and advancing a year's rations at rates that took at least five years to pay off. Opium smoking (Peru) and alcoholism (Trinidad) deepened the debt trap (Chapters 10 and 11). Contract workers found that work conditions and systems of coercion were largely directed to negating the one guarantee of free legal status the contract appeared to confirm – its limited duration.

These structures were reinforced at the work-place, on large-scale plantations in particular, by the multiplication of white management personnel and by the elevation of contract workers to privileged positions. Employers also played the race card here at discretion, employing free black foremen for Chinese workers in Peru, for example; otherwise they relied, as in Trinidad, on confidential contract workers who also served as charge hands distributing wages, as storekeepers and (from 1868) as police constables (Chapters 10 and 11). The superior wages of confidential contract workers enabled them to see their way, in contrast to their slave counterparts, out of the system; they were consequently under no absolute necessity to be Janus-faced and to serve at times their constituency of fellow workers. They emerged from contract status to form a petit bourgeois element engaged as traders and barbers, for example, in Cuba and Peru or as recruiting agents for the planters, re-contracting expired contract workers to deliver them back to the plantations. In Trinidad they were also able to set themselves up as cocoa planters and cane farmers (see below).

The body of contract workers, moreover, were necessarily divided among themselves by infinite and arbitrary gradations of work-loads determined by task and irregular wage rates obscurely recorded – methods used in Peru and made into a fine art in Trinidad by employers determined to maintain profit margins during a depression by slicing into wage bills (Chapter 11). Contract workers were also divided by the option their contract provided of a return passage home after ten years. This escape hatch was used by no less than 25 per cent of Indian immigrants, though it is not clear to which strata they belonged. The comparative powerlessness of contract workers to enforce their contract terms is clearly indicated by their recourse, like their slave predecessors, to suicide and flight and by the widespread use of covert methods of labour withdrawal, systematic malingering (persistent and well organized in Peru) and endemic sabotage, theft, arson and machine breaking (Chapter 10).

Overt attempts at labour bargaining by strike action met with sharp disciplinary action: disputes tended to be suppressed, not mediated and this proved the case where contract workers comprised either a minority or a majority of the work-force. Chinese contract workers in Peru comprised a significant proportion of the plantation labour force and were consistently contentious; on the smaller properties in particular collective action protested, as in chattel slave regimes, against excessive and unjust punishment of individuals and subsistence levels. They appear, however, to have met with success only in conditions of long-term or seasonal labour shortages and where their position was strengthened by competition from non-contract Chinese who could negotiate individual wage rates in addition to rations which represented several months' earnings for contract workers.[21] Japanese families, imported from 1898–1923 as a result of political lobbying by the sugar interest, were no more successful. They fought hard to keep control of their earnings and avoid debt at the company stores and bitterly contested their employers' relentless drive to reduce wages by substituting task work for day wages. The employers however simply deported the leaders and ruled that 'approaching a supervisor in a group constitutes an uprising' (Chapter 10), a regulation more draconian than any practice customary within the slave labour system.

In Trinidad Indian immigrants composed 90 per cent of sugar estate workers and the centralization of sugar production put 78 per cent of them (by 1897) in the power of six large firms. Sugar ceased to expand in the 1880s, but new immigrants continued to be imported, so that contract and non-contract workers competed at similar low rates for existing work. Employers ruthlessly manipulated pay scales, and strike action became endemic. Confrontations with the police and military generated 'collective bargaining by riot'; procedures for collective bargaining with mediation were not established. The intense discontent among a rural work-force of such substantial numbers precipitated (1884) the creation of a para-military police force, modelled on and recruited from the Royal Irish Constabulary.[22]

European sharecroppers in Sao Paulo in the 1850s who attempted to secure their contract terms also had their leaders expelled, but from the property rather than the country. Sharecroppers, however, with subsistence plots and, from the employers' point of view, with cash debts as well as labour rent to pay, had an alternative strategy to employ: they shifted their energies to subsistence production and trade, a form of labour withdrawal which prompted employers to devise a new form of contract for incoming immigrants which made the use of subsistence plots contingent on the number of coffee trees cultivated and harvested (Chapter 9).

The employers' confrontational treatment of the workers' attempts to bargain collectively for the fulfilment of their contract terms put a premium on their rights as persons of free legal status to carry their grievances outside the work-place to company or state officials. Swiss sharecroppers (1856) appealed to their diplomatic representative for mediation, with success: and Japanese contract workers to the emigration company officials, with none (Chapters 9 and 10). The Chinese in Cuba worked hard to prompt state intervention on their own behalf and succeeded in getting the official prohibition of punishment by flogging which had been sanctioned by earlier government regulations (1860). In Trinidad the state machine included officials apppointed to defend contract workers in court; their utility was marginal, but their presence encouraged appeals to the authorities including the Colonial Governor (Chapter 11). It was a well-timed petition to the Governor from 25 Indians who had worked their way through ten years' indenture which secured the contract workers what was, arguably, their only significant bargaining gain: taking advantage of a new government policy to open Crown lands to small settlers they offered to exchange their right to a return passage to India for land. The governor granted them 10 acres each; this scheme, in place until 1880, together with independent purchases, enabled increasing numbers of ex-contract workers to move from the estates as smallholders, or tenant farmers.[23] The majority of plantation workers in Trinidad, as in Cuba, achieved this goal, however, primarily because the modernization of sugar production offloaded an increasing proportion of cane growing onto small farmers and tenants who, by 1921 grew 50 per cent of the cane.[24]

Publication of grievances and petitions did little more, however, than provide a vent for anger and despair. The Indians in Trinidad with their increasing numbers and continuous contact through fresh imports with their home society, were unusual in being able, like their slave predecessors, to develop the politics of cultural resistance. Contract workers claimed as of right, rather than by negotiation, full religious toleration and made their religious festivities an affirmation of their political presence and importance. It was rumours of new restrictions on religious activities together with widespread increases in the size of the task that prompted the most notable explosion of collective rage in this period (1884) when a popular public Hindu festival became a demonstration against the established order and was put down by the armed police assisted by the military. Thirteen were killed and numbers maimed and wounded.[25]

The role of the state as the employers' ally prompted contract workers, as opportunity arose, to ally themselves with its enemies; in Cuba this meant joining with slaves to fight in the first national war of independence against the armies of Spain and its Cuban allies. In Peru, it led the Chinese to support the invading Chileans (1880) during the War of the Pacific and to the subsequent massacre of some at the hands of enraged black Peruvian peasantry whose wage rates and employment opportunities they undercut (Chapter 10).

Contract workers, these case studies suggest, attempted to secure their contract terms by the methods of labour bargaining used by chattel slave workers, with one addition: as persons of free legal status they had the right to present grievances to state and immigration company officials in the hope of redress and with protection, in law, from retribution. They took opportunities where they could to pursue individually favourable deals and attempted to conduct collective bargaining. The evidence suggests, however, that they did not in fact succeed in establishing work-place procedures to mediate grievances.

Overt work-place protests, in the form of written petitions (from European sharecroppers) or oral complaints to lower management, were treated characteristically as manifestations of indiscipline to be repressed. Bargaining processes leading to improved work conditions seem to have been countenanced in Peru only by small-scale, contract-work employers with narrow capital margins who were confronting seasonal or long-term labour shortages. While further research may well reveal greater diversity in the outcome of collective confrontations in the societies represented here, the evidence as it stands captures some essential features of the system.

Contract workers who comprised a minority element at the work-place (Chinese in Cuba, Europeans in Sao Paulo, Japanese in Peru) were on the whole in a weak bargaining position. The sharecroppers' initial bargaining advantage – the capacity to withdraw their labour from coffee cultivation to their subsistence plots – was whittled away by employers who in the 1860s devised contracts which tied the use of family subsistence plots to quantified coffee tree cultivation and weeding – the *colonato* system (Chapter 9). This technique also served in late nineteenth-century conditions of labour surplus (generated by state subsidized immigration and emancipation) to intensify dramatically rates of labour extraction.

The evidence suggests, however, that the crucial factor was the employers' determination to extract labour at the cheapest rate – a determination which to different degrees required state support. Contract workers were imported as cheap labour and the pay rates for contract workers were intended to impact on wage levels in general. They were a captive labour force with the potential to recapture resident workers for the same or closely related wage rates (Chapter 11). Employers needed to hold the line on contract worker wages and conditions to validate their importation and maximize its benefits.

Collective bargaining within the slave system by contrast took place in a context in which slave labour was a separate category from, rather than a special category of wage labour. In such a framework there was scope for individual and collective deals effecting significant variations in work conditions and rewards which only in limited special circumstances either attained the same rates, or threatened to increase the rates for wage work. The terms and conditions of wage workers in general set a ceiling, economic, customary or legal, on either overall gains or individual pay scales for slave workers.

Employers for the most part commanded the coercive mechanisms to suppress strikes by their own workers and called in the military to crush rebellion. The scale of the immigrant work-force in Trinidad, however, and the level of protest generated by work conditions, meant the employers required more assistance from the state laws and law-enforcement agencies to sanction and supplement work-place discipline for contract and wage workers alike. Employers in Sao Paulo also required state support when immigration increased in the 1880s and work conditions made strikes endemic. Planters employed armed guards to suppress their own employees, organized to support one another, and called on the police to confront large-scale strikes. In 1913 the government made all forms of protest other than the presentation of grievances to officials appointed for the purpose illegal.[26] These methods secured the cheap wage policy contract workers were introduced to sustain: coffee *colonos* wages in Sao Paulo and sugar workers' wages in Trinidad remained stable until 1913 and 1919 respectively.

Bonded wage work, like chattel slavery, was ended by state intervention; supplies were cut off at source by the workers' country of origin: by China in 1874, India in 1917 and Japan in 1923. The Chinese trade had always been illegal and was actively opposed at a local level; the government's move to enforce its own laws reflected both its own increasing stability and British-inspired pressure (Chapter 10). The Indian government was also eventually stirred by national pride, but by 1917 the trade had more than fulfilled its promise from the Trinidad employers' point of view and the same can be said of Japanese contract workers in Peru where tens of thousands of Peruvian peasants had been transformed into plantation workers.

The official decision to end the contract trade to Peru also reflected, however, as the evidence here makes clear, the increased bargaining power of Japanese contract workers. The impact of high food prices and inflation which followed World War I and the success of massive urban demonstrations in Lima-Callao for an eight-hour working day, prompted alliances with Peruvian workers already claiming a legal right to organize. Manifestations of contract-wage worker solidarity in the context of a widespread working-class movement forced managers to make limited concessions. The utility of contract work for the employers was clearly at an end and a new phase in the history of labour bargaining had begun.

The contract workers' one clear legal right, the right to complain and petition authority was offset by methods of coercion which in Cuba and Peru gave employers a double lash to their whip: flogging and fines. Their legal claim to terminable bondage was also offset by indebtedness. More significantly, in late nineteenth-century conditions, at the end of their contracts workers found themselves forced to accept the same low wages to serve their subsistence needs.

The struggle for subsistence conducted by workers with free legal status is investigated in the final section of the volume which deals with three Caribbean societies, Martinique, St Kitts-Nevis and Jamaica (Chapters 12, 13 and 14). Each case confirms the importance to the ex-slaves as free persons of the customary right to labour bargaining procedures established under slavery and demonstrates their limited utility in economic circumstances which exposed them to the fluctuations of international trade and the new instruments of coercion perfected by employers and the colonial state.

At the moment of emancipation the labour bargaining position of workers in these societies was sharply differentiated. The workers in St Kitts, driven to accept the Apprenticeship contract by military intervention, found themselves tied into labour tenancies. The estates monopolized the cultivable land and commanded adequate labour supplies. Workers who lived in estate housing (the position of 70 per cent of the rural workforce until 1930) and refused to work on the estate on the terms employers dictated, were evicted. The employers as island legislators subsequently (1849) reinforced their hand by a version of the Masters and Servants Act which remained in force until 1922, punishing by fine, or imprisonment with hard labour any worker's breach of a written, or oral work contract – a law backed up informally by blacklisting of labour activists.[27] These workers became and were perceived to be, contract workers (Chapter 14).

Like contract workers their sole legal means of defence against wage decreases and task increases was their right to petition employers and the colonial authorities. In conditions of labour surplus and hedged in by coercive laws, this method proved ineffective. When the subsistence crisis created at the turn of the nineteenth century lowered cane cutting rates 25 per cent first in 1896 and again in 1905, they resorted to island-wide strikes. The 1896 strikers used every weapon they could short of outright rebellion including, like slaves, collective intimidation, parading the island in mass demonstrations, confronting employers in person and destroying crops by arson; they were suppressed, as in 1834, by the marines. In 1905 they tried a more pacific approach which proved equally ineffectual. Employers yielded to neither tactic; collective bargaining by wage workers as well as by contract workers could be simply suppressed.

Workers so strictly bonded had recourse, from the mid-nineteenth century, to exporting themselves, at first for annual work stints in neighbouring islands, but later on a more permanent basis as employment opportunities opened up throughout the Caribbean and the United States. The descendants of African immigrants coerced by slave traders became immigrants coerced by subsistence needs, relieving employers of transport costs and imposing on themselves the traumas contingent on leaving home and country.

Sugar workers in Martinique found themselves, in the immediate aftermath of abolition, by contrast in a comparatively strong bargaining position. Their numbers were not in excess of the planters' needs and labour bargaining procedures, combined with regulations laid down by the imperial government had already established on many estates a task work system which secured slaves some time every day for their grounds; as slaves they had also conducted a series of strikes and go-slows in an attempt to secure implementation of an imperial government guarantee of a five-day working week and to limit the use of the relay system during crop.[28] A rebellion which staked their claim to free legal status early in 1848 was suppressed, but the arrival of the Abolition Decree, issued in fact by the imperial government before the rebellion, created the pleasing illusion that it had been effective. It also arrived at a useful moment for the workers, in the middle of the sugar harvest. The workers made good use of their momentary advantage; since most planters lacked the resources to tempt them with good wages, but were anxious to keep them on the estates, they concluded sharecropping contracts which allowed them to keep their houses, grounds and five-day week in return producing sugar on shares – the value of one third, or one half of the crop to be divided among the work-force (Chapter 12).

This deal secured the workers' basic subsistence and persuaded as many as two-thirds of them to remain on the estates, in preference to moving to the mountains or to the towns, and work for day wages on estates of their own choosing or at hours and days of their own choosing at their place of residence on shares. The imperial government, in an attempt to recapture the work-force for regular work on the estates, sent an official (on whose report this study is based) to attempt to rationalize and regulate the existing situation by a new, standard, legally enforceable sharecropping contract. In the contract as formulated the employers made occupation of house and grounds contingent (as in St Kitts and Sao Paulo) on work on the estates: the price of crop-sharing was five nine-hour work days a week. The contract also incorporated terms which reflected some of the workers' demands: the contracts were to be renewable yearly and administered by an elected workers' council to mediate worker-planter conflicts. This gave official recognition to labour bargaining procedures and injected a republican and democratic form by introducing an election process.

The democratic form did not persuade the workers that sharecropping on these terms was worthwhile. They continued to divide their time between estate work and the provision grounds, showing a clear preference for wage work when available. They tended to put in five-hour days on the estate – a pattern which can be traced throughout the provision ground colonies in the British Caribbean (Chapter 14). Longer hours required new methods of coercion: eviction, vagrancy laws and disciplinary labour gangs, which in conditions of labour shortage the employers hesitated to apply (Chapter 12).

In these circumstances effective occupation of house and grounds allowed the workers to distribute their labour as they thought best suited their advantage, a distinct advance on their condition as slaves and at the very moment when, in the heartland of industrial development, wage slaves were fighting to impose a legal maximum ten-hour working day.

The sugar estate workers in Jamaica were also, at the moment of emancipation in 1838, able to contest their employers' terms of work; labourers were in short supply, land was available for settlement and the employers' attempt to cut wage rates 50 per cent and collect rent for houses and the continued use of their provision grounds prompted strike actions island wide. By 1865 their bargaining position had been thoroughly undermined; their numbers were surplus to the needs of a sugar estate sector which had shrunk by 50 per cent. At the same time, the small settler strata which had emerged after emancipation found new land was unavailable for settlement and customary property rights disputed by a landlord class determined to engineer a land shortage by legal process as essential to their control of labour (Chapter 13). Land hunger affected peasant freeholders, wage workers with exhausted provision grounds and a broad stratum of 1–5 acre people accustomed to supplement their subsistence with wage work. The wage workers' bargaining power was also diminished overall by this diversification of the working population as well as the use of contract labour.[29] The 1860s subsistence crisis – two years of drought, increased food and clothing prices, reduced wages as sugar fell to the lowest price of the century – drove a people already staggering under a punitive tax load to nakedness and starvation[30] and emphasized the extremely limited political instruments at their disposal. As in St Kitts only one legal recourse was open to the majority: they could appeal to people in authority in the hope of a sympathetic response – in Jamaica this included Assemblymen sensitive to the small number of freeholders who were registered voters or, in the particular case of the member for St Thomas in the East, George William Gordon, concerned with the welfare of working people in general. Their only other recourse, as in St Kitts, was collective pressure of numbers and intimidation to resist, for example, surveyors sent to reclaim land they occupied or even, as at Morant Bay on the eve of the rebellion, to defend their fellows by intimidating the magistrates in court – a tradition established during the Apprenticeship period. These methods occasionally succeeded, but led more characteristically as demonstrated in the evidence here, to legal charges, court cases, imprisonment and hard labour (Chapter 13).

Jamaicans turned in these circumstances like their forefathers to their churches, now organized publicly under their own leaders, such as Paul Bogle, for both solace and political self-expression. The religious revival which swept the island 1860–1, like the revival which preceded the 1831 rebellion, was an affirmation of hope that, as the slaves put it, better must come, as much as an expression of despair.

The rebellion was provoked first by the actively repressive policy of the employers and of every level of the colonial government. Symptomatic of this regime was the rise in prison convictions (82 per cent increase in 1863–4 over the 1861–2 figures mostly on charges of petty larceny) and the extension, early in 1865, of punishment by flogging (limited as in the Slave Codes to 39 lashes) to larceny cases. Then came, miraculously, the promise of relief in the form of the imperial government's apparently sympathetic response to petitions from the naked and hungry made on their behalf by Edward Underhill, Secretary of the Baptist Missionary Society. Preachers and politicians were galvanized into holding mass public meetings, launching radical critiques of the government, charging it with class legislation, passing resolutions, multiplying petitions and raising expectations to the highest pitch, arguably since 1831, when the free paper was expected to arrive at Christmas. This hope was then snuffed out by the circulation of 50,000 copies of the 'Queen's Advice', the imperial government's 'supercilious message' in reply to a petition from St Ann advising the people that their prosperity depended as in other countries on 'working for Wages . . . steadily and continuously'.[31]

At this juncture, blocked of all hope of redress at the hand of the imperial government, there was only one option for action, to take over the land. There were immediate rumblings of rebellion in the western parishes, scene of the 1831 Baptist War, and warships were sent. But rebellion came in St Thomas in the East where all the rich valley bottom land was still monopolized by the sugar estates and where, as slaves, workers had established collective bargaining and experienced forms of workers' control. It was led by the Native Baptist minister Paul Bogle, political heir and successor of Sam Sharpe, organizer of the 1831 rebellion, who had been, publicly, leader in the Montego Bay Baptist mission church and clandestine leader of the popular sects.

The *cinéma vérité* account of the first day of the rebellion presented here (Chapter 13) vividly conveys the powerlessness of workers – short of rebellion – in conditions of labour surplus and land shortage. Employers could get people to work for them and then refuse payment. The black builder and vestryman Charles Price was one of them. 'He not pay us', a rebel woman cried, and he paid with his life. The Chief Magistrate and the Anglican clergyman also paid low, irregular wages, imposed long tasks and exacted fines for indiscipline. They met the same fate. As one observer commented, 'The negro know who fit for retribution'. The police by contrast, recruited from their own ranks, few in number and untrained, were simply stripped of their uniforms when the jail was emptied.

The rebellion revealed the organizational weakness of part-time wage workers and small settlers. Paul Bogle, as compared with Sam Sharpe, enjoyed as a person of free legal status liberty to run his own public church and become the political agent for the local Assemblyman. He could not like Sam Sharpe address himself to a network of headmen and drivers to mobilize their semi-industrial work units into a general strike in support of armed revolt and extend the rebellion beyond Blue Mountain valley. The reduction of the estate sector of the economy had also weakened the political formation rooted in the work-place which slave workers had established and no new political growth among workers with free legal status had replaced it.

At the same time, the removal of legal disabilities combined with new systems of coercion and a continued struggle for subsistence had by no means diminished and possibly heightened class and race awareness.

The slave workers' expectation that wages and abolition spelt improved subsistence and improved status for blacks had proved illusory and the polarization of society was no less acute. The rebels had no power to invoke other than their own numbers, colour for colour, which as the decision to kill Price demonstrated, meant class for class.

The Morant Bay rebellion, consequently, though small-scale, touched vital political nerves: it claimed land and justice for the black majority and reached for a second Black Republic. The challenge was countered first by slaughter, pillage and the exemplary execution of Assemblyman George William Gordon, noted friend of the people. It was a convincing demonstration of the legal and military power of the colonial state. The elimination of the limited form of representative government embodied in the Assembly followed: and a form of direct rule, the Crown Colony, which became the characteristic form of government in the British Caribbean until the twentieth century, was substituted. The move confirmed and elevated into constitutional form the victory of the landlords over the rebels. Wage workers remained without collective bargaining rights, small settlers at the mercy of government policy, and the Jamaican population as a whole disenfranchised and excluded from positions of political power.

Wage workers in the British Caribbean at the end of the nineteenth century had one largely ineffectual method of labour bargaining: by petition. The employers' legal methods of coercion hedged them about with a regular thicket of regulations, courts and prisons and a military with improved fire-power. Punishment by flogging at the work-place was the only weapon missing from the traditional armoury. In the long depression (on present evidence) no effective new worker or peasant formations appeared and labour bargaining other than by riot was at a halt. The wage workers' one advantage over contract workers was the right to move themselves in pursuit of higher wages. At the work-place, contract and wage workers were equally powerless.

This deadlock was not definitively broken in the British Caribbean until the 1930s. The demand for collective bargaining rights was formulated in the widespread upheavals stirred by the combined impact of World War I, price hikes, post-war layoffs and the new political horizons generated by emigration, military service and the first globally significant revolution of the twentieth century. Symptoms of new levels of worker solidarity appeared across the Americas in this period, from Peru to Nova Scotia. In St Kitts the first indigenous attempt at trade union formation was made by a disappointed 1896 striker-turned-US-immigrant who went home to politicize his fellow countrymen; the initiative was easily suppressed by law (Chapter 14). A legal right to collective bargaining was conceded only as part of the fall-out from the massive explosions of rage and despair detonated throughout the region by the second long depression of the century among a population which included both hungry peasants and rural workers (as in the 1860s) and large-scale conglomerates of urban poor, an immediate menace to the propertied middle classes. In these circumstances, middle-class propertied and professional people, by this date already involved in nationalist organizations demanding constitutional reform, put themselves forward to mediate between the enraged people and the imperial government. They acted as spokespersons for some popular demands and pushed their own constitutional priorities.[32]

The scale of the crisis, the emergence of middle-class leaders perceived as essential to the development of parliamentary democracy, plus strategic concern for securing Trinidad's oil fields,[33] all contributed to an imperial policy which in sharp contrast to the repression which followed Morant Bay, implemented constitutional and trade union reforms. Workers throughout the British Caribbean were suddenly invested with collective bargaining rights, the first increase in bargaining power since 1838.

This gain was offset by the fact that by this date trade union reform was simply one more weapon in the imperial government's arsenal for regulating colonial as well as domestic labour relations. Strenuous efforts were made to try and ensure that the workers would be led by actual, or at least aspiring members of the middle class and conducted according to the British model of 'responsible' unionism as compared to the syndicalist, anarcho-syndicalist and communist unions characteristic of Cuba and much of the Americas. In St Kitts this meant deliberately by-passing experienced, radical Black leaders in favour of the propertied professional coloured bourgeoisie who already served as elected members of the new legislative council introduced by the 1936 Constitutional reforms (Chapter 14).

The reforms, nevertheless, placed British Caribbean wage workers on a new footing. They no longer necessarily faced military reprisals or prison sentences for strike action; their risks and losses became primarily economic, gambling the actual loss of their subsistence on strike against the hope of a pay rise sufficient to compensate them. The employers on the other hand, gambling on profit margins, could calculate the best moment to secure the cheapest possible settlement.

In political terms unionization enabled work-place leaders to emerge, gain power within the organization and shape an independent political trajectory for the union which addressed the central issues of wages and work routines. It also led, in due course, to 'the most important strategic innovation of the trade union era', the direct involvement of the labouring population in politics. Mass mobilization to demand universal suffrage and independence in the 1940s was led by union leaders; when universal suffrage was finally conceded in 1951, the union and its allies won all the elective seats in the presidential legislature and in 1956 internal self-government made the union president become chief minister.

The union doubling as government became necessarily the sugar industry's confidential slaves, sitting on joint committees with industry representatives to discuss methods of reducing absenteeism on Sundays and

Mondays and of teaching the workers to regard 'the extinction of fires as a permanent duty'. It was an early version of Tripartism.

The workers, thrown back on traditional methods, turned like their forefathers to arson which in the 1950s destroyed increasing quantities of cane, from 2,000–70,000 tons, and challenged directly both their employers and the union leadership. They also resorted, yet again, to emigration, this time not to seasonal or short-term work in the Americas, but primarily to life-long exile in Britain. It was this haemorrhage of people which 'broke once and for all the planter's control of estate labour'. The best guarantee of subsistence standards for chattel and wage slave alike was, evidently, to be themselves in short supply for their exploiters' needs.

The validity of the demarcation between slave and legally free labour is in some respects confirmed by the findings here. The destruction of property rights in persons effected by abolition thrust slave workers into a new system of labour extraction which differentiated between their persons and their labour power and released them into the labour market. The ex-slaves were free to sell their labour power, not like slaves on hire for a portion of its market price, but for its full cash price.

Consistent with this change, methods of labour discipline changed and focused on the workers' wages rather than their persons. Punishment of their persons required legal process and imprisonment. Workers' lives continued to be endangered by what are now termed health and safety issues, but exposure to injury and death in the process of bargaining was occasional.

The use of legal mechanisms was symptomatic of another important new development: the employers' capacity to rely on the increasing coercive power in the hands of the colonial and post-colonial state – a development which often, as in the United States, preceded abolition and has continued to the present.

Abolition also opened the way for ex-slaves to struggle for the civil rights associated with free status. The arena defined for them by the new system of labour extraction provided only one legal recourse for the redress of grievances – to petition. Substantively, their position was that of the contract workers. In a sense the ex-slaves confronted at abolition a new version of the situation they had dealt with on arrival in the Americas: they had to establish nodes of rights to deal with their new situation. The difference was that the rights could be defined in law, rather than custom, and had to be established in conflict with existing laws. The ex-slaves were endowed with an improved legal status which permitted them to commence battle for citizen status.

The legal modification of slave status, however, left untouched the workers' fundamental problem, how to secure subsistence. This battle was to an extent complicated by their new status as sellers of labour power. As slaves, whatever the exchange rate for their labour, its use was assured.

Abolition exposed them to the local, national and international labour market. The struggle for subsistence now dictated finding a market for their labour. Their circumstances had altered but the purpose of their struggle remained the same, securing subsistence.

The eventual achievement of legal collective bargaining rights put a new instrument in their hands. But the basic work-place tactics available to them as trade unionists were the tactics they had used as slaves – overt and covert withdrawals of labour – and their success was contingent on the factors which influenced success within the slave system – demand for labour contingent on high prices and maintaining social stability. The power of trade union organizations themselves – even in the late twentieth century when they became corporate capital entities in their own right – was subordinate to the state. Trade unions at best assisted the maximization of wage increases during upswings in the world economy; in downswings their power base diminished and they provided the workers' wages little if any protection. In the last resort they commanded the arguments to support a fair day's wage for a fair day's work, but not the power to supply it.

These studies of the labour bargaining process confirm that the fundamental linkage between chattel slaves and wage slaves is that by barter, or sale, the whole of their active lives are consumed in pursuit of subsistence, in the effort to secure the necessities for life itself.

Notes

1. B.W. Higman, *Slave Population in the British Caribbean, 1807–1834*, (Baltimore and London), 188.
2. Mary Turner, 'Slave Workers, Subsistence and Labour Bargaining: Amity Hall, Jamaica, 1805–1832' in *The Slaves' Economy, Independent Production by Slaves in the Americas*, eds Ira Berlin and Philip D. Morgan (London, 1991), 94.
3. John Campbell, 'A "Kind of Freeman"?: Slaves' Market-Related Activities in the South Carolina Upcountry, 1800–1860', *Slaves' Economy*, 131–69.
4. Rebecca Scott, *Slave Emancipation in Cuba, The Transition to Free Labour, 1860–1899* (Princeton, 1985), 14.
5. Mary Turner, 'Slave Workers, Subsistence and Labour Bargaining', 101–2, *Slaves' Economy*.
6. P.P. (Lords) (no. 127) 1831–2, 306:646 evidence of Rev. P. Duncan.
7. Mary Turner, *Slaves and Missionaries: the Disintegration of Jamaican Slave Society, 1787–1834* (Urbana and London, 1982), Chap. 5.
8. Selected contributions include: S.W. Mintz, 'The Question of Caribbean Peasantries: a Comment,' *Caribbean Studies*, 1 (1961); *Caribbean Transformations*, (Chicago, 1974); 'Was the Plantation Slave a Proletarian?' *Review*, 2 (1978); Richard Frucht, 'A Caribbean Social Type: Neither "Peasant" nor "Proletarian"', *Social and Economic Studies*, 13 (1967); E.D. Genovese, 'Class, Culture and Historical Process', *Dialectical Anthropology*, 1 (1975).
9. See *The Slaves' Economy*, 1.
10. W.L. Burn, *Emancipation and Apprenticeship in the British West Indies*, (London, 1937) remains the definitive study on this period.
11. David Eltis, 'Free and Coerced Transatlantic Migrations: Some Comparisons', *American Historical Review*, 88 (1983) 255–7; Stanley L. Engerman, 'Contract labour, Sugar and Technology', *Journal of Economic History*, 43 (1983), 641, 644.
12. Donald Wood, *Trinidad in Transition* (London, 1968), 148.
13. Hugh Tinker, *A New System of Slavery, the Export of Indian Labour Overseas, 1830–1860* (London, 1974), 63.

14. Bridget Brereton, *A History of Modern Trinidad 1783-1962* (London, 1981), 105; Verena Stolke, *Coffee Planters, Workers and Wives, Class Conflict and Gender Relations on Sao Paulo Plantations, 1850-1980* (Oxford 1988), 15.
15. Michael Gonzales, 'Chinese Plantation Workers and Social Conflict in Peru in the Late 19th Century', *Journal of Latin American Studies*, 21 (1989), 393, 397.
16. Brereton, *A History of Modern Trinidad*, 107.
17. Tinker, *A New System of Slavery*, 89-90.
18. David V. Trotman, *Crime in Trinidad, Conflict and Control in a Plantation Society, 1838-1900*, (Knoxville, 1986), 194.
19. Evelyn Hu-Dehart, 'Chinese Coolie Labour in Cuba in the 19th Century: Free Labour or Neo Slavery?', *Slavery and Abolition*, 14 (1993), 82.
20. This applied until 1895; subsequently returnees paid a proportion of the cost. K.O. Laurence, *Immigration into the West Indies in the 19th Century*, (Barbados, 1971), 59.
21. Gonzales, 'Chinese Plantation Workers', 403, 415.
22. Howard D. Johnson, 'Patterns of Policing in the Post Emancipation British Caribbean', in *Policing the Empire, Government, Authority and Control, 1830-1940*, eds D.A. Anderson and D. Killingray (Manchester, 1991), 79-81.
23. Wood, *Trinidad in Transition*, 274-5.
24. Brereton, *Modern Trinidad*, 207.
25. Kusha Haraksingh, 'Control and Resistance among Indian Workers 1875-1917', in *India in the Caribbean*, eds David Dabydeen, Brinsley Samaroo (London, 1986), 74.
26. Verena Stolke, *Coffee Planters, Workers and Wives*, 34-6.
27. Master and Servant laws used throughout the British Caribbean in the post-emancipation period characteristically made breach of contract by a worker a criminal offence and by the master a civil offence. This followed the pattern set by the proto-type British Master and Servant law which was repealed in 1875 as a result of trade union pressure. Daphne Simon, 'Master and Servant', in *Democracy and the Labour Movement*, ed. John Saville (London, 1954), 160.
28. Dale W. Tomich, *Slavery in the Circuit of Sugar, Martinique in the World Economy, 1830-1848*, (Baltimore and London, 1990), 245-6, 255-7.
29. 4,565 contract workers were imported 1860-3 as crisis mounted. William A. Green, *British Slave Emancipation, the Sugar colonies and the Great Experiment 1830-1865* (Oxford, 1976), 382.
30. Import duties on staple foods for the working population became the revenue source of choice 1840-65; duty on herrings rose 166 per cent, on salt fish 366 per cent, on mackerel 433 per cent. Taxes were also loaded onto small settlers (e.g. for cart and donkeys) while plantation supplies were imported duty-free by 1865. Don Robotham, 'The Notorious Riot': the Socio-Economic and Political Bases of Paul Bogle's Revolt', *Anales del Caribe* (Havana) 3 (1983) 77, quoted in Thomas S. Holt, *The Problem of Freedom, Race, Labor and Politics in Jamaica and Britain, 1832-1938*, (Baltimore and London, 1992), 275.
31. Douglas Hall, *Free Jamaica, 1838-1865* (New Haven, 1965), 244-5.
32. Richard Hart, 'Origin and Development of the Working Class in the English-speaking Caribbean Area, 1898-1937', *Labour in the Caribbean*, eds Cross and Heuman (London, 1988), 50-75.
33. Howard D. Johnson, 'Oil, Imperial Policy and the Trinidad Disturbances, 1937', in *The Trinidad Labour Riots of 1937*, ed. Roy Thomas (St Augustine, Trinidad, 1987), 141-81.

I
Negotiating Slavery

Informal Contracts
&
Cash Rewards

1

Chattel Slaves into Wage Slaves

A Jamaican Case Study

MARY TURNER

Slaves were distinguished from other categories of labour by being persons whose labour was denied exchange value. They faced as workers, however, fundamentally the same problems as serfs, or wage workers; they were forced to spend their lives expending labour over and above what was necessary for their own subsistence. Improvement in work conditions for all categories of workers meant improving rewards for labour extracted and cutting down on the coercive power(s) of the owners of the means of production. The question arises, therefore, whether these fundamental similarities in the nature of exploitation and in the goals of the exploited indicate some similarities in their methods of struggle?[1]

The structure of slave based sugar production in the British Caribbean suggests this possibility. The plantations were set up as specialized, export oriented, agro-manufacturing units of 200–600 workers, supervised by a skeleton staff of owners and their waged employees as an integral part of an economy characterized by wage labour. These specialized export crop production units developed as part and parcel of a commercial economy with internal and external market connections in which the slaves themselves were gradually integrated through the development of their provision grounds. These plots, allocated for subsistence to cut production costs, generated surpluses necessary to the development of the colonial economy and provided the body of slaves, as petty producers, with cash rewards. Skilled slaves, hired out for payment as the towns grew, became proxy wage earners. Supplying labour in response to direct physical coercion in societies characterized by wage labour and from workers involved in the cash economy, dictated struggles over the degree of coercion and the quantities of reward.

This chapter investigates, in relation to Jamaican sugar estate workers, the dynamics generated by this contradiction. It is based on estate papers for the parish of St Thomas in the East, one of the most important sugar producing parishes in Jamaica with a slave population, in 1832, of 23,000.[2] It shows that the forms of class struggle which characterized contract and wage sugar estate workers, such as group and collective verbal protests as well as' appeals for mediation backed up by strike action, were adopted by slaves and contributed to undermining the slave labour based economy.

Early labour protest and strikes

The fundamental impetus which generated collective organisation among the slaves, these records suggest, was the struggle for survival. The provision ground system, usually regarded as in itself a mitigation of the slaves' work conditions, represented simply an alternative use of the slaves' labour by the owner who dictated that the slaves subsist the labour power they used. In the early stages of estate development this system subjected the slaves to additional problems. Blue Mountain estate, for example, was developed for sugar in the latter half of the eighteenth century in a fertile interior valley by an influx of predominantly male Africans who increased the estate labour force from 170 to 350.[3] The demands for estate work were such that only some of the more privileged and longest settled slaves were able to establish provision grounds.

This situation surfaced in 1787 after Jamaica had been pounded by successive hurricanes and was suffering the effects of new trade restrictions with the United States. Consequent food shortages dictated that, in the Jamaica Assembly's own estimate, 15,000 slaves died.[4] Conditions at Blue Mountain contributed to this death toll. The 1786 hurricane destroyed the slaves' plantain walks; emergency supplies of potatoes and black-eye peas brought in from Kingston proved inadequate. As a result, the great gang could not carry out its routine. Cane holing, which was particularly strenuous work on the heavy soil of a valley bottom, was curtailed because the workers were beginning to 'drop off fast'.[5]

In these circumstances the planting attorney, William Sutherland, in charge of the estate between 1780–1804, discovered that the 'better sort' of slaves had established grounds and were using the 'poorer sort' to work them in return for a share of the produce. The system broke down when provisions were scarce and the 'poorer sort' required subsistence from the estate.[6] Sutherland's terminology clearly suggests that the 'better sort' were skilled and confidential slaves and the policy he pursued confirms this. He did not challenge the system directly. The fight for subsistence had created a slave village interest bloc which could not be simply disciplined out of existence. He proposed, rather, to provide the 'poorer sort' with the means to develop their grounds by supplying all their food for a year.[7]

No such arrangement was made. Substantial losses to the work force threatened if the provision ground problem was not resolved, but despite Sutherland's pleas that the 'odd slice' of salt pork saved lives, the owner refused to undertake the expense involved. When the same subsistence problem surfaced a decade later during a prolonged drought, Sutherland strongly recommended more drastic action, recruiting 'a small gang of about 15 or 16 Negroes ... for the sole purpose of raising provisions'; in other words, workers should be withdrawn from sugar production to specialize in food production. Again, nothing was done; the workers were left to subsist themselves as best they could.[8]

The slave village interest bloc underpinned efforts to exert some control over work conditions and, in particular, to protest unjust and excessive use of coercion by overseers. Blue Mountain attorneys tried to minimize this problem by stocking the estate with new Africans; Jamaican born workers with 'bad habits' and 'connections outside the state', that is those familiar with local labour conditions and protest patterns, as well as experienced American slaves on sale after the revolution, were excluded.[9] Their method calls into question the rebellious qualities commonly attributed to 'wild Africans', but is, of course, consistent with industrial employers' preference for unorganized immigrant labour.

Despite these precautions Blue Mountain slaves effected the removal of two overseers between 1795 and 1800. In one case the action they took is not specified; in the paternalist language attorneys used, the overseer, William Grant, was described as having lost their (the slaves') affections. He had a 'peevish temper' and 'teasing methods' and his successor was recommended as a man of 'mild disposition'.[10] In this instance the slaves timed their protest well. The planters' fight against the Maroons, itself partly inspired by fear of revolutionary infection spreading from Haiti at the instigation of French agents, was in progress. Martial law, which drew overseers and bookkeepers away from the plantations was still in force and, when Grant was dismissed, had been extended for another month.[11] It was a moment which put a premium on management maintaining the 'affections' of the work-force.

In the second instance, the attorney masked the slaves' success by delaying the overseer's departure until the crop was over so that his removal appeared to be part of the turnover customary for white estate personnel.[12] The overseer, his reputation as a good planter (i.e. maximum sugar producer) at risk in an excessively rainy crop season, extracted labour 'by harsh ... bordering on cruel treatment of the Negroes, particularly the Pregnant Women'.[13] The pregnant women, despite the fact that they had most to lose by physical punishment, resisted work demands beyond their capabilities and won enough support among their fellows to make the overseer's position untenable.

The earliest and most developed form of labour protest in these records, however, took place at Grange Hill estate in 1770 during the attorneyship of

Malcolm Laing (1759–78) who first developed Blue Mountain estate for sugar. The Grange Hill slaves' struggle was facilitated by two circumstances: the land was only marginally suitable for sugar so its anticipated profit margins were lower than at Blue Mountain and, more significantly, the estate slaves were intertwined with the wage work economy of Manchioneal, a port and market town where the demand for skilled workers and the ready sale of ground provisions demonstrated the cash value of labour.[14]

By 1770 the slaves, some 200 strong, had secured terms of service distinctly in advance of existing slave code provisions: they had Thursdays as well as Sundays to work their provision grounds[15] and estate artisans enjoyed material benefits which reflected their value as wage earners: benefits intended, presumably, to curb any ambition for free status. Carpenter Joe, for example, lived in Kingston at Laing's house for three months every year, perhaps at his own insistence,[16] either to be hired out or to earn something for himself. His services on the estate earned the same rations of meat, salt fish and rum as the white managers had.

An artisan, once valued at a rate comparable to white wage earners, naturally appealed in the event of dispute with them, to the land owner's representative and, since an artisan was less replaceable than an overseer or a bookkeeper, such an appeal was likely to succeed. The Grange Hill records exemplify this process. Joe, in a dispute with the overseer, instantly appealed to the attorney who 'gave credit to the Carpenter' and sacked the overseer. The success of this grievance procedure naturally afforded 'a great triumph' and set a useful precedent to the whole work-force.[17]

In February 1770 a new overseer, David Munro, an ex-soldier with a military man's view of slave labour, took charge. He considered 'the same Discipline and Subordination ... proper to slaves, as is practised in the Army and Navy, and without which they can't be kept to their Duty ... It is a well known Maxim that a relaxation of Discipline, has the same effect on Slaves which it has on Soldiers: inclining them to Dissolute Indulgence and Loose passions'.[18]

The slaves' response to Munro's methods was to strike; early in September they took to the woods and sent four delegates 60 miles to Laing in Kingston to state their case. What ill-usage sparked the strike does not emerge; Laing had a clearly articulated policy of listening to both sides of 'Negro Stories' and his reaction to the crisis suggests that it was not, in his experience, altogether unusual. He told the slaves to return to work, told the overseer to withhold any punishments and promised to investigate affairs in two weeks' time when he had attended to business in Clarendon parish. In the upshot Munro, the military style disciplinarian, was sacked.[19]

The struggle for informal contract terms

In all these cases management, by judiciously responding to an immediate grievance, conceded very little and won a great deal. Laing, for example, by placating the work-force before crop commenced in December, secured his income and reputation, and prevented another flight to the woods which risked the permanent loss of some slaves, the disruption of neighbouring estates and the threat of small-scale rebellion. At the same time, the attorney impressed on propertyless whites respect for property in slaves. This class conflict was reflected also in the island courts; Laing himself took a white mason who shot one of the slaves in his charge to court 'as if the Man had perpetrated Murder'. Laing lost the case and the accused was awarded £5* for shooting a rebellious negro. As Grange Hill attorney, however, Laing had no intention of allowing Munro liberties with live investments and was perfectly prepared to give what the overseer termed 'glaring encouragement' to the slaves' 'contempt of Authority and of the White Colour'.[20]

Slave protests against the overseer's use of his coercive powers neatly exploited this class division and contributed to the turnover rate of white estate personnel. More significantly, this bargaining process secured the slaves material advantages which constituted informal contract terms, always disputed, but always likely to be reconfirmed and possibly improved upon. The bargaining process contributed, as Munro observed, to developing their political consciousness.

Island-wide developments fed and watered this consciousness in the early decades of the nineteenth century. The abolition of the slave trade in 1807 did not effect the transformation of the slave labour system the abolitionists hoped for, but it cut off the plantation owners' capacity to increase their effective labour force (i.e. workers aged 18–49) at will. The fixed labour force, with its own internally determined age structure, dwindled in numbers with the highest rates of loss on the sugar estates where the proportion of effective workers was reduced to some 40 per cent of the population by 1832.[21]

These circumstances generated new areas of struggle for the slave work-force and contributed to important new gains. In the first place, efforts to rationalize the available labour power removed workers wholesale from marginal to more profitable properties.[22] This robbed the workers of property (houses and grounds) and of the burial plots which contained their history. Removals prompted widespread resistance and induced some careful managers to offer compensation – houses and grounds already prepared at the new location – but conflict and coercion were always anticipated.[23] Thousands of slaves were removed; some however, as one of the cases discussed below indicates, secured *de facto* occupation of their estate.

The overall labour shortage, however, in some ways improved the slaves' bargaining position. Coloured slaves claimed by custom a right to differentiated functions as skilled and domestic as opposed to field workers; estates short of blacks for field work advertised coloured slaves for exchange.[24] More significantly, a substantial proportion of slaves secured, like the Grange Hill workers, more time for the provision grounds.

Their success was reflected in the 1816 Slave Code in which planters officially designated 26 days a year in addition to Sundays for provision ground cultivation. The slaves made it clear that they regarded the grounds and the time to work on them as a form of wages for their work on the estate. 'The slave thinks he has a right to those grounds on account of his labour on the property to which he belongs', one observer commented; at the same time, work on the grounds secured the slaves' foothold in the island's commercial economy and strengthened their bargaining position on the estate.[25]

The slaves' capacity to connect themselves to the island's commercial economy and to contribute to the export trade exacerbated the tension between coerced labour and 'waged' labour. Consciousness was raised, struggles with management intensified and, as a result, slave workers were able to establish customary norms for estate work and respect for their expertise. As Robert Scott, proprietor and attorney (1802–26) for 4,000 slaves in the important sugar producing parish of Trelawny commented:

> They are excessively impatient of control, if you exact more from them than you ought to do, *they will not submit to it*, but they know very well what duty [i.e. informal contract obligation] they have to do on a plantation and if no more is exacted, they are very easily managed and require no harsh treatment whatever.[26] (emphasis and brackets added)

Labour bargaining and re-negotiation of informal contract terms consequently took place whenever new overseers took charge. Overseers expected to 'encounter opposition' rather than, as in the cases reviewed, stir it up, and claimed that the whip was an essential weapon in their initial struggle to determine terms of work, including work loads.[27]

The establishment of work norms opened the way to demands for task work, sharpening the division between masters' time and slaves' time and led to forms of outright wage bargaining. The slaves pressed for time, food or cash payments for work over and above the production routine, such as the repair or extension of the existing infrastructure, roads, buildings, fences, bridges and ditches.

Task work characterized coffee and pimento production in Jamaica just as it characterized lowland rice cultivation in central South Carolina because, as Philip Morgan argues, this was the most efficient form of labour organization.[28] Investigation may prove, however, that the task work system reflected worker demands as much as staple crop 'requirements'. Certainly, no later than the 1820s slaves were pressing for task work in sugar production, traditionally characterized by gang labour and team work. The method seems to have been limited to cane holing, but it was suitable for both planting and cutting as continental experience in low country rice production demonstrated.[29] From management's point of view, task work, while recognizing work norms, also promoted productivity and reduced jobbing costs; the danger for the slaves, as some slave foremen realized, was that established work norms would be undercut.[30] Task work opened the way, however, to the demand for wages.

The slaves were always ready, as one observer put it, to work for pay. The slaves paid each other wages; Sunday work on the provision grounds, for example, could earn 1s. 8d per day plus breakfast. Sunday work on an attorney's garden might earn 2s. 11d plus breakfast; and cash payments were incorporated into task work deals. The planters faced the uncomfortable realization, articulated to the 1832 Commons Committee on Slavery, that they simply could not afford to pay both wages and maintenance.[31] From their foothold in the island's commercial economy, the slaves attacked directly the form of exploitation to which they were subjected.

The political implications of the struggle to secure free time and cash rewards for estate work were clearly spelt out for the slaves by the free coloured and black population which more than quadrupled (10,000–46,000) between 1800 and 1834. Freedmen, traditionally urban based, jostling with the slaves at market, now appeared in little colonies adjacent to some plantations, on land rented from ruinate estates. They worked as small producers and traders, and, in some cases, established family connections with estate slaves.[32] They translated into material terms the slaves' vision of the future implicit in the provision grounds, and their campaign for full civil rights which succeeded in 1830, extended that vision to embrace citizen status, a hope also fostered by the Protestant missionaries and the abolition campaigners.

The planter class rallied to hold back the creeping tide of economic and political pressure undermining their economy by improving management techniques. *The Jamaica Planter's Guide* (1823), for example, explicitly advocated security of tenure for occupations usually dominated by coloured slaves (artisans and domestics) and dismissal of overseers who wantonly interfered with the authority of drivers and head men; it celebrated the expertise of sugar boilers and their crucial role in production and specified, as great gang requirements, good tools, rum rations in wet weather and shelter from persistent rain.[33]

The challenge to white authority

The impact of these general circumstances and the limitations of management techniques are well illustrated by developments at Grange Hill and Blue Mountain which were in the hands (1825–9) of a reforming attorney, Charles Lewsey, imported by the absentee owner from Barbados to make his Jamaican properties pay. Lewsey's correspondence, suffused with awareness of labour problems, contrasts sharply with that of Laing and Sutherland and suggests one measure, though refracted through Barbadian experience, of the shift in the balance of power between workers and owners since the end of the slave trade. The estate workers indicate the new spectrum of these relations: one work-force bargaining within the parameters set by demands for sugar production while the other challenged those parameters.

The slave population at Blue Mountain in 1825 was just 176 – about the size it was before sugar production developed, a reduction Lewsey unhesitatingly attributed to malnutrition and mismanagement after studying the estate records.[34] Cultivation was carried on with the assistance of jobbing gangs. The use of jobbers could mean that estate slaves had successfully transferred part of the work load to hired gangs; at Blue Mountain it was symptomatic, rather, of estate slaves working, in industrial terms 'at stretch', in planter terminology, being subjected to 'the pushing system'. The 'pushing system' served merchant rather than planter interests by pushing for maximum profit crop by crop, at the expense of the owners' reputedly long-term profit interest.[35]

The slaves, nevertheless, had consolidated their village life and had their own social centre, a religious meeting-house with a regular priest, an elderly African, in charge. The priest is not characterized as an obeah man, perhaps because Lewsey did not wish to risk the effects of taking legal action against him, but may have been one of the syncretic sect leaders engendered by the Black Baptists (active since the 1780s) and the missions established in St Thomas in 1802. Whatever the case, the slaves made it clear to Lewsey that their religion was their own affair by resisting his efforts to make them good Anglicans; very few consented to be baptised even at the ceremony held for Lewsey's own infant daughter.[36]

On the estate, apparently under the leadership of Becky, the head driver, the slaves used a variety of methods to limit white authority and to assert their own expertise. They threatened strike action in response to manifestly unjust as well as cruel punishment. Conscious that the take-over period was a testing time for managers and workers Lewsey, in good Barbadian fashion, set out to establish that he ran a tight ship; in pursuit of economy and efficiency he systematically attacked infringements of estate property rights and consequently curtailed traditional slave property rights. One such move sparked instant collective protest: he ordered the slaughter, without warning, of hogs found straying in the cane. Outraged property owners surrounded Lewsey, long discussions ensued, and though the slaves finally (in Lewsey's account) admitted they were wrong to let the hogs stray, the attorney was left in no doubt as to the injustice of his action.[37]

The slaves had their revenge; the head driver, Becky, made a mockery of Lewsey's efficiency campaign by demonstrating the incompetence of his assistant, overseer Parkinson, a trainee planter also from Barbados. Ordered to close up a drain trench that needed to be open, Becky defied the order. Parkinson compounded his error and called the second driver to take Becky to the stocks. Lewsey, who met the punishment detail on the way, instantly recognized 'all is done here with Mr Parkinson ... The negroes find out he knows nothing'. Slave expertise had discredited white management; Lewsey raged privately that 'it was the overseer that ought to be put in the stocks'. Publicly, he tried to save face, told Becky he would 'beg Mr Parkinson for him' and put the trainee back on probation.[38]

Becky's exposure of Parkinson, nevertheless, undermined his authority. When he tried to solace himself by commanding new sexual favours and sent male slaves to solicit for him, they did not meet with instant success. Customarily, slave women sought alliances with white managers for there were immediate material benefits and the children were whitened. Parkinson, however, already had a resident 'housekeeper' and some male relatives of the girls solicited, concerned perhaps to assert their family's autonomy or to comment obliquely on Parkinson's career prospects with Lewsey, refused on their behalf. The three girls who were recruited were made a common laughing stock by field women next day. Parkinson, desperate to assert his authority, took advantage of Lewsey's absence in Vere and had the women flogged, 18 lashes on their naked shoulders.

The women, an important component in the first gang, sent a delegation to Mrs Lewsey and threatened to walk off the job to go to Vere and complain to Lewsey. Mrs Lewsey played mediator; she sent for Lewsey and promised Parkinson would cease all punishments if the women returned to work. Lewsey in contrast to Laing who, confronted by an actual strike could order the slaves back to work on the promise of an investigation two weeks later, was on the spot in 48 hours, heard all parties and immediately sent Parkinson off the estate.[39]

The intensity of the contract bargaining process at Blue Mountain permeates the correspondence and it is clear that agreement was reached chiefly because labour shortages forced Lewsey to rationalize production; this meant reduced work loads and improved work routines. The land laid out in sugar was 'beyond the strength' of the estate workers and jobbers were expensive: great gang work cost 2s. 1d, caneholing 2s. 6d per day per worker, or £7.10s. an acre and their use tended to be cumulative, from clearing land, to cane holing, weeding and cutting.[40] Lewsey reduced the acreage in cane and organized sugar production to cut down on night work during crop. The Blue Mountain slaves became part of an experimental routine which attracted comment throughout the parish and was brought to the attention of the House of Commons Select Committee on Slavery in 1832. The mill was shut down for 6–8 hours every week night and from Saturday evening until Monday morning. This gave a 16–18 hour production day, worked in spells, but allowed for 6–8 hours sleep every night.[41]

The slaves at first regarded these innovations with suspicion and scepticism, suspecting that some new loss of privilege or property would make them pay for apparent improvement. As the new work routine continued, however, the reduced acreage to hole and weed and a reduced working day at the mill achieved co-operation. The benefits to management were measured when the 1826 crop was taken off. Like the crop of 1800, it was done in the face of heavy rains which fell from January through to July; 'not two days together have we had in those months fair'. The weather made extra work: the cattle pens became swamps and had to be moved seven or eight times. But, in marked contrast to 1800, the workers' health and spirits stayed good. They let Lewsey know they were trying their best; 'Let us put our shoulder to the wheel and break out a good crop for Massa'. Lewsey took the hint and put up an old steer (value £8cy) to fatten for the harvest home. Almost lyrical with success, he wrote, 'It is truly gratifying to see we can make such an improvement [in the quality of sugar] in the same copper and with the same people'. All this was achieved without a single case of insubordination or a single complaint 'presenting itself for some months'.[42]

The benefits to the slaves were described by the head driver. Lewsey, characteristically, asked him if the cane cutters did more work after they had a night's rest.

> He said that the Negroes did not require to be *Drove* that frequently *before time* when the officer had to look for the people in the morning they would find 5 or 6 absent, or Gone to some cane piece to sleep, that those that had *Heart* to take the Flogging would come up and receive it and go to work and those that had none would *Run*.

The results had been bad sugar, bad returns and 'disgraceful depopulation on this estate'.[43]

The slaves at Blue Mountain, as sugar workers, had something to gain from improved contract terms; at Grange Hill they had everything to lose. Grange Hill slaves had successfully cut down on estate work and devoted themselves to provision ground production and marketing. On their grounds they employed, for payment in cash or kind, slaves from other estates and runaways and took the produce to market on the estate mules. Manchioneal was no longer their main outlet; they travelled 30 miles to Morant Bay and shipped from there to the Kingston market.[44]

It is not clear how all the slaves fitted into this system; certainly some enjoyed a higher than average standard of living. Slaves usually owned a few chickens, a hog and sometimes a goat, but only headmen had mules to ride. At Grange Hill slaves commonly owned donkeys with a market value of £8cy.[45] Sugar production was marginalized; the 'Engine ground the Cane juice and the Coppers Stewed the same into what they call Sugar'. Local jobbing gangs did most of the work, not because the estate slaves were subjected to the 'pushing system', but because they had minimized their work loads and 'enjoyed a Life of Idleness'.[46]

Lewsey initially held his predecessor ('a sinecurist') responsible for this state of affairs but experience taught that his real enemy was John Reay, the head driver. Reay had a reputation in the parish as a man of good character – a court case was settled in his favour on that account – and his support among the Grange Hill work-force made him, virtually, ruler of the estate. Lewsey's efforts to tighten discipline and improve production met with collective non-cooperation. His threat to sell the slaves if runaways were found on the provision grounds was met by silence, possibly of disbelief, since slave prices were low. The promise of cash rewards ($1 a head) and the threat of the work house for Reay if he was not the first to inform on culprits, produced no results.[47] The threat to rent out their provision lands and supply them with corn instead (the practice in Vere parish) provoked, however, a strong verbal response; drivers and people in a grand chorus, nicely calculated for the ear of a man himself devoted to their owners' service, begged for forgiveness, and promised to work their lands. Led by the drivers they pleaded with special fervour that Lewsey not 'write and inform *Master* of their bad conduct'.[48]

The chorus of assurance expressed primarily, as Lewsey rapidly discovered, the collective determination to defend the status quo. Lewsey resorted to physical punishment of individuals; slaves identified as 'trouble makers' were weeded out periodically and sent to 'cool' in the work house. The punishment of individuals did not provoke any overt retaliation from the slaves and no work stoppages or grievance meetings ensued. Management hopes of 'redeeming this property from ruin' were sustained.[49] But such punishments did not alter the power structure on the estate; Lewsey's threats against Reay intensified – he promised to destroy him by sending him from one work house to another through the island, 'unless an immediate emendation takes place in the conduct of the people' – but he never judged it appropriate to do so. The only slave to lose office, in fact, was the woman driver of the productively least important third gang. Mary Tait was 'broke from her Office' for 'winking at the Idleness of those under her charge and for not paying attention to the children and reporting the dirt eaters to the Overseer and the Head Man'.[50] Lewsey made no attempt, either, to move the slaves collectively to Blue Mountain. Although desirable in economic terms, this threatened resistance at Grange Hill and disruption at Blue Mountain. Transfers were individual and voluntary and on this basis ten young men, prime workers, moved to Blue Mountain.[51]

The processes which undermined productivity and with it white authority, are illustrated by the case of Mr Fry the bookkeeper. Sent with a driver and the head watchman to clear a yam piece, he left at least half the yams in the ground 'and those the pick Yams of the whole piece', the overseer reported that 'they took good care not to dig one good one for me'. This 'neglect of duty' by the bookkeeper, together with similar instances, and an old grievance against his 'shameful conduct in attempting mauling a female in the Hot House' secured his dismissal.

The bookkeeper's 'neglect of duty' may have been just that; the circumstances suggest, however, that the level of disaffection among the slaves made it more politic to leave a job half done than coerce them to complete it. Mr Fry did not make an issue of the yam digging and neither, in fact, did the overseer; he sacked Mr Fry, but makes no mention of punishing the slaves.[52] The bookkeeper and the overseer seem to have agreed that, given the state of labour relations on the estate, disciplinary action was not appropriate.

The slaves won this round in the struggle; Lewsey reluctantly concluded he could never promote at Grange Hill 'the Great Work of Reform' achieved at Blue Mountain. Surrounded by 'A set of subjects which meet me on every Quarter with Low Cunning and Vile Cant' efficient sugar production was out of the question; he could only 'extinguish it' as a sugar estate.[53] The property was turned to pasture and livestock, which complemented the slaves' provision ground production and rationalized the economic transformation they had effected.

Conclusion

The slaves at Blue Mountain and Grange Hill demonstrate that the methods of struggle customarily identified with wage workers were first developed by slave workers cognisant of the crucial value of labour power. Collective withdrawal of labour, the presentation of grievances and the use by owners and managers of mediation were methods developed by 1770. Group action by slaves with particular grievances was also used, notably by women, and secured positive results. Skilled and confidential slaves pioneered these processes and the head men on both estates emerge as instigators and, by inference, organizers of group and collective action.

The immediate cause of action was physical coercion: the whip used to extract more intensive, or longer hours of labour and to exert arbitrary authority. The protests recorded were directed against the slaves' immediate oppressors, a realistic objective given the sharp class difference between owners and their representatives and their hirelings. It is clear, however, that the slaves also fought to command their own labour and their own produce, including a 50 per cent share in the estate yam piece. The records reflect primarily the *results* of these struggles which were facilitated by long term trends – the diminution in the labour force and the expansion of the internal market. The *methods* used can also be inferred – 1770 style strike action together with informal 'deals' and 'understandings' between head men and overseers. The problems presented by 'managing' slaves practically dictated that overseers were either strict disciplinarians (like Munro), or time servers. In either case, their transience assisted the modification of work loads and increased rewards. The attorneys themselves were no more than occasional visitors whose self-interest, like Laing's, was often best served by acceding to the slaves' demands – a pattern sufficiently common by the 1820s for attorneys to attempt to conceal from the slaves their key role in overseer dismissals.[54]

The Blue Mountain and Grange Hill experience suggests more than one parallel with nineteenth-century Russian serf bargaining procedures. Many serfs were also owned by absentees, supervised by stewards (attorneys) and managed by bailiffs (overseers). Deterioration of work conditions, excessive work demands, excessive punishments, removal of livestock, and seduction of women, also prompted grievance procedures. In this case, written petitions to a higher authority – the owners, a local official (magistrate) or even the Tsar – were carried by delegates who risked flogging. Complaints often focused on the bailiff and, if nothing was done, the serfs went on strike until a special land court composed of local officials (a form of Council of Protection) reviewed the complaint. The end result, which affected the fortunes of several hundreds of thousands of workers on vast estates, was frequently armed resistance and military confrontation.[55]

The slaves' use of strike action and their long tradition of bargaining for informal contract terms places in a new perspective the role played by strike action in slave rebellions (e.g. the 1831 Jamaica rebellion) and invites revision and re-assessment of small-scale events currently labelled 'rebellion'. Small-scale outbreaks may represent spontaneous reactions to the failure of mediation processes.

The struggle of the Jamaican slaves also places in context their astonishing performance as apprentices. The Apprenticeship scheme, implemented in August 1834, incited the workers to bring to bear on a published contract all the skills they had acquired in making, maintaining and developing informal contract terms. The new contract, which established the working week at $40\frac{1}{2}$ hours a week and also rolled back customary allowances to the levels sanctioned by the slave code, resulted in island-wide confrontations. For several months Jamaica teetered on the verge of some form of general strike. The crisis was only resolved when, with crop season looming, 'all the prominent attorneys' and all the big sugar producers conceded the old allowances for the shorter working week.[56] The part-time wage slaves' first task, under the new contract, was to consolidate the gains they had made as chattel slaves.

The records also demonstrate the crucial role in these developments of the slaves' connection with the world of wage labour outside the plantation. The differences between Grange Hill and Blue Mountain derive to a large extent from the fact that Grange Hill slaves were closely intertwined with that economy no later than 1770. Their access to cash returns for labour on their provision grounds exacerbated the tension between coerced labour on the estate and exchange-valued labour on the grounds. In the last decade of slavery these workers were able to carry this struggle a significant step further and take the estate out of sugar production. Grange Hill represents, perhaps, one extreme of a spectrum with Blue Mountain, a profitable sugar property where workers still bargained for terms as sugar producers, at the other.

By 1832 Jamaica's gross domestic product was worth £5.5 million sterling of which exports from the plantation sector represented just under 50 per cent (£2.2 million). The slaves' contribution to the economic pie 'outside the canefields' has been calculated at £1.5 million and included almost complete dominance of food production for local consumption (£847,000 of £900,000) as well as contributing arrowroot and ginger, for example, to the export trade. No less than 27 per cent of Jamaica's total agricultural output came from the slaves' provision grounds and was the product of waged labour. The slaves in Jamaica were bursting the bonds of the coerced labour economy by the same processes which undermined the serf economy in western Europe.[57]

The slave labour system, instituted by capitalists to foment rapid capital accumulation, was undermined by the slaves' participation in the capitalist economy they were intended simply to serve. This development reached its apogee in the 1831 rebel slaves' demand, reinforced by the destruction of a million pounds' worth of their owners' crops and property, for wages. In the context created by the re-formation in 1832 of Britain's own ruling class, the Jamaican slaves' militancy destroyed slave labour as a separate category throughout the British Empire and forced acknowledgement of their right to wages for their work.

Notes

* £1 sterling = £1.4cy

1. Slave labour is more usually considered a 'peculiar institution': E. Foner for example, in *Nothing But Freedom*, (Baton Rouge, University of Louisiana Press 1983) writes of the slave plantation as generating 'a distinct system of social relations as well as its own characteristic class system and political economy' (p. 9). This analysis was presented in April 1986 at the Association of Caribbean Historians' Conference, Nassau, Bahamas and published in *Labour in the Caribbean*, M. Cross and G. Heuman (eds), (London, 1988). While any shortcomings remain my own I am indebted to friends and colleagues for encouragement and advice, including Nigel Bolland, Paul Burgwin, Stanley Engerman, Gad Heuman, Barry Higman, Woodville Marshall, Sidney Mintz and Robert Shenton.
2. Fitzherbert Papers 239M/E, Derbyshire County Record Office, Matlock, Derbyshire; Barry Higman, *Slave Population and Economy in Jamaica 1807–1834*, (Cambridge 1976), 53, Table 6: 123, Table 24.
3. Fitzherbert Papers 239M/E 17766, William Sutherland (planting attorney) to Jacques and Fisher (mercantile attorneys) 24 Nov. 1783; hereafter referred to as 239M/E.
4. Hurricanes struck Feb., Oct., 1780: Aug. 1781: Oct. 1786. Richard S. Sheridan, 'The Crisis of Subsistence in the British West Indies during and after the American Revolution', *William and Mary Quarterly*, 33: Oct. 1976, 625, 632.
5. 239M/E, 17787, 17803, Sutherland to Jacques and Fisher, 29 Aug. 1785; 9 April 1787.
6. 239M/E 17803, ibid., 9 April 1787.
7. Ibid., Great Britain, Parliamentary papers, (Commons) *Report from the Select Committee on the Extinction of Slavery Throughout the British Dominions*, (no. 721) 1831–2, 20: Q: 6398, William Shand (hereafter cited as P.P. (Commons) (no. 721), 1831–2, 20) corn took 4, yams 8, and plantains 11 months to mature.
8. 239M/E 17843 Sutherland to Sir William Philip Perrin (absentee owner), 14 Jan. 1798. Some sugar estates (e.g. Worthy Park) resolved the subsistence problem by importing Jamaican food, (yams, cocos, plantains) from specialized provision grounds. It is not clear, however, that the slaves' conditions there were significantly better than at Blue Mountain. Michael Craton and James Walvin, *A Jamaican Plantation: The History of Worthy Park, 1670–1970*, (London, 1970), 135.
9. 239M/E 16972–3, Jacques and Fisher to Perrin, 24 April 1783; 17766, Sutherland to Jacques and Fisher, 24 Nov. 1783; 17143, Jacques to Perrin, 28 Feb. 1794.
10. 239M/E, 17177, Jacques to Perrin, 7 Sept. 1795.
11. 239M/E, 17177, 17179, Jacques to Perrin, 7 Sept., 6 Oct., 1795.
12. 239M/E, 17322, Jacques, Laing and Ewing to Perrin, 26 July 1800; Craton and Walvin, *A Jamaican Plantation*, 145.

13. 239M/E, 17323, Jacques, Laing and Ewing to Perrin, 26 July 1800.
14. 239M/E, 17084, Jacques and Fisher to Perrin, 12 April 1785; 17733, James Blaw (overseer) to Mrs Frances Perrin, 7 Feb. 1775.
15. 239M/E, 17717, David Munro (overseer) to Mrs Frances Perrin, narrative account.
16. Charles B. Drew, 'David Ross and the Oxford Iron Works: a study in Industrial Slavery in the early nineteenth century', *William and Mary Quarterly*, 31: April 1974, 205. c.f. case of Billy Bacon, skilled slave who insisted on being hired out in Richmond; his owner had to employ a white miller to replace him.
17. 239M/E, 17717, Munro, narrative account.
18. Ibid.
19. 239M/E, 17711, Malcolm Laing (planting attorney) to Munro, 11 Sept. 1770. US planters recognized that disciplinarian overseers had the greatest difficulties in managing slaves. Wm. K. Scarborough, *The Overseer*, Baton Rouge, Louisiana State University Press, 1966, 79–80.
20. 239M/E, 17717, Munro, narrative account.
21. Higman, op. cit., 206.
22. Ibid. 224–5.
23. P.P. (Commons) (no. 721), 1831–2, 20: Q. 25, W. Taylor; Q. 513, J.B. Wildman.
24. Higman, op. cit., 208–9.
25. P.P. (Commons) (no. 721), 1831–2, 20: Q. 1406, 1495, Rev. P. Duncan.
26. Ibid. Q. 5283, Robert Scott.
27. Ibid. Q. 510–11, William Taylor.
28. Higman, op. cit., 23, 29, 220; Philip S. Morgan, 'Work and Culture: The task system and the World of Low Country Blacks 1700–1880', *William and Mary Quarterly*, 39, Oct. 1982, 563–99.
29. Ibid. p. 583.
30. P.P. (Commons) (no. 721), 1831–2, 20: Q. 63, 90, William Taylor.
31. Ibid., Q. 89, 90, 111, 570, William Taylor.
32. Ibid., Q. 129, William Taylor.
33. T. Roughley, *The Jamaica Planter's Guide*, (London, 1823), 82, 97,101–2, 340–1.
34. 239M/E, 21021, Lewsey to Fitzherbert, 9 May 1826.
35. 239M/E, 21032, Lewsey to Fitzherbert, 2 July 1826.
36. 239M/E, 20992, Lewsey to Fitzherbert, 9 Aug. 1825.
37. 239M/E, 20985, 20987, Lewsey to Fitzherbert, 12 June, 18 July 1825.
38. 239M/E, 20985, Lewsey to Fitzherbert, 12 June 1825.
39. 239M/E, 20993, Lewsey to Fitzherbert, 25 July 1825.
40. Higman, op. cit., p. 238, Table Al, 1.
41. 239M/E 21021, Lewsey to Fitzherbert, 9 May 1826; P.P. (Commons) (no. 721), 1831–2, 20: Q. 563, William Taylor.
42. 239M/E, 21032, 21021 Lewsey to Fitzherbert, 9 May, 2 July 1826; Higman, op. cit., 237.
43. 239M/E, 21021, Lewsey to Fitzherbert, 9 May 1826.
44. 239M/E, 20986, Lewsey to Fitzherbert, 18 July 1825.
45. Higman: op. cit., 238.
46. 239M/E, 20139, Lewsey to Fitzherbert, 22 Aug. 1826.
47. 239M/E, 20985, 20986, 20987, Lewsey to Fitzherbert, 12 June, 8, 18 July 1825.
48. 239M/E, 20986, Lewsey to Fitzherbert, 8 July 1825.
49. 239M/E, 21004, Lewsey to Fitzherbert, 28 Feb. 1826.
50. 239M/E, 21039, Lewsey to Fitzherbert, 22 Aug. 1826.
51. 239M/E, 21021, Lewsey to Fitzherbert, 9 May 1826.
52. 239M/E, 21004, William Duncan (overseer) to Lewsey, 28 Feb. 1826.
53. 239M/E, 21039, Lewsey to Fitzherbert, 22 Aug. 1826.
54. P.P. (Commons) (no. 721), 1831–2, 20: Q. 6510, William Shand.
55. Peter Kolchin, 'The Process of Confrontation; Patterns of resistance to Bondage in 19th Century Russia and the United States', *Journal of Social History*, vol. 11, 1977–8, 459–63.
56. W.L. Burn, *Emancipation and Apprenticeship*, London 1970, 176–7.
57. M. Craton, ed., *Roots and Branches*, Toronto 1979, S.W. Mintz, 'Slavery and the Rise of Peasantries', 231 quoting A.J.G. Knox, 'Opportunities and Opposition, The Rise of Jamaica's Black Peasantry and the Nature of Planter Resistance', *Canadian Review of Sociology and Anthropology*, 14, 1977, 386. c.f. Robert Brenner, 'Agrarian Class Structure and Economic Development in Preindustrial Europe', *Past and Present*, no. 70, Feb. 1976, 30–75.

2

Strategies of Slave Subsistence

The Jamaican Case
Reconsidered

RICHARD B. SHERIDAN

To the Arawaks, the first known inhabitants, Jamaica was a land of streams
and forests. It is also a land of mountains, savannas, fertile valleys, coastal
plains, the lower basins and deltas of the larger rivers which have rich
alluvial soil, and 'karst' lands known as the Cockpit Country. At some risk
of oversimplification, it can be said that in slave days the larger sugar plantations or estates occupied fertile, lowland areas; cattle pens, the savannas and
hills; coffee, the hills and mountains; minor staples and slave provision
grounds, areas of sparse population and broken terrain. Jamaica was Britain's
richest colony in the eighteenth and early nineteenth centuries, linked by
trade and shipping to the metropolis, West Africa, North America, and
Latin America. While coffee growing became important in the 1790s and
early 1800s, sugar cane planting and processing was the base on which was
erected Jamaica's great wealth and income. What was needed in land and
physical equipment for a profitable sugar estate was a large extent of level,
fertile and well watered land to grow sugar cane, provision grounds for the
slaves, pastures for livestock, and woodland for fuel and building materials.
At a central location on the estate were the sugar works consisting of
the mill for crushing the canes, a boiling house, curing house, rum distillery,
hothouse or slave hospital, and various outbuildings. The planter's great-
house was generally built on rising land overlooking the sugar works and
the village of huts occupied by the slave workers, and at an intermediate
point stood the houses of the white overseer, bookkeepers, and skilled
craftsmen.

Most crucial to the functioning of the sugar estates and other labour using
activities were the African West Indian slaves who were known as the
'sinews of empire'. As the planting frontier of Jamaica expanded from the

48

late seventeenth to the early nineteenth centuries, masses of labour were needed to clear new land, construct sugar works, slave quarters, great-houses and grow and process sugar canes and other export staples. Slave trade statistics show a total of 828,185 African slaves imported into Jamaica in the period 1702–1808, of whom 193,597 were re-exported to other markets, leaving 634,588 to labour on the island. Slave population estimates for the island are 45,000 in 1700, rising to 300,000 in 1800. This meant that some 575,000 (634,588 less the 58,505 slaves imported in the period 1801–8) new labourers were needed during the eighteenth century to increase the population by 250,000, or a ratio of about two imported slaves to one net addition to the island's slave population.[1]

To feed this work-force owners and managers had to import food or have the slaves produce it, either as part of the regular work of the estate or on their own account. The second course, where practicable, was more economical and less risky. In Jamaica, although imported foodstuffs and estate-supervised production of provisions played a part in subsisting the slaves, the dominant system came to be one of unsupervised production of food crops by the slaves. They were allotted parcels of land, unsuited to the growing of sugar cane and other export staples to produce a variety of foods, 'such as tree crops, vegetables, and edible herbs and roots, as well as craft materials'. In time, they came to produce surpluses which they took 'to local markets and exchanged for other commodities or sold for cash'.[2]

The Jamaican provision ground and internal marketing system was characterized by the largely unsupervised food growing and marketing by slaves who were allotted small plots known as 'yards', 'house plots', or 'kitchen gardens', near their huts in the slave village, and on the outskirts of plantations larger plots known as 'provision grounds', 'negro grounds', or 'polincks'. This system of largely self-organized subsistence production, it is argued, benefited masters and slaves. It saved masters much trouble and expense and was a means of guaranteeing cheap labour; it kept the slaves usefully employed in seasons of slack demand for plantation labour; it minimized the risk of food shortage and famine at times of natural disasters and wartime shipping embargoes.

At the same time, the provision ground system enabled the slave to get away from the oppressive plantation environment and work with family members and interact socially with other slaves. It increased the slave's capacity to function independently and intelligently, is said to have provided him and his family with a better diet, a small income from the sale of foodstuffs and other products, and gave him a feeling of proprietorship in the land. Sidney Mintz and Douglas Hall, authors of the pioneer monograph on the origins of the Jamaican internal marketing system, argue, among other things, that the provision grounds and markets helped to make the slaves less discontented, less likely to run away, and less prone to rebel. Mintz, in a later publication, uses the term 'proto-peasant' to characterize those activities that provided slaves with agricultural skills, craft techniques and other essentials by which a peasant-style life was created, in spite of the repressive conditions of slavery.[3]

'Jamaica', according to Orlando Patterson, 'was the first of the West Indian islands to utilize the provision ground system as the main source of supplying the slaves with their subsistence and it was the island in which the system was most highly developed'. Evidence of rudimentary provision grounds can be found as early as the period 1671–5, when Governor Sir Thomas Lynch gave detailed instructions for establishing a cocoa plantation on which he said there was a need for provision grounds for both white indentured servants and African Jamaican slaves.[4]

It was openly acknowledged, however, that the provision ground system in fact at times fell short of satisfying the slaves' basic needs. The results were vividly described by Governor Sir Edward Trelawny who wrote in 1746 that 'some of the poor Creatures pine away and are starved, others that have somewhat more spirits, go a stealing and are shot as they are caught in Provision Grounds; others are whipt or even hang'd for going into the Woods, into which Hunger and Necessity itself drives them to try to get Food to keep Life and Soul together'. Subsistence crises followed drought, storm, hurricane and wartime shortages of imported supplies. A combination of successive hurricane years (1780, 1781, 1784, 1785, 1786) and wartime shortage produced an outright famine officially estimated to have killed 150,000 slaves.

It is clear, however, that in other seasons some slaves had produce to sell. Slaves brought their provisions and other articles to markets established for the white community, the first of which was held at Spanish Town in 1662, seven years after the English occupation. Marketing activity increased in subsequent years, so much so, in fact, that in 1735 an act of the Assembly of Jamaica provided that 'Slaves may carry about, and sell, all manner of provisions, fruits, fresh fish, milk, poultry, and other small stock of all kinds, having a ticket from their owner or employer'.[5] This article investigates the contradictory evidence relating to the provision ground system and brings to question its adequacy as a method of slave subsistence.

Leading Jamaicans asserted, in a report from the Committee of the Assembly (23 November 1815), that the treatment of slaves had improved markedly both before and after abolition of the transatlantic slave trade. The laws now afforded protection to the slave in the important points of life, that is, 'exemption from cruel and excessive punishment, or severe labour, and secures to him food, raiment, and a fair trial for offenses, involving the punishment of death, transportation, or protracted confinement to hard labour'.[6]

Lending credence to the above committee report is the recent work of John R. Ward. He estimates that the productivity of slaves engaged in sugar production in the older British West Indian colonies (which include

Jamaica) increased about 35 per cent between 1750 and 1830. This rise in productivity he attributes chiefly to improvements in the quality of the labour force, for experience showed the planters that 'a better-fed, self-reproducing labour force was superior in efficiency to contingents of half-starved Africans'. Ward adds much to our understanding of technical changes which contributed to the increased productivity of labour and to planter-directed measures to ameliorate the condition of slaves on sugar estates.[7]

In his historical survey of the slave laws of Jamaica, Orlando Patterson finds that 'for almost three-quarters of the period of slavery Jamaica did not possess a proper slave-code. All that existed between 1655 and 1788 was a series of *ad hoc* laws, most of which were prompted by sheer necessity, and were largely confused, vague, in parts, even contradictory'. Codifying or consolidating the laws relating to slaves was undertaken after 1782, in response to pressure from the abolition movement in England to ameliorate the condition of the slaves and also the slave rebellion in Saint Domingue.[8]

Bryan Edwards had the Consolidated Act of Jamaica, passed 2 March 1792, printed in his *History of the British West Indies*, which was first published in 1793. Clause II provided that 'every master, owner, or possessor, of any plantation or plantations, pens, or other lands whatsoever', should allot a sufficient quantity of land for every slave in his possession, 'and allow such slave sufficient time to work the same, in order to provide him, her, or themselves, with sufficient provisions for his, her or their maintenance'. Furthermore, all such masters, owners or possessors were required to 'plant at least one acre of land for every ten negroes that he shall be possessed of on such plantation, pen, or other lands, over and above the negro-grounds aforesaid; which lands shall be kept up in a planter-like condition, under the penalty of fifty pounds'. A note attached to this clause said that in the former act of 1782 an acre of ground provisions was to be planted for every four Negroes, 'but it was found an exorbitant and unnecessary allowance'.[9]

Clause III of the 1792 slave act provided that slave-owners, masters, chief managers, and overseers should 'personally inspect into the condition of such negro-grounds once in every month at the least, in order to see that the same are cultivated and kept up in a proper manner, of which oath shall be made, as in this act is hereafter directed'. Where lands proper for growing provisions were not available to the masters, owners, or possessors, they were to 'make good and ample provision for all such slaves as they shall be possessed of, equal to the value of two shillings and six-pence currency per week for each slave, in order that they may be properly supported and maintained, under the penalty of fifty pounds'. Clause IV prohibited masters, owners, possessors, attorneys, guardians, and trustees from discarding or turning away 'any slave or slaves, on account of or by reason of such slave or slaves being rendered incapable of labour or service' because of 'sickness, age, or infirmity; but every such master, owner, or possessor, as aforesaid, shall be, and he is hereby obliged ... to find and provide them with wholesome necessaries of life ...' Owners who failed to provide for such slaves and allowed them 'to wander about, or become burthensome to others' suffered a penalty of ten pounds for every such offence.[10]

Several clauses in the act of 1792 specified the holidays allowed during the year, the days allowed to slaves to cultivate their provision grounds, and the hours of work and breaks for meals for field slaves. Clause XVIII allowed holidays to all slaves on Christmas-day and the day following, and a single day at Easter and Whitsuntide, provided that, apart from Christmas, no two holidays should be allowed 'to follow or succeed immediately one after the other', thus prohibiting long weekend holidays. Clause XIX made compulsory the 'usual and customary practice of allowing slaves one day in every fortnight to cultivate their own provision-grounds (exclusive of Sundays), except during the time of crop [or harvest]'. A penalty of £50 was levied for infractions of this clause. Clause XX stated that 'every field-slave on such plantation or settlement shall, on work days, be allowed, according to custom, half an hour for breakfast, and two hours for dinner'; and no slave be compelled to perform field-work 'before the hour of five in the morning, or after the hour of seven at night, except during the time of crop, under the penalty of fifty pounds, to be recovered against the overseer, or other person having the care of such slaves'.[11]

The slave act of 1816 modified the act of 1792 in three particulars. It increased the time allowed to cultivate provision grounds to at least 26 days in the year other than Sundays and the season of harvesting the crop. It directed that slaves should not be compelled to perform estate labour on Sundays, even in crop time; it prohibited the sugar crushing mills from operating during the period from about 7 p.m. on Saturdays to 5 a.m. on Mondays. It also provided that slaves belonging to masters who were without land to serve as provision grounds should be served with 'good and ample' provisions to the value of three shillings and four-pence currency per week.[12]

Jamaicans resisted the Orders in Council issued by the Colonial Secretary in Whitehall during the decade of the 1820s. The island's Assembly protested strongly and enacted only a few of the amelioration measures they were pressured to adopt. Although the power of the planters was officially limited by the slave codes enacted by the Assembly, no machinery was in place to enforce the clauses designed to protect the slaves.

The virtues of the provision ground system were first expounded by Bryan Edwards, the planter-historian and leader of the West Indian lobby in the House of Commons. His two-volume (1793) history supplied the public with the following 'idealized' picture of the provision ground and internal marketing system in Jamaica:

The practice which prevails in Jamaica of giving the Negroes lands to cultivate, from the produce of which they are expected to maintain themselves (except in the times of scarcity, arising from hurricanes and droughts, when assistance is never denied them) is universally allowed to be judicious and beneficial; producing a happy coalition of interests between the master and the slave. The Negro who has acquired by his own labour a property in his master's land, has much to lose, and is therefore less inclined to desert his work. He earns a little money, by which he is enabled to indulge himself in fine clothes on holidays, and gratify his palate with salted meats and other provisions that otherwise he could not obtain; and the proprietor is eased, in a great measure, of the expense of feeding him . . . if the owner's territory is sufficiently extensive, the Negroes make it a practice to enlarge their own grounds, or exchange them for fresh land, every year. By these means, having quicker and better returns, they raise provisions in abundance, not only for their own use, but also a great surplus to sell.

The misfortune is, they trust more to plantain-groves, corn and other vegetables, that are liable to be destroyed by storms, than to what are called *ground provisions*; such as yams, eddoes, potatoes, cassada [cassava], and other esculent roots; all which are out of the reach of the hurricanes; but prudence is a term that has no place in the Negro-vocabulary. To obviate the mischiefs which fatal experience has proved to flow from this gross inattention, the *Slave Act* of Jamaica obliges, under a penalty, every proprietor of lands to keep, properly cultivated in ground provisions, one acre for every ten Negroes exclusive of the Negro grounds.

In Jamaica, the Negroes are allowed one day in a fortnight, except in time of crop, besides Sundays and holidays, for cultivating their grounds and carrying their provisions to market . . . The most industrious of the Negroes do not, I believe, employ more than sixteen hours in a month in the cultivation of their own provision grounds (leaving all further care of them to the beneficence of nature) and in favourable seasons, this is sufficient.

Sunday is their day of market, and it is wonderful what numbers are then seen, hastening from all parts of the country, towards the towns and shipping places, laden with fruits and vegetables, pigs, goats, and poultry, their own property. In Jamaica it is supposed that upwards of 10,000 assemble every Sunday morning in the market of Kingston . . . I do not believe that an instance can be produced of a master's interfering with his Negroes in their *peculium* thus acquired. They are permitted also to dispose at their deaths of what little property they possess; and even to bequeath their grounds or gardens to such of their fellow-slaves as they think proper. These principles are so well-established, that whenever it is found convenient for the owner to exchange the negro grounds for other lands, the Negroes must be satisfied, in money or otherwise, before the exchange takes place. It is universally the practice.[13]

My research on the demographic, medical, and economic history of Jamaica has led me to question what Edwards called the 'happy coalition of interests between the master and the slave' by which the bondsman laboured on his provision ground to feed himself and family and earn a little money at the market to indulge himself in 'fine clothes' and 'salted meats' he could not otherwise obtain, while his master was relieved in great measure of the cost of feeding him. In the following pages I will draw on contemporary evidence supplied by planters, plantation attorneys, overseers, missionaries, abolitionists and modern authorities to shed light on the following questions concerned with the provision ground and internal marketing system in Jamaica. 1. Did the typical field hand have a large enough allotment of land to feed himself and his family? 2. Were the slaves given ample time away from plantation labour to cultivate their provision grounds? 3. Did they have the energy and will to grow food for themselves and their families? 4. How great a distance separated the slave quarters from outlying provision grounds and the Sunday markets where surplus produce was bartered and sold? 5. Were adequate reserves set aside for periods when food production and imports were interrupted by inclement weather, embargoes on trade and shipping, and other emergencies? 6. Were adequate measures taken to prevent theft, pilfering, and trespass of livestock on the provision grounds? 7. Was the provision ground and marketing system adapted to the needs of the young, infirm, and improvident slaves? 8. Did the typical field hand grow crops of sufficient variety and have access to foodstuffs that would provide a balanced and nutritious diet? 9. Did the typical field hand grow a surplus of foodstuffs for sale at the Sunday market?

Jamaica, with its comparatively large land area and mixture of coastal plains and river deltas, interior valleys, savannas, and mountain areas, was considered ideal for combining staple production with the growing of provisions and the raising of livestock. The amount of land allotted to the typical field hand, according to contemporary accounts, ranged from as little as a quarter of an acre to as much as four or five acres or more. William Beckford, sugar planter and author of a descriptive account of Jamaica, asserted that a provision ground of a quarter of an acre was fully sufficient for the supply of a moderate family and with a small surplus to carry to market. But Beckford hedged his claim with qualifications that made its credibility highly suspect. The quarter-acre plot of ground, he said, 'must be of a productive quality, be in a situation that cannot fail of seasons, be sheltered from the wind, and protected from the trespass of cattle, and the theft of negroes'. Moreover, he said the land needed to be regularly planted, well cultivated, and kept clear of weeds.[14]

James Stephen, leading abolitionist and one-time barrister in the sugar island of St Kitts, believed that in Jamaica the case for subsisting slaves by providing provision grounds was, 'for the most part, much better than in any of our other sugar colonies'. It was not because the planters of Jamaica were more liberal, he said,

> but there is, in most districts of that island, a much greater quantity than elsewhere of seasonable land fit for the growth of provisions, and unemployed in the culture of canes; so that few of the planters there comparatively, are under any great temptation to stint their slaves improperly in the quantity of their allotments, or to assign them in a barren soil, though they often lie at an oppressive distance from the home stall.

Stephen went on to caution that the best provision grounds would not suffice to prevent want, unless time and strength enough were allowed for their cultivation.[15]

James Simpson, attorney for several absentee-owned estates in eastern Jamaica from 1804 to 1828, stated in 1832 that,

> It is not customary in Jamaica to make any survey of the land cultivated by the negroes, and they generally cultivate it in a straggling way, here and there where they find the best soil; if they had land enough to go upon, they cultivate that which is most easily cultivated and most productive, so that it is impossible to form a judgment of the extent of it in the aggregate.

Simpson's reference to cultivation 'in a straggling way' can be construed as swidden, slash-and-burn, or shifting agriculture which was widely practised by the slaves on their provision grounds. This entailed the strenuous labour of clearing or partly clearing primary or secondary forest in hilly and mountainous land and burning it over before putting in a crop. High yields were limited to a few years, after which the nutrients in the soil and wood ashes were exhausted. Moreover, the growing crops required frequent weeding. 'In effect', writes Robert Dirks, 'time available for weeding imposes the primary constraint on the extent of production' by the swidden method of cultivation.[16]

Regarding the time allowed to cultivate the provision grounds, it is obvious that the best grounds would not suffice unless time and strength were allowed by the masters for their cultivation. That the time was frequently insufficient is the burden of testimony of numerous contemporaries. The Reverend John Thorpe, who testified before the House of Commons Select Committee on the Extinction of Slavery in 1832, had been Assistant Curate of the Anglican church in the parish of St Thomas-in-the-East. In reply to the question, 'Do you conceive the time allowed by law to be generally sufficient for the maintenance of the slaves?' he said, 'No, I think not'. His grounds for believing the time was insufficient were: 'Because they are compelled to work in their grounds on a Sunday, and the provisions which they cultivate on the other 26 days is not sufficient to maintain them as they ought to be maintained, in proportion to the severe labour they have to undergo; it would enable them to cultivate on land of fair quality a sufficiency of vegetable provisions, but not other things'.[17]

Labour demands were particularly onerous during the four to six months of the sugar harvest. Chiefly from testimony given to Select Committees of the Commons and Lords, it is evident that all available workers were pressed into the campaign and the pace accelerated to finish the crop before the onset of the May rains. Under instructions coming down from plantation attorneys and higher up, overseers generally ordered more canes cut in a given day than the crushing mill could process in the daylight hours, and because the cut canes fermented and spoiled within 24 to 48 hours, the work continued around the clock, six days out of seven, in the mill house and boiling house. Robert Scott and other leading planters who testified before the Select Committee of the House of Commons in 1832, described this system of both day and night work in some detail. Scott said that some estates had all their able-bodied, non-specialist slaves divided into two spells or shifts and others into three spells, according to the size of their labour force. Daytime labour extended over six days from Monday through Saturday in crop time and for 12 hours daily, less a half-hour for breakfast and two hours for dinner (or lunch). Under the two spell system each spell was subdivided into two divisions. On day one, say, the first division of the first spell would work the night shift from eight to midnight, when it would be relieved by the first division of the second spell which would work from midnight to 6 a.m., when it would be relieved by daytime factory workers. Upon being relieved, these first division, second spell slaves would go to the field and work until sunset, taking time off for breakfast and dinner. They would then have the night off, work all the following day in the field, after which they would work the eight to midnight shift. By dividing the night workers into four groups, each slave worked and rested on alternate nights. In the aggregate, each slave laboured approximately 72 hours each week during crop time, after allowing two-and-one-half hours daily for meals. But even the dinner hour was not always free from labour, for, as Patterson has noted, 'If the provision grounds were not very far away some slaves attended them during the two-hour break at lunch; and a few of the very industrious even went to them at nights'.[18]

Planters frequently remarked that their slaves were cheerful and robust during harvest, chiefly because they consumed unrestricted quantities of raw cane juice and chewed ripe canes in the field. But the Reverend Hope Masterton Waddell, a Presbyterian missionary in Jamaica, observed that the slaves were lively at the beginning of the crop and seemed to thrive on the sweet cane juice, of which they had a plentiful supply. 'But 'ere the season closed they began to suffer, were fagged and sickly from excessive toil and want of proper food'.[19]

Sunday labour was common for the slaves, especially during the sugar harvest season when it was the only day they had to tend their provision grounds, take produce to market, and supply their family needs. Writing in 1774 the Jamaica planter-historian Edward Long complained 'that the sabbath-day, as at present it is passed, is by no means a respite from labour; on the contrary, the Negroes, either employing it on their grounds, or in travelling a great distance to some market, fatigue themselves much more on that day, than on any other in the week'. The Reverend Peter Duncan, a Methodist missionary, said he believed it was 'indispensably necessary for the Negroes to labour on Sunday'. He never expected to see slaves at any of the chapels where he conducted services more than once a month, even when their masters and owners favoured missionary endeavour among their slaves.[20]

William Taylor, a merchant and plantation attorney in Jamaica, was asked by the House of Commons Committee, 'Do you think that if a Negro were to devote the whole of Sunday to repose, he could maintain himself and his family upon the surplus time given him in the 26 weeks?'

> Certainly not [he replied]. I should think not on the 26 days, seeing that the 52 Sundays and the 26 days are for the great majority of them, generally consumed in marketing and in their grounds; I certainly should infer that if they strictly observed the Sunday and only had the 26 days, it would not be sufficient, because in the mission stations, I remember that, on Sundays when they had not [been allowed to work for themselves the previous day], the people never would attend service, and I have heard the clergymen complain that on those Sundays they could not get congregations generally.

Mary Turner notes that 'when drought affected the provision grounds, as in 1825, the people were left short of food and money and were too depressed to show any enthusiasm for church going'.[21]

Gilbert Mathison, an estate owner, returned to Jamaica in 1808 after an absence of 13 years in England. Although he saw improvement in the tone of colonial life, he deplored the mismanagement of sugar estates and the harsh treatment of slaves. The degree of labour required of slaves was, he believed, generally kept within the limits of fair and good regulation; however, he complained that cane hole digging and keeping spell (or night work) during crop were the most laborious and depressing duties on a sugar estate. Elderly and 'weakly' people were said to be exposed to the pressure of unsuitable hardship and fatigue during the crop season. Moreover, Mathison railed against the 'prevailing disposition on the part of overseers to squeeze every possible degree of labour from the Negroes; no tenderness is felt for them, and no relaxation admitted of. If they are not working for themselves, they must work for their masters'. Similarly, Benjamin McMahon, an overseer and bookkeeper in Jamaica, wrote that he knew of plantations where the labourers' provision grounds were 'almost entirely neglected, from their being unable, after the toil and barbarity to which they had been subjected by their task-masters for six days out of seven, to cultivate them'.[22]

It would be wrong to assume that labour on the provision grounds was consistently less arduous than that on sugar estates and coffee plantations. In fact, Beckford wrote, 'The manner in which the Negroes occupy themselves in their grounds is rather an employment than a toil, particularly if the wood be felled, and the land is cleared: but if they have heavy timber to cut down, the labour will be much, and the danger will be great; for they often get maimed or killed in this precarious operation, in which are required not only strength but likewise foresight'.[23]

The distances walked by slaves to their provision grounds and the Sunday markets varied widely. James Stephen remarked, 'Even the laborious walk to and from the provision grounds must, in many cases, suffice to deter the poor slave from going to them, and make him or her truant to the Sunday task. In Jamaica they are very commonly distant several miles from the homestall, and on hills of steep ascent'. In the infancy of a plantation the provision ground was generally near the slave quarters and sugar works. However, the extension of a plantation often made it necessary to open new grounds farther away. Barry Higman writes that some planters purchased separate areas for such grounds, 'requiring the slaves to travel distances up to 15 miles to tend their crops. In some cases the provision grounds comprised marginal, unproductive land; in others the soil was ideal for food crops'.[24]

Regarding the Sunday markets, William Beckford regarded a distance of 'five or seven miles, or more' as making the journey backwards and forwards to the market 'a day of labour and fatigue', but if, on the contrary, the market was within 'any tolerable reach', it was a day of both enjoyment and rest. Reverend Thomas Cooper, former missionary to slaves in Jamaica, was asked by the House of Commons Committee, 'Were the Negroes in the habit of carrying the provisions which they cultivated to market upon a Sunday?' 'Yes they were,' he replied, 'all the surplus provisions, and frequently provisions which they ought not to have sold, they constantly took to market on the Sunday'. To the question, 'What number of miles have you ever known them to travel with their provisions upon a Sunday?' he replied, 'I think 13 or 14 and back again'. Methodist missionary John Barry testified before the same committee that he knew slaves who travelled 25 or more miles to market, travelling overnight to reach the Sunday market, and taking the greater part of the Sabbath to return home.[25]

Providing reserve stocks of foodstuffs was difficult because of spoilage in a tropical climate, weevil and other vermin and theft. To Mathison it was a humane deed for the Assembly of Jamaica to pass the act of 1792 requiring slaveowners to have 'land planted in ground provisions, and kept in good condition, in the proportion of one acre for every ten Negroes, upon all plantations'. He said the law was intended to serve as a precaution against famine resulting from hurricanes, 'but as no hurricanes have happened for a long course of years, the law is universally disregarded, and is now no better than mere waste paper'. Higman says that 'one of the arguments presented by the planters of Barbados and the Leeward Islands in favour of the system of estate cultivation of food crops and rationed allowances was that it reduced the possibility of famine resulting from drought, hurricanes, or interruptions to trade'.[26]

We have seen that the slave act of 1792 required monthly personal inspections of Negro-grounds. One purpose of the inspections was to ascertain the extent of and take measures against theft. Theft was an especially acute problem owing chiefly to seasonal, if not chronic hunger and the attitude of slaves toward the property of their masters. Roderick McDonald writes that slaves were consistent in their rationalization of 'stealing' from the plantation or the planter. 'Their common attitude argued "What I take from my master, being for my use, who am his slave, or property, he loses nothing by its transfer"'. Slave watchmen on sugar estates were intended by their masters to guard export crops, livestock, pastures, orchards, kitchen gardens, and provision grounds from theft, arson, or the depredations of livestock. But Beckford complained that the watchman was often a slave who had become an invalid from age, accident, or other infirmity, and that 'much was expected from his vigilance, and more from those exertions, which, in fact, from bodily infirmity, he is not able to make'.[27]

Inspection of provision grounds was also undertaken to see that the slaves were providing adequately for their own sustenance. Whereas the slave act of 1788 contained a clause requiring such inspection on a monthly basis, Robert Hibbert, Jr, a planter wrote in 1825 that the overseer or his deputy, a bookkeeper,

> Should never omit a single week to examine accurately the Negro grounds, which may not only prevent neglect, but will also give the overseer the earliest notice of any failure of crop, which may entitle any Negro to the indulgent support of his master; for with all care, such support will occasionally be necessary, and unless the overseer fully inform himself, he will be apt to give to the undeserving what he should deliver with a less sparing hand to the unfortunate.

That Hibbert's advice often went unheeded is suggested by John Ward who writes that 'the overseers on some estates claimed at the time of emancipation that the provision grounds were regularly inspected, as required by law, but many admitted their ignorance of what they clearly regarded as the slaves' private arrangements'.[28]

Writers of various persuasions and experience were convinced that the provision ground and marketing system were not well adapted to the needs of young, aged, infirm, and improvident slaves. Mathison asserted that the slaves were exposed to a thousand hazards. 'If it should happen that, through idleness, or sickness, or old age, or in consequence of too numerous a family of children, the provision-ground should be neglected, or become unproductive or insufficient', he wrote, 'the Negro is not allowed to expect, nor, in point of fact, does he obtain, assistance from the stores of the plantation'. He added that while there were many exceptions to this state of affairs, he felt compelled 'to state it *broadly* that such is the *general* practice from one end of the island to the other'. James Stephen wrote that he could not see 'how the weaklier slaves in Jamaica, or in colonial language, the less industrious, can be exempted from often suffering under a scarcity of food, though in a less degree, perhaps, than those in other colonies'.[29]

Hibbert claimed that 'good Negroes' provided for themselves except 'in the day of calamity', but he had known instances 'where the indolence of the Negroes was so great as to make it necessary for the overseer to put the idlers into the regular gangs, and make them cultivate their own grounds, as they were the work of the estate'. It was customary on many plantations to issue weekly rations of salt and pickled fish and herrings. But these and other allowances, such as rum, were made to head slaves in larger portions than to ordinary field slaves. 'Special allowances other than those given on holidays were distributed chiefly to head people on sugar estates,' writes Higman, 'further buttressing the hierarchy of status and increasing the potential nutrition of those performing the smallest amounts of heavy manual labour'.[30]

We have seen that salt fish and herrings were highly valued by the slaves and were often purchased at the Sunday markets. According to the *Journal of the Assembly of Jamaica* for 11 March 1801, a committee appointed to inquire into the situation of the trade of the island called attention to 'the alarming situation the island is placed in with regard to salt provisions, whereby our slaves will be deprived of a food absolutely necessary to correct the ill effects of a diet entirely vegetable'; it was recommended that a committee be appointed 'to prepare an address to his honour the lieutenant-governor on a subject of so much importance'. Again, on 10 July 1805, at a time when the herring fishery on the coasts of the British Isles had failed, the Assembly sent a representation to Lieutenant-Governor George Nugent, part of which follows:

> Salted provisions are the chief corrective of the vegetable diet of the Negroes, and a want of them inevitably brings on dysentery and disorders of that class, which, whenever prevalent, never fail to carry off great numbers. By being deprived of what they know to be absolutely necessary, and have been accustomed to consider their right, discontents are excited, and there have already been instances of gangs of negroes leaving the plantations, to complain to the civil magistrates of the usual allowance being withheld.

But such 'allowances' were not only withheld in periods of war, as above, but as I have demonstrated in *Doctors and Slaves*, herrings and salt fish were considered an 'indulgence' and not an 'allowance' by the planters of Jamaica in both war and peace, and 'the whole system of indulgences operated upon the Negro population as a stimulus to good conduct, because they were withheld whenever their conduct was not good'. Although slaves raised poultry, pigs, goats, and occasionally had cows, the evidence suggests that most of their livestock was sold to the white inhabitants and transients. All-in-all there was marked dietary imbalance for the slaves of Jamaica, one that was deficient in protein and fat, on the one hand, and weighted heavily on the side of vegetable carbohydrates on the other.[31]

Notwithstanding the colourful and functional aspects of the Sunday markets, it may be questioned to what extent the average field hand was involved in market transactions. William Shand was a plantation attorney who had charge of estates in almost every parish and from 18,000 to 20,000 slaves in the years from 1791 to 1823. He was asked by the Select

Committee of 1832, 'Do not the larger proportion of the Negroes, having provision grounds, raise surplus provisions and carry them to market?' He replied, 'The larger proportion of the Negroes do not, but they may do it; they all have the same means upon an estate'. In reply to a follow-up question, 'Did the greater number of the Negroes under your charge raise surplus produce for sale or not?' Shand replied, 'I should say that a larger proportion raise surplus produce but as to the quantity it is difficult to speak; more than a moiety [about a half] of the adult part of the Negroes raised more than was sufficient for their own consumption.' From a wide reading of the literature on the internal marketing system it seems evident that much the greater part of the 'surplus' from the provision grounds went to purchase pickled and salt fish that should have been supplied to the slaves as allowances from their masters. Patterson says that most slaves carried a load weighing between 30 and 50 pounds on their heads; but a few of the more prosperous had asses to assist them. He finds the assertion of a pro-slavery writer that an industrious couple could earn between ten and eleven shillings per week (or from £26 to £29 currency per annum) as clearly a preposterous overstatement. Moreover, he finds a general consensus among many writers that 'the slave earned just enough to enable him to buy his salt for a week, i.e. salt, fish and beef, and on a few occasions, some pieces of cloth and a few trinkets'. In fact, Patterson asserts that very few slaves managed to save anything.[32]

From the testimony and writings presented above, 'the happy coalition of interests between the master and the slave' that Bryan Edwards regarded as judicious and beneficial was, in fact, far from a happy arrangement for great numbers of slaves in Jamaica. With relatively few exceptions, it was the duty of the slave to feed himself and his family. During the long crop season he was burdened with day and night work and allowed no week days to tend his provision ground and market his produce. Hence, Sunday was the only day he had to work for himself and family. The evidence suggests that slaves frequently lacked the energy and will to feed themselves, that they were removed from their provision grounds and the markets by considerable distances, had limited reserves of foodstuffs to fall back upon in periods of scarcity, and were plagued by theft, pilfering, and the trespass of livestock. Moreover, while industrious, able-bodied slaves could withstand the rigours of life and labour on sugar estates, the young and old, infirm and improvident were often neglected. Malnutrition, disease and death often followed, in part because of dietary imbalance resulting from defects in the system of food production and distribution. Finally, the typical field slave seems to have had only a small surplus to take to market, the greater part of which he laid out for salt fish which he should have received as a rationed allowance from his master. In the final analysis it is clear that insufficient time and energy for the slaves to properly cultivate and market their provisions were criticisms most often cited in the literature on sugar slavery in Jamaica.

If the provision ground and internal marketing system is viewed from the standpoint of the slaves attached to sugar estates where their condition had been ameliorated, there are grounds for believing the system had certain positive aspects. Matthew Gregory ('Monk') Lewis who visited his estates in Jamaica in 1815–17, told of an evening drive when he met his slaves returning from their grounds in the mountains carrying baskets of provisions sufficient to last them for a week. Noting that he had given them extra time to tend their grounds, he wrote, 'it enables them to perform their task with so much ease as almost converts it into an amusement; and the frequent visiting [of] their grounds makes them grow habitually as much attached to them as they are to their houses and gardens'. Provision grounds, kitchen gardens, houses and yards were areas of relative freedom, privacy, and social interaction for the slaves. They were spaces where they could relax from the rigours of plantation labour. On these spaces they worked without compulsion, often in family units or with friends. Here they reportedly worked more diligently than in the canefields, expending an amazing amount of energy. Moreover, they enjoyed pride of workmanship in traditional handicrafts and quasi-ownership of land which helped to build their self-esteem. 'Before emancipation', writes Higman, 'slaves on large plantations generally lived in separate household units surrounded by small garden plots and formed into villages, with populations typically in excess of 200 persons. The community life and kinship networks of plantation villages created strong ties of attachment to these locations . . . .'[33]

According to Barbara Bush, the establishment of provision grounds stemmed from the reluctance of West Indian planters to provide their slaves with sufficient food. 'Paradoxically', she writes, 'this failure on the part of West Indian planters to supply their slaves with the basic material necessities of life was instrumental in the development of a resilience and independence among the slaves which gave their otherwise depressing lives meaning and purpose'. Mary Turner contends that the provision grounds vitally influenced the slaves' family organization and their relation to the slave system itself. The slaves customarily cultivated their grounds in household groups which were usually represented by families. 'The focus for family life was the provision grounds, which the families worked in common . . . Family households with their common property interest in the grounds and houses enabled the slaves to establish a nucleus of family solidarities to sustain them in the vicissitudes of life'.[34]

The role of slave women in plantation agriculture, which has become a topic of increasing scholarly interest, in itself was an obstacle to the creation of family units. The condition of Black women probably deteriorated during the last quarter-century of slavery in Jamaica. Lucille Mathurin Mair finds that the negative rate of natural increase of the Jamaican slave population, coupled with closure of the Atlantic slave trade, led to an increased proportion of women concentrated in unskilled areas of agriculture where their work output was expected to equal that of men. Mair contends that the treatment of women did not improve in the later period of slavery; in fact, conditions may have worsened. 'Sexual exploitation and violence were inescapable features of the Black woman's condition'. Furthermore, 'the degree of sustained manual output required by the plantation of its labour force was inconsistent with the physical demands made on women by menstruation, pregnancy, lactation, infant and child care'. The Black woman was not without bargaining power, however; in the period of pro-natalist 'amelioration' policies she was strategically placed as a costly work-unit to 'hold the estate to ransom by not working, or not breeding'.[35]

Marietta Morrissey in her study of *Slave Women in the New World* finds that Caribbean slave women were gradually deprived of their role in the household economy domain of family life and horticulture, becoming more nearly units of agricultural labour, like men. Their lack of access to skilled agricultural work diminished their social status and authority. Morrissey suggests that it was not the inefficiency of slave production that brought slavery's end, but the near impossibility of sustaining the slave population and increasing productivity. She contends that women made a disproportionate proportion of an aging population of slaves, and that they were forced to bear too many burdens in domestic, subsistence, and commodity production.[36]

The research of Barry Higman and Michael Craton tends to support the findings of Mair and Morrissey. Higman shows that while the Jamaican economy was dominated by sugar on the eve of emancipation, the slaves also produced coffee, pimento and other minor staples, and they worked on livestock pens. Variations in the rate of natural increase were related to crop types, size of estates, and the work performed by slaves. While the slaves on small non-sugar properties tended to increase by natural means, those on sugar estates with about 250 slaves had the highest mortality. Conversely, the birth-rate was higher on small properties than it was on large sugar estates. The ratio of female to male slaves in Jamaica increased after 1807 and females came to dominate the field gangs on sugar estates where they were expected to perform the same tasks as males. Higman says that 'masters found it necessary to indulge females who became pregnant once they had to depend on natural increase to maintain their slave labour force'. Craton's study of Worthy Park estate in Jamaica reveals that while slave mortality rates declined, fertility rates remained abnormally low despite efforts by the proprietor and overseer to encourage family life and reproduction. A major reason for increasing the proportion of women in the field labour force from 58 per cent in the 1790s to 65 per cent in the 1830s was the monopolization by men of the elite jobs of drivers, headmen, craftsmen, and other specialized occupations. Women were normally expected to perform the arduous tasks of digging and cutting, writes Craton, 'as well as the lesser jobs of weeding and carrying that books on slave husbandry advised as most suitable for their limited strength'.[37]

Much light can be shed on the merits and demerits of the provision ground system by comparing the radically different systems of subsisting the slaves in Barbados and Jamaica. Barbados, after the destructive hurricanes of the 1780s, turned away from dependence on imported foodstuffs and slave provision grounds and gardens. In the course of a few decades the planters adopted the ration-allotment system, whereby the slaves were subsisted chiefly on food rations, both estate grown and imported, and distributed by estate owners and managers. These rations were supplemented by foodstuffs grown by slaves in garden plots. The system called for the supervised labour of slaves on both the fields that grew canes and those planted in food crops. Since very small plots of land were allotted to the slaves to grow their own produce, they provided only a fraction of the average diet and little or no surplus to market and earn a cash income. The Barbadian system was described by the plantation attorney of the Codrington plantations to one of his principals in England. He wrote that the system of feeding the slaves differed from that in every other West Indian colony. In fact, the cultivation of provisions formed a considerable part of the system of management on every plantation. In raising provisions, 'at least one-third of the labour of all the slaves on every estate is expended, producing a sufficient quantity of corn, yams, potatoes, &c. for the year's consumption, which is carefully stored, and afterwards dealt out to them in daily rations, and when the crop is short, an additional quantity is purchased'.[38]

It is interesting that Barbados and Jamaica experienced contrasting trends in their slave populations after 1807. 'Of the sugar colonies', writes Higman, 'only Barbados managed to maintain a positive natural increase, a position it probably achieved by about 1810'. The island's slave population had a positive natural increase of + 4.8 per thousand in 1817–20, and + 14.4 per thousand in 1832–4. Jamaica, by contrast, had a negative net increase of –0.7 per thousand in 1817–20, and –4.8 per thousand in 1829–32. Another comparison indicating a less rigorous labour regimen in Barbados than in Jamaica is Higman's rough calculation of total hours worked by first-gang field slaves. 'This results in an average annual 3,200 hours for the Barbadian slave, and 4,000 for the Jamaican. The Barbadian slave spent less time than the Jamaican in estate labour out of crop, and the contrast was even greater during crop. Thus, the provision ground system was simply an added imposition for the Jamaican slave, in no way compensated by extra "free days",' Higman asserts.[39]

Another interesting comparison is that between the parish of Vere, Jamaica, and the island as a whole. Whereas Jamaican slaves as a whole had a negative natural increase, sugar estate slaves in Vere moved from a position of negative natural increase to one of consistent positive increase between 1817 and 1832. Here the slaves were generally required to grow food crops as part of estate labour, and they received rationed allowances from their masters. They had little or no cane hole digging and their work loads were generally lighter than those of other slaves in Jamaica. Moreover, as Higman points out, 'In Vere the slaves did not have provision grounds but were provided with Guinea corn and salt fish and pork, and they used their corn to raise poultry which they sold in Spanish Town or to hucksters who came from Kingston by boat. They were said to be "exceeding well off" '.[40]

The provision ground system emerges from this analysis as an essentially uncertain method of slave subsistence. Its successful operation was always contingent on many physical variables: drought and hurricane, quality and quantity of land, distance from the slave village. It was no less contingent on plantation management practices such as the time allowed for work on the grounds and on the circumstances of individual slaves in terms of age, health and household labour power. All these factors affected the production of both subsistence and surplus for marketing. Opportunities, even, to market surplus were also contingent on geographical and personal circumstances and the participation of the average field hand in these processes has yet to be demonstrated. The demographic contrast between Jamaica and Barbados, between Vere as a ration-allotment parish and the provision ground parishes of Jamaica casts strong doubt, in itself, on the system as a 'judicious and beneficial' method of slave subsistence. Subsistence crises continued to afflict individual estates throughout the slavery period and drought and hurricane induced regional subsistence crises – one of which, in the particular political circumstances of 1831, precipitated rebellion. It is interesting to note, moreover, that the slaves themselves did not intend that rebellion to make them simply peasant proprietors. Their first hand, practical experience of the uncertainties and limited benefits of provision ground production led them to claim freedom in the form of wages for work on the estates. Regular cash earnings at reasonable rates were perceived as the only certain route to improve the material standard of living represented by the provision grounds.

Notes

I am indebted to Mary Turner, Douglas Hall and Barry Higman for helpful comments and valuable advice in preparing this paper.

1. Michael Craton, *Sinews of Empire: A Short History of British Slavery* (Garden City, NY, 1974); R.B. Sheridan, 'The Slave Trade to Jamaica, 1702-1808', in B.W. Higman (ed.), *Trade, Government and Society in Caribbean History 1700-1920. Essays Presented to Douglas Hall* (London, 1983), 1-16.
2. Sidney W. Mintz, *Caribbean Transformations* (Chicago, 1974), 180-99.
3. Sidney W. Mintz and Douglas G. Hall, *The Origins of the Jamaican Internal Marketing System*, Yale University Publications in Anthropology, No. 57 (New Haven, 1960), 3-26; Mintz, *Caribbean Transformations*, 151-9.
4. Orlando Patterson, *The Sociology of Slavery: An Analysis of the Origins, Development and Structure of Negro Slave Society in Jamaica* (London, 1967), 15-23; John M. Parry, 'Plantation and Provision Ground: An Historical Sketch of the Introduction of Food Crops into Jamaica', *Revista de Historia de America* (Mexico), 39 (1955), 1-20.

5. (Edward Trelawny), *An Essay Concerning Slavery* (London, 1746), 38; Edward Long, *The History of Jamaica*, 3 vols (London, 1774), 2: 492.
6. 'Report from the Committee of the Assembly of Jamaica on the Bill to Prevent the Unlawful Importation of Slaves', *Journal of the Assembly of Jamaica* (cited hereinafter as *J.A.J.*), 12 (23 November 1815), 791–3.
7. J.R. Ward, *British West Indian Slavery 1750–1834: The Process of Amelioration* (Oxford, 1988), 3, 13–37, 190, 206–8.
8. Patterson, *Sociology of Slavery*, 70–2.
9. Bryan Edwards, *The History, Civil and Commercial, of the British Colonies in the West Indies*, 2 vols (Dublin, 1793), 1: 233–6, 2: 131; Patterson, *Sociology of Slavery*, 73–92.
10. Edwards, *History of British West Indies*, 2: 146–7.
11. Ibid., 2: 157–9.
12. Patterson, *Sociology of Slavery*, 83–4; Brathwaite, *Creole Society*, 292–3.
13. Edwards, *History of British West Indies*, 2: 123–5.
14. William Beckford, *A Descriptive Account of the Island of Jamaica*, 2 vols (London, 1790), 2: 185–7.
15. James Stephen, *The Slavery of the British West India Colonies Delineated*, 2 vols (London, 1830), 2: 271.
16. *Account and Papers (Parliamentary Papers)*, 1831–2, XX (721), 385: 'Report from the Select Committee of the House of Commons on the Extinction of Slavery', (cited hereinafter as *House of Commons Report*, 1831–2), evidence of Simpson; Robert Dirks, *The Black Saturnalia: Conflict and its Ritual Expression on British West Indian Slave Plantations* (Gainesville, 1987), 69–70, 75.
17. *House of Commons Report*, 1831–2, 168, evidence of Thorpe.
18. Ibid., 332–4, evidence of Scott; Patterson, *Sociology of Slavery*, 67–9.
19. Hope Masterton Waddell, *Twenty-Nine Years in the West Indies and Central Africa* (London, 1863), 21–2; Ward, *British West Indian Slavery*, 87–90.
20. Long, *History of Jamaica*, 2: 492; *House of Commons Report*, 1831–2, 110–11, evidence of Duncan.
21. *House of Commons Report*, 1831–2, 25, evidence of Taylor; Turner, *Slaves and Missionaries*, 82.
22. Gilbert Mathison, *Notices Respecting Jamaica in 1808, 1809, 1810* (London, 1811), 37–40; Benjamin McMahon, *Jamaica Plantership* (London, 1839), 145.
23. Beckford, *Descriptive Account of Jamaica*, 2: 151.
24. Stephen, *Slavery of British West India Colonies*, 2: 269; B.W. Higman, *Jamaica Surveyed: Plantation Maps and Plans of the Eighteenth and Nineteenth Centuries* (Kingston, 1988), 204.
25. *House of Commons Report*, 1831–2, 135, evidence of Cooper; Ibid., 68, evidence of Barry; Beckford, *Descriptive Account of Jamaica*, 2: 151–3.
26. Mathison, *Notices Respecting Jamaica*, 32; B.W. Higman, *Slave Populations of the British Caribbean 1807–1834* (Baltimore, 1984), 214; (David Collins), *Practical Rules for the Management and Medical Treatment of Negro Slaves in the Sugar Colonies* (London, 1803), 93–4; Dirks, *Black Saturnalia*, 58, 81; Kenneth F. Kiple, *The Caribbean Slave: A Biological History* (Cambridge, 1984), 67–71.
27. McDonald, 'Goods and Chattels', 75–87; Higman, *Slave Populations*, 175; Beckford, *Descriptive Account of Jamaica*, 2: 17–18.
28. Robert Hibbert, Jr, *Hints to the Young Jamaica Sugar Planter* (London, 1825), 11; Ward, *British West Indian Slavery*, 110.
29. Mathison, *Notices Respecting Jamaica*, 30–1; Stephen, *Slavery of British West India Colonies*, 2: 271–7.
30. Hibbert, *Hints to Jamaica Sugar Planter*, 11; Higman, *Slave Populations*, 207.
31. *J.A.J.*, X, March 11 1801, 567; *J.A.J.*, XI, July 10 1805, 315–16; R.B. Sheridan, *Doctors and Slaves: A Medical and Demographic History of Slavery in the British West Indies, 1680–1834*, (Cambridge, 1985), 162–4, 216–19; Kiple, *The Caribbean Slave*, 77–83, 89; Ward, *British West Indian Slavery*, 284–5.
32. *House of Commons Report*, 1831–2, 459–60, evidence of Shand; Patterson, *Sociology of Slavery*, 228–9; Mintz, *Caribbean Transformations*, 198–200; Beckford, *Descriptive Account of Jamaica*, 2: 187.
33. M.G. Lewis, *Journal of a Residence among the Negroes in the West Indies* (London, 1861), 41, quoted by Mintz in *Caribbean Transformations*, 202–3; Higman, *Jamaica Surveyed*, 17.
34. Barbara Bush, *Slave Women in Caribbean Society 1650–1838* (Kingston, London and Bloomington, Indiana, 1990), 46–7; Turner, *Slaves and Missionaries*, 44–7.
35. Lucille Mathurin Mair, 'A Historical Study of Women in Jamaica from 1655 to 1844', Ph.D. Diss. (University of the West Indies, 1974), 286–324.
36. Marietta Morrissey, *Slave Women in the New World: Gender Stratification in the Caribbean* (Lawrence, Kansas, 1989), 60.
37. Higman, *Slave Population and Economy*, 12–17, 71–80, 122–38, 208; Michael Craton, *Searching for the Invisible Man: Slave and Plantation Life in Jamaica* (Cambridge, Mass., 1978), 75, 87, 142–4.

38. F.W.N. Bayley, *Four Years' Residence in the West Indies* (London, 1830), 136–7, quoted in Sheridan, *Doctors and Slaves*, 174–8.
39. Higman, *Slave Populations*, 188, 307–11; Woodville K. Marshall, 'The Establishment of a Peasantry in Barbados, 1840-1920', in *Social Groups and Institutions in the History of the Caribbean*, Sixth Annual Conference of Caribbean Historians (Puerto Rico, 1974), 85–104.
40. Higman, *Slave Population and Economy*, 122; Mary Turner, 'Slave Workers, Subsistence and Labour Bargaining: Amity Hall, Jamaica, 1805-1832', Ira Berlin and Philip D. Morgan (eds), *The Slaves' Economy*, in *Slavery and Abolition*, 12 (1991), 92–106.

3

Slave Economic Strategies

Food, Markets
& Property

MICHAEL MULLIN

Planters, as businessmen, continually searched for ways to reduce expenses. One means was to have slaves grow their own food at the cost of giving them land and the time off to do so. This method of slave maintenance became *the* slave institution in the Caribbean, especially in such mountainous and volcanic islands as Jamaica and the Ceded Islands where only a portion of land was suitable for sugar cane; the remainder – the slope, the ridges of the interior spine – was given over to the slaves as their 'mountain', where they could grow their own food.

Through hard work, luck, and holding on grimly to the advantage of providing for themselves (other than allowances of salt fish and imported grain) the mass of West Indian blacks in time accumulated amounts and kinds of property that are startling if one begins (as I did) with a perspective of slave maintenance that was based on the antebellum South. Slaves on all islands owned flocks of fowl and such small stock as pigs and goats, which, along with other marketable products such as fodder (Guinea and Scotch grasses), firewood, fruit, vegetables, and fish, generated the Caribbean's justly famous large and flourishing slave-dominated markets. This enterprise, as Sidney Mintz and Douglas Hall argue in a seminal essay,[1] was important for the future as well. It provided the base for the modern internal marketing system in the West Indian islands. No equivalent development occurred in the American South, where generally slaveholders, not their slaves, controlled surpluses including livestock, and did not allot provision grounds anywhere close to the size and distance from the home plantation which was the case in the Caribbean.[2] The argument is not that there was not a certain amount of slave-controlled food production in the South, or even some scratch marketing, but rather that it was negligible when compared to the cluster of social developments that stemmed from the internal economies of Caribbean plantation societies.[3] The argument here is that plantation authority was a function not so much of paternalism or of plantations as prisons, but rather more directly of the slaves' experience of the organization of maintenance. Through time Southerners came to realize that the cultivation and distribution of food as 'allowances' conveniently and effectively controlled slaves. West Indians agreed, but were often unable to use food in this manner because their slaves provisioned themselves.

Slaves who grew much of their own food and marketed surpluses, constantly and readily travelled beyond plantation boundaries. Those who did not, namely the mass of Southern slaves, were susceptible to stifling organizational schemes (as described in the 'Management of Negroes' in nineteenth-century agricultural journals) which were designed to make plantations 'their only home'. In the South, slaves were fed allowances, a practice that enhanced views of them as chattels, while enforcing a slave's sense of being confined and dependent. By contrast, where blacks fed themselves, as in much of the British Caribbean, the process diluted white power, and slaves acted as if planters owned only their labour, not their lives or personalities.

Hence, it is the social dimensions of food production and distribution that make the regional contrast so important. The exclusively Caribbean features of slave maintenance deserve emphasis in three respects. The first was the mobility of the ordinary slave (women in particular) from plantation to mountain to market, creating sizable and usually expanding hinterlands that were beyond the routine control of whites. The second, the rise of the slave family estate, gave slaves a stake in the plantation, the promise of a future, and in time the means and determination to defend that future. Third, the provision ground system provided opportunities for slaves to accumulate the surpluses and property that sustained families and autonomous religions that were African in character.

Systems of slave maintenance were set in motion the moment Africans arrived on the plantation and seasoning began. In both Southern and Caribbean usage 'seasoning' comprised the familiar idea of acclimatizing incoming Africans to new and often dangerous weather and disease environments. However, in the Caribbean an additional and paramount meaning was to establish a new Negro's maintenance, which was principally a matter of housing, food, and training. 'When a new Negro has been two or three years in the country', explained a plantation physician, 'and acquainted with the language and manners of it, and has got his provision ground in such a state as to supply himself with food, we consider him then as a seasoned Negro'.[4]

New Negroes in the Caribbean were introduced to plantation life not by whites but by other Africans who were often the new arrivals' countrymen. These seasoned Africans either went on board slave-ships or went into the merchant yards, where they tried to quiet fears and tell new Negroes in their own language what to expect. Once on the plantation, the Africans were placed for several months in the households of established slaves. The white supervisors allowed them to work on their mentors' provision grounds and be fed by them or by the estate until their own plots were bearing. Provisioning new Africans by 'hand-feeding' or by having them tend the gardens of the established residents contributed to the slaves' economy, which centred on their provision grounds.

The pattern of cultivation in Jamaica was described by Governor Balcarres:

> This Country [Jamaica] differs from all European Settlements. *There* the Vallies are fertile, & produce the necessaries for the sustenance of Man. *Here* it is exactly the reverse; the Vallies produce nothing but Sugar Canes, the sustenance of Man is received from the Mountains ... Every Settlement on the Low Grounds has a Mountain as its appendage, that is parcelled out to the Slaves, and every Negro has his particular Lot apportioned to him for raising his Provisions, which is absolutely his Property, and his whole dependence.[5]

Provision grounds were an acre or more in some Caribbean societies, merely 'bits' and 'pieces' in others. Their origins are obscure, but snippets indicate a haphazard development from local and practical deals worked out between slaves and supervisors in a distinctively West Indian system of plantation authority that was diffuse and shared. A witness at the Parliamentary slave trade hearings in the late 1780s mentioned that his Grenadian estate incurred heavy expenses from feeding slaves imported grain until 'after some years', when estate grounds were full and bearing, the slaves proposed feeding themselves – salt provisions such as beef, pork, and fish excepted – if in return they were given Saturday afternoons off. He agreed, and occasionally, when his slaves asked for fresh land, he directed the gang as part of their regular routine to clear a new section, thus suggesting that the task was too difficult for slaves in small numbers and in their own time.[6] The practice of allowing slaves provision grounds caught on, and in both St Vincent and Grenada planters came to rely on slave-grown produce, and imported quantities of food only during droughts.

A few of the actual layouts of allotments, which overseers or owners in the Caribbean sketched on the spot, have come to light. One plan from 1777 for a small pen in St Ann's parish Jamaica indicates that corn was grown throughout, and potatoes next to Quashy's allotment, which was one of 26. Most allotments were made to individuals, including women, only one of whom was paired, Eve with Good Luck; the other five or six were on their own.[7]

Plans for Lord Penrhyn's estates in Clarendon parish indicate no grounds in 1750, either because they were as yet undeveloped or else located at some distant and unmarked mountain. By the 1760s, however, Penrhyn's people had developed Bullard's Pen of 1,200 acres, 230 of which were in pasture

Map of Denbigh New Works, Jamaica:
old and new slave provision grounds

and Negro houses, and two of the three possible food crops were close to
the houses: cornfields ('pieces') of respectively 23, 25, and 12 acres. Another
plan, for Denbigh New Works, features 650 acres in cane, five acres in
pasture surrounding the works, 100 acres in pasture and Negro houses,
and one section, marked with a diamond shape of 139 acres the 'New
Slave provision grounds', and another, marked with a heart shape of 214
acres, 'Old Negro Grounds in Pasturage' (see figure above).[8]

Assigning grounds individually and to women as well as to men were
radical departures for Africans who came from societies where land was
owned collectively and usually by patrilineal groups but sometimes by
matrilineal ones as well. The slaves' swidden methods, which could engross
large sweeps of plantation upland, were also African. Reminding an
absentee that new fuel sources of logwood and bamboo might not be
available to stoke the sugar boilers, William Sutherland, a manager wrote:

> the Negroes on the Estate have occupied all the Mountain land with their
> Provision grounds. You may observe that surely they have too much land for
> the provision grounds. But the case is this. Their ground provisions such as
> Yames, cocos, Potatoes &c will not bear except in new land [cut] out of the
> woods, or in such land as has been allowed to lye over for several years & grow

up with Bushes. The way that the Negroes do is – After they take one or two crops of Cocos or Yames from their grounds they then allow that ground to grow up for several years in bushes & in the mean time they clear & plant some other land, by which means they occupy a much larger quantity of land than one would think was necessary for them.[9]

While admitting that such methods at first view seemed wasteful and left little upland for general use, Sutherland advised against restricting grounds and making do with plantain walks (groves). Planters agree, he continued, that every encouragement must be given to slaves to plant ground provisions and depend less on plantain walks; consequently, slaves are to be given as much land as possible and, once it was cleared, 'never' be deprived of it. This attitude was general and reinforced by the terrible hurricanes of the 1780s that set planters against the cultivation of plantains (hitherto a major food source) because the tall and graceful trees shattered in high winds.[10]

Provisions grounds in Jamaica were often some miles distant from the home plantation. For slaves who lived on a pen or settlement, grounds may have been only a walk of less than an hour, but if the 'mountain' served an estate on the coastal plain, it may have been several hours away – and many were. The grounds for Monk Lewis's Cornwall Estate and for Perrin's Blue Mountain, for example, were about eight miles off. Slaves may not have regarded distances of this kind as a hardship, however. Food-collecting meant leave to travel, often for a good portion of the weekend, and along the way slaves cultivated the 'connexions' that crop up in so many advertisements which refer to those who 'harboured' fugitives. Provision grounds were also settings for such unsupervised activity as trading and other dealings with maroons, runaways, and slaves from other estates.

Food supplies from the provision grounds were not, however, consistent. Ground provisions, like sugar cane, were adversely affected by drought. Thomas Thistlewood, manager of a Jamaican plantation and a diarist, recorded the effects of one such year (1754) on his estate in Westmoreland. By early June the drought was severe. 'Gave' the Negroes Saturday off and 'made them' work in their grounds, Thistlewood wrote for several weeks running.[11] By mid-July Thistlewood cut the allowances of rice, corn and fish given to eight new slaves being seasoned to six fish each, to which he added two bitts apiece, expecting them to buy sustenance.[12]

Hungry slaves, however, foraged for food and for goods to trade. Thistlewood's Egypt Plantation attracted foragers because its bountiful margins of morass and river teemed with food and fuel. Beginning Saturday afternoon and into Sunday, neighbouring slaves tested Thistlewood's vigilance by fishing and gathering the grasses and reeds that fed stock and cooking fires and mended their houses.[13] As the drought wore on depredations increased. One Saturday afternoon Thistlewood and a few slaves confiscated a gun and powder from a Negro cutting timber and, from another, a canoe, 30 bunches of fodder, crabs, crabbing baskets, a calabash, ropes, four knives, a shirt and frock, flints and punk for lighting tobacco pipes, and six bitts. The loot was distributed among the slaves: to mulatto Sam, a shirt, crab baskets, a knife, one of the punks, and two bitts 'in money'; to Crookshanks the clerk, his choice of the knife 'he liked best'; and a knife each to two other slaves.[14]

Foraging, however, was persistent, and when challenged the poachers sometimes pulled a knife or stabbed at Thistlewood with a fish gig.[15] A strange slave caught poaching could be handled roughly, stripped of his possessions and clothing, whipped, and put in the stocks overnight before he was sent away. If owned by a neighbour, however, the slave was usually treated more circumspectly. After one incident Thistlewood wrote: 'rode to Captain Forests' Maismore Estate and had a discourse with Mr. Smith about Yaw taking Quacco's 7 bitts worth of fish. They agreed to make satisfaction'.[16] (Seven bitts in spring 1759 was not inconsiderable; it would buy 135 plantains, two or three of which constituted a meal.) Meticulous by nature, Thistlewood sometimes made shopping lists before he interceded on behalf of his slaves. When some of his men and women were robbed by Retrieve Plantation slaves, he noted carefully:

> Big Doll had 5 Bitts worth of Plantanes took from her . . . by Akoi
> Mountain Lucy 2 bitts worth of plantanes & 1 bitt of Fish, by one of the White People
> Cubba 4 Bitts worth of fish, by Quasheba
> Betty 5 Bitts worth of fish, by white people, in Billey's house
> Casar 2 bitts worth of Fish & Plantanes by Cork, in the Road[17]

The manager of Retrieve's promise – to make inquiries 'and get redress if possible' – was accomplished a few days later.[18]

Thistlewood struggled to protect his slaves' supply of provisions and played an active role in getting compensation on their behalf from the owners of the slaves who robbed them. Accordingly, about twice a month in dry, bad years, goods circulated among slaves and whites as Thistlewood sought to 'recompense' slaves who had been robbed by Negroes from other plantations. Traps, nets, baskets, knives, and bills passed among the Egypt women and men who accompanied the whites on their Sunday forays. Catching trespassers and 'making prize' was sport of sorts. It was also an important way of convincing slaves, new Negroes especially, of such notions and practices as the merits of individual possessions, and that the plantation was their territory to be defended against interlopers.[19]

In more prosperous years the provision ground production allowed the slaves to participate in a wide range of trading activities on their own behalf as well as on behalf of the planter. One of the most interesting elements in these trading patterns is the extent to which the slaves became active participants in networks etched by gifts and barter.

Slaves acquired money and gifts by way of tips. Thistlewood, for example, on his way to dinner, gave necklaces to two women, a bitt to a washerwoman, and two bitts and a snuff box to a stable keeper. Arriving at Egypt Plantation, he gave the former overseer's fishing boat to an old driver.[20] At times Thistlewood gave slaves food, rum, old clothing, such tools as pen and pocket knives, as well as ducks and fish and even alligator teeth. Bottles of rum went to slaves who delivered messages; and to Ambo, a driver, a secondhand greatcoat made in London in 1744. Several times he paid Phibbah and other slave women for making or mending his clothing. Many little gifts, but most often a bitt or two, went to slave women for sexual services.

When Thistlewood left Egypt Plantation and established nearby his own place, Breadnut Pen, gift exchanges immediately began, mostly in Thistlewood's direction, both from his own and neighbourhood slaves, and from local slaves to his. Phibbah and Egypt Lucy sent butter, bread, goat peppers, potatoes and a pineapple; Harry at Egypt sent two cats, presumably as mousers. When slaves delivered their little statements personally, Thistlewood was uncommonly social: 'Kirkpatrick [Pen] Old Quashie, brought me 2 alligator Pears [avocadoes], gave him dinner, punch &c'. Phibbah also loaned him cash for supplies, hardware, and work which required hard cash (which Thistlewood used to buy a firkin of butter, window hinges, and window framing by Cumberland). A gift of land turtles for the newly dammed duck pond – to help the little settlement get off the ground – may be construed as a sign of the kind of sentiments, interests, and forces that held so many West Indian plantations together[21]. In general, gift giving demonstrated slaves' determination to make a potentially soul-destroying situation manageable by reminding their supervisors that tribal ways of maintaining allegiances, obligations, and duties could work in Jamaica as well as in Africa.[22]

In more conventional ways the slaves engaged in substantial trade among themselves and with the planter. Thistlewood's house-keeper, Phibbah, owned a mare cared for by an estate driver who received every third foal as payment; foals were sold to other slaves for between £4 and £7.[23] The managers themselves sometimes could rely on slaves to supply such livestock as a Spanish horse worth £10, or a mule worth £18.[24] Estate accounts indicate such transactions were not unusual. In Hampden Estate's 1779 accounts, the 'Increase and Decrease of Stock' lists as 'Bought of the Estate's Negroes': two mule colts, ten mares, two horses, one colt, and six fillies.[25] One visiting proprietor, Matthew Gregory 'Monk' Lewis, noted that the slaves' livestock was pastured with his own, a practice he estimated cost the estate about £12 a year per animal. The slaves, expecting Lewis to be the 'general purchaser' of their marketable cattle, set a price of £15 regardless of quality for every three-year-old horned creature. As a result, Lewis decreed that each slave should own only one large stock animal.[26] It is not surprising to find that the slaves' valuation of their provision grounds and stock was substantially above estate valuations. A wealthy stone mason and slave owner found in 1791 that when he sold his Windsor estate, the provision grounds were appraised at £280. He allowed the slaves, however, to put a value on their grounds and some stock, and paid more than three times that sum, or £1,000.[27]

Skilled slaves could, of course, make money working in their own time. On John Tharp's York estate in the 1780s, for example, mule men, a carpenter for Sunday work on a Negro's house, and a slave who brought home a runaway from the Spanish Town workhouse, were paid cash. Eighteen slaves were even paid 2s. 6d each for Sunday work during crop time. When skilled workers were employed in gangs without cash payments their owners and managers took good care to ensure that they would be well fed; good rations were intended to compensate for lack of cash payments. In these cases the contractual element in slave labour relations is explicit; less explicit but no less important were the informal contacts made by jobbing gangs for work on the estates. When jobbing slaves were hired at Thistlewood's Egypt Estate, for example, gifts were usually exchanged between the manager, the gang's driver, and sometimes the woman water carrier – a bottle of rum or a coconut – to seal the terms of the informal contract. There are numerous instances of jobbers, when the unmentioned ground rules were breached, returning home abruptly in the early afternoon. Many such exchanges were necessary to keep gears greased, and routines running as smoothly as possible in what was a highly exploitive, and occasionally violent, setting.

Provision grounds, trade networks, and different forms of wages paid for labour all contributed to generating status differentials among the slaves. One critical factor in this process was the availability of labour for the provision grounds. The seasoning process itself exposed newcomers to being used by established slaves to work their grounds. The experienced Jamaican attorney Simon Taylor warned against established slaves making 'slaves' of newcomers. Another observer wrote that competition for a newcomer's labour could be 'violent, and troublesome in the extreme', because 'every negro in his garden, and at his leisure hours [is] earning much more than what is necessary to feed him'. An additional hand would make a larger 'surplus for sale, market, and for feeding his stock'.[28]

The use of slaves by other slaves for work on provision grounds was not limited to the use of newcomers. Managers observed the difference between the propertied and the 'poorer sort' of slaves, some of whom 'never work grounds for themselves':

> ... it is a custom for the better [s]ort of Negroes to get as many of the poor, worthless n[egroes] [torn] possible to work their grounds for them on Sundays [and in return] generally give them as much Provisions as they can eat. But when a time of Scarcity comes and when Provisions are selling high they wont give them a morsell, the consequences of which are that the better sort of Negroes in times of scarcity are not only wallowing in Provisions but are selling them while the poorer sort are absolutely starving.[29]

When 'Principal Negroes' stopped taking care of their provision grounds – as happened in 1791 – the slave owners feared insurrection. As a governor commented at the time:

> . . . had the observation respected only the poorer kind of Negroes, it might have been attributed to that indolence and neglect that had occasioned them to be poor, but when those who by superior skill in culture, and habitual industry have become comparatively rich and acquired a superiority of consequence with the other Negroes all at once cease their industry and neglect their only source of wealth and consequence, there must be some cause.[30]

Differences in slave prosperity were reflected in estate housing. In contrast to the typical antebellum South barrack-row housing, Caribbean slaves often built their own dwellings. Two rooms were reported to be customary except for 'the better kind of Negroes', whose houses were timbered, boarded and shingled. Sir Phillip Gibbes, a Barbadian absentee and author of *Instructions for the Treatment of Negroes*, wrote about 'Negroes of the first distinction' who had longer houses of 'two very good chambers & a good sized room for a kitchen'. As for framed houses, they should be 'at least 18 feet long' and given only to the principal Negroes as 'the inferior Negroes Will not take care of them'. Principal Negroes, Gibbes explained, required the extra 'apartment', which could be used to lodge an 'inmate whom the master of the house receives to do the drudgery of the Family', or be further divided into a storeroom or kitchen. Barry Higman calls attention to an 1818 account from Jamaica in which head slaves, people 'entrusted with duties of responsibility or skill', owned houses that were, in some instances, situated in the centre of an actual compound or enclosure, and 'in general very superior to the others'.[31] On some estates there were individuals and families who through 'the practice [of] beques[ts]' had accumulated 'several' houses and 'numerous' garden plots.[32]

There is no equivalent in the records of slavery in the United States to a reform that the British government promoted in 1826 for 'The Establishment of Savings banks for the better protection' of slave property, defined in a note as including the right to dispose of land, money, cattle, tools and furniture of any value, but not weaponry and ammunition. Finally, another clause – calling attention to an important political feature of slave property and enterprise (or its absence) – stipulated that slaves could declare heirs whose names were to be recorded.[33] The most important long-term effect of this development is readily summarized by Douglas Hall. Emancipation, he explains, 'did not create any group of landless labourers [in Jamaica] who were entirely dependent on wage labour for a living'.[34] By contrast, sharecropping and peonage, which stemmed from landlessness, were the lot of Southern freedmen.

Pervasive and conspicuous slave marketing, dominated by women traders, characterized the Caribbean to a degree which had no precise parallel in the Southern states where such developments were manifested only irregularly, in Georgia and South Carolina for example.[35] Slaves in the South were constantly engaged more or less legally in trade and barter with their owners, river traders and storekeepers as well as on their owners' behalf. But the slaves did not in general enjoy the publicly sanctioned monopoly of the local provision market so widely commented on by eighteenth- and nineteenth-century travellers in the Caribbean.

It was the activities generated by the slaves' work on their provision grounds which inspired reformers like Joshua Steele to envisage slaves as wage earners living as tenants, even before the slave labour supply began to dwindle after 1807. Provision grounds and markets provided the framework for a free-market perspective on the problem of slavery.

Notes

This chapter includes material from Michael Mullin's *Africa in America, Slave Acculturation and Resistance in the American South and the British Caribbean*, Copyright 1992 by the Board of Trustees of the University of Illinois Press. Used with the permission of the University of Illinois Press. The editor thanks the press for permission to republish.

1. Sidney W. Mintz and Douglas Hall, 'The Origins of the Jamaican Internal Marketing System', in *Papers in Caribbean Anthropology*, Mintz (ed.), Yale University Publications in Anthropology, no. 57 (New Haven, 1960).
2. The 1781 Jamaican Consolidated Slave Act required owners to allot provision grounds to each slave, along with time to work them. In addition one acre per four Negroes was required for plaintain walks and ground provisions 'exclusive' of the slaves' own holdings. Slaves were also to be given a day off every two weeks (Sundays and crop times excepted) to grow their own food. The act was revised in 1787, and included a penalty of £50 and a clause that required an oath to be taken before the parish vestry accompanying an account of the quantity of land (over and above the slaves' regular allotments) which had been set aside for 'the Use of their slaves, & when land was not available an account of how they proposed maintaining them'. See Committee Report, Henry Shirley, Nov. 12 1788, *Votes of Assembly*, 80, 88, C.O. 140/73.
3. Barbara J. Field, 'The Nineteenth-century American South: History and Theory', *Plantation Society in the Americas*, 2 (April 1983): 9, 9n, argues that most slaves in sugar and rice areas 'and perhaps more than we now realize in cotton-producing areas – had possession if not ownership of garden plots and livestock'. She concludes, however, that although slaves engaged in local provision markets and sold produce to their owners, they 'stood outside the realm of market relations.' Cf. Roderick A. McDonald, *Goods and Chattels: The Economy and Material Culture of Slaves on the Sugar Plantations in Jamaica and Louisiana* (Baton Rouge and London, 1993), 52. There was little selling by slaves off the Plantation. The planter instead was their intermediary, and the plantation replaced the town as the slaves' retailing and purchasing outlet. For the Carolina low country, the most persuasive case for a modicum of slave selling, based on the claims of freedmen to the Southern Claims Commission, is Philip Morgan's in 'Work and Culture: the Task System and the World of Low Country Blacks, 1700 to 1800', *William and Mary Quarterly*, 3d ser., 39 (Oct. 1982): 587 ff.
4. House of Commons Sessional Papers (1790), 29/218, 29/144, 189: Gordon Turnbull, *An Apology for Negro Slavery*, 2nd edn (London, 1786), 21 ff, 25.
5. Lt. Gov. Balcarres to the Duke of Portland, Dromilley near Wills (Jamaica), Nov. 16, 1795, C.O. 137/96.
6. House of Commons Sessional Papers (1790), 29/101-3.
7. Oct. 26 1779 entry in a small daybook, 1776-9, Alexander Johnston Books, 1782-7, box 29B, Powell Family Collection, Historical Society of Pennsylvania, Philadelphia.
8. Denbigh Estate plans, no.2790 (1781), Coates's and Denbigh's Outbounds, Penrhyn Papers.
9. William Sutherland to William Philip Perrin, Greenwall, St Davids, Dec. 20 1795, no. 17814, Fitzherbert-Perrin Papers.
10. Ibid. A good description of cultivating plantain trees appears in the House of Commons Sessional Papers (1790), 29/143.
11. Ibid., May 18, 25, June 7, 15, mid-July, 1754.
12. Thistlewood's Journal, Monson 31, Lincolnshire Record Office, Lincoln, March 20-21, 1754. See also March 28, 29, 1754.

13. Ibid., May 1, 3, 4, 13, 17, 1751; April 8, 1754; see also Aug. 4, 1750, April 12, 1759.
14. Ibid., June 15, 1754; see also Sept. 10, 1758.
15. Ibid., June 12, 16, 1754.
16. Ibid., Sept. 10, 1758, Nov. 30, 1767, July 3, 1759; see also Aug. 1, 1752, April 18, 1756, May 30, 1762, Oct. 27, 1763, June 25, July 30, 1758, March 18, 1754.
17. Ibid., March 19, 1764.
18. Ibid., March 24, 25, 1754; see also Feb. 1, Sept. 7, 1761.
19. Ibid., May 4, 1755.
20. Ibid., June 23, 1750; Sept. 22, 27, 1751.
21. Ibid., Sept. 4, 8, 17, 25, Oct. 7, 9, 18, Nov. 18, 19, 1767.
22. Ibid., Oct. 2, 3, 8, Nov. 8, Dec. 2, 1780; see also Aug. 3 1785. The inhabitants of Westmoreland parish wrote to the council president (Aug. 11 1781) that 'the dread of famine absorbs all other considerations', C.O. 137/81, f. 12v. Robert LeVine notes that a feature of being African is an emphasis on material transactions (of food, particularly) in interpersonal relations. See 'Patterns of Personality in Africa', in *Response of Change: Society, Culture, and Personality*, George A. DeVos (ed.) (New York, 1976), 121 ff. For another side of gifting, as displaced aggression and marking territory, see Bruce Chatwin, *Songlines* (New York, 1987), 113.
23. Thistlewood's Journal, May 27, 1758; Jan 27, April 5, Sept. 28, 1760.
24. Account book 1791, 3/e/5, Gale-Morant Papers; cf. Thistlewood's Journal, Jan. 27, 1760.
25. 'Account Increase and Decrease of Stock . . .', Jan. 1, 1779, Account book, 1775–81, Accounts and Plan for Hampden Estate, T-SK 22, Sterling Family of Keir and Cawder, Strathclyde Regional Archives, Glasgow.
26. M.G. Lewis, *Journal of a West Indian Proprietor, 1815–17*, Mona Wilson (ed.), (London, 1929), 166–7.
27. July 7, 1783 account of attorney, Edward East, Hope Estate Plantation Accounts, 1777–83, Stowe MS, uncatalogued, Henry E. Huntington Library, San Marino, Cal.; Deposition of John Whitaker, Montego Bay, Jan. 11, 1792, C.O. 13/90, ff. 35–6, 40.
28. John Tharp to the Trustees, Sept. 12, 1785, June 17, 1786, Account book, 1786, 8v, 3/e/2, 1790, 9v, 3/e/4, Gale-Morant Papers, Roborough Library, University of Exeter; Simon Taylor to Chalonder Archedeckne, Kingston, June 11, 1782, box 2, bundle 11, Vanneck MS, Manuscripts Room, Cambridge University Library. Sir Christopher Codrington, a Barbados proprietor, directed his attorneys to assign new negroes to live in the houses of seasoned workers, to give every slave Friday afternoons to work their grounds, and to provide new Negroes with their own grounds rather than placing them in those of older residents. Codrington to Thomas Jones and John Lightfoot, June 27, 1715, c-2, microfilm 347(1), Codrington Papers, Gloucestershire Record Office, Gloucester.
29. William Sutherland to William Philip Perrin, April 9, 1787, E17803, Fitzherbert-Perrin Papers. See also a Jamaican manager's note concerning provisions for new Negroes and 'thin people', 775/948/2, 16(1799), Dukenfield Hall Papers, Middlesex Record Office, London; and an attorney's request for woollens, especially for the 'poorer sort of Negroes', who have 'only what is given to them', Mainsweet Walrond to Clement Tudway, Aug. 25, 1774, bundle 4, box 11, Tudway MS, Somerset Record Office.
30. John Whitaker, 'Affidavits of white People and confessions of Negroes', enclosed in J.L. Winn, chairman of the St James Parish Committee of Security and Safety, Jan. 13, 1792, 35–6 in Lt. Gov. Adam Williamson to the Sec. of State, Feb. 12, 1792, C.O. 137/90, ff. 1–2.
31. Sir P[hillip] Gibbes to Sir William Fitzherbert, June 9, 1788, bundle marked 'Sir P[hillip] Gibbes – Negro Houses', Turner's Hall, Barbados, pre-1821 box (now as a separate document E20555), Fitzherbert-Perrin Papers. Also see clothing distribution lists indicating larger allotments to 'Principle Negroes': Mr Concannon to R.H. Elletson, Hope Estate (Jamaica), May 6, 1779, MS29aa, Institute of Jamaica, Kingston; Barry W. Higman, *Slave Population and Economy in Jamaica, 1807–1834* (Cambridge, 1976), 169; Higman, 'Household Structure and Fertility on Jamaican Slave Plantations: A Nineteenth-century Example', *Population Studies*, 27 (1973): 537, 541; and Douglas V. Armstrong, *The Old Village and the Great House: An Archaeological and Historical Examination of Drax Hall Plantation, St Ann's Bay, Jamaica* (Urbana, 1990), ch.4, esp. 93 ff.
32. Lewis, *Journal of a West Indian Proprietor*, 333–4.
33. Orders-in-Council 'for Improving the Condition of Slaves in Trinidad', in Bathurst, Downing Street, May 11, 1826, C.O. 137/163.
34. Douglas Hall, *Free Jamaica, 1838–1865: An Economic History* (1959; repr. London, 1969), 158.
35. Cf. e.g. John Campbell, 'As "A Kind of Freedman?"': Slaves' Market-Related Activities in the South Carolina Upcountry, 1800–1860', p. 132 and Roderick A. McDonald, 'Independent Economic Production by Slaves on Ante-Bellum Louisiana Sugar Plantations', p. 194, in *The Slaves' Economy, Independent Production by Slaves in the Americas*, Ira Berlin and Philip D. Morgan (eds) (London, 1991).

4

'Never on a Sunday?'

Slavery & the Sabbath in Lowcountry Georgia 1750–1830

BETTY WOOD

When Governor James Wright of Georgia visited England in the early 1770s he left the management of his rice plantation in the capable hands of his friend James Habersham. Planter absenteeism in the Georgia and South Carolina Lowcountry tended to be more infrequent and for shorter periods than was often the case in the sugar islands, but there was nothing particularly unusual about the arrangement made between these two eminent planters. What makes their arrangement of more than passing interest is an episode which occurred in the summer of 1773.

Habersham reported to Wright the difficulties he had encountered when trying to move twenty 'good Hands' from one of the Governor's plantations to another 'for a complete Week'. Habersham was clearly taken aback when the slaves concerned refused to comply with his wishes. Unfortunately we know nothing about the bondmen and women who so disconcerted James Habersham. What we do know is that Habersham found he had no alternative but to negotiate terms with them. Here were slaves who adamantly refused to travel or work on the two Sundays which would have been involved in their transfer without first ensuring that they would be recompensed. How long the negotiations took and who negotiated on behalf of the workforce is unclear, but in the end Habersham agreed to pay these slaves 'half a Crown a Piece for the two Sundays' and a 'Dram Each' upon their arrival at their temporary work-place. Habersham assured Wright that his money had been 'prudently bestowed, as it will make the People happy, and save [you] a great many barrels of Rice'.[1]

This episode has a dual importance. Firstly, bearing in mind that slavery was not sanctioned in Georgia until 1751, it is the earliest evidence from that colony of direct negotiations between slaves and their owners concerning the terms under which the former would agree to work. Secondly, it reveals quite explicitly that what in Georgia had begun in 1751 as the gift or privilege of Sunday as a day of rest from the work demanded by owners, was by 1773 being claimed as a customary right by the colony's bondwomen and men. James Habersham was among the first in a long line of Georgia owners to learn just how highly prized that right was by slaves and what compensation they would require for relinquishing it.

Negotiations between slaves, their owners, and other whites by the early 1770s had emerged, as in the other plantation colonies, as an integral feature of Georgia's evolving slave society. Such negotiations, and the struggle for black self-assertion which they epitomized, were by no means limited to the world of work. They were to be profoundly important in the struggle to preserve the integrity of the slave family, in forging the patterns of religious behaviour which slaves sought to create or to recreate, and in defining the character and scope of their informal economic activities and leisure-time pursuits.[2] They were negotiations which entailed rather more than direct verbal discourse with owners and overseers. Slaves were able to force concessions by running away, by malingering and feigning illness, by the misuse or destruction of property and, as might have been the case in the incident involving Habersham, by taking advantage of owners who prided themselves on their Christian benevolence. When faced with black demands an economic pragmatism, which may or may not have been tinged with a sense of themselves as Christian masters, persuaded most owners that they had little choice other than to negotiate with individual slaves or with their workforce as a whole.

This chapter will focus on an increasingly significant and controversial aspect of the negotiations which were conducted within and between the white and black communities of Lowcountry Georgia between the mid-eighteenth century and 1830 – those involving the spare time pursuits of slaves and, more specifically, the ways in which they perceived and sought to employ the Sabbath.

Slave owners in the Southern mainland subscribed from the mid-seventeenth century onwards to the convention that only under exceptional circumstances would they require work from their bondmen and women on Sundays. This gift of Sunday owed everything to economic self-interest and nothing to Sabbatarianism, or the belief that this would be an appropriate day on which to instruct slaves in the tenets of Christianity.

The meanings which Lowcountry slaves attached to Sunday, their assertion of their right to that day, and the ways in which they elected to employ it, were firmly rooted in material rather than spiritual, or at least in Christian, imperatives. The Georgia slave code of 1755 and those enacted subsequently remained silent on the question of how slaves ought to spend the Sabbath. But, as in the other plantation colonies, the unspoken assumption was that they would be forced to spend at least part of that day, as well as such time as the task system permitted during the week, working to subsist themselves. This practice had been introduced into the Georgia Lowcountry during the early 1750s by South Carolina planters and their slaves.[3]

Most planters allocated each of their slave families or households, 'as much land as they can handle' for their own use and the crops cultivated in these gardens, or patches, together with the poultry raised by many slaves, added variety and nourishment to the often meagre rations distributed by owners.[4] But from the outset plantation slaves had another objective – to produce surpluses which could be traded as part of an on-going endeavour to raise their standard of living above bare subsistence. This endeavour depended upon maintaining the opportunity to employ Sundays, and the hours after the weekdays' tasks had been completed, as they pleased.

There were, of course, other reasons why the retention of the right to Sunday assumed the significance it did for slaves. Indisputably the most important of these revolved around the slave family. Given the willingness of owners to separate slave husbands and fathers from their wives and children, Sunday was the one day of the week when many couples and families could hope to be reunited, if only for a few hours. It was patently obvious to owners that, with or without their permission, men would travel many miles, usually on foot, to visit their wives and children at the weekend. Most owners found that they had little choice but to acknowledge as a right that which slaves had already claimed as such.[5]

Even if they were not separated during the week, Sunday was the one day when slave families and friends could gather together for any length of time to tend their gardens or to engage in various recreational pursuits. Little detailed evidence has survived from this period concerning the precise ways in which slaves deployed their time on Sundays. Successive white commentators noted that on that day they 'plant for themselves', but did not reveal how much of that day was occupied in this way. The hours spent cultivating gardens no doubt varied, not least according to the season. As we have seen in the case of Governor Wright's bondwomen and men, another option open to many plantation slaves throughout this period was to hire out their labour for all or part of the Sabbath. In addition, the handicraft industries which sprang up on many plantations, including basket making and the construction of canoes, together with hunting and fishing, also took up leisure time. Prior to the late eighteenth century attendance at divine worship was noticeable by its absence from the Sunday agendas set for themselves by all bar a handful of Lowcountry slaves.

The right to employ Sundays as they wished involved slaves in negotiations with their owners; the ways in which they actually employed that day involved negotiations between themselves – between men and women, within and between families. Tantalizing snippets of evidence suggest that through the early years of the nineteenth century traditional West African beliefs and assumptions concerning gender roles played a significant part in shaping patterns of spare time work and leisure. Charles Ball, for example, related the story of Lydia, a country-born bondwoman who had been 'compelled' to marry an African-born man who claimed 'to have been a priest in his own nation, and never taught to do any kind of labour'. This man was forced to work as a field-hand during the week, but 'refused to give his wife the least assistance in doing anything'. Lydia was 'obliged to do all the little work that it was necessary to perform in the cabin and also to bear all the labour of weeding and cultivating the family patch'.[6] In Ball's experience the demands made by Lydia's husband were atypical, but the requirement that she tend 'the family patch' and the labour this entailed would have been entirely familiar to many West African-born women.[7]

The persistence of West African practices is also suggested by the fact that bondwomen assumed a major role in the marketing of surpluses. Petty marketing in the Lowcountry was neither an exclusively female activity nor one which was confined to Sundays, but there is ample evidence that by the late eighteenth century female vendors predominated in Savannah's Public Market.[8] As in many West African societies, and in the other plantation colonies, women assumed a vital responsibility for securing the cash income at the disposal of their families. Less clear from the surviving evidence is the degree of control they exercised over patterns of expenditure.

Petty marketing and the patterns of consumption associated with it became of increasing concern to some white commentators around the turn of the eighteenth century.[9] Much of this concern focused on Savannah and the Sabbath or, to be more precise, Savannah on the Sabbath. An aggressive Sabbatarianism, together with the belief in some quarters of white society that it was proving particularly difficult to maintain tight racial discipline in urban environments, threatened to bring about dramatic changes in the ways in which those slaves who lived in, or within striking distance of, Savannah employed their Sundays.

By the early 1770s Georgia owners were discovering that which had long been known to their counterparts elsewhere in British America – costs might be trimmed by forcing slaves to spend part of their time working on their own behalf, but this entailed costs of another kind, not only to themselves but arguably to the broader interests of white society as a whole. Part of that cost has already been alluded to – the erosion of the total authority claimed by owners as slaves successfully resisted attempts to make them work for nothing in their spare time. Increasingly, however, other costs came to be identified which stemmed not from slave idleness but from slave industry which manifested itself in the production of surpluses for barter or sale. The exchange of surpluses within the slave quarters and the negotiations which these transactions entailed aroused no interest on the part of owners. But when slaves sought to extend their trading networks beyond the plantation, intervention rapidly became the order of the day.

From the 1760s onwards owners waged a generally unsuccessful struggle to restrict the trading activities of their slaves to the confines of the plantation. Some sought to do this by offering what amounted to a guaranteed market for surpluses. On larger estates this might take the form of a plantation store where slaves and masters negotiated terms of sale. Other owners during the 1760s, including Henry Laurens, acted as a factor for their bondmen and women. Even so, as Laurens appreciated, if the slaves thought it advantageous they would trade elsewhere.[10] All owners throughout this period were the weaker partners in negotiations over the disposal of the surpluses produced by their slaves. They might establish plantation stores, exhort their overseers to clamp down on illicit trade, resort to man traps and hire armed guards to patrol their estates, but such strategies failed to prevent slaves from forging links with outsiders.[11]

Slaves had little difficulty in finding trading partners, white as well as black. From the outset the Lowcountry's informal slave economies depended on white complicity with slave initiatives. Some whites were keen to do business and were not averse to socializing with slaves and it is not surprising that some of the strongest, although not always the most influential, opponents of Sabbatarianism were drawn from these sections of white society.

Whereas slaves were in a strong bargaining position vis-a-vis their owners, in that they could always seek trading partners off the plantation, their negotiations with the crews of passing river boats, country store-keepers, or Savannah retailers were not without their difficulties. What was in some respects their undeniably weak bargaining position – they could scarcely complain if they were underpaid or overcharged – undoubtedly encouraged some whites to run the risk of a fine and do business with them. But, as some commentators pointed out, there was another side to the coin. Slaves, they argued, so monopolized the supply of certain foodstuffs that they could charge whatever prices they wished.[12]

For obvious reasons a good deal of illicit trading took place after dark. Owners were simply unable to impose watertight curfews and, as Charles Ball explained, slaves were considered such valuable customers that many store-keepers were 'ready to rise at any time of the night to oblige them'.[13] Much the same was true of Savannah, where slaves were frequently seen shopping or visiting dram shops and taverns in the evenings. These night-time excursions vexed owners, but increasingly attention also came to be focused on the day-time activities of slaves, especially those who lived in and around Savannah.

Predictably, plantation slaves sought to exploit the urban demand for their surpluses, and in practice the legal stipulation that they must have written permission from their owners and display badges before they could sell 'Fruit, Fish and Garden Stuff' in Savannah counted for little.[14] Once in Savannah slaves had little difficulty in disposing of their wares in the Public Market, in the streets and alleys or, as sometimes happened, by going from door to door. It was in an attempt to control this illicit trade, whilst at the same time satisfying the demands of both urban consumers and local planters, that the Savannah City Council drafted Ordinances permitting two slaves per plantation to come to the city on Sundays to trade. Most owners would not readily consent to their slaves visiting Savannah on business of their own during the week, but realized that with or without their permission they would make their way there on Sundays. Of course, the Savannah Ordinances by no means guaranteed that the limit of two slaves per plantation would be observed.

Savannah also offered slaves, and not least runaways, many opportunities to acquire cash by negotiating for the sale of their labour.[15] Much the same was true in the countryside, but there were important differences. Plantation slaves negotiated terms with either their owner or a neighbouring planter for Sunday work and, generally speaking, owners knew of any arrangements for outside work made by their slaves. The main difficulty in Savannah was in differentiating between those slaves who had their owners' permission to work out and those who did not. The badge system which was introduced in 1774, and the simultaneous attempt to establish rates of pay for bondmen and women who were hired out by their owners, did little to remedy the situation.[16]

The sale of commodities and of their labour secured many Lowcountry slaves a variable cash income and they encountered few difficulties in spending their hard earned money. In Savannah, as in the countryside, many retailers were perfectly happy to do business with slaves as were tavern keepers and the proprietors of dram shops.[17]

Within a decade or so of the introduction of slavery, Georgia slave owners, like those of the other plantation colonies, were caught in a cleft stick. Their insistence that bondwomen and men work in their spare time to subsist themselves made sound economic sense. But by the imposition of such a requirement they had opened the way for the rapid development of a complex range of quasi-autonomous economic activities which they found both worrisome and virtually impossible to control.

By the 1760s the slaves' economic activities were the target of many criticisms. It was claimed that to allow slaves to trade on their own behalf was tantamount to encouraging theft, that the slaves' monopoly of certain foodstuffs grossly inflated prices in Savannah, and that their earnings were frittered away on alcohol and gambling, and used by bondwomen in particular to attire themselves in a manner scarcely befitting their servile status. Some owners also protested vehemently at the losses they were incurring as the result of the illicit hire of their slaves.[18]

Complaints in the 1760s and 1770s seldom focused, however, on the Sabbath per se and the occasional comments which were made about 'disorderly' behaviour were as likely to be levelled against poor whites as they were against slaves.[19] Critiques which reflected the essentially pragmatic considerations continued to be voiced during the half-century after the

American Revolution and were stimulated in particular by the St Domingue Revolution (1791), and the Prosser (1800) and Vesey (1822) rebellions. By the mid-1780s white and black perceptions of the leisure time pursuits of both blacks and whites began to be informed by essentially new religious imperatives. An increasingly systematic and acrimonious debate on the necessity and desirability of those pursuits was generated which took place both within and between the white and black communities and produced some strange alliances.

The roots of this specifically religious concern with the activities and conduct of slaves were located in the rapid growth of the Baptist and Methodist churches in the Lowcountry during the years after the War for Independence. This development constituted a social revolution. Throughout the middle years of the eighteenth century, Anglican planters on the mainland, like their counterparts in the British Caribbean, staunchly opposed any and all attempts to convert their slaves to Christianity. Far from seeing this as a Christian duty or, more pragmatically, as a useful weapon to secure slave submission, their constant refrain was that conversion made slaves proud rather than humble, less rather than more willing workers, and encouraged them to question, if not to actively resist, their servile status.

Anglican churchmen frequently asserted that slaves were eager for instruction but were thwarted by the indifference or hostility of their owners. In fact, the evidence strongly suggests that the reverse was true – that so far as most slaves, and especially African-born persons, were concerned the denial of Christianity was not a source of grievance. As Sylvia Frey has argued so persuasively for the revolutionary and early national phases of Southern history, bondwomen and men made choices, not least in respect of their religious beliefs and affiliations.[20] Precisely the same was true of the colonial period. Most plantation slaves chose not to embrace that version of Anglicanism deemed fit for their consumption on those comparatively rare occasions when it was presented to them. Instead, they maintained and developed as best they could their own traditional West African beliefs and rituals.

Bishop Gibson in 1727 considered one of the greatest obstacles to the Anglican missionary endeavour in the plantation colonies was that 'grown persons' imported from West Africa were 'accustomed to the Pagan Rites and Idolatries of their own Country [and] prejudiced against all other Religions, particularly the Christian'.[21] The 'prejudice' identified by the Bishop of London did not mean that slaves were unfamiliar with the belief systems of their European owners, or that when occasion permitted they were in any way reluctant to try and turn the Christianity of those owners to their own advantage. Christian benevolence, or a Christian conscience, could well be exploited by men and women who had little interest and saw even less utility in internalizing the role of dutiful Christian servants.

The possibility that Georgia might deviate from this pattern and coerce owners into assuming the obligations of Christian masters and expose their slaves to regular Christian teaching had arisen in 1750. The Trustees then agreed to sanction slavery in the colony, but only upon conditions which included the novel demand that owners send their slaves for instruction at some time on the Sabbath.[22] At the same time the Trustees negotiated with the Society for the Propagation of the Gospel for the appointment of a catechist to provide primarily this instruction.[23] As a result, in 1751 Joseph Ottolenghe took up his post as catechist to a population which numbered fewer than 3,000 Europeans and 600 Africans.[24]

Within weeks, Ottolenghe discovered, as Bishop Gibson had done, that Georgia's 'penurious Masters' claimed that 'a Slave is ten times worse when a Christian, than in his State of Paganism'. Moreover, the colony's predominantly African-born population was strongly attached to 'the old Superstitions of a false Religion'.[25] The Trustees' regulation, which was flouted with impunity by the South Carolinians who flooded into Georgia once the ban on slavery had been lifted, was superseded by the slave code enacted by the Assembly in 1755, a year after the introduction of Royal government. Like the South Carolina slave code of 1740 upon which it was modelled, the legislation omitted any reference to the religious lives of slaves.[26]

A few Anglican planters, however, including James Habersham and William Knox, arranged for the regular instruction of their slaves.[27] Clearly, the latter remained free to accept or reject the dogma presented to them, but they had little choice other than to attend the meetings arranged for their edification. Comparatively few Anglican owners followed the example set by Habersham and Knox – they neither made provision for the private instruction of their slaves nor sent them for that offered by Ottolenghe and the Reverend Bartholomew Zouberbuhler.[28]

The most sustained attempts to convert slaves in the years before the War for Independence were made by the Salzburgers at Ebenezer and the South Carolina Congregationalists who, beginning in the mid-1750s, settled in the District of Midway. But even in these two centres relatively few bondmen and women could be persuaded to uncritically accept the religious beliefs of their owners.[29] There is no record of how many adult slaves were converted to Christianity by Anglicans, Lutherans or Congregationalists, or how many of their children were baptized regardless of the wishes of their parents. The evidence which has survived, however, strongly suggests that only a minuscule proportion of the slave population, which by 1776 totalled around 18,000, opted for Christianity in any form.[30]

The Baptist revivals which began in the Savannah area in the mid-1780s, and gathered pace and strength after the great revival of 1802, attracted new church members and revitalized the old.[31] The moral and social demands being made of the Lowcountry's inhabitants, white and blacks, by the spiritually reborn were quite explicit – society as a whole must go through the cleansing process of rebirth and regeneration and, if necessary, the forces of government as well as those of the churches must be directed towards the attainment of that end. Nowhere was this spiritual and moral decay more in evidence, nowhere was the need for action more urgent, than in Savannah or, as Henry Holcombe termed the city, 'This emporium . . . Satan's strong hold'.[32]

The whites' religiously inspired concern with the so-called irreligion and immorality of slaves, as evidenced not least by their behaviour on the Sabbath, had a practical objective. Whether by the spiritual rebirth of slaves and their owners, by government dictate, or a combination of both, their proposed reformation of black behaviour was to secure more obedient and consequently more productive slave workers. Few whites in the Lowcountry would have quarrelled with those objectives. What many did quarrel with, however, were the costs of a course of action which sought not merely to regulate, but to suppress many of the spare time activities of slaves.

The demand that what were widely regarded as two of the more common leisure time pursuits of poor whites and slaves in Savannah, drinking and gambling, which sometimes they indulged in together, be rigorously stamped out, met with little opposition. Urban and rural owners alike had long complained about the comparative ease with which slaves were able to secure hard liquor, and the proprietors of dram shops, and others who retailed alcohol, found no support when in 1808 and 1810 the fines for selling or giving liquor to slaves were increased.[33] Similarly, the Savannah Ordinance of 1818, which sought to prevent slaves from gambling, met with no significant opposition.[34] It was a different matter entirely, however, when the City Council was urged to clamp down on those who since the 1760s had been conducting perfectly harmless, if not always strictly legal, transactions with slaves – Savannah's shop keepers. The City Council had traditionally allowed both the Public Market and retail stores to remain open until 9 a.m. on Sundays, and it was this convenient practice which those who argued vociferously for the total observance of the Sabbath sought to rescind.[35]

The Sunday trading issue bitterly divided white society in the 1820s. Arguments were rehearsed in the press, petitions and counter-petitions were presented to the City Council. At one end of the spectrum stood those who argued for pragmatic or religious reasons, and sometimes a mixture of both, that all the informal economic activities of slaves and not just Sunday trading must be ruthlessly suppressed. At the other extreme the retailers were supported by those who claimed that there were at least three good reasons why a closely supervised amount of quasi-independent black economic activity actually served white interests. Slaves, they argued, would be most unlikely to run away, or behave in any other way which might jeopardize the possessions they could accumulate as a result of their industry. Moreover, to acknowledge such industry might encourage slaves to be more industrious when working for their owners. Finally, as one commentator pointed out, even if Sunday trading was prohibited slaves would still make their way to Savannah on that day, where they would find whites willing to deal with them. These 'unprincipled' slaves, he continued, would 'encourage a species of traffic, calculated to corrupt the morals of Negroes and endanger the interests of their masters by promoting drunkenness and purchasing stolen items'. It would be far better, he concluded, to persist with a system which did not greatly threaten the physical security of white society and one which provided slaves with 'inducements to industry'.[36]

The status quo was defended on other grounds. How, asked one commentator, could Sunday trading be considered 'obnoxious to public devotion because long before the churches are open the shops are closed, the market is cleared, and every vestige of worldly traffic is removed from observation'. This same anonymous author objected vehemently to what he described as the 'pious tampering' of 'a few sectarian reformers' with Savannah's 'temporal concerns'. Here was an invidious 'attempt to unite religion and politics, and revive an influence which has ever been withering to the liberties of the people'.[37]

Matters came to a head in 1829 when the Savannah City Council elections turned on the single issue of Sunday trading. Ten of the fourteen Aldermen elected had run on the 'People's Ticket' which, according to its 'Independent Ticket' opponents, had been 'got up for [the] particular purpose' of prohibiting the same. The newly elected council not only banned Sunday trading, but also enacted a comprehensive ordinance 'for enforcing the observance of the Sabbath'. With one or two exceptions, work and trade of any kind were forbidden on Sundays as were any 'public sports or pastimes', including 'hunting and fishing . . . singing, fiddling or other music for the sake of merriment'.[38] This legislation, which remained on the statute books for the remainder of the ante-bellum period, did not lay to rest the many questions posed by the informal economic activities of slaves or result in a universally acceptable solution to the thorny problem of Sunday trading. On the contrary, these matters remained divisive and at election times often violent issues in Savannah politics for the next 30 years.[39]

The Sabbatarianism which secured such a political triumph in 1829 was not imposed on an unwilling and hostile slave community. It was rather warmly embraced by many slaves who together with free blacks assisted in generating it themselves. Nevertheless, it is important to emphasize that this impulse, with all that it implied for the slaves' right to use Sundays as they pleased, was by no means uncontested in the slave quarters of the Lowcountry.

Slave Sabbatarianism was firmly anchored in the spiritual, moral and social imperatives which informed the quite remarkable growth of Afro-Christianity in the Lowcountry during the decade following the American Revolution. The content and appeal of the evangelical religion, initially presented to slaves by white Baptists and Methodists, but increasingly by black preachers, and the manner in which they 'critically appropriated' that religion for their own purposes, have been brilliantly illuminated by the recent work of Sylvia Frey and there is no need to rehearse her arguments in detail here. However, two of her findings have a particular bearing on the present discussion – the ever-increasing number of slaves everywhere in the early National South who chose to become members of the Baptist and Methodist churches, and the fact that in most racially mixed churches they comprised a significant proportion of the total membership. As Professor Frey argues, 'black Christians were major participants in the shaping of southern religious life' and in what she describes as 'the transformation' of that region's 'religious cultures' in the years following the American Revolution.[40]

During the quarter century before the War for Independence the bond-women and men of Lowcountry Georgia had won marketing rights – they had established themselves as wage and cash earners. By the mid-1780s they were also claiming the right to have religious beliefs, to practise public worship and to organize their own churches. The impressive growth in the number of Afro-Methodists and, more especially, Afro-Baptists in early National Georgia is well documented. In the Lowcountry, for example, there was at least a tenfold increase in African-American membership of the Baptist church between the mid-1780s and 1829. By 1829 the five African churches affiliated to the Sunbury Association reported a total membership of 4,264. Even more remarkable is the fact that by the 1820s, if not before, Afro-Baptists comprised at least 70 per cent of the total membership of that Association.[41]

As was the case at the Sunbury Baptist Church, organized in 1806 with an initial membership of two whites and 68 blacks, some Afro-Baptists worshipped alongside their white co-religionists. However the vast majority of those who lived in or close to Savannah chose to worship in their own independent churches. Andrew Bryan led a tenacious struggle to secure that right during the 1780s, and the support he received from some of Chatham County's most influential citizens was a by no means unimportant factor in both the securing and the retention of that right.[42]

The opening of the First African Church in Savannah in 1787, with an initial membership of under 300, was followed 15 years later by the constitution of two more independent black churches: the second African, also in Savannah; and the congregation which organized itself at Ogechee, 14 miles to the south of the city.[43] In 1819 churches were formed in the immediate neighbourhood of Savannah at Abercorn and White Bluff, but in terms of membership the two Savannah churches remained pre-eminent. Between 1803 and 1829 their combined membership increased from 600 to 3397, and together they accounted for between 70 and 80 per cent of the total membership of the five black churches affiliated to the Sunbury Association.[44]

The Afro-Baptists who were concentrated in and around Savannah comprised an ever-increasing proportion of the local slave and free black population, and this was to be of crucial importance in respect both of the forging and the subsequent spread of the Sabbatarian impulse. Unfortunately there is no record of the gender, age, or place of residence of these church members. However, it would seem reasonable to suggest that the catchment area of Savannah's two independent African churches was essentially similar to that of the city's Public Market. If they so wished, and depending upon the means of transport available to them, slaves living within a 15 or 20 mile radius of Savannah could make their way to the city in time for at least one of the services held on Sundays. Precisely the same was true of those affiliated to the churches at Abercorn, White Bluff and Ogechee. In theory, most of Chatham County's black population was within reach of an independent Afro-Baptist church.

Between 1790 and 1830 Chatham County's slave population increased by just under 1,000, from 8,201 to 9,052, and the number of free blacks, concentrated mainly in Savannah, from 112 to 456.[45] It is possible that some slaves crossed from South Carolina to attend church in Savannah and that the Ogechee church might have attracted some of its members from neighbouring Liberty County, but Chatham County probably accounted for virtually the entire membership of the Lowcountry's five independent Afro-Baptist churches. Assuming that this was the case, the proportion of the county's slaves who chose to become affiliated to these churches increased from around 9 per cent in 1800, to roughly 35 per cent by 1820, to somewhere in the order of 47 per cent by 1830. Rather more difficult to enumerate with any degree of precision are those slaves who opted to join the racially mixed Methodist congregation in Savannah and the smaller number who worshipped alongside their owners in the city's Presbyterian, Episcopalian, Lutheran and Roman Catholic churches.

The choices open to slaves elsewhere in the Lowcountry were far more limited. True, depending upon where they lived, by the 1820s slaves in Liberty County could choose to become members of the Baptist churches in Sunbury, Darien and Pleasant Grove. In the same county the Congregational church at Midway attracted a growing number of black members during the first quarter of the nineteenth century. Yet the fact remains that the 462 slaves (261 women and 201 men) and eight free blacks (six women and two men) who were baptized and admitted to full communion by the church between 1800 and 1829, compared with the 74 admitted between 1756 and 1789, must be put in the context of a Liberty County slave population which during this same period increased from 3,940 to 5,602.[46] In the other Lowcountry counties, whose combined slave populations increased from 5,952 in 1790, to 6,906 in 1820, and 13,107 in 1830, the possibilities of church membership and attendance were virtually non-existent. As Julia Floyd Smith has observed, before 1830 and the plantation missionary endeavour 'the large majority of rural slaves . . . remained outside the reach of the institutional church'.[47] There was a very real sense in which during the first third of the nineteenth century Afro-Christianity in the Lowcountry was concentrated in and around Savannah and, to a lesser extent, around the smaller towns of Sunbury and Darien.

The leaders of the independent African churches appreciated from the first the practical necessity, if not the spiritual desirability, of forging links with their white co-religionists and chose to affiliate themselves with the Baptist Associations formed in the Lowcountry. As was the case with white and, by the early nineteenth century, racially mixed congregations, each of the African churches sent two delegates, usually the pastor and a deacon, to annual meetings which concerned themselves with formulating church policy on a range of issues, not least of which was that of drawing up guidelines for the moral conduct of its membership.[48] But inter-racial discourses at this level, and on this subject, were not limited to two or three days a year. The dialogue continued in a less formal vein throughout the year. From the outset, Afro-Baptists appear to have played a central and continuing role in defining the rigorous standards of morality demanded of all church members, white as well as black, and those which through the first third of the nineteenth century their white co-religionists sought to impose by political means on the Lowcountry as a whole.

Both within the formal structure of the churches and less formally in the slave quarters, these moral demands were made more often than not of black audiences by black preachers and exhorters. As Sylvia Frey has argued, growing numbers of bondwomen and men found within this evangelical message a profoundly significant sense of spiritual independence, a sense of meaning for the present, and hope for the future.[49] The willingness of so many to try and lead their lives according to the exacting moral standards demanded of them was to be crucially important in shaping and re-shaping many facets of black life, and not least in enhancing both the individual and collective concept of self-worth, dignity and purpose. At the same time it perhaps also fostered a sense of spiritual and moral superiority over the unregenerate, regardless of their colour and status.

Church membership necessitated various choices, some of which were probably easier to make than others, about the use of leisure time and patterns of consumption. Even before the strident Sabbatarianism of the 1820s the rural slaves' decision to attend church could mean that little, if any, of Sunday was available for either recreational or material ends. For those who lived on the outer fringes of church catchment areas most of their Sunday was taken up with travelling to and from services. If they attended church regularly, and unfortunately there are no detailed records of church attendance, this meant finding time during the week for tending gardens. Similarly, by choosing to attend church many slaves effectively ruled out the possibility of securing a cash income by hiring out their labour for all or part of the Sabbath.

What they did not necessarily rule out before the 1820s, however, was the possibility of combining their spiritual and material needs on their weekly visits to Savannah. The fact that the Public Market and retail stores remained open until 9 a.m. on Sundays at least offered them the opportunity to trade before attending divine worship. How many plantation slaves took advantage of this situation is impossible to ascertain. What is certain is that by the mid-1820s they were being exhorted by their leaders not to do so and by the early 1830s could not do so, at least not legally. Although not easily documented, it is entirely possible that slaves who found themselves in this situation re-oriented their trading practices in ways which involved them in more dealings and negotiations with their owners and, when within reach, country store-keepers. In practice, of course, it was perfectly simple for their urban counterparts to comply with demands that they not trade on the Sabbath. They had innumerable opportunities to do so on weekdays.

Regardless of whether they chose to attend church on a regular basis, church membership involved adjustments in the budgets of both rural and urban slaves. For example, the building and maintenance of churches involved congregations in expenditure which might take the form of cash or unpaid labour. Sometimes, as was the case with the congregation of the First African Church in Savannah, members clubbed together to buy plate and other adornments for their church. Money also had to be found to help support local preachers and sometimes to pay the expenses incurred by visiting speakers.

Church attendance may have involved additional expenditure on clothing. Standards of clothing, and the pride clearly taken by many slaves in their appearance, did not necessarily correlate with church membership but there is evidence that bondwomen and men thought it important to dress themselves as well as they could when about the business of their Lord. One white resident of Liberty County, for instance, recalled that on Sundays slaves were to be seen 'clean and neatly dressed and . . . in their best' making their way to church, often 'on foot carrying their shoes and stockings'.[50]

Contrary to the impression conveyed by many white commentators, the majority of slaves did not simply drink or gamble away all their hard earned income although, as Charles Ball conceded, some might purchase 'an occasional bottle of rum'.[51] However, Baptist and Methodist morality ruled out the possibility of even the 'occasional' use of alcohol and was equally uncompromising on the sin of gambling. In some cases compliance with these requirements would have resulted in changing patterns of expenditure as well as of behaviour.

Afro-Baptists combined with their white co-religionists in the definition of Baptist morality, but the independent African churches were solely responsible for ordering their own moral priorities and ensuring that their members lived up to the spiritual and moral demands being made of them. They and they alone assumed the responsibility for disciplining their

Going to market in Savanna, Georgia
(Harper's Weekly, *1875*)

members and, if they thought it necessary, excommunicating the recalcitrant. That there were those who were either unwilling or unable to conform to the standards being set for them by their black co-religionists is evident from the fact that between 1794 and 1829 the independent African churches excommunicated at least 382 of their members, of whom 207 were subsequently restored to full church membership.[52] What the records do not reveal are the numbers who were disciplined, but who avoided excommunication by repenting and mending their ways. Neither is there any indication of the range or comparative frequency of the offences committed by those who were disciplined, although it may be safely inferred that they almost certainly included drunkenness, gambling, sexual misdemeanours and, possibly by the 1820s if not earlier, ignoring the strictures against Sunday trading.

Some Afro-Baptists could not live up to the high moral expectations and patterns of behaviour that church membership imposed upon them. Several of their compatriots in the slave quarters saw little virtue in trying to do so. That Afro-Christianity, and more especially the evangelical churches, made great inroads in and around Savannah between the mid-1780s and 1830 is indisputable. However, Chatham County's slave population also continued to include men and women who for a variety of reasons rejected Protestant Christianity regardless of who it was that presented it to them. In 1830 this was true of maybe as many as one-third of Chatham County's black population. These women and men were coming under increasingly heavy pressure, not least from other slaves, and sometimes from those closest to them, to re-order their lives. In the process one of their most cherished rights was also coming under intense threat – not their right to Sunday *per se*, but their right to use that day as they wished. By 1830 there were important senses in which, at least in theory, those slaves who lived in and around Savannah had been deprived of that right by Afro-Baptists and Afro-Methodists acting in concert with their white co-religionists.

Before 1830 most of the slaves who lived outside Chatham County and parts of Liberty County were immune from this pressure, a situation which was to change quite dramatically with the inauguration of the plantation missionary movement. During the next 30 years virtually every bondwoman and man in the Lowcountry would be confronted with precisely the same spiritual, moral, social and economic choices, if not dilemmas, as those long familiar to their compatriots in Chatham and Liberty Counties. The battles within and between the enslaved and free populations of Lowcountry Georgia over the spare time pursuits and behaviour of slaves, and particularly the ways in which they employed their Sundays, did not end in 1830 but thereafter the front line advanced with ever-increasing speed from town to countryside.

Notes

My deepest thanks go to Professor Sylvia Frey for her generosity in allowing me to consult three of her unpublished manuscripts prior to their publication, and to cite her findings. Professor Frey also read an earlier draft of this essay, as did Professor Mary Turner. I am most grateful to them both for their incisive comments. Any errors of fact or interpretation which may remain are my, rather than their, responsibility.

1. *Letters of the Honorable James Habersham, 1756-1775*, Georgia Historical Society, Collections, (Savannah, 1840-19-), 6 (1904), 190-9.

2. The slaves' spare time, or leisure time, is here defined as those hours and days when they were not legally or customarily required to work for their owners. In addition to the variable amounts of time they had at their disposal after the completion of their daily tasks and the Sabbath, plantation slaves were usually given one or two days off work at Christmas.

3. Klaus G. Loewald, Beverly Starika and Paul S. Taylor, (trans. and eds), 'Johann Martin Bolzius Answers a Questionnaire on Carolina and Georgia', *The William and Mary Quarterly*, 3rd Series, XIV, (1957), 236, 258-60; Philip D. Morgan, 'Work and Culture: The Task System and the Work of Lowcountry Blacks, 1700-1800', Ibid., 4 (1982), 563-99. Some contemporary reports suggested that on rice plantations the day's tasks might be completed by midday or 'by two o'clock'. Basil Hall commented that 'this is rare . . . the work generally lasts till four or five o'clock'. He claimed to have seen 'gangs of Negroes at work till sunset'. Jeremiah Everts Papers (1822), Georgia Historical Society, Savannah; Basil Hall, *Travels in North America in the Years 1827 and 1828*, 3 vols (Edinburgh, 1829), III, 223.

4. Writing in the mid-1750s Pastor Bolzius reported that slaves cultivated 'corn, potatoes, tobacco, peanuts, water and sugar melons, pumpkins [and] bottle pumpkins' in their gardens. Charles Ball's list of the crops grown around the turn of the eighteenth century was essentially similar. The only additional items noted by later commentators were 'garden vegetables', which probably included legumes, cabbages and turnips, and according to one description of Cumberland Island, sugar cane. Loewald, Starika and Taylor (trans. and eds), 'Bolzius Answers a Questionnaire', 259; Charles Ball, *Fifty Years in Chains* (New York, 1970 edn), 166-7; William Grimes, *Life of William Grimes the Runaway Slave* (New Haven, 1855), 46; Felicity Calhoun (ed.), *Pleasure and Pain. Reminiscences of Georgia in the 1840s* (Savannah, 1978), 36-7; *Early Reminiscences of Camden County, Georgia. By An Old St Mary's Boy In His 82nd Year, 1914-1915* (Kingsland, Ga., n.d.), 8.

5. R.Q. Mallard, *Plantation Life Before Emancipation* (Richmond, Va., 1892), 51-2.

6. Ball, *Fifty Years in Chains*, 263-4.

7. For an extended discussion of this point see E. Boserup, *Women's Role in Economic Development* (London, 1970 edn) and C. Meillassoux, *Maidens Meal and Money: Capitalism and the Domestic Economy* (Cambridge, 1981).

8. Betty Wood, '"White Society" and the "Informal" Slave Economies of Lowcountry Georgia, c.1760-1830', *Slavery & Abolition* 11, 3 (1990), 320-2.

9. Ibid., 321-6.

10. Philip M. Hamer, George C. Rogers, et. al. (eds), *The Papers of Henry Laurens*, 9 vols (Columbia, SC, 1968-81), IV, 319, 616.

11. The public laws of slavery prohibited bondwomen and men from trading off their plantations without the express written consent of their owner or overseer. Whites who contravened this regulation were liable to a fine. Wood, '"White Society"', 315-16.

12. For allegations that slaves monopolized the supply of poultry, eggs and dairy produce and overcharged their white customers see *The Georgia Gazette*, 5 Feb. 1795 and *The Republican and Savannah Evening Ledger*, 9 July 1812.

13. Ball, *Fifty Years in Chains*, 190-1.

14. For the regulations governing the purchase and display of badges, which were similar to those of South Carolina, see Allan D. Candler and Lucian L. Knight, (eds), *The Colonial Records of the States of Georgia*, 26 vols (Atlanta, 1904-16), 19, pt 2, 23-6; XIX, pt 2, 256-62 (hereafter *Colonial Records*); *The Georgia Gazette*, 26 June 1787, 7 Oct. 1790, 8 Nov. 1792; *The Republican and Savannah Evening Ledger*, 8 July 1812 and *The Savannah Republican*, 22 Sept. 1818.

15. Wood, '"White Society"', 318-20; Betty Wood, 'Some Aspects of Female Resistance to Chattel Slavery in Lowcountry Georgia, 1763-1815', *The Historical Journal*, 30, 3 (1987), 607-8.

16. For the regulations governing the hire and payment of slaves in Savannah see *Colonial Records*, XIX, pt 2, 23-30; *The Georgia Gazette*, 26 June 1787, 7 Oct. 1790, 8 Nov. 1792 and *The Georgia Republican and State Intelligencer*, 3 Jan. 1803. These regulations served also to define the rates of pay for slaves who worked without their owners' permission as well as those of their white competitors.

17. Wood, '"White Society"', 330 (note 50).

18. Philip D. Morgan, 'Black Life in Eighteenth-Century Charleston', *Perspectives in American History*, New Series, I, (1984), 187-232; Wood, '"White Society"', 320-1, 329 (note 34).

19. Wood, '"White Society"', 323-4.
20. For the elaboration of this theme see Sylvia R. Frey, '"The Year of Jubilee is Come": Black Christianity in the Plantation South in post-revolutionary America', in R. Hoffman and Peter J. Albert (eds) *Religion in a Revolutionary Age* (Charlottesville, 1994); '"Shaking the Dry Bones": The Dialectic of Conversion', in Ted Ownby (ed.) *Black and White Cultural interaction in the Antebellum South* (Jackson, Miss., 1993); and *Water from the Rock. Black Resistance in a Revolutionary Age* (Princeton University Press, 1991).
21. Edmund Gibson, *Two Letters of the Lord Bishop of London. The First to the Masters and Mistresses of Families in the English Plantations abroad: Exhorting them to Encourage and Promote the Instruction of their Negroes in the Christian Faith. The Second, to the Missionaries there: Directing them to Distribute the said Letter, and Exhorting them to give their Assistance towards the Instruction of the Negroes within their several Parishes* (London, 1727), 5.
22. Betty Wood, *Slavery in Colonial Georgia, 1730-1775* (Athens, 1984), 74-87; *Colonial Records*, I, 59.
23. John C. Van Horne, ed., *Religious Philanthropy and Colonial Slavery. The American Correspondence of the Associates of Dr Bray, 1717-1777* (Urbana and Chicago, 1985), 16-20.
24. Wood, *Slavery in Colonial Georgia*, 89; James B. Lawrence, 'Religious Education of the Negro in the Colony of Georgia', *The Georgia Historical Quarterly*, 14 (1930), 41-2.
25. Van Horne (ed.), *Religious Philanthropy*, 112, 116.
26. For the movement of South Carolinians into Georgia after 1750 see David R. Chesnutt, 'South Carolinian Expansion into Colonial Georgia', (Ph.D. Diss., The University of Georgia, 1973). For the South Carolina slave code of 1740 see Thomas Cooper and David J. McCord (eds), *The Statutes at Large of South Carolina*, 10 vols (Columbia, SC, 1836-1841), 7, 397-417. For the Georgia code of 1755 see *Colonial Records*, 18, 102-44.
27. *Letters of the Honorable James Habersham*, passim.   28. Wood, *Slavery in Colonial Georgia*, 239.
29. Records of the Midway Congregational Church (typescript), Georgia Historical Society, Savannah; James Stacy (ed.), *History of Midway Congregational Church. Liberty County, Georgia* (Newnam, Ga., 1903); A.G. Voigt (trans. and ed.), *Ebenezer Record Book* (Savannah, 1929); G.F. Jones (trans. and ed.), *Detailed Reports of the Salzburger Emigrants who Settled in America . . . Edited by Samuel Urlsperger*, 15 vols to date (Athens, 1968-90).
30. Wood, *Slavery in Colonial Georgia*, 159-65.
31. Frey, '"Shaking the Dry Bones"', passim; 'The Year of Jubilee is Come', passim; *Water from the Rock*, 284-325.
32. Henry Holcombe, *The First Fruits. In a Series of Letters* (Philadelphia, 1812), 62.
33. Augustin S. Clayton (ed.), *A Compilation of the Laws of the State of Georgia Passed by the Legislature Since the Political Year 1800. To The Year 1810 Inclusive* (n.p., 1813), 457-8.
34. *The Savannah Republican*, 28 Sept. 1818.   35. Wood, '"White Society"', 324.
36. Ibid., 325.   37. Ibid., 326.
38. Charles Henry, comp. *A Digest of All The Ordinances of the City of Savannah Which Were of Force on the 1st July 1854* (Savannah, 1854), 310-13.
39. For an elaboration of this point see R.M. Haunton, 'Savannah in the 1850s', (Ph.D. diss., Emory University, 1968).
40. Frey, '"The Year of Jubilee is Come"', 15; '"Shaking the Dry Bones"'; *Water from the Rock*, 241-325.
41. *Minutes of the Sunbury Baptist Association*, 1818 (n.p., n.d.); 1820 (Savannah, 1820); 1821 (Savannah, 1821); 1823 (Savannah, 1823); 1824 (Savannah, 1824); 1825 (Savannah, 1825); 1827 (Savannah, 1827); 1829 (Savannah, 1829); 1830 (Savannah, 1830). (Hereafter *Sunbury Bpt. Ass.* 1818-30.)
42. James S. Simms, *The First Colored Baptist Church in North America* (New York, 1969 edn); Frey, 'The Year of Jubilee is Come', 9-10; *Water from the Rock*, 287-9.
43. Frey, '"The Year of Jubilee is Come"', 10.
44. *Sunbury Bpt. Ass.* (1810-30); *Minutes of the Georgia* [Baptist] *Association*, 1788 (Augusta, n.d.); 1814 (n.p., n.d.); 1830 (Charleston, 1830). (Hereafter *Ga. Bpt. Ass.* (1788-1830)); *Minutes of the Savannah River Baptist Association*, 1812 (n.p., n.d.); 1814 (n.p. n.d.), 1830 (Charleston, 1831). (Hereafter *Sav. Riv. Bpt. Ass.* (1812-30).)
45. Julia Floyd Smith, *Slavery and Rice Culture in Low Country Georgia* (Knoxville, 1985), 217.
46. Ibid. Records of the Midway Church (typescript), Georgia Historical Society, Savannah.
47. Smith, *Slavery and Rice Culture*, 158.
48. For attendance of African-Americans at Baptist Association annual meetings see *Sunbury Bpt. Ass.* 1818-30; *Ga. Bpt. Ass.* 1788-1830; *Sav. Riv. Bpt. Ass.* 1812-1830.
49. This theme is elaborated in the works cited in note 20 (above).
50. Mallard, *Plantation Life*, 83.   51. Ball, *Fifty Years in Chains*, 190-1.
52. These figures are derived from *Sunbury Bpt. Ass.* 1818-30; *Ga. Bpt. Ass.* 1788-1830; *Sav. Riv. Bpt. Ass.* 1812-30.

5

Work & Resistance in the New Republic

The Case
of the Chesapeake
1770–1820

LORENA S. WALSH

In the American Chesapeake, a region including the present states of Virginia, Maryland and West Virginia, tobacco was at one time an important export crop. However, the degree of reliance on this staple became more varied across the eighteenth century and in the older eastern areas, slave owning was widely, but thinly, spread. By the 1780s about two-thirds of rural householders owned slaves. Although a few large planters possessed 100 or more bondspeople, most householders owned fewer than ten. In addition, in the 1780s, roughly half of householders in older areas owned land; the median holding was about 200 acres. In the more recently settled western sections, the proportion of householders owning land was slightly higher, landholdings were larger, and the proportion owning slaves slightly lower.[1]

The period 1770 to 1820 was a time of profound change in the Chesapeake, change that had a marked impact on the nature and pace of slaves' work, modes of resistance and aspirations for the future. I will begin with a brief summary of these changes and then consider the implications for slaves. First, it was a period of international instability. In the Chesapeake, wars at home brought invasion, destruction and trade stoppages, while wars abroad both disrupted traditional channels of trade and occasionally afforded Chesapeake farmers nearly unprecedented opportunities for profit in agricultural products. Second, these events prompted marked changes in the agricultural system. In long-settled parts of the Chesapeake, a shift from tobacco, the traditional staple of the region, to grains necessitated a shift from hoe culture to plough culture and an intensification of year-round work. Third, the period was one of rapid geographic expansion, as many residents of older areas moved to new lands. Fourth, rapid growth of hitherto small and relatively unimportant towns and cities in the region expanded the range and numbers of non-agricultural occupations, afforded farmers new markets for lumber and perishables, and offered slaves new outlets to find work and to sell produce they raised or goods they stole. Fifth, and last, it was a period of deep political change. The North American colonists revolted from Britain and began working out a new political order that incorporated elements of egalitarianism. By and large southern whites had no intention of extending the rights and privileges of free men to blacks, although for a short time after the American Revolution some slave-owners manumitted some or all of their bondspeople. But slaves too adopted egalitarian ideology and adapted it to their own ends. As the struggle for liberty and equality spread to the Caribbean, expressed most dramatically in the Haitian revolution, Chesapeake whites increasingly feared slave insurrections, and sought to tighten control over their slaves and to curb the slaves' aspirations for freedom.

Slave Diet

The exchange of food for labour is fundamental to the operation of any work extraction process. Food was particularly important for slave workers, since coupled with shelter and clothing, it was the basic recompense they received. The slaves' claim to adequate subsistence was a fundamental reason for work-place confrontation and other forms of protest. Chesapeake planters supplied slaves with the basic rations they considered necessary for six full days of plantation labour and one day of rest. Hence slaves had to carve most opportunities to augment their rations out of their scant 'leisure' time. While the basic rations generally provided sufficient calories to meet work requirements, they were by no means generous, may have been nutritionally inadequate and did not include a variety of foods that slaves wanted to eat. The shift from tobacco to grain impacted profoundly the nature of slave work and work conditions, but had little effect on Chesapeake slave diet which hardly changed across this period.[2] Slave foodways and related aspects of culture associated with and expressed in foodways, demonstrated greater continuity than did other aspects of the slave experience.

What did slave-owners supply? Evidence for slave diet comes from two main sources – planters' records and archaeology.[3] These sources provide different and sometimes contradictory evidence which is not always easy to reconcile. Maize clearly formed the bulk of the slave diet. The standard ration of one peck of shelled corn per adult per week and half a peck for old people and for children between the age of weaning and under 16 was well established. This allotment had become the rule of thumb for all Chesapeake residents, bound or free, by the mid-seventeenth century. The slave ration was close to the standard ration for indentured servants. One peck per week comes to 13 bushels a year; three barrels (15 bushels) of maize was the norm for servants and freedmen and was considered sufficient to supply food for a year plus seed and a small reserve to feed poultry or to fatten a hog.[4] By the later eighteenth century, planters generally had the grain ground at a plantation or other local mill and the allotment was delivered in the form of meal.[5] The maize ration was, as Richard Sutch concluded, 'neither excessive nor generous', but was 'adequate to provide sufficient energy to enable one to work like a slave'.[6]

Allotments of other grains were uncommon in the Chesapeake. Usually, enough maize was available for purchase should there be a localized shortage due to adverse weather conditions. In a few years when the corn crop was short throughout the region and the price high, some planters substituted wheat and legumes raised on the plantation for part of the maize ration in order to save the trouble of purchasing corn from distant sources and to avoid outlays of cash. This practice remained uncommon since farmers did not want to expend part of their wheat, a major cash crop, for on-farm consumption, and preferred to reserve peas and beans for trade to the Caribbean. (These could be bartered to ship captains for supplies of molasses, sugar, and rum.) Benjamin Latrobe reported that George Washington had tried substituting wheat for maize for slave rations, 'and had found that though the negroes, while the novelty lasted, seemed to prefer wheat bread as being the food of their masters, [they] soon grew tired of it'.[7] Perhaps. More likely the consideration that if the slaves ate wheat or rye bread, they would have to 'have a considerable addition to their allowance of meat' in order to do the same work, had greater weight.[8]

The amount, composition and quality of slaves' meat diet is more problematic. Lower south, long-staple cotton and rice planters and Caribbean sugar growers were notoriously stingy with meat rations, and in these areas slaves had to catch small wild mammals, turtles and fish in order to enjoy any regular source of protein. Chesapeake planters did provide regular rations of preserved meat, although the amount seems to have differed widely from plantation to plantation. The minimum ration appears to have been $\frac{1}{2}$ pound of salt meat or fish per adult per week, and some plantation accounts suggest a weekly ration of one to two pounds of meat per adult. (For comparison, ordinary free whites probably ate about four pounds of meat per week, and some privileged white labourers were allotted as much as six pounds a week. Meat consumption among the gentry was lavish by any standard.)[9] It is less clear whether planters usually supplied proportionate meat rations for children, or allotted meat only to workers; again, practices seem to have varied. If slave families had to subsist on workers' meat rations alone, they were almost certainly short on proteins.

However, plantation records usually take into account only distributions of preserved meat – primarily salt pork and fish. Inferior cattle and sheep were also slaughtered for fresh meat, and the archaeological evidence shows that these were often substantial additions. A consistent finding from all later seventeenth-, eighteenth- and early nineteenth-century archaeological sites is the importance of beef in the diets of all groups. This is a major revision of the evidence from documents. From estimates of the weights of meat represented by recovered bones, beef and pork were eaten in roughly equal proportions. Most beef was eaten fresh in late fall and early winter, and fresh beef distributed to slaves is very likely under-represented in accounts of standard rations; most slave sites show the same relatively equal proportions of beef and pork that appear in free households.[10]

There were almost certainly distinctions between the quality of the meats provided to slaves and other bound labourers and the cuts that free whites generally ate. Elite planters clearly kept the more desirable parts of slaughtered animals for themselves. Slaves and servants probably ate beef from low quality cuts, especially heads and feet. Crude butchery techniques on occasional larger bones suggest that slaves had limited familiarity with more desirable parts of animal carcasses.[11] Some planters also issued slaves only coarse pieces of salt pork, appropriating the hams from the hogs reserved for 'the people' for themselves.[12] But planters did distribute any butchery offal and fat they did not choose to consume, a supplement that leaves few detectable traces in the archaeological record.[13] Virginia planter Joseph Ball, for example, ordered in 1744 that his slaves were to get the hog haslets and all the fat that could be spared, as well as 'the head and pluck or the value of it' from slaughtered cattle and sheep.[14] Fifty years later (suggesting a continuing practice), George Washington directed that 'The insides of the Hogs, that is, the hastlets, Guts (after the fat is stripped off) &ca. is given among the other Negroes at the different places'.[15]

So far there is not enough archaeological evidence available to prove that consumption of fish and shellfish increased after the Revolution. However, I think that the documentary evidence is so strong that this will prove to be the case. My research in Maryland and Virginia agricultural account books and planter correspondence shows an increase in seine fishing both in Chesapeake Bay and in freshwater streams. Salt fish did not appear in slave rations until the 1760s, but were increasingly common after the Revolution. Much of the fish was caught and processed locally, but planters also bought salt fish from New England ship captains and later from Baltimore merchants.[16] In rural pre-revolutionary probate inventories, seines and oystering and crabbing equipment appear very infrequently. But in inventories from tidewater areas for the years from 1790 to 1820, fishing and/or shellfishing paraphernalia is present in about a quarter of the inventories, perhaps on nearly every farm located along waterways.[17] This likely increase in use of marine resources probably reflected both a response to growing urban markets and a shift among farmers to lower-cost sources of protein in a period of rising grain prices. High grain prices raised the cost of meats and farmers may either have fattened fewer animals, or else have sold a greater proportion of surplus stock.

The amount of milk to which slaves may have had access is another unresolved question. In the early eighteenth century when planters did not pursue butter making to any extent, slaves were sometimes allowed to use the milk of cows not needed to supply the planter's table and to 'manage it as they see fit'.[18] Given the large numbers of cattle planters kept, some surplus milk would normally have been available. This allowance is again mentioned in the early nineteenth century when, for example, on one plantation 'women that had yung children had a pint a pice as soon as it [the cow] was milked'.[19] On another large estate in the late 1790s most slave families had a cow to milk for themselves during the summer.[20] After the revolution, many planters began pursuing dairying more systematically, both for their own tables and for sale in urban markets. On these plantations, the proportion of milk available to the slaves must have been less. Here they may have received the residual buttermilk, but the planters might also have used it to feed hogs.

Planter records also mention occasional issues of salt and small amounts of molasses and alcohol. On some plantations there were fairly regular distributions of salt, while on others it was doled out only occasionally, usually to preserve meat or fish. Sweeteners clearly were not regularly supplied to most Chesapeake slaves. At childbirth, slave women were given some sugar and rum, as were sick slaves. Cider rations are infrequently mentioned, but on plantations where there were extensive orchards, cider consumption may have been more common than the records indicate.[21] Rum (and more commonly after the revolution domestically-produced whisky) was an occasional holiday present and was regularly issued during the wheat harvest. On the other hand, slave-owners considered European status beverages inappropriate for slaves. Before 1820 tea and coffee were not included among occasional treats and plantation accounts show no evidence of slaves choosing to buy such beverages on their own account.

What foods did Chesapeake slaves secure for themselves? First of all, they insisted that owners supply full customary maize rations. Slaves considered this amount an entitlement; any change was protested, as George Washington found when he attempted to make minor changes in rations in 1793. At Mount Vernon, every working negro had received one heaped peck of unsifted meal and all others except sucking children half a peck, at which, Washington asserted, no one complained. 'Since the meal has been given to them sifted, and a struck peck only, of it, there has been eternal complaint; which I have suspected arose as much from the want of the husks to feed their fowls, as from any other cause, 'till Davy [a slave overseer] assured me that what his people received was not sufficient, and that to his certain knowledge several of them would often be without a mouthful for a day, and (if they did not eke it out) sometimes two days'.[22] Washington quickly returned to the usual ration: 'in most explicit language I desire they may have plenty; for I will not have my feelings again hurt with Complaints of this sort, nor lye under the imputation of starving my negros and thereby driving them to the necessity of thieving to supply the deficiency. To prevent waste or embezzlement is the only inducement to allowancing of them at all, for if, instead of a peck they could eat a bushel of meal a week fairly, and required it, I would not withhold or begrudge it them'.[23] Slaves also demanded that they get whatever meat or equivalent rations were customary to a particular plantation or estate. However, slave consumption of meat, whatever its source, was almost certainly lower than among most whites, except perhaps among urban labourers.

Second, slaves used free time to raise or gather vegetables and fruits to supplement and vary monotonous owner-supplied rations. Vegetables and fruits were never part of the rations a slave-owner provided. Planters cultivated fruits and vegetables for their own tables, used fallen fruit to fatten hogs and by the end of the eighteenth century raised vegetables such as turnips, jerusalem artichokes, carrots and pumpkins for feeding livestock. Only when there was an unexpected glut of a particular vegetable did planters mention distributing produce to the slaves. For example, in 1819 Anne Arundel County, Maryland, planter John Francis Mercer raised a bumper crop of 3,224 pounds of exceptionally large, but ill-tasting pumpkins in his cornfield. The 1,000 pumpkins he sent to Baltimore for sale glutted the town market. After reserving a supply for livestock feed, Mercer allowed 'his people' to use the remainder 'freely' for food for themselves and for their hogs.[24] Nonetheless, whatever the planters' policies, it seems likely that hungry slaves could readily pilfer some fruits and vegetables from their owners' fields and orchards and do so with small risk of detection.[25]

In general, slaves were expected to raise whatever vegetables they wanted to eat in their own garden plots in their 'free time'.[26] The vegetables they raised included white and sweet potatoes, onions, peas, beans, greens and squash. Slaves stored the root crops in pits under their cabins. Some were careful to save seed for the next season, for planters often bought starts of potatoes and onions from them for spring planting. Aside from melons, slaves did not usually grow fruits, although they probably ate and occasionally dried fallen apples and peaches from the planters' orchards. Some also harvested wild fruits and nuts which they might either eat or sell to whites.

It is unclear how much of a supplement to the slaves' diet gardening and gathering provided. New archaeological techniques for studying plant remains and analysis of human skeletons may eventually help to provide an answer. Studies of plant remains promise better evidence of the vegetable part of the diet. Skeletal analysis can reveal much, not only about diseases and nutritional stress, but also about the ratios of various plants and animals eaten during the lifetime of an individual.[27] Doubtless much depended on the health and industry of the slaves, upon whether or not slave-owners allowed them an occasional Saturday afternoon off to tend their gardens at critical planting times, and upon whether slaves chose to eat the produce or instead to sell much of it for clothing, liquor and other goods. Before the revolution, the only daylight hours that most slaves could count on for tending their gardens were on Sundays. By the 1790s, some plantation work records begin to note that slaves also had two or three Saturday afternoons a year free for planting their gardens or harvesting the produce. Perhaps slave-owners were more willing to allow slaves more time for gardening because vegetables were becoming a more important part of everyone's diets. However even in this case masters expected slaves to produce the greatest volume of food that could be raised within the least time; they were especially likely to allow extra time for planting Irish potatoes, a crop that produced high yields with little work.

Most Chesapeake slaves also raised chickens, and many families dealt frequently with their masters and with neighbouring whites in fowl and eggs, as did free blacks. Some large planters seem to have decided that their tables would be better and more regularly supplied if they paid their slaves to raise chickens than if they tried to raise an adequate stock of easily pilfered fowl themselves; at least one planter ensured a ready supply of poultry by requiring that his slaves sell their surplus chickens and eggs only to him.[28] To the extent the slaves ate their chickens and eggs, this would have helped to make up deficiencies in owner-supplied meat rations, and archaeology does show poultry remains on slave sites. On the other hand, slave chicken sales were so ubiquitous that it seems likely the slaves sold more than they consumed, relying instead on less readily marketable wild game for supplemental protein. Where meal rations were closely monitored, slaves may have stinted themselves in order to raise a marketable product. Whites considered slave poultry raising as an indication of generous cereal rations; this is of course their perspective.

Slaves also made use of wild resources to supplement their diets. Some acquired a thorough knowledge of the game available in the area, especially those whom planters sent out to fish and hunt to supply the great house table. Archaeological remains, however, show that when it came to filling their own cooking pots, slaves did not range far from home. Given limited time, limited mobility, and the fact that they did not often have the use of boats, nets and guns, slaves had to rely on the wild species that they could catch or trap near their quarters. On plantations as widely scattered as Washington's Mount Vernon and the Georgia sea islands, slave deposits have more small fish caught in shallow waters with hook and line, while planter household refuse contains more deep-water fish caught with seines and boats. Remains of large game animals, primarily deer, similarly appear in planter trash pits, while slaves were more likely to eat more easily caught opossums, squirrels, rabbits or turtles. Upland slaves, in contrast to those living in the tidewater, had access to a narrower range of wild resources, for which planters may or may not have compensated with larger rations of domestic meats.[29]

By the early nineteenth century, tidewater Chesapeake slaves (and free blacks as well) appear to have turned more often to the nearby waters for supplemental protein. This is probably related to a decline in other wild resources attributable to environmental changes brought about by the shift from tobacco to grains. Once planters began to clear more woodlands in order to enlarge grain fields or else to market more lumber and firewood, some forest game species became scarcer. And as woodland range diminished, planters had to pen and more carefully watch domestic livestock, making it more difficult for the slaves to pilfer stray animals. Some tidewater planters began to grant slaves an occasional Saturday afternoon off for crabbing and oystering, and many who owned seines or fishing landings (worked directly or rented out each weekday), let slaves use the equipment on Sundays.[30] Free blacks also appear more often in planter account books selling fish and shellfish, resources on which their families doubtless also relied.

To supplement the potables their owners occasionally doled out, slaves could also purchase alcohol, and did so with relative ease. Planters paid rum and whisky to their own and to their neighbours' slaves in return for produce or for sums owed for work performed in 'leisure' time. Dealers in stolen goods frequently paid slave pilferers with liquor, and slaves who went to town on errands had little trouble buying drink there. Slave-owners were perhaps more apprehensive about the kinds of social and economic contacts between blacks and whites that the trade in alcohol fostered than they were about slave drinking *per se*.[31]

To summarize this section, slave cereal rations were probably sufficient to avoid outright hunger on most Chesapeake plantations. The meat supplied by the owners was often less than adequate for the amount of work required, and perhaps increasingly so, as work requirements intensified. Fruits and vegetables might be had in season, but by and large the slaves had to raise or gather them in their scant free time. Slaves harvested whatever wild foods they could procure near their quarters and most raised poultry. Access to foods not raised or found on or near the plantation was limited, with the exception of alcohol. What is unclear is how satisfactory were the supplements the slaves raised or procured either to provide a sufficiency of protein or to supply nutrients absent in corn and salt meat rations. Incentives to raise foodstuffs on their own time provided slaves some chance to supplement inadequate rations or to add variety to their diet. On the other hand, since gardening and poultry raising were about the only avenues through which ordinary field workers could obtain cash or credit, many slaves may have decided to sell much of their own produce for non-food items.

While most Chesapeake slaves appear to have had a more adequate diet than did those living in the American lower south and in the Caribbean, their marginal subsistence standard is demonstrated by at least three kinds of evidence. The first is cooking methods. The archaeological record shows that most slaves had few storage or cooking vessels. As with lower class whites, meals had to be prepared simply, primarily by boiling, and most of the food the slaves secured was eaten promptly. While the cooking methods made the most of what was available, long cooking and frequent reheating of foods doubtless lost much of the vitamin content. Analysis of faunal remains shows that slaves hacked available meat into small pieces for cooking, and thoroughly scraped or pulverized the bones to extract the marrow.[32] Such cooking methods suggest scarcity rather than abundance of food and especially short supplies of meat.

The second kind of evidence comes from records of slave crime. Slaves often pilfered foodstuffs from their home plantations, and such thefts were a matter for the owner to investigate and punish. In addition, slaves who were brought to trial for thefts off the plantation were most often accused of taking livestock or preserved meat. Stolen foods might be used to satisfy immediate hunger or else served as an underground currency that could be traded for other goods.[33]

The third kind of evidence comes from the extra food slaves received during the harvest season for small grains. At this critical moment, planters encouraged their labourers to maximum effort by supplying extra amounts of bacon and freshly killed mutton, as well as liquor in quantity (hired harvest workers got a pint a day and slaves perhaps nearly as much). By the end of the eighteenth and especially in the early nineteenth century some planters, influenced by the temperance movement, sought to discontinue liquor at harvest. This the slaves resisted, as George Washington noted in 1793: 'Although others are getting out of the practice of using spirits at Harvest, yet, as my people have always been accustomed to it, a hogshead of Rum must be purchased'.[34] Slaves thought some special compensation was required for long hours of hard work in the intense heat of mid-summer. In addition, many larger planters raised more wheat than their own slave work-forces could cut and hired a number of free white labourers for the harvest. This forced planters for a few weeks at least to compensate their slaves with food rations equivalent to those free workers demanded.

Change and Resistance to Change

What work were Chesapeake slaves expected to do, and how did work demands change with altering economic conditions? First, international instability brought periodic warfare to the region and produced rapidly shifting climates of boom or bust. Slave-owners' fortunes alternated between years of high prosperity and years of straightened finances. They made rapid changes in crop mix that entailed abrupt changes in slaves' daily and seasonal work routines. During the American Revolution, with most markets cut off, planters suffered a precipitous drop in farm revenues. Many slaves suffered shortages of clothing, shoes, salt and medicine. Some embraced the greater opportunities to escape their masters that the periodic presence of British troops afforded. Peace brought more plentiful supplies of clothing and provisions, but planters' efforts to make up for revenues lost during the revolution, and later to produce ever larger wheat crops to take advantage of windfall profits as neutral traders to wartorn Europe, led to demands for more and more intense work from the slaves. War, the threat of war, periodic trade embargoes, closing and opening of markets, and years of economic expansion followed by severe contractions (especially in 1819), produced a climate of uncertainty, with planters' outlooks alternating between hope and despair. With their own well-being so closely tied to the fortunes of their masters, the uncertainty of the times must have caused slaves heightened anxiety.[35]

Changes in the agricultural system had an even more immediate impact on slaves' work conditions. The shift from tobacco to grain entailed much more than the substitution of one cash crop for another. Cultivation techniques, systems of field and livestock management, and the mix of secondary crops all had to be altered. Hence the crop shift did not diminish labour requirements; rather it entailed a longer work day, more off-season labour, and more intense work during the growing season. Chesapeake planters extended the slaves' work day by the addition of night chores such as husking and shelling maize, sorting and tying hands of tobacco, and picking seeds from cotton raised to produce slave clothing. Women domestics had to sew clothing for their families in their own time, and most mothers had to make clothes for their infants after work. Individuals were expected to complete a given evening's 'task' and often whipped if they failed.

During the winter months, in earlier years a season of relative leisure except for clearing land and cutting firewood for plantation use, slaves had to plough ground for spring grain crops (weather permitting), to thresh and clean small grains from the previous harvest, to clean meadows and sow forage crops, to mend the increased number of fences necessary to enclose cultivated land, and to cut extra firewood and building timber for sale to town markets.[36] Slaves could not refuse outright to do such work, although they might escape during the most inclement weather, when their clothing and shoes often provided inadequate protection against the elements. Overseers frequently pleaded unwillingness to force slaves to do winter work that might endanger their health as a reason for falling behind schedule. The overseers themselves were doubtless averse to going out to supervise workers in bad weather. They were also unwilling to risk good crop hands falling sick from doing outside chores that did not directly contribute to producing the next year's cash crops. Virginia overseer William Claiborne voiced the pressure he and his hands were under to do winter work in February, 1817: 'I am almost a Mad Man now, here is the 24th of Feby and snow[in]g too as if the winter was just set[tin]g in, and not a solitary furrow run'd towards a new [corn] crop, and hardly half rails enough gotten to do up the crop fence'.[37]

Grain culture and the other farm activities associated with it also required intense work during the growing season. Since most planters grew both wheat and maize, and sometimes other small grains as well, crop hands were fully occupied between March and November with ground preparation, planting, cultivating and harvesting. With the aid of ploughs, more acres were put into cultivation than had been cropped before the revolution. In addition, planters raised more hay, oats and imported grasses to feed the greater numbers of draft animals required for ploughing and waggoning. Seeding the next year's wheat crop and threshing and cleaning the current season's harvest extended the period of high pressure work well into the autumn. Other activities, such as growing and processing fibre crops for slave clothing whenever war threatened a shortage of imported cloth, took up additional time. The agricultural year was filled, leaving no season of leisure except in the worst winter weather.[38]

Slaves, especially those on large plantations, also began to experience a marked increase in the sexual division of labour, a division that enabled planters to extract more labour from almost all workers. The new crops and routines required new tasks that were both varied and often involved some degree of skill – managing draft animals, sowing and mowing grain, ploughing, harrowing, carting, ditching, lumbering, fishing and milling, for example. These new jobs were assigned primarily to slave men. By the end of the eighteenth century many men were performing a greater variety of tasks, and even on large plantations they sometimes worked on special projects by themselves or with only one to two mates and not always under constant supervision. While such men gained greater autonomy in performing their work, they could also be held to more arduous standards since they were no longer working in company with less skilled or weaker hands.

The great majority of slave women continued to perform unskilled manual field labour – hand hoeing and weeding – more often without the help of their menfolk, or only with the help of young boys. The new jobs assigned to women (or the old jobs formerly shared with men) included many of the least desirable chores – building fences, grubbing swamps in the dead of winter, cleaning winnowed grain of weed seed, breaking up new ground too rough or weedy to plough, cleaning stables, and loading and spreading manure. On large plantations slave women's work was less varied than that of the men, and they often laboured together in gangs under the direct supervision of an overseer.[39] The separation of skilled from unskilled workers, and of men from women and boys made it easier for planters to demand more effort from men and to more completely regiment the work of women and boys.

Changes in crop mix and cultivation techniques thus offered new opportunities for some slaves, but entailed worsening conditions for others. Large planters engaged in wheat culture and general farming needed more specialized labourers. Those who gave over tobacco often found themselves with too many unskilled hoe hands. Consequently some began to reduce or at least to stabilize the size of their labour forces by selling the less productive workers, by employing more slaves in non-agricultural pursuits, by hiring out surplus hands, by apprenticing out youngsters, and some, by selective manumissions.[40] Most slave-owners who chose to manumit bondspeople freed only women and children immediately, or after a few additional years of work, while requiring prime age men to serve from five to ten years longer than women. This reduced the planters' costs by eliminating the charge of maintaining the least productive workers while expropriating the most productive years of the strongest workers. But without the help or earnings of the husband, many of the freed women, who had few resources with which to support their children, and few chances for much waged work in rural areas, led a most precarious existence.[41]

The shift from tobacco to grains involved some technological changes which required slave workers to acquire new skills. Beginning in the 1790s, small as well as large slave-owners began using ploughs and carts, and by 1820 almost all did.[42] Thus more slaves gained skill in handling draft animals. Planters must have relied on older slaves to teach adolescent boys (and occasionally girls) how to guide the animals while older workers drove the plough. By the early nineteenth century planters entered into annual contracts with overseers that required them to provide each working farm with a specified number of adult workers, one or two teams of draft animals, and one or two 'plough boys'. Slaves on small farms most commonly drove horses and, increasingly in the early nineteenth century, slower (but more cheaply fed) oxen as well. Both horses and oxen had long been present on plantations, but heretofore not used so extensively as work animals. Before 1820 use of mules was limited to large plantations of 20 or more slaves. Mules were superior to horses or oxen for some kinds of cultivation, but were relatively expensive, and their breeding, training and management was a new skill slave workers as well as planters had to learn.

Slave workers on the whole adjusted well to these important changes in agricultural technology and there is little evidence to suggest that they mistreated draft animals.[43] At the same time the planters' interest in horse breeding and racing, mule raising and coach travel opened up new privileged job opportunities for a fortunate few as grooms, ostlers, jockeys and coachmen.

Slave workers on large farms were also expected to use some labour-saving machinery such as wheat fans, seed drills and corn shellers. These relatively complicated mechanical devices were constructed, usually, by white artisans, but they were maintained by the slave craftsmen who helped to build them. The slaves' response to these innovations, however, was variable. Planters tended to be more enthusiastic about new machines – which often did not work well and broke down frequently – than were either slaves or overseers.

Planters had long complained that slaves were negligent of tools of any sort, and doubtless there was some truth in their belief. If essential tools were lost or broken, work could be delayed or perhaps avoided altogether. Most overseers had little or no knowledge of improved European farming practices, and little use for the agricultural experiments, labour-intensive improvements and new devices which some of their employers were avidly pursuing. Workers and supervisors preferred known routines to the new and unproven, and perhaps did not want to risk falling behind schedule should untested machines break down, or to risk a short crop should experiments fail. Planters faulted 'ignorant negroes, and careless overseers' equally.[44] George Washington commented of a former manager in 1795, 'finding it a little troublesome to instruct the negros, and to compel them to the practice of *his* modes, he slided into theirs'.[45] Examples Washington cited included the use of hoop poles instead of flails to thresh grain, and treading out grain in the barnyard rather than using the threshing floor in a new barn Washington had put much effort into building.[46]

Slave workers, on the other hand, quickly learned to use new tools whose utility was readily apparent, such as scythes and cradles and improved ploughs. Planters who actually laboured alongside their slaves, who saw how the new tools worked (or did not work), and who accepted their slaves' suggestions for modifications, had more success than those who kept their distance from the fields.[47] Slaves thus were able to control to some extent, sometimes positively and sometimes negatively, the introduction of new machinery and other new technologies.

The primary struggle between slaves, overseers and slave-owners in this period was over control of the pace of work. Large planters attempted to force their workers to become more productive – to work more efficiently at all times, more steadily within each day, and more regularly across seasons. Some began to view time as money, resenting any slackening of the work pace or failure to complete tasks within the limits of a prescribed schedule as a form of theft. They expected their slaves to work 'as much in the 24 hours as their strength without endangering the health, or constitution will allow of'.[48] Large planters increasingly adopted schemes of multi-year field rotations, detailed annual plans of work, daily monitoring of tasks accomplished, and hourly measurement of work output with watches – in short, applying 'method' to agriculture that had long been governed more by season, weather conditions and individual task[49]. Slaves probably continued to think of their work within a much shorter time frame – such as what was a reasonable day's task. At most slaves might think of the set of tasks that had to be completed during the growing season.[50] Overseers could plan a more comprehensive cropping strategy for a given year, but seldom took very seriously more ambitious multi-year schemes, the results of which they might not be present to see.[51]

Slave field-hands resisted this close regulation of work time and attempts to speed up work by reverting to a slower pace when observers were absent, or by not working at all. For example, a planter's wife wrote to her husband in February 1815 that cold and snowy weather was keeping the overseers indoors, so 'the people go to work late, and go on thro' the day, at their own ease'.[52] Slaves clung tenaciously to the task requirements and work pace that had become customary on a given plantation. Whenever a new overseer attempted to change established work routines, he encountered stiff resistance. The slaves, many complained, had become accustomed to doing little work or were accustomed to working as they pleased.[53] For example, Charles Dabney, an estate manager, told his employer that slaves on a distant plantation had won extraordinary privileges under one Wingfield, a good-natured but lazy overseer: 'The Negroes are very unwilling to give up the privileges they were allowed in Wingfield's time. Indeed they seem to be determined to Maintain them & because Smith [the new overseer] has Endeavoured to keep them to there duty they have fell upon every plan they possibly could to get him turned off'. When they could obtain no satisfaction from Dabney, several slaves travelled repeatedly to their owner's home plantation in the tidewater to press complaints, and the manager had eventually to agree that 'as the Negroes has taken such a dislike to Smith he is to go off in the fall'.[54]

So long as the results satisfied reasonable expectations, overseers found it much easier not to rock the boat. Planters sought an 'active' overseer, since, as George Washington observed, the slaves 'are not so ignorant (knowing this is required of him) as not to relax as he relaxes, and be idle in proportion as he is idle; because all of them have discernment enough to know that no man can, with propriety, or a good conscience, correct others for the fault he is guilty of'. Many overseers lacked method, pursuing a slow pace until confronted with more work than could be readily accomplished. Then they tended to panic and tried to do everything at once, losing much time in 'marching and countermarching'.[55]

When the slaves slowed work beyond an acceptable pace, many overseers then resorted to brutal whippings administered in the heat of passion. This course was usually counterproductive. When one or two slaves were punished for reasons most considered unfair, the others slowed down even more, as well as running off to press complaints against the overseer to the slave-owner. The owners, in turn, often forbade hot-tempered overseers to administer punishments without prior consultation. In this way the owners sought to prevent incapacitating beatings and widespread discontent among their workers, but increased their own vexations by having to adjudicate frequent disagreements between slaves and overseers.

Slaves who did not work in the fields – artisans and 'jobbers' (teams of slaves who worked at various and often far-flung tasks on several quarters such as ditching, quarrying stone, fencing, road building, timber cutting, brick making and the like) – found other ways to control the pace of their work and the tasks they performed. Slave artisans worked most willingly at the tasks they preferred, and if their white supervisor did not intervene, various members of a team managed to 'carve out such jobs as they like'.[56] They clearly often did 'what they would', taking advantage of any failure of overall direction or planning among the whites. Other slave artisans, especially millers, sawyers, smiths, wagoners, carters and boat hands, had even greater autonomy, usually working on their own without supervision. Many slaves would not have worked to the owners' satisfaction without direct oversight. But those slaves who had specialized skills and who valued autonomy could sometimes carve out niches in which they could work as they would a good deal of the time.

When slave and white artisans worked together, they often co-operated in slowing the work pace. Free white craftsmen, for example, were often employed to direct teams of slave carpenters or masons. Working alongside the hands each day, some of the whites identified more with the workers than with the master. White artisans found it even more counterproductive to push or punish skilled slaves than did field overseers to drive or punish crop hands.[57] Many slave-owners were frustrated at the slow pace with which mixed slave and free artisan groups completed particular projects. They thought the teams drew out more complicated projects to an unconscionable amount of time, with many of the artisans working at whatever pace they chose, concentrating on short-term, more easily performed tasks, and neglecting more complex jobs.[58]

While some ordinary slaves thus gained a degree of control over the work pace, and a privileged few had considerable autonomy, most were unable to halt the continued intensification of work requirements, nor were they able to negotiate additional compensating free time. Slaves had few holidays to which they could look forward. From the second quarter of the eighteenth century, regular holidays were limited to three events each year – Christmas (the duration of the break was a matter for the discretion of the master), and three days each at Easter and Whitsuntide. In addition, for almost all slaves, Saturday was a full work day. Some masters allowed their slaves an occasional Saturday afternoon off to tend their gardens or to go fishing or oystering and, less often, women were allowed part of the afternoon to wash the family's clothing. But these respites depended upon the owner's inclinations, and were not a customary right on which the slaves could rely.[59] Nor could they stop work to celebrate or commemorate rites of passage within their own community. Weddings and funerals had to be postponed until the slaves were 'at leisure'.

The slaves did establish, however, that on Sunday they were free from farm and plantation work and this customary right could not be arbitrarily violated. The sabbath had been a day of rest in the Chesapeake colonies from the outset, where for at least the initial 50 years after settlement English-born indentured servants had predominated in the bound labour force. Chesapeake slaves, especially those born in Africa, did not often accept Christianity and most Anglican planters, as in the lower south, were indifferent and sometimes openly hostile to attempts to convert their slaves. Theoretically planters might compel non-Christians to labour seven days a week, but this was impractical so long as work-forces included a mixture of blacks and whites. Later, slave-owners' religious sensibilities enjoined them from 'mak[ing] our people work too much of a Sunday'.[60] And as elsewhere in the Americas, most slaves employed Sundays for socializing, visiting separated family members, and hunting and gardening to supplement allotted rations. By the mid-eighteenth century, Chesapeake slaves had converted that practice into a right. Occasionally a master might demand that his slaves do pressing work on the lord's day, but did so only if he compensated them for their lost free time with extra food or a little cash.

Forced Mobility, Urban Growth and Worker Response

The slaves' struggle to exert some control over work conditions took place in a context in which they lived under increasing threat of sale or transfer within the region, or of forced moves to the expanding frontier hundreds of miles away from home and kin.[61] Removal and sale were processes over which the slaves could be expected to exert little control. They managed, nevertheless, in some circumstances to negotiate, in effect, terms for removal and forced some planters to acknowledge family rights. The slaves' chief instruments were withdrawal of labour, inefficient labour, and undermining work-place discipline in order either to re-unite with their partner, or to change owner and location.

Planters who established western quarters from a tidewater base tried to minimize these problems either by shifting whole families, or, most often, by moving teenaged and single young adult workers. Communications between the two groups were often limited to biennial trips east that one or two slaves made each spring and fall to obtain plantation supplies, and to drive western livestock to tidewater plantations or deliver crops. Sometimes news the slaves themselves exchanged was supplemented by whatever messages overseers and owners passed along in their correspondence. Tidewater slaves sold to western traders lacked even these scant means of communication, and were forced to move too far away to maintain contact with their families or to have a chance of running back home. Such moves were traumatic, both for those forced to migrate to a place many days' journey away and for those left behind.

Husbands and wives usually worked badly when separated and the men frequently ran away. Experience taught prospective buyers or their representatives to interview slaves they were considering buying, and to decline purchasing those likely to be so discontented with a move involving family separations that the slave would not work willingly and would be inclined to run off to his or her kin. One Virginia planter, for example, decided to sell off some surplus women, children and old people. His overseer responded that one of the candidates for sale, old Peter, 'will not sel for much with out he can get to winchester ware his wife is for he wold let on that he cold do nothing for he can put on the worst face I Ever saw with out it should be what mite sute him'.[62] In some cases planters on the move arranged local sales of spouses who would otherwise be parted by their owners' removal. For example one planter who moved from southwestern Virginia to the city of Richmond in 1809 gave his field slaves the option of accompanying the white family to Richmond where they would be hired out to various townspeople as artisans, domestics or day labourers, or of finding new masters in the locality willing to purchase them.

Slaves who wished to change their masters (and consequently where they lived) repeatedly ran away. Most got a whipping and a period of close confinement whenever they were recaptured, and they also ran a risk of being sold west. But those able to bear the punishment often caused their owners so much aggravation and expense in repeatedly searching them out, and so often spread greater discontent among those who remained on the farm, that the owner would rather sell the slave to his or her master of choice than to 'be plagued with a runaway negroe'.[64] Some runaways, recovered in distant localities where they had gone to find kin or where they had formed attachments while they eluded capture, asked that they be sold in the place to which they had gone, and had their wishes thus far accommodated.[65]

Discontented slaves could sometimes also force owners to let them work at a preferred occupation. Ned, for example, a Kent County, Maryland, field-hand, in 1800 informed his overseer that he had 'a great desire to be hired out to go by water [i.e. to work on boats] & says that he will not stay hear if [you] will [not] let him go for he says that he tires of working on the land'. His owner chose to arrange the transfer rather than risk Ned's running if he did not comply.[66]

Outrageous behaviour rather than running away was often the women's chief weapon. Peg Cooper, for example, a slave on Maryland's eastern shore, had behaved so 'outrageously' that her owner determined that she be sold out of the county so she could no longer foment discontent on or anywhere near the family's farms. Yet her master allowed Cooper and three of her youngest children to travel to Baltimore on their own to look for a buyer.[67]

The pressures slave plantation workers brought to bear against forced migration were also used by slaves hired out for urban work in the region's growing network of towns and cities. Few slave-hirers were willing to engage a 'notorious runaway', or would hire such a slave only conditionally, for example, that 'we pay only for the time he stays in our service'.[68]

The emergence of a layer of hired slaves was symptomatic of the ways in which the developing post-revolutionary economy afforded new opportunities for slaves to earn cash rewards for their labour and offered some a wider range of occupations. Individual skilled artisan and domestic slaves found more chances for short-term, waged positions in Chesapeake cities, and more youngsters were apprenticed to town craftsmen. Those who were able to find reasonably regular work were often allowed to keep some portion of their wages for themselves. Slaves working on their own in larger cities like Baltimore had more control over their living arrangements and could mingle freely with rapidly growing numbers of free black urban residents. Slave runaways also had a greater chance of losing themselves in a city among the free blacks who often helped to conceal them.[69] Urban employments also afforded some skilled slaves a chance for self-purchase. Carpenters, for example, who were allowed to work for wages in booming cities like Baltimore, Richmond, and Washington, DC, could sometimes earn enough to purchase themselves, as well as the liberty of other family members.

The expansion of the slave hire system, most pronounced in towns, but also to a lesser extent in the countryside, did not benefit all slaves. Some hired slaves suffered increased miseries. Those who were seized by the courts for their owners' debts had to go to work for the creditors or else, along with slaves belonging to less caring masters, were auctioned off each year to whomever bid the most for their services. These slaves might work for a different master every year, and had to move so often that they had scant chance to form lasting unions or to maintain much contact with kin.[70]

Expanded urban markets for food, fodder and fuel did allow a significant element in the slave population to work occasionally as traders either on behalf of their owners or on their own account. Before the revolution slaves usually sold the produce they tended or gathered in their own time – chickens, eggs, oysters, fish, fruits and vegetables – to their owners or to other nearby white families. Slaves who traded with neighbouring families, who knew them personally and who knew what sorts of dealings their owners sanctioned, were much less likely to be accused of stealing their wares and they did not need a pass to go to town. If the slaves sometimes peddled goods in town, either on their own account or for other slaves, it went unmentioned in surviving records, and it seems likely that such traffic was limited. The small size of most Chesapeake towns was apparently the main reason, coupled with planters' attempts to limit their slaves' movement. There were no legal restrictions imposed on slave traders aside from the requirement that they have their owners' permission.

After the war urban demands for perishables, hay, diary products, meat, firewood and timber for building rose. Improved roads, and by the 1810s, regular water transportation, increased the possibilities of marketing perishables. Produce like potatoes, apples, and even turnip greens, which earlier had no value since almost every rural household raised them, suddenly became valuable market crops, and planters deep in the hinterland as well as those near cities began rearing livestock for urban markets. Astute slave salesmen and women were assigned the job of peddling the produce in town, sometimes weekly, occasionally daily. Market days must have been a welcome time, affording some slaves a chance to escape the plantation and work without supervision, manage cash, and perhaps find ways to make a little money for themselves.[71]

Black hucksters were considered superior to white. 'A black man is much better for this business than a white man', Richard Parkinson, an English immigrant who raised produce and dairy products for the Baltimore market at the turn of the nineteenth century asserted. 'Although they are in general ignorant, they are impudent'. Selling produce was 'an employment which they like, viz. riding to market in a cart, drinking whisky, and cheating you out of part of the money they get for the *truck*'.[72] Slave or free black marketeers acting as agents for the planters sometimes made a few pennies by devious methods, for example by under-reporting sales, by watering the milk they were sent to sell, or by trading a bit of produce for whisky that they consumed on the trip home. Slave-owners who lived at a distance from the towns where their slaves traded tried to keep such expropriations to a minimum by requiring the slaves to account with a resident merchant, and to turn over the proceeds to the representative. Slaves also conducted a clandestine trade in stolen goods with town receivers; at least many owners suspected this was the case.

By the end of the eighteenth century, Chesapeake townspeople began to pass local ordinances regulating the activities of slave peddlers. Some of these laws were aimed at curbing urban disorders, and may also have represented attempts by white traders to diminish competition from blacks. Examples include an order by the Norfolk, Virginia, Common Council prohibiting slaves from selling beer, cakes and the like on city streets, and restrictions on slave traders in the Petersburg, Virginia, municipal market. However, most of the new municipal rules seem to have been intended to curb trading in stolen goods by requiring the slave have the owner's written permission to sell a stated list of goods. It was not until after 1800 that the Virginia legislature adopted state-wide regulations requiring all slaves to secure their owners' written permission to trade.[73]

More significantly, as planters diversified farming operations, slaves began to spend more time tending fruits and vegetables and making butter to feed townsfolk. White families everywhere began to eat a more varied diet, and many were increasingly willing to pay others to raise or catch vegetables, wildfowl, fish and shellfish. Slaves kept abreast of market prices whether or not they sold in nearby towns and began to regulate their dealings accordingly. As a Fairfax County slave told an English traveller in 1801, his mistress ' "always gives me the price of the Alexander market" ' for the poultry and vegetables he raised on his own time.[74]

Political Dimensions

Slave pressures within the system interacted with other factors, such as geographic expansion, urban growth, changes in crop mix or cultivation techniques, to allow more opportunities for cash and wage earning and a wider range of activities for slave labour. Struggles between slaves, overseers and slave-owners over control of work, of family life and conditions of servitude took place, moreover, in the context of a larger political struggle which assisted some planters to see that positive incentives might improve labour standards.[75]

A few planters in the early nineteenth century, for example, attempted to improve the care of meat hogs by assigning slaves more responsibility, either by rewarding the hogkeeper with one of the animals if he did well, or else allowing individual families to tend particular hogs, assigned for the annual meat ration, during the months before slaughter. A few well educated, progressive, but not exceptionally rich planters with smaller plantations attempted to involve their slaves in improving agricultural routines. One Virginian, for example, engaged his eight field-hands in experiments with maize. Each man had an individual plot to tend, all planted in slightly different ways. Small payments to some of the slaves for maize and corn fodder suggest the planter rewarded those who produced the most.[76] One Maryland farmer divided up his wheat field into rows that he and a slave seedsman alternately sowed. He then watched the crop to see who was the better and more economical sower.[77] Finally, John Coalter, a Virginia judge, left the management of his farm in the hands of his slaves while he was gone on long trips attending court in 1809 and 1810. He discussed the work to be done with the slaves before he left, and periodically sent additional instructions to his wife who read the letters to Old Ned, their leader. His directions included a new method for shocking corn that the judge had observed in his travels and which he considered his slaves capable of carrying out from the verbal description his wife passed on. The slaves in turn relayed suggestions for improving on the owner's plans through their mistress.[78]

Such cases were the exception. In general slaves were not expected to respond positively to incentives. While the master expected a preferred slave to serve his owner's interests, what the slave often saw was an opportunity to serve him or herself or to help other slaves. Dairymaids, for example, took some of the butter they made to feed their families. Spinners appropriated some of the wool they were issued to process. Carpenters and jobbers sold nails and tools when they had the chance. Men in charge of distributing weekly rations left the cornhouse unlocked so that other slaves could help themselves to more than their weekly allotment, or appropriated grain intended for feeding livestock to their own uses. And so on. The incentives to which the slaves responded were not always those the owner intended. Paradoxically, the most powerful incentive that slave-owners could offer their bondspeople was the chance to cease being a slave. The slaves who worked the most diligently were those who had the opportunity to purchase their own freedom or that of other family members. Only when slaves could alter their condition were they likely to regard 'incentives' in the same way as might free men and women. The nature of the transition is captured in an incident involving two slave men, Jack and Dick, who had left a distant western quarter and come to their master, Robert Carter of

Nomini, to complain about their overseer. Carter had formed a plan for eventual manumission of all his slaves, including Jack and Dick. He persuaded the men to agree to return to the quarter and to work there during the coming year in part by arguing that their conduct 'did not comport with expectations of men who were to become free, and then would be citizens of the United States'.[79]

Changes in the political system, however, which made more offices elective rather than appointive, may have had some effect in mitigating slaves' daily living and working conditions. Slave-owners who aspired to election began to be concerned about their reputation as a master among their constituents. George Washington, for example, was disturbed at the way the maize ration controversy on his own estate reflected on his reputation (see above). And Edward Lloyd IV, a prominent Maryland politician, went to extraordinary lengths in 1793 when a minister attacked him publicly as 'a Cruel and hard Task Master who neither feeds nor Cloaths sufficiently his Black Family of People'. Lloyd believed the attack had been politically motivated; he went so far as to try to counter the charges with a public address to the citizens of his home county, accompanied by 23 detailed affidavits from current and former stewards and overseers attesting to his good treatment of his slaves.[80] Other office seekers – this includes most large slave-owners – may have become somewhat more careful about the way they provided for their slaves and about how they responded to their complaints in order to prevent the circulation of rumours prejudicial to their reputations. More importantly, however, the ideology the white colonists used to justify their revolt from Britain could not be confined to white minds. Although slave-owners intended to limit application of the egalitarian political philosophy underlying the Declaration of Independence to white men, slaves quickly adopted it to their own ends. Before the revolution in most cases the masters' laws were the only ones that counted for slaves. But with whites in the process of changing the rules of government for themselves, slaves had reason to learn about lawyers, courts, legislatures and anti-slavery movements. These they too might utilize to change the rules in their own interest and soon after the war some slaves began the attempt, often in quite sophisticated ways. They could now appeal to universal natural rights and not just to the questionable generosity of individual .masters. Slaves presented petitions for freedom to state legislatures, initiated suits for freedom against their masters, ran away, and above all questioned their status.[81] Thereafter, that questioning did not cease, whatever the outcome of slaves' attempts to gain their freedom. One plantation manager noted that during the revolution the slaves were so encouraged by the success of some who ran away that he had to 'be more severe than I would wish ... without that they could not be managed'.[82] Grumbling and expressions of discontent continued over the years, to the increasing frustration of slave-owners. In 1798 George Washington observed that 'Negros are growing more and more insolant and difficult to govern'.[83] Similarly, in 1802 Maryland planter John Galloway, plagued by runaway and all too assertive slaves, stated that 'property in Negroes is becoming more precarious and less valuable every day and the management of them exceedingly difficult'.[84] The next year, one of Galloway's overseers, James Eagle, quit his lucrative post in frustration. 'I am now drawing towards 50 years of age. I have spent 21 of that time on this place the first part of it much more agreeable than the latter'. The slaves he supervised had decided they too had an inalienable right to freedom. Eagle found 'they Get much more Dissatisfied Every year & troublesome for they say that they ought all to be at there liberty & they think that I am the Cause that they are not'. He could not cope with their changed behaviour: 'by that means [they] Gaves me all the trouble that they can which keeps me one half of my time in hot blood & when that is the Case I Cannot Conduct my business as I ought to do'.[85]

For a brief time in the 1780s and 1790s Chesapeake slaves' opportunities for freedom greatly increased. Some slave-owners repudiated the institution and freed their slaves, and state legislatures and courts liberalized manumission codes and more readily entertained freedom suits. Rapid growth of a free black population in the upper south raised the expectations of those still enslaved. Although many slave-owners changed their minds about manumission in the early nineteenth century, the slaves had no doubts but that all should be 'at there liberty'.[86] The slave-owners' demands that slaves continue to do their duty faithfully and quietly fell on increasingly deaf ears.

Notes

This paper is based on preliminary results of a study on plantation agriculture in the Chesapeake region from 1620 to 1820. The primary sources are planter correspondence, plantation account books, and selected probate inventories throughout all parts of the region where tobacco was at one time an important crop. The bulk of the evidence comes from a few middling and many large servant and slave-owners, although small planters are taken into account. The project draws especially on the work of Lois Carr, Paul Clemens, Carville Earle, Lewis Gray, Allan Kulikoff, John McCusker, Russell Menard, Edward Papenfuse, David Percy, and Joseph Robert, as well as upon numerous county studies, studies of individual planters, and works on Chesapeake merchants and the Chesapeake economy. I am indebted to all, though there are a number of areas where my interpretations differ from theirs. For a bibliography of recent literature see John J. McCusker and Russell R. Menard, *The Economy of British America, 1607–1789* (Chapel Hill, 1985), ch. 6.

1. Allan Kulikoff, *Tobacco and Slaves: The Development of Southern Cultures in the Chesapeake, 1680–1800* (Chapel Hill, 1986), 131–57.
2. Discussion of the slave diet – its composition, adequacy or inadequacy, and the relative contributions of slaves and slave-owners to that diet – should be placed in the context of changes in the diet of the free population at the beginning of the nineteenth century. Among the free population, levels of meat consumption, relatively high in the Chesapeake since the seventeenth century, did not change significantly. The main source of protein was domestic livestock, with all groups eating beef and pork in roughly equal proportions. In contrast to the early eighteenth century, when wild foods contributed only about 10 per cent of the meat diet, consumption of fish and to a lesser extent shellfish increased throughout older parts of the country after the revolution. Production of dairy products, especially butter, rose in the upper south. Wheat flour was

increasingly substituted for other cereal grains among the upper classes. All economic groups began to eat more vegetables. Consumption of alcohol rose dramatically between 1790 and 1820. Coffee drinking increased as well, while tea drinking, a practice in most households, remained relatively constant. The social connotations of using these two beverages (especially tea) continued to be a prime consideration for their adoption, separate from their nutritional role. Cooking and food preservation technology remained basically unchanged for all groups until the 1830s. However, food supplies became somewhat less dependent on season as improved systems of harvesting and distribution and marginally improved preservation techniques afforded a greater range of foods across the calendar year. On the whole, there was probably some improvement in the fare of middling and upper-class whites, but the diets of the rural and especially the urban poor likely declined in quantity and quality, as more poor people lacked access to land for raising livestock or garden produce. (Lorena S. Walsh, 'Consumer Behaviour, Diet, and the Standard of Living in Late Colonial and Early Antebellum America, 1770-1840', in Robert E. Gallman and John Wallis (eds) *American Economic Growth and Standard of Living before the Civil War* (Chicago, 1992).

3. Evidence from planters' records comes from my study of plantation agriculture; the sources are too numerous to cite in full here. The archaeological literature is summarized and cited in Walsh, 'Consumer Behaviour, Diet, and the Standard of Living', and in Theresa A. Singleton, 'The Archaeology of African American Life: A Critical Review and Bibliography', in Theresa A. Singleton and Mark Bogard (comps) *Guides to the Archaeological Literature of the Immigrant Experience in America, no. 2* (Society of Historical Archaeology, forthcoming). See also Stacy Gibbons Moore, '"Established and Well Cultivated": Afro-American Foodways in Early Virginia', *Virginia Cavalcade*, 39 (2) (1989): 70-83, for an account of slave diet utilizing some of the same materials, and especially, for the ante-bellum period, interviews with former slaves in the Federal Writers' Project collections. Moore's findings underscore the many elements of continuity over time. The Chesapeake slave diet is a topic of continuing concern among historians, archaeologists, curators and foodways experts at the Colonial Williamsburg Foundation. I am particularly indebted to Patricia Gibbs of the Research Department for sharing unpublished findings.

4. Lois Green Carr, Russell R. Menard, and Lorena S. Walsh, *Robert Cole's World: Agriculture and Society in Early Maryland* (Chapel Hill, 1991), ch. 2.

5. Earlier in the century, most people ground their maize at home using mortars and pestles.

6. Richard Sutch, 'The Care and Feeding of Slaves', in P.A. David, et. al., *Reckoning with Slavery: A Critical Study in the Quantitative History of American Negro Slavery* (New York, 1976), 268.

7. Benjamin Henry Latrobe, *The Journal of Benjamin Henry Latrobe, Being the Notes and Sketches of an Architect, Naturalist and Traveller in the United States from 1796 to 1820* (New York, 1905), 60.

8. This paper makes extensive use of George Washington for quotations. This is because he often wrote more explicitly, more clearly and more grammatically about numerous aspects of slave management than many contemporaries. I have used Washington materials only in those instances where my research indicates these were representative of other large planters. Ways in which Washington was a typical or an atypical planter are discussed in Lorena S. Walsh, '"To Labour for Profit": Plantation Management in the Chesapeake, 1620-1820', manuscript in process.

9. Carr, Menard and Walsh, *Robert Cole's World*; Walsh, 'Consumer Behaviour, Diet, and the Standard of Living'; and Philip Ludwell Lee, MS Ledger, 1743-83, Perkins Library, Duke University, Durham, NC (hereafter, Duke).

10. Henry M. Miller, 'Colonization and Subsistence Change on the 17th Century Chesapeake Frontier' (Ph.D. Diss., Michigan State University, 1984); Henry M. Miller, 'An Archaeological Perspective on the Evolution of Diet in the Colonial Chesapeake, 1620-1745', in Lois Green Carr, Philip D. Morgan, and Jean B. Russo (eds), *Colonial Chesapeake Society* (Chapel Hill, 1988): 176-99; and Henry M. Miller, 'Kingsmill Plantation Faunal Analysis Preliminary Statement', (typescript, n.d.). Cf. P.H. Garrow and T.R. Wheaton, Jr. (eds), 'Final Report Oxon Hill Manor Archaeological Site Mitigation, Project I-95/MD 210/I-295' (typescript, 1986), vol. 2, 570-1, 640-2.

11. William M. Kelso, *Kingsmill Plantations, 1619-1800: Archaeology of Country Life in Colonial Virginia* (Orlando, 1984), 176-97; John Solomon Otto, *Cannon's Point Plantation 1794-1860: Living Conditions and Status Patterns in the Old South* (Orlando, 1984); and Elizabeth J. Reitz, 'Urban/Rural Contrasts in Vertebrate Fauna from the Southern Atlantic Coastal Plain', *Historical Archaeology*, 20 (2) (1986), 49-58.

12. Plantation Records, 1787-97, Cheston-Galloway Papers, Ms. 1994, Maryland Historical Society, Baltimore, MD (hereafter MHS).

13. Walsh, 'Consumer Behaviour, Diet, and the Standard of Living'.

14. Instructions About My Affairs, 18 February 1744, Joseph Ball, Ms. Letterbook, 1744-59, Manuscripts Division, Library of Congress, Washington, DC (hereafter LC).

15. George Washington, *The Writings of George Washington from the Original Manuscript Sources, 1745-1799*,

John C. Fitzpatrick (ed.), 39 vols (Washington, DC: 1931–44), vol. 33, 195–207.

16. Walsh, 'Consumer Behaviour, Diet, and the Standard of Living'.

17. Lorena S. Walsh, 'Report on Selected Agricultural and Food-Related Items in York County, Virginia, and St Mary's County, Maryland Inventories, 1783–1820', (Colonial Williamsburg Foundation, typescript, 1991).

18. Instructions About My Affairs, 18 February 1744, Ball Letterbook, LC.

19. Alexander Wood to Lawrence Lewis, 4 May 1818, Lewis Family Papers, Ms. Duke.

20. Edward Lloyd IV, Treatment of Slaves, 1793, Reel 40, Lloyd Papers, Ms. 2001, MHS.

21. Instructions About My Affairs, 18 February 1744, Ball Letterbook, LC.

22. Washington, *Writings*, vol. 32, 470–7.

23. Ibid., 434–8.

24. *The American Farmer* (Agricultural Periodical), John S. Skinner (ed.), (Baltimore, MD: 1819–34), no. 25, 17 September 1819; no. 35, 26 November 1810.

25. Moore, '"Established and Well Cultivated"', 74, indicates that later in the nineteenth century planters may have included vegetables in slave rations and allowed slaves to gather orchard fruits. This may reflect earlier practices, but I have not found any evidence for the early nineteenth century.

26. I have found no evidence about the size of Chesapeake slave garden plots, but suspect, given slaves' limited free time, that most slave gardens were relatively small. So far I have found no slave garden areas depicted on period plantation maps. Probably the plots were shifted from year to year, and were often sited either on 'old fields' temporarily abandoned from cash crops, or else on newly cleared land not yet ready for cropping.

27. Marley Brown III, 'Digging the Urban Places of Colonial Virginia: The Perspective of Environmental Archaeology', (Colonial Williamsburg Foundation, typescript, 1990); and Elizabeth J. Reitz, Tyson Gibbs, and Ted A. Rathbun, 'Archaeological Evidence for Subsistence on Coastal Plantations', in Theresa A. Singleton (ed.), *The Archaeology of Slavery and Plantation Life* (Orlando, 1985), 163–91.

28. Edward Lloyd IV, Treatment of Slaves, 1793, Reel 40, Lloyd Papers, MHS.

29. Reitz, Gibbs and Rathbun, 'Archaeological Evidence for Subsistence'; Dennis J. Pogue, '"Washington's View of Mount Vernon": Transformation of an Eighteenth-century Plantation System', (paper presented at a conference on Re-Creating the World of the Virginia Plantation, Charlottesville, VA, 1990); Joanne Bowen Gaynor, 'Preliminary Notes on the House for Families Faunal Assemblage', (typescript, 1989); and Martha A. Zierden, Lesley M. Drucker and Jeanne Calhoun, 'Home Upriver: Rural Life on Daniels Island, Berkeley County, South Carolina', (contract study produced for the South Carolina Department of Highways and Public Transportation by Carolina Archaeological Services and The Charleston Museum, 1986).

30. Walsh, 'Consumer Behaviour, Diet, and the Standard of Living'; and Walsh, '"To Labour for Profit"'.

31. Eugene D. Genovese, *Roll, Jordan, Roll: The World the Slaves Made* (New York, 1974), 641–7.

32. Barbara Davis, 'Faunal Analysis', in Theodore R. Reinhart (ed.), 'Material Culture, Social Relations, and Spatial Organization on a Colonial Frontier: The Pope Site (44N180), Southampton County, Virginia', (typescript, 1987), 85–96; William M. Kelso, 'The Archaeology of Slave Life at Thomas Jefferson's Monticello: "A Wolf by the Ears"', *Journal of New World Archaeology*, 6, no. 4 (1986), 5–20; Kelso, 'Mulberry Row: Slave Life at Thomas Jefferson's Monticello', *Archaeology* (1986), Sept./Oct, 28–35; Kelso, *Kingsmill Plantations*, 176–97; Larry W. McKee, 'Delineating Ethnicity from the Garbage of Early Virginians: Faunal Remains from the Kingsmill Plantation Slave Quarter', *American Archaeology*, 6 (1987), 31–9; and Reitz, Gibbs, and Rathbun, 'Archaeological Evidence for Subsistence'.

33. Philip J. Schwarz, *Twice Condemned: Slaves and the Criminal Laws of Virginia, 1705–1865* (Baton Rouge, LA, 1988), 118–36.

34. Washington, *Writings*, vol. 32, 470–7.

35. Ira Berlin, 'The Revolution in Black Life', in Alfred F. Young (ed.), *The American Revolution* (Dekalb, IL, 1976), 348–82; Benjamin Quarles, *The Negro in the American Revolution* (Chapel Hill, 1961); Quarles, 'The Revolutionary War as a Black Declaration of Independence', in Ira Berlin and Ronald Hoffman (eds), *Slavery and Freedom in the Age of the American Revolution* (Charlottesville, VA, 1983), 283–301; Lorena S. Walsh, 'Rural African Americans in the Constitutional Era in Maryland, 1776–1810', *Maryland Historical Magazine*, 84 (1989): 327–41; Walsh, 'Chesapeake Planter Response to Market Incentives, 1770–1820: Capitalist Transformation or Historical Accident?' (Paper presented at the Annual Meeting of the Economic History Association, 1990); and Walsh, '"To Labour for Profit"'.

36. Lois Green Carr and Lorena S. Walsh, 'Economic Diversification and Labour Organization in the Chesapeake, 1650–1820', in Stephen Innes (ed.), *Work and Labour in Early America* (Chapel Hill,

1988), 144–88; and Lorena S. Walsh, 'Slave Life, Slave Society, and Tobacco Production in the Tidewater Chesapeake', in Ira Berlin and Philip D. Morgan (eds), *Cultivation and Culture: Labour and the Shaping of Slave Life in the Americas* (Charlottesville, VA, 1993).

37. Claiborne to George W.P. Custis, 24 February 1817, Lee Family Papers, MS1L51, b 33–38, Virginia Historical Society, Richmond, VA (hereafter VHS).

38. Lois Green Carr and Russell R. Menard, 'Land, Labour, and Economies of Scale in Early Maryland: Some Limits to Growth in the Chesapeake System of Husbandry', *Journal of Economic History* 49 (1989): 407–18; Carr and Walsh, 'Economic Diversification and Labour Organization'; Lorena S. Walsh, 'Enlightened Practice or Egregious Blunder: Agricultural Change and the Chesapeake Ecology, 1650–1820', (paper presented at the Annual Meeting of the Social Science History Association, 1988); Walsh, 'Slave Life, Slave Society, and Tobacco Production'; and Walsh, '"To Labour for Profit"'.

39. Carr and Walsh, 'Economic Diversification and Labour Organization'.

40. Peter J. Albert, 'The Protean Institution: The Geography, Economy and Ideology of Slavery in Post-Revolutionary Virginia', (Ph.D. Diss., University of Maryland, 1976); Berlin, 'The Revolution in Black Life'; Richard S. Dunn, 'Black Society in the Chesapeake, 1776–1810', in Berlin and Hoffman (eds), *Slavery and Freedom in the Age of the American Revolution*, 49–82; Lorena S. Walsh, 'Plantation Management in the Chesapeake, 1620–1820', *Journal of Economic History*, 49 (1989): 393–406; Walsh, 'Rural African Americans in the Constitutional Era'; and Walsh, 'Chesapeake Planter Response to Market Incentives'.

41. Thomas E. Davidson, 'The Demography of Freedom: Manumission Practices and the Shaping of the Eastern Shore's Free African American Population, 1776–1810', paper presented at a conference, 'Freedom Fettered: Blacks and the Constitutional Era in Maryland 1776–1810', Morgan State University, 1987; Barbara Jeanne Fields, *Slavery and Freedom on the Middle Ground: Maryland during the Nineteenth Century* (New Haven, 1985), ch. 2; and Sarah S. Hughes, 'Slaves for Hire: The Allocation of Black Labour in Elizabeth City County, Virginia, 1782 to 1810', *William and Mary Quarterly*, 3d ser., 25 (1978): 260–86.

42. Walsh, 'Report on Selected Agricultural and Food-Related Items'.

43. There are a few scattered complaints of slaves abusing draft animals, but planters and overseers generally agreed that draft animals performed poorly because they had insufficient food. (Walsh, 'Slave Life, Slave Society, and Tobacco Production in the Tidewater Chesapeake'.)

44. For example, Washington, *Writings*, vol. 36, 37–8.

45. Ibid., vol. 34, 101–6.

46. Ibid., vol. 31, 336–8, vol. 34, 101–6.

47. For example, J.F.D. Smyth, *A Tour in the United States of America . . .* (London, 1784; New York, 1968), 110–22.

48. Washington, *Writings*, vol. 30, 175–6.

49. Walsh, 'Plantation Management in the Chesapeake'; and Walsh, 'Slave Life, Slave Society, and Tobacco Production in the Tidewater Chesapeake'.

50. Mechal Sobel, *The World They Made Together: Black and White Values in Eighteenth-Century Virginia* (Princeton, NJ, 1987), chs 1–5.

51. Sobel, *The World They Made Together*, chs 3–5, presents a perceptive discussion of African, African-American, and Anglo-American attitudes towards time. I agree that the struggle over use of time was in part a clash between early modern and traditional world views. However, I disagree with her assessment that 'time in Virginia was slowing down rather than speeding up' (p. 55). The elite's increasing concern about use of time towards the end of the eighteenth century is not an indication that 'it was apparent they were fighting a losing battle with their children, their white servants and their African slaves' (54–5). Rather, struggles over use of time intensified because planters *were* increasing the duration and intensity of labour. Productivity measures demonstrate the degree of their success. Throughout the Chesapeake, for example, mean wheat output per slave labourer trebled between 1750 and the end of the century, and on large plantations the rise was sevenfold, from about 10 bushels at mid-century to over 70 bushels by the 1780s. (Walsh, 'Slave Life, Slave Society, and Tobacco Production in the Tidewater Chesapeake').

52. A.B. Cocke to J.H. Cocke, 4 February 1815, Box 19, Cocke Family Papers, Ms., Alderman Library, University of Virginia, Charlottesville, VA (hereafter UVA).

53. Walsh, 'Slave Life, Slave Society, and Tobacco Production in the Tidewater Chesapeake'.

54. Charles Dabney to [John Blair] [1769], Charles Dabney Papers, 1744–1900, Ms., Southern Historical Collection, University of North Carolina, Chapel Hill.

55. Washington, *Writings*, vol. 33, 221–4. Cf. 5–12, 141–3; vol. 32, 245–50, 278–84; and vol. 36, 110–14.

56. Ibid., vol. 33, 188–95.

57. Stefano Fenoaltea, 'Slavery and Supervision in Comparative Perspective: A Model', *Journal of Economic History*, 44 (1984): 635–68.
58. Washington, *Writings* vol 32, 462–7; vol. 33, 61–6, 212–4; and Sobel, *The World They Made Together*, ch. 4.
59. In the seventeenth century, white indentured servants claimed a free Saturday afternoon as a customary (though not legally sanctioned) right transferred from England. By the early eighteenth century, when slaves predominated among bound labourers, planters had succeeded in making Saturday a full day of work.
60. William Byrd, *The Secret Diary of William Byrd of Westover, 1709–1712*, Louis B. Wright and Marion Tinling (eds) (Richmond, VA, 1941), 202, 208.
61. Allan Kulikoff, 'Uprooted Peoples: Black Migrants in the Age of the American Revolution, 1790–1820', in Berlin and Hoffman (eds), *Slavery and Freedom in the Age of the American Revolution*: 143–71.
62. Alexander Wood to Lawrence Lewis, 23 March 1816, Lewis Family Papers, DUKE.
63. William Mumford to Sally Mumford, 29 December 1809, Letters 1786–1831, George W. Mumford Division, Mumford Ellis Family Papers, Ms., Duke. Cf. Dunn, 'Black Society in the Chesapeake'.
64. John Hanson to Philip Thomas, 14 February 1782, 5 March 1782, 10 March 1782, John Hanson Letters, Ms. 1785, MHS.
65. For example, no. 12764, Galloway-Maxcy-Markoe Papers, Ms., Manuscripts Division, LC.
66. Ibid., no. 13286.
67. Ibid., no. 13328.
68. Journal, 1808, Kennan Papers, Ms., UVA.
69. Berlin, 'The Revolution in Black Life'; and Robert L. Hall, 'Slave Resistance in Baltimore City and County, 1747–90', *Maryland Historical Magazine*, 84 (1989): 305–18.
70. Hughes, 'Slaves for Hire'.
71. Walsh, 'Slave Life, Slave Society, and Tobacco Production in the Tidewater Chesapeake'.
72. Richard Parkinson, *A Tour in America in 1798, 1799 and 1800* (London, 1805), 175–6, 218–19; for fuller documentation, see Walsh, 'Slave Life, Slave Society, and Tobacco Production in the Tidewater Chesapeake'.
73. I am indebted to Michael Nicholls, Department of History, Utah State University, for this information.
74. John Davis, *Travels of Four Years and a Half in the United States of America, during 1798, 1799, 1800, 1801, and 1802* (Bristol, 1803), 388.
75. This section treats only political change. During these same years, an upsurge in evangelical religion also profoundly affected master-slave relations. See for example, Rhys Isaac, *The Transformation of Virginia, 1740–1790* (Chapel Hill, 1982); Sobel, *The World They Made Together*.
76. Charles Dabney Commonplace Book, 1811–25, Ms. 5:5 D1124:1, VHS.
77. James Wilson Farm Account Book, 1770–96, Ms. 915, MHS.
78. Brown, Coalter, Tucker Papers, MS, Swem Library, College of William and Mary, Williamsburg, VA, box 3, folios 4–16.
79. Carter to Robert Newman, 25 December 1792, Robert Carter Letterbook, 10 July 1792–April 1793, Ms., DUKE.
80. Edward Lloyd IV, Treatment of Slaves, 1793, Roll 40, Lloyd Papers, MHS.
81. Berlin, 'The Revolution in Black Life'; *Maryland Historical Magazine*, 84 (1989) (special issue on African-Americans in the Constitutional Era); and Walsh, 'Rural African Americans in the Constitutional Era'.
82. Certificate of Richard Grayson, 23 August 1793, Edward Lloyd IV, Treatment of Slaves, Roll 40, Lloyd Papers, MHS.
83. Washington, *Writings*, vol. 36, 443–7.
84. Galloway-Maxcy-Markoe Papers, no. 13328, LC.
85. Ibid., no. 13412.
86. Berlin, 'The Revolution in Black Life'; and David Brion Davis, *The Problem of Slavery in the Age of Revolution, 1770–1823* (Ithaca, 1975).

6

Proto-Proletarians?
Slave Wages in the Americas

Between Slave Labour
& Free Labour

O. NIGEL BOLLAND

In slavery the *labourer* is a commodity, while in wage labour the *labour power* of legally free labourers is the commodity. Hired labour, as distinct from slave labour, 'implies the conceptual abstraction of a man's labour power from the man himself'.[1] Marx, distinguishing between slave and wage labour, draws attention to the difference between the appearance and reality of these forms of labour.

> In slave labour, even the part of the working day in which the slave is only replacing the value of his own means of subsistence, in which he therefore actually works for himself alone, appears as labour for his master. All his labour appears as unpaid labour. In wage-labour, on the contrary, even surplus labour, or unpaid labour, appears as paid. In the one case, the property-relation conceals the slave's labour for himself; in the other case the money-relation conceals the uncompensated labour of the wage-labourer.[2]

This analytical distinction between systems of labour control and exploitation, in which some people work more or less involuntarily for others, is crucial for the conceptualization of various forms of compulsory labour.[3] But what does this analytical distinction really mean when applied to the actual social relations in which people are engaged in the labour process, relations which rarely conform to social scientists' ideal types and which change over time?

Marx, in a letter to P.V. Annenkov in 1846, criticizes the French philosopher Proudhon for failing to see that '*economic categories* are but *abstractions*' of the real relations in which people engage in the course of their productive activities, and therefore 'they are truths only in so far as those relations continue to exist'.[4] Such economic categories are not the 'eternal laws' that bourgeois economists believe them to be, but 'historical laws only for a given historical development, a specific development of the productive forces'. So, when Marx goes on to say that slavery is 'an economic category of paramount importance', he means, on the one hand, that it is the basis of colonial trade and hence of the emergence of capital industrialism, and on the other hand, that it is but an abstract expression of the actual relations in which particular people engage in their productive and social life, corresponding to their specific, transitory historical development, and not an eternal law.

'Slaves' and 'masters' are not particular kinds of people, but social roles, defined and bolstered by institutional arrangements. To examine the nature of slavery we must examine *relationships*, not the attributes of individuals. To say that some people are slaves is to say that there are other people who have a peculiar kind of claim over them, a claim that not only denies them rights and honours but also denies any rights of people other than the slave-owner in them. A slave is thus a 'socially dead person',[5] one who has no socially recognized existence except through his master. Slavery, then, is a relationship, 'one of the most extreme forms of the relationship of domination, approaching the limits of total power from the viewpoint of the master, and of total powerlessness from the viewpoint of the slave'.[6] This abstraction, or ideal type, of slavery as a relation of total domination/subordination was, in reality, contested in all kinds of ways – overtly and covertly, individually and collectively, psychologically, culturally and militarily – in the dialectical practice of everyday life. Consequently, while slaves and masters inherited their social relations and ideas about such relations as social structures and ideologies from preceding generations, they themselves, in the course of their social lives, which necessarily consisted of real antagonism, were actually maintaining and transforming their relations. This is what Marx means when he says 'the economic forms in which man produces, consumes and exchanges are *transitory and historical*'.[7]

To understand the profane origin and history of categories such as 'slavery' and 'freedom' it is necessary to locate them in practical life, that is, in the real relations and activities of people in a particular time and place, thereby revealing their historical specificity. For example, when Marx distinguishes between slave labour and wage labour in the passage in *Capital* cited above, he does not do so in order to make eternal verities of these categories but in order to clarify, even to expose, the contemporary bourgeois usage of these terms. Hence, he writes of 'capitalism's illusions about freedom', that it is a trick of 'vulgar economics' to make the 'actual relation' of wage labour invisible by making it all appear as paid labour, as distinct from slave or unpaid labour.

The task of historical sociology, seen in this light, is to reveal ways that the activities and relations of real people reflect and create social developments. For example, when Sidney Mintz raised the question 'Was the Plantation Slave a Proletarian?'[8] he did so partly in order to raise theoretical and conceptual questions about the abstract categories themselves, but also to understand the forms of labour, and the nature of the society in which they existed, in a specific time and place. Thus, in the Caribbean, 'labour forms other than slavery were usually combined with slavery itself, in practice'.[9] On the one hand, slaves who cultivated and marketed provisions on their own account engaged in labour not usually associated with slavery. These slaves Mintz refers to as a 'proto-peasantry'.[10] On the other hand, some legally free people, working alongside slaves, were often coerced.

While the utility of the categories we use depends on keeping the analytical distinctions clear, we need to remember that they are, after all, abstractions. The people whom Mintz calls 'proto-peasants' are not, in essence, 'slaves' or 'peasants', but people working in relationships in which they act, more or less, in ways that we mean by 'slavery' and 'peasantry'.

A 'wage' is generally construed to be the payment made to a worker for a period of time during which he is to be at his employer's disposal, thereby implying that the worker is otherwise *free* to dispose of his own time. Consequently, 'paying wages in return for labor is generally conceived of as the very antithesis of slavery',[11] because the slave is considered to be *entirely* at his owner's disposal. This paper investigates situations in which slaves received payment for their labour, situations that are anomalous in so far as they imply a conceptual abstraction of the slave's labour power from the person while, *at the same time*, the slave remains a commodity. If reality conformed to our categories, such situations would be impossible because 'slave labour' means 'unpaid labour', and hence slaves, by definition, receive no wages. However, the custom of slaves receiving payments for their labour, though by no means common, was quite widespread in the Americas, particularly in connection with skilled and industrial labour and urban life, but also among unskilled and agricultural labourers. The payment of slaves for their labour has been viewed, on the one hand, as a sign of 'quasi-freedom' for the slave and the imminent disintegration of slavery, and on the other hand, as an incentive system designed to get more out of the slaves and to control them by rewards as well as traditional punishments.

The investigation of this topic will also throw light on the question of the emergence of a labour market, or what is often called 'the transition' from slave to wage labour. This transition was not a sudden shift from slave to wage labour, conceived as two mutually exclusive categories, but a 'succession of different mixes of forms of labor exaction . . . as parts of a worldwide capitalism'.[12] The capitalist system depended on a *combination* of free and coerced labour, with the former emerging first among workers in the core countries while the latter predominated in the periphery.[13] Mintz argues 'the integration of varied forms of labor-exaction *within* any component region addresses the way that region, as a totality, fits within the so-called world-system. There was give-and-take between the demands and initiatives originating with the metropolitan centres of the world-system, and the ensemble of labor forms typical of the local zones with which they were enmeshed'.[14] The specific ways that a region is integrated into the world-economy, as well as the specific local responses to different forms of labour control, affect the manner and timing of the transition from slavery to some other form of labour in that local economy. While different forms of labour may co-occur in local economies, as these economies become increasingly integrated in and dominated by the world capitalist system, there is a general tendency for wage labour to prevail. The categories of 'slave' and 'proletarian' were not only 'linked intimately by the world economy' that gave birth to them in their modern form,[15] but they also coexisted at times in *the same people*. Whether or not slaves who received wages are usefully considered as 'proto-proletarians', the existence of the practice of paying slaves wages is further evidence that 'slavery rarely occurred in absolutely pure form'.[16]

In general, the payment of cash to slaves, in a variety of forms more or less resembling wages, is an aspect of the process of commodification, 'by which formerly non-market-mediated activities come to take the commodity form'.[17] Labour, like land, undergoes different kinds and degrees of commodification within the logic of capitalism. Slave labour, which 'is more commodified than serfdom, and is more manipulable and congruent with the logic of profitable commodity production',[18] gives way to the commodification of labour power. The payment of slave wages constitutes a degree of commodification of the slave's labour time or labour power as distinct from the labourer as a commodity. For the capitalist, whether owner or hirer of such slave labour, this offers a degree of flexibility along with control, while for the slave it offers a degree of autonomy along with the promise of material benefits. Less fully commodified than free wage labour, where the capitalist buys only the labour power he needs, 'slave wages' may be seen as an intermediate category and a transitional phase in the long-run commodification and proletarianization of labour.

I will, first, survey the evidence of varieties of slave wages in the Americas, then evaluate their meaning both for the slaves and their owners, and, finally, discuss the significance of this phenomenon in relation to the transition from slave to wage labour. Through examining these examples of slaves who received wages, we gain further understanding of how, in the nineteenth century, the institution of slavery was changing from within, because of the actions of the slaves and their masters, in relation to the ways these local economies based on slave labour were integrated into the capitalist world-economy.

Varieties of Slave Wages

Similar tendencies in relation to slave wages appear throughout the Americas, increasingly in the nineteenth century, as slaves received payment from their owners as reward for good work, payment for working in their own time, or for working more than a normal task. Varieties of payments, more or less resembling wages, are distinguishable by the circumstances in which they were given. First, a variety of payment was in the form of bonuses, either as gifts or as incentives. Second, there were payments associated with the practice of slave-hiring. Generally, the cash payment made for slave-hiring was given to the slave-owner, almost as a rent for the lease of his slave. The market transaction between the person hiring the slave and his or her owner excluded the slave from the negotiation, but some slaves received a portion of the money paid their owners. In other cases the slaves were responsible for hiring themselves and then gave their owners a portion of their wage, retaining the rest for themselves. In the latter cases slaves were actively involved in market transactions concerning the monetary value of their own labour power. Third, there was payment made for extra work in task systems or for working overtime, suitably called overwork. In these cases, too, there was often an opportunity for slaves to engage in some bargaining regarding what were considered normal tasks or the owner's time, beyond which they expected some remuneration.

First, we will examine the bonus payments. Throughout the Americas it was a common practice to reward valued slaves with favours, whether in goods, special opportunities or cash. The bonus, as a reward for good conduct or for loyalty, such as informing on other slaves, was often simply a special favour, given arbitrarily as a way to increase the owner's paternalistic control. Christmas gifts, for example, could be a reward for productivity or good conduct,[19] so could be seen by both slaves and masters as a simple form of remuneration. Thomas Thistlewood, an overseer and then slave-owner in eighteenth-century Jamaica, generally gave slaves money after having sex with them.[20] Sometimes bonuses were given regularly, as an additional, and often annual, allowance to an especially skilled, reliable or favoured slave. Drivers on the Codrington and Newton plantations in Barbados received annual rewards of as much as £20 and two pairs of shoes,[21] for 'good behaviour and attention to the Negroes'.[22] Savannah, Georgia, provides an unusual example of incentive payments among slave fire-fighters: 'As a spur to greater enthusiasm a bonus of one dollar was given to the first to arrive on the scene of a blaze, and the second and third received fifty cents apiece'.[23] This could be considered an incentive to arson.

Some bonus schemes more closely resembled a regular wage system. A Tennessee turnpike company in the 1850s paid each of its slaves between 40 cents and $3, as 'Stimulant & Reward money'.[24] On the sugar estates of colonial Brazil, monetary incentives and other rewards were common. The account books of one estate were filled with small payments to slaves as rewards for various minor chores.[25] Many slaves on the sugar estates of Louisiana received cash payments as compensation for goods and services, such as woodcutting and harvest work, as regular bonuses. Skilled slaves were paid for their services according to their level of skill and responsibility during the harvest. In the mid-1840s, the sugar-maker received $30 and his deputy $15, while the chief engineer and the kettle-setter each got $10, and the firemen, kettle-tenders and the second engineer each got $5 for their harvest season work.[26]

Bonuses did not generally resemble wages as they were not usually given regularly, nor was the amount of payment fixed, but 'varied according to the liberality of the master'.[27] Slaves may have begun to see such bonuses, given in the context of a holiday or as a reward for some special behaviour or activity, as a right, like their rations and shelter, but the masters did not see them that way. To the extent that bonus payments were regarded as 'a master's exclusive prerogative',[28] they offered little scope for bargaining.

Second, there were payments made in relation to slave-hiring. The widespread practice of slave-hiring created something resembling a labour market. However, we should distinguish between, on the one hand, those cases where the slave-owners and slave employers arranged the rate of hire over the slave's head, and, on the other hand, the situation of a slave actively seeking and negotiating his or her own hire. The slave's opportunity to influence his work conditions and rewards was much greater in the latter case, which often amounted to a slave bargaining directly about his or her own wage rates.

Slave-hiring occurred in Virginia at the time of the revolution. A Scottish indentured tutor on a Virginia plantation hired a slave woman to spin for him, on nights and Sundays, and he sold what she produced. He paid her 'three shillings the pound'.[29] As slave labour became increasingly scarce and expensive in Virginia, the cost of hiring rose, from $45 to $50 per year per slave in the 1820s, to $135 to $150 for 'good hands' in the mid-1850s.[30] Slave-hiring increased in the nineteenth century and was an important aspect of slavery in the ante-bellum South where owners hired out their slaves for annual payments between 12 and 15 per cent of their value. As the cost to hirers, or employers, was usually less than that of free labour, 'The tobacco factories, the saltmakers, the iron and coal industries, the railroad and canal builders and steamboat owners were calling urgently for hired hands'.[31]

Clement Eaton writes that slaves 'who worked in the factories had many privileges which made plantation Negroes eager to work there. In addition to being able to choose their masters, they were given a small sum of money each week by the manufacturer to find their meals and sleeping quarters. This was, to them, almost an emblem of freedom'.[32] While the slaves could not always choose their masters, their owners sometimes took their preferences into account at hiring time, but wages were often fixed and could not be easily influenced by the slaves. In 1858, for example, a North Carolina court declared that the practice in Craven County of giving hired slaves a weekly allowance of 25 cents 'was sanctioned by public as well as private policy'.[33] For skilled slaves, allowances were much higher. Joshua Crews, a hired slave who held an important supervisory post at a Virginia ironworks, was paid $5 a month.[34] Simon Gray, a hired slave who was captain of a lumbering firm's flatboat on the Mississippi in the 1840s and 1850s, received a bonus of $5 for each trip between Natchez and New Orleans on top of a salary of $8 per month. While he remained a slave in the eyes of the law, he engaged in a profitable business on his own account which enabled him to purchase his family's freedom.[35]

Hired slaves in Latin America also received cash payments. In Cuba, hired slaves could not be physically punished and they 'received part of the money paid for their hire'.[36] In the Colombian Choco, slaves were hired out to work in gold mines where few whites or other free men were willing to work. Many owners permitted certain slaves to rent themselves independently, paying one peso per working day to their owner, a sum officially stipulated in 1719 as 'the average amount a healthy slave could produce through one day's labor'.[37] One young male slave, working entirely on his own for six years, paid his owner 1,634 pesos for this privilege.[38] The owners benefited from such income during slack periods when they could not put the slaves to useful work themselves, those who rented the slaves paid for them only when they specifically needed them, and 'incentives to enter such an agreement were high for healthy slaves since they could keep what they earned above the stipulated one peso a day',[39] which was the rate for free labourers.[40]

In Brazil, hired slaves were commonly allowed to retain a portion of their earnings. This was true on sugar estates[41] and, in particular, in urban Brazil. There was a considerable range of relationships between masters and their slaves in a highly flexible system. Sometimes slaves received a daily wage which had to be turned over to the master, who might choose to return an allowance. If the master did not contribute to the slave's upkeep, he was expected to remunerate him. The master sometimes provided room, board, clothing and medical treatment. When he offered only room and medical treatment, or he left the slave entirely on his own, the slave had only to pay his master a fixed daily sum, 'determined in such a way that it would have been difficult for the slave to save much of what he earned'.[42] So, while some hired slaves had to accept whatever bonus or allowance their owners chose to give them, others were more involved in negotiating their employment and remuneration. Unlike the hired slaves in North Carolina, whose weekly allowance was fixed, these Brazilian slaves competed with each other and with free workers in a labour market, though they were neither entirely free to operate, nor legally entitled to all their earnings.

The practice of slaves hiring themselves out existed in the eighteenth century and seems to have increased in many places in the nineteenth century. In the Chesapeake, an increasing number of slave artisans hired out their own time after the 1760s. So widespread was the practice in 1782 that residents of Henrico County, adjacent to Richmond, complained that 'many persons have suffer'd their slaves to go about to hire themselves and pay their masters for their hire and others under pretence of putting them free set them out to live for themselves and allow their Masters such hire as they agree on'.[43] In Baltimore, in 1820, slaves who hired their time from their owners earned 75 cents a day, plus their food, and paid their owners $2 a week.[44] An observer in Louisville, a small town in 1820, commented that there were at least 150 slaves who hired their own time and paid their owners $20 per month, as well as slave women who paid $4 to $6 while supporting three or four children each.[45] In 1845 a grand jury in Savannah declared that the practice of slaves hiring their own time or working for themselves was 'an evil of magnitude . . . striking directly at the existence of our institutions'.[46] Similar complaints were heard from St Louis and Charleston. What they feared was that slaves who could choose their employers were avoiding the supervision of their owners. The *New Orleans Daily Picayune* opined that the practice 'has weakened the close connection of master and servant, producing the most serious change in the latter'. As the ties binding master and slave are weakened, the latter 'become intemperate, disorderly, and lose the respect which the servant should entertain for the master . . . [T]heir example is contagious upon those who do not possess these dangerous privileges'.[47]

Despite legislation against slaves hiring themselves in all the slave states of the USA, there was no slackening of this practice in the 1850s.[48] The state of Georgia attempted to tax these slaves out of existence in 1850, but a tax of $100 on slaves hiring themselves could not be enforced; in South Carolina grand juries repeatedly complained that laws against slaves hiring their own time were so 'grossly and habitually violated' that stricter laws were needed.[49] The reason why the practice could not be eliminated was simply that it suited too many people – masters, employers and slaves. Certainly, 'owners received more from slaves hiring themselves out than they did by leasing them through annual contracts'.[50] This is exemplified by the payments made by Yellow Jim, a Louisville slave, who was allowed to be on his own provided he paid his owner, James Rudd, $5 a week. Rudd's account books reveal steady and prompt payments of between $202.35 and $271.55 a year, totalling nearly $1,900 between 1847 and 1853, while the prevailing hiring rates averaged around $100 annually and rarely reached $200. Yellow Jim finally had enough of these privileges, as the ledger records: 'Dec. 11, 1853. Ranaway'.[51]

The idea that slaves could search for work, bargain for wages, dispose of their own time, and be responsible for their own food, clothing and shelter, appears so anomalous in the institution of slavery, yet we should not jump to the conclusion that such slaves enjoyed real autonomy. Urban slave artisans who lived on their own and found their own work 'might well count this a privilege worth fighting to secure and retain', but it is 'highly doubtful', as Barbara Jeanne Fields warns, 'that slaves hired for unskilled agricultural labor enjoyed any greater independence while living with employers than they did while living with their owners'.[52] She refers to Frederick Douglass's bitter comment when he hired himself out and had to pay his owner three dollars each week: '"Master Hugh seemed to be very much pleased ... with this arrangement", Douglass commented sardonically, "and well he might be ... [W]hile he derived all the benefits of slaveholding ... without its evils, I endured all the evils of being a slave, and yet suffered all the care and anxiety of a responsible freeman"'.[53] While there were some obvious advantages to slaves in these arrangements, Douglass found when the ante was raised to $9 that he could not make ends meet, as he had to provide all his own tools as well as his means of subsistence.

The situation was similar in Latin America, except that the slave's property was more likely to be protected and the slave was more likely to be able to use his or her savings to purchase freedom. In Brazil, for example, many urban slaves worked for wages or sold goods in the streets and could keep for themselves whatever they earned above a specified sum they gave their masters. In the seventeenth century, this practice did not provide many slaves the opportunity to earn enough to buy their freedom, but by the nineteenth century urban slaves participated in a wide range of occupations. Unskilled slaves who worked as porters, stevedores, boatmen, oarsmen and sailors, sometimes accumulated enough from their wages to buy their freedom within nine or ten years.[54] Most skilled occupations in urban Brazil were in the hands of male slaves, working for wages. Masters apprenticed young slaves to a trade in order to increase their earning power and then lived off their wages. In such cases, a slave had less choice regarding his occupation, though 'the degree of his skill was often his responsibility, as well as whether he used his skills to earn the price of his freedom'.[55] Skilled slaves worked at all the metal crafts – iron, tin, copper, gold and silver – and 'frequently commanded some of the highest prices and earned good wages'.[56] Others worked for wages as tailors, seamstresses, musicians, painters, sculptors, barbers and prostitutes, splitting their earnings between themselves and their masters. Though such slaves experienced some freedom of movement and choice of occupation, along with opportunities to earn money and buy their freedom, they could be punished and were even driven to suicide for failure to meet their owners' requirements. A slave barber in Rio de Janeiro, for example, earned his own wages, but when he could not earn enough to please his master he was flogged, and as a result he killed himself with a razor. This master, who was said to be 'barbarous and remorseless', forced his slaves to earn money for him and 'had already whipped thirteen of his slaves for not earning enough money, when the barber killed himself'.[57]

In Cuba, a slave wage-earner (*jornalero*) 'personally signed on at a sugar mill for a certain figure and ... periodically handed part of his wages to his nominal owner as payment for the status of a semifreedman with the right to sell his services freely'.[58] Though this passage appears to exaggerate the slaves' rights, such slaves could use their earnings to buy their freedom through gradual self-purchase (*coartacion*), if they did not spend them on food, luxuries, liquor or gambling, as they were encouraged to do. In Matanzas, the centre of the Cuban sugar economy in the nineteenth century, skilled slaves even hired themselves out for wages 'without the knowledge or permission of their owners', while others 'garnered valuable skills and were paid cash wages with the approval and encouragement of their masters'.[59] A seventeen-year-old slave who was apprenticed to a mason for four years, received a salary of 1 peso daily in the final year, and then, presumably, became a wage-earning skilled slave.

These practices are found throughout the Caribbean. In Martinique in the 1840s, 'slaves earned money by hiring themselves out during their free time, either on or off the plantation' and 'some slaves used their earnings to hire other slaves or freedmen to work in their gardens'.[60] In the British Caribbean, slaves who worked independently and made fixed periodic payments to their owners were 'common in the towns but rare in the rural areas', where they were mostly skilled slaves.[61] In Jamaica, a slave-jobber generally contracted with other free persons for the lease of his slaves, but 'sometimes', Barry Higman says, 'he found it convenient to simply ask a fixed weekly or monthly payment from his slave and permit the slave to employ himself to others for a wage ... To a certain extent the system allowed the slave to choose his occupation as well as his employer, and this also suited the slave-owner'.[62] This system applied to a whole range of occupations in the towns, including prostitution. Some Jamaican slaves even paid each other wages: 'Sunday work on the provision grounds, for example, could earn 1/8 per day plus breakfast'.[63] In the Bahamas, with the collapse of the cotton-based plantation system, slaves were increasingly hired out or permitted to hire themselves out, and some of them saved enough from their wages to buy their freedom.[64] What these Caribbean examples share is the notion that, in certain fairly specific and limited contexts, slaves had a right to sell their own labour power and to receive remuneration – often as cash payments resembling wages – for at least a portion of their work.

The third kind of slave wage, after bonuses and slave-hiring, occurred when the slave-owner paid his own slave for special work or extra work, beyond a customary amount of time or work. Such payments for overwork, as it was appropriately called, implicitly acknowledged a limit to the slave-owner's right to his slave's labour power and the slave's right to remuneration. Some slave ironworkers in Virginia, for example, received a small allowance, 'in effect a regular wage for, evidently, assuming responsibility for various phases of the furnace or forge operation'.[65] There are numerous examples of owners paying their slaves for extra work in the slave societies of the Americas, beginning in the eighteenth century and increasing in the nineteenth century, particularly among skilled and industrial labourers.

Overwork payment was widespread in many industries in the southern United States, because it had obvious advantages for the slave-owners. As Robert Starobin emphasizes, rewards for overwork benefited the slave-owners by increasing the productivity of their slaves. 'Since bonuses never accrued until after the slave's required day's tasks were completed, masters also insured that a certain amount of work would be done *before* overtime outlays took effect'.[66] Slaves who were self-hired artisans and industrial workers were relatively privileged so long as there was a shortage of their skills. In the Chesapeake region, for example, slave worked alongside whites at the iron forges and furnaces. By the 1750s, slaves were replacing skilled white workers and, by the 1770s, between 30 and 50 slave ironworkers constituted about one per cent of the adult slaves in the region. 'They were paid for work done on their own time and purchased rum and other goods at company stores with the money they earned'.[67]

This concept of 'their own time', time that belonged to the slave, not the owner, is one aspect of the system of overwork, while working beyond a specified task or quantity of work is another. Slave ironworkers in Virginia 'who did more than their required amount of work were rewarded with payment, in either cash or goods'.[68] By the ante-bellum period, the system of overwork payments had spread as an incentive scheme to unskilled workers associated with the ironworks. 'Compensation for extra work was almost a universal feature of the labor system at slave-manned furnaces and forges in the Old South'.[69] Slaves who chopped wood over and above their task of $1\frac{1}{2}$ cords were given credit on the company's books at the rate of 40 cents per cord, the same rate as free white wood choppers. This system operated for other jobs: for skilled slave ironworkers who produced more than their quota of iron, ore-bank hands who mined and washed extra ore, colliers who tended the charcoal pits in their time off, and shoemakers who made additional shoes. Even unskilled hands earned credit, at the rate of 50 cents per day, for working at night, on Sundays and the traditional Christmas holidays, and in emergencies.[70]

Slaves could choose the method of payment for overwork at Buffalo Forge, Virginia, whether in cash, in credit at Weaver's store, or to secure time off. Though Weaver almost never granted his slaves the opportunity to purchase their freedom, they took advantage of this system to materially improve their own lives and their families'. The skilled forge workers were in the best position to benefit from the overwork system, some receiving between $3 and $5 per ton for their overwork. One heater at Weaver's forge, Henry Towles, earned $31.80 in 1852, $36.16 in 1853, $55.28 in 1855, and $93.53 in 1856, and was credited with $102.53 in his account at the company store in 1858.[71] Sam Williams, Weaver's slave forgeman, regularly made over $50 a year in the 1850s. In 1855 and 1856 he earned $92.23 and $103, respectively, while his wife, Nancy, earned overwork pay by running her owner's dairy. In 1856, they had accounts in a Lexington bank; Sam's held $91.31 and Nancy's $61.96.[72] They used the money they earned to buy extra food, furniture for their home, clothes for their children, presents for each other and their relatives, and little luxuries, but they could not buy their freedom.

The overwork system appears in other occupations and regions in the United States. The tobacco factories of the Chesapeake, for example, required a slave to do a task of 45 pounds of pressed tobacco in a ten-hour day. Slaves who did more than this task received compensation of at least $5 and sometimes over $20 a month.[73] A turpentine distillery paid cash sums ranging from $2 to $14 annually to slaves who exceeded their required tasks.[74] In coal pits near Richmond slaves received between $12 and $14 a year for their overwork.[75] Jim Matthews, a slave who worked as a raftsman on the Mississippi, was paid for extra work performed at night or on holidays. Other slaves owned or hired by the same lumber firm were paid $1 a day for extra work as well as a cash bonus at Christmas.[76]

Overwork payments were also made to slave agricultural workers, both in the task system, for ditching and leveeing, for ginning, pressing and baling cotton, and for Sunday and holiday work, and 'special marketing tasks'.[77] In Louisiana, the Spanish custom of allowing slaves to work for themselves on Sundays was continued into the American period. Slaves were paid at the rate of 50 cents for Sunday work, a provision said to have been upheld by the courts.[78] On sugar plantations in Louisiana, slaves who cut wood on their days off received between 50 and 75 cents per cord. Planters paid their slaves to dig ditches on a task basis in their time off, at rates varying with the depth of the ditch. Plantation slaves were paid by their owners to make shingles at $3 per thousand, staves at $5 per thousand, pickets at $1.25 per hundred, and boards at $2\frac{1}{2}$ cents per four-foot board. They were paid to make hogsheads and barrels at $2 each, hauled wood for 75 cents a day, collected fodder for 1 cent per bundle, and other tasks in their time off from regular plantation labour. Other slaves were paid to make bricks, shuck-collars, baskets, rails and handbarrows. A slave named Thornton got $20 for making a cart in his own time.[79] The slaves' participation in an internal economy not only enabled them 'to enjoy substantial material benefits', but they also 'derived satisfaction from controlling a portion of their own lives'.[80]

Cash payments for overtime or overwork were also known in the Caribbean and Latin America. In Barbados, for example, skilled slaves such as masons, carpenters and even unskilled field slaves, were paid small amounts for 'specific job work or for labor on customary free days'.[81] In Belize (British Honduras), it was observed in 1809 that 'Saturday's labour, invariably the privilege of the slave, and which is generally engaged by his owner', was customarily paid for at the rate of 3s. 4d. per day, or £8 13s. 4d. annually. It was added, however, that this nominal rate 'seldom actually amounts to anything like so much', as the owners substituted goods – 'slops, trinkets, or liquors, of the most inferior kind' – at inflated values, from their stores.[82] In Martinique in 1845, the 'Mackau Law' specified that male and female slaves who had to work beyond an obligatory and legally specified maximum number of hours, should be paid at least 10 centimes per hour or 5 francs per month. During the intense harvest season, 'Money was given to the slaves according to their ability to work'.[83] Many urban Brazilian slaves earned money through extra work. Slave women in Rio de Janeiro earned wages, after they had completed their household tasks, as street pedlars, hired cooks, wet nurses and prostitutes. A good cook 'often peddled examples of her culinary skills in order to earn extra money for herself or her owner'.[84]

To the extent that it was conceded that slaves had time that was theirs to dispose of as they saw fit – in working extra for their owners, working for themselves, or in leisure activities – this was socially and psychologically important for the slaves. However, as the slaves' rewards began only after they had completed their regular tasks or hours, they were working a great deal more for their owners for little compensation. It was a way for the slave-owners not only to keep their slaves' labour up to the mark but also, quite literally, to overwork them. Negotiations around such issues as the slaves' time and tasks were not limited to material rewards but occurred within the larger context of slaves' aspirations to gain more control over their lives.[85]

The widespread emergence throughout the slave systems in the Americas of several varieties of remuneration, more or less resembling wages, indicates the evolving nature of relations between masters and slaves. The threat of physical punishment remained the core of this cruel system of labour control, but some small rewards were found by the masters to secure more cooperation and extra work, and to the slaves they meant a difference in the material quality and meaning of their lives. Most important, however, was the recognition, implicit at least, that the master's right to his slave's labour power was not absolute and that, by the same token, the slave should receive some compensation for work that did not belong to his master. The payment of remuneration to slaves, in any form, acknowledged that they could be motivated by desire for gain as well as fear of punishment. Such acknowledgement of individual self-interest meant a degree of independence for the slave, however implicit and prescribed. In such a situation, 'work was not a sphere of total domination by the master but an arena where meaning and motivation were contested'.[86] Masters could still, by law and force, establish the parameters of the relationship, but by manipulating a system of rewards as well as punishments they were opening up new opportunities for the slaves to bargain and negotiate.

Negotiating Work and Wages

Slaves seized, and often created, opportunities to negotiate their rewards and work conditions. Negotiations sometimes took the form of explicit bargaining. Mechanics and craftsmen in the United States who hired their own time could 'choose their own masters and make their own arrangements . . . When they were particularly efficient or when the demand for their trade ran high, they could drive good bargains and pocket substantial earnings'.[87] When slaves were paid for overwork, norms regarding what the slave owed his master and what the master should pay his slave for work done beyond such norms were established through a process of mutual accommodation. So we find slaves making deals, reaching understandings, bargaining about the value of their time and about what constitutes a fair task, with their owners and employers. Slaves who negotiated in this way engaged in a market transaction about the value of their own labour power, as a consequence of which they were able to improve their material standard of living and sometimes even to purchase their freedom, or the freedom of others, with the proceeds of their labour. Such slaves resemble a kind of 'proto-proletariat', engaged in subtly transforming their relations with their masters.

There are numerous examples of slaves negotiating their work and wages. In 1831, slaves on the Codrington estates of Barbados, who were owned by the Society for the Propagation of the Gospel in Foreign Parts, were allowed to purchase 'free' days on which they would subsequently be paid for their labour. Once the door to bargaining had been opened, the slaves discussed the terms and conditions of their free days and of task work with Bishop Coleridge. The bishop said that they displayed 'no want of shrewdness' in wishing to know 'who would pay the doctor' if they fell ill on their free days, and how much the Society would charge them for each of their free days. 'With respect to task-work', which they called job-work, Coleridge reported, 'they agreed that it could not be well adopted on the Estate, from the difference of *soils*, the different state at the *same time* of the same soil, the difficulty of saying what quantity of canes was a fair day's work to cut from the *entangled* and *trailing* state in which they were often lying & other reasons enumerated by themselves'.[88] The paternalistic bishop and his estate manager had to negotiate with their slaves when they tried to implement their scheme of gradual emancipation and, as a result of the difficulties the slaves raised about practically defining 'a fair allotment of work', the idea of task labour was abandoned.

In Jamaica, the practice of establishing informal contracts with jobbing gangs opened the way to general wage bargaining by the estate workers: 'The slaves pressed for time, food or cash payments for work over and above the production routine'.[89] In Cuba, in the 1860s and 1870s, chattel slaves pursued cash payments in competition with non-slave labour. Gangs of Chinese, white and mulatto workers received wages for the same work slaves did, and this became the chief reason for work stoppages. Consequently, minimal wages were frequently demanded and routinely paid to slaves as the 1870s progressed, for a variety of tasks. Without such incentives, the increasing militancy of slaves would have made it impossible to complete the harvests.[90]

Skilled slaves in construction, metal and clothing crafts, barbering and painting, in urban Brazil, were either placed in jobs by their owners or exercised their own initiative to find better, and more highly paid, jobs. Slaves who joined brotherhoods (*confrarias*) consisting of people who practised the same crafts (such as that of Sao Jorge, the patron of blacksmiths and locksmiths)[91] probably used these as networks to obtain information about employment opportunities and as a basis for bargaining with their owners about the going rates. Masters did not interfere with such organizations, 'whose goal was to help slaves win their daily struggle to earn a living',[92] because they acquired a share of whatever their slaves could earn.

> Generally speaking, men of different 'nations' gathered at different cantos, or streetcorners, to await their clients . . . At the cantos freed men were often joined by slaves practising the same trade, and the friendships that grew up between members of the same ethnic group who did the same kind of work proved solid and durable. They were responsible for the foundation of many manumission societies and religious confraternities, which helped to encourage solidarity and mutual aid among urban slaves.[93]

On the one hand, these organizations could divide the black community into factions that competed with each other. On the other hand, they united some free and slave workers in something resembling employment agencies. These slaves participated in a labour market in which the remuneration rate for their labour was influenced by and influenced the wages of free workers, and they combined in order to limit competition between themselves and so raise their wages. As a result, some slaves obtained sufficient wages to buy their freedom and become property owners, even owning other slaves.[94]

There is ample evidence from the United States that slaves negotiated with their owners about their working conditions and remuneration. Hired slaves who were 'frequently allowed the choice of a master, could use this privilege for bargaining'.[95] Such slaves could choose not only to avoid those employers who had a reputation for ill-treating them, but also to obtain some allowance for their personal use, beyond what was paid to their owner. The better their own reputation, the better they were able to bargain. Eaton calls this 'an incipient state of wages', which developed 'a habit of bargaining between bondsmen and prospective hirers'.[96] Hired slaves, particularly in industry, customarily negotiated payments for their overtime work in the 1850s. Tobacco manufacturers in Virginia 'flirted with the idea of raising the standard tasks and thus eliminating overwork, but there is no evidence that they ever managed to break the long-standing custom of incentive wage payments'.[97] Though bargaining about the terms and conditions of labour between slaves and their hirers was often implicit, slaves clearly 'learned how to manipulate the system in order to win advantages or concessions for themselves'.[98]

Among Virginia's ironworkers the masters retained their legal right to punish their slaves, but the latter 'did anything but sit passively by while their fate was decided'.[99] The slaves 'could do extra work if they wished, or they could take their time off as leisure. Even in the simple act of accepting or rejecting the overwork system, they were achieving, in at least one small phase of their existence, some measure of self-choice. If they did choose to do additional labour, the sums they earned were theirs to control'.[100] In the summer of 1860, Sam Williams, the Virginia forgeman, used the credit he had earned through overwork to take four weeks off. Sam waited until his underhand could replace him in order not to disrupt the work at the forge, but he did not ask permission to take his break. There was no confrontation, however, because his master 'tacitly recognized that Sam had the power to force reasonable, limited, and temporary changes in his work regimen', and also 'because his challenge to the system was guarded and oblique and had a limited objective – rest from work'.[101] Slaves' rights to their own time, to fair tasks, and to remuneration for their overwork, were achieved and defended in such everyday struggles.

Charles Dew argues that the ironmasters would have found it risky 'to increase work quotas or to abolish compensation for overwork' for their skilled workers.[102] The potential for sabotage, for example, 'gave slave foremen considerable protection against an increase in their tasks and helped them preserve their right to earn compensation for themselves'.[103] This does not mean that slaves explicitly threatened sabotage in their negotiations, but there was a tacit understanding that they would cooperate provided their master kept his side of the bargain. The master simply could not afford to risk alienating his reliable slave workers. In the forges and furnaces of Virginia, where the success of the slave-owner's enterprise was 'in many ways, controlled by the slaves he employed, measures like compensation for overwork grew into features of primary importance in the functioning of his slave system'.[104]

Slaves who hired themselves out or who were paid by their owners for overwork, did not have formally equal standing in the transactions regarding their own labour with their employers and owners, who were legally free. When slaves engaged in a market transaction concerning their own labour time or capacity for labour, they used whatever means they had available to improve their situation and redefine their relations with their owners. The complex relationship between master and slave, though defined close to the master's ideal of total domination in the abstractions of the law, was contested in the myriad struggles of everyday life. In this continuous tug-of-war, compromise and accommodation played a part along with coercion and physical force.

Slavery, Wage Work and Freedom

This section assesses what may be learned through the study of slave wages in the Americas about the transition from chattel slavery to wage labour.

There are two distinct but related questions regarding this transition. The first, at the level of interpersonal relations, concerns the status of those slaves who received wages: were they themselves, by virtue of the fact they received wages, in a state of 'quasi-freedom', half-slave, half-proletarian? And the second, at the level of the social system, concerns the relation between the spread of this practice within local economies and the increasing predominance of wage-labour in the capitalist world-economy: did the fact that some slaves earned wages reflect global economic transformations and erode the system of slavery from within? These questions are distinct because the answer to either one is not contingent upon the answer to the other, but they are also surely related because the labour forms in the components of the world-economy are related to the evolution of the entire system.

Slaves who could negotiate bonuses and allowances, choose employers and manipulate work conditions, it is claimed, were 'almost free'.[105] The systems of hiring out and overwork payments in the late ante-bellum period indicate a 'trend toward upgrading slaves into a shadowland of quasi-freedom'.[106] Robert Starobin, to the contrary, argues that payments were 'part of a complex system of discipline-by-reward ... a technique of slave control which had long existed and which supported the slave system'.[107]

> Entrepreneurs who consciously used cash incentives to control their industrial bondsmen and to increase slave productivity clearly had no intention of 'liberating' their slaves. A Tennessee iron manufacturer, for example, kept account of breaches of discipline and subtracted them from his slaves' credit sheets.[108]

This is the other side of the coin, so to speak: having earned money or credit, the slaves had to be on good behaviour in order to actually receive it from their masters. The Black Code of Louisiana seems to have been exceptional in the United States in giving slaves legal right to their earnings for Sunday labour. The Supreme Court of that state ruled in 1836: 'According to ... law, slaves are entitled to the produce of their labor on Sunday; even the master is bound to remunerate them, if he employs them'.[109] When masters were not legally bound to pay, however, slaves found it hard to insist on what they undoubtedly saw as their right, even when cash payments had taken deep root in custom. So long as payments to the slaves remained a concession rather than the legal right of the slaves, they would be used to improve discipline and productivity.

To the extent that slaves began to resemble wage labourers, they became subjected to similar disciplinary procedures, such as fines and withholding wages. The ways that cash earnings were used in a system of labour incentive/discipline are suggested by some contemporary observers. One employer asserted that slaves 'work with as much steadiness and cheerfulness as the whites, and the fear of losing their ten cents, if they are lazy or inattentive, saves all the expense of overseers'.[110]

Starobin, on the one hand, underlines the arbitrary quality of the system of payment which, he claims, was 'so firmly under control of the masters that it could be abandoned at any time without consulting the slaves'. The masters continued to regard cash payments as their exclusive prerogative, not as the slaves' right. Starobin may be too one-sided in emphasizing the masters' power, rather than the slaves' ability to shape a compromise. Dew, on the other hand, while recognizing that the overwork system aimed 'to make the industrial slave a disciplined and productive worker without having to rely heavily on physical coercion',[111] also draws attention to the active role of the slaves and the more or less explicit bargaining between the two parties. The slaves were doing their masters' bidding, but they also let their masters know that it was in their self-interest to give them fair rewards because if they did not the slaves could make trouble, or choose to do no more work beyond their assigned tasks.

The payment of slave wages indicates that economic methods of exploitation and discipline were utilized alongside the political methods that were more characteristic of slavery. Some slaves were able to benefit, albeit to a limited extent, from such mutual accommodation even while it furthered their exploitation. We should not forget that ironworkers and other industrial slaves were enjoying limited privileges within an essentially coercive system. This is well illustrated by the fate of Henry Towles, Sam Williams's underhand and one of Weaver's key forge workers. In December 1859, just after John Brown was hanged, patrollers set out to intimidate the slaves of Buffalo Forge. For an unknown reason they singled out Towles for victimization and he was severely whipped. It was ten days before he had recovered enough to return to work.[112] The slave regime still depended heavily upon physical punishment and terror. Such evidence of continuing outright repression indicates that slaves who were able to negotiate their work and wages from time to time were not, in consequence, 'almost free'.

At the level of interpersonal relations, some slaves who were hired or received wages were in an intermediate status between chattel and wage slavery – a 'proto-proletariat' – but they were still chattel property. Nor did self-purchase constitute a road to freedom for most slaves. In Cuba, gradual self-purchase 'created an intermediate status between slave and free' in theory, but in practice, as slave prices rose in the 1860s, self-purchase was 'far beyond the reach of almost all slaves'.[113] In the United States, also, self-purchase was not easy. While urban skilled slaves' opportunities to earn cash increased in the 1850s, so did their value, so 'only the most industrious urban bondsmen could hope to buy their liberty'.[114]

Such limited modifications of the master/slave relationship did not necessarily mean that the slave societies were consequently being transformed from within, as some have argued. Eaton, for example, views slave hiring as 'an important step toward freedom'.[115] However, the stability and efficiency of the slave regime generally appear to have been reinforced rather than threatened by such modifications of pure slavery. To identify remuneration for labour as contradictory to the essence of slavery, in so far as the latter is defined as unpaid labour, is not the same as to say that this practice was effectively undermining the system of control on which slavery rested. While slave wages often contributed to the economic system organized by the slaves – their internal economy – so long as the practice was not common, it may have provided sufficient flexibility at the edges of slavery to actually make the system more rather than less stable and, in so doing, to help ensure an orderly adjustment from slave to wage labour – when that transition resulted from altogether different causes.

Certainly, there was a relationship between the remuneration for slave labour and the development of a labour market for legally free wage labour. Where slaves were hired, whether or not they received any payment themselves, they had a depressing effect on the wages of free workers with whom they competed. In seventeenth-century Barbados, for example, slave artisans 'performed the same work for lower wages than freemen'.[116] In eighteenth-century Virginia, slaves and white men were paid the same wages as stevedores, while whites who worked with slaves in building a schooner received higher wages,[117] though probably less than they would have earned if slaves had not been available. Hired slaves not only depressed the wages of free labourers, they were also used to discipline free workers when they were hired as strikebreakers. In Richmond, Virginia, in the 1850s, an ironmaster paid $150 a year for hired slaves, and 'rewarded them for working overtime by as much as $10 to $15 a month' to break a strike by white workers.[118]

Racial discrimination, as well as market forces, affected the slaves' employment opportunities and ability to bargain. In Brazil, by the 1840s, 'slaves began to lose their prominent place in the crafts to white competitors'.[119] Their vulnerability to competition and racism meant, as Douglass knew, that such slaves suffered the vicissitudes of market forces while continuing to endure 'the evils of being a slave'.

What these examples indicate is that, in practice, slave and wage labour were not two separate labour systems, but were intimately interlinked, just as the colonial economies of the Americas were interlinked with the emerging capitalism of western Europe. The capitalist world-economy, as it developed, increasingly dominated the forms of labour in the Americas, including slavery. What is generally called the transition from slave to wage labour was not a single event, but a process which lasted for about a century, and was marked by slave rebellions, struggles between metropolitan and colonial elites, civil wars and the mass immigration of indentured labourers to substitute for the slaves. The outcome of this prolonged process, then, was as much a function of *political* factors as of economic forces. It is more sensible to think of a number of *transitions* taking place, in a variety of circumstances, rather than a single event. To mention just a few examples, the ways that slavery ended in Haiti, the British West Indies, the United States, Cuba and Brazil, were very different, in part because of the influence of each preceding case upon its successors. What the comparative evidence suggests is that, with some considerable local variations in the circumstances and process of emancipation, there is no simple linkage of cause and effect between the payment of wages during slavery and the transition to 'freedom'.

The examples of Cuba and the United States illustrate the importance of specific local conditions in these transitions. In Cuba, where the transition from slave to wage labour was prolonged,

> slaves were able to widen the dimensions of their lives substantially by demand-ing and gaining access to cash in the 1870s. They also hastened the trans-formation of slavery in its waning days and played an active role in the transition to new forms of labor exploitation. Plantation owners were forced to adapt to new socioeconomic parameters. Rather than simply resorting to repression and harsh punishment in order to extract labor from their slaves, now impossible because of the scale of resistance, positive incentives were utilized to accomplish the same ends.[120]

Slaves in Matanzas sought cash in the 1870s in order to purchase their freedom, which is why 'wages were the single most important demand motivating work stoppages in the 1870s'.[121] From the slaves' viewpoint, wages did not in themselves destroy the system of slavery. Rather, receiving wages meant an opportunity to make a down-payment on a contract for gradual self-purchase and thus the hope of manumission. What changed the slaves' legal status was not that they received money, but that they *paid* money to their owners, and they were free only when the total price was paid. Though slaves who had such a contract had some limited rights, the option of self-purchase 'led to liberty for only a small fraction of the slave population'.[122]

Despite the widespread payment of wages to slaves in Cuba, slavery persisted into the 1880s and, 'the anticipated rural-proletarianization process did not take place after abolition. It was one thing to abolish slavery; but the emergence of a free labour market was something entirely different'.[123] Moreno Fraginals argues that the 'anomalous situation' of different kinds of labour 'acted as a break on capitalist industrial develop-ment: the Law of Abolition was a means to the end of rationalizing the confused labour system efficiently'.[124] But the labour market was not, in fact, so swiftly rationalized. The structures of social, economic and political power kept people of colour at the bottom of the society long after emancipation. As in other former slave societies in the Americas, systems of domination persisted after slavery.[125]

In the United States, different regions experienced variations in the process of legal emancipation. Familiarity with the overwork system eased the transition at Buffalo Forge, Virginia. The slaves were freed by order of the military authorities on Friday, May 26 1865, and the next day quit work as they considered themselves free. They were told that they had no 'claim whatever upon, or rights in connection with the property of former owners', that they were as free to make contracts or agreements as a white man, but they were 'equally bound to abide' by them. They were also bluntly told not to move to 'the already over-stocked city' but to stay and work where they were. Consequently, 43 men and women, almost the entire work-force, promptly accepted labour contracts. Dew observes, 'Both skilled and unskilled workers in appreciable numbers made the transition to a wage basis at the jobs they had held as slaves'.[126] In the circumstances, the ex-slaves appear to have had few options. The chief point, however, is that although the experience of the overwork system eased the transition to wage labour, it was the Civil War that undermined slavery and the victory of the Union armies that brought emancipation to Buffalo Forge. Without the defeat of the Confederacy, people like Sam and Nancy Williams might well have continued producing overwork as slaves for the rest of their lives, as their owner was unwilling to allow them to purchase their freedom.

Whatever effect the payment of wages to slaves had upon their personal relations with their owners, in the sense of redefining the conditions and relations of servitude, the abolition of slavery was chiefly the result of other factors in Cuba, Virginia and elsewhere. Though slave wages were a precursor of a free wage system and sometimes eased the transition to such a system, the spread of this practice per se did not cause the evolution of a free labour market.

Conclusions

The comparative study of emancipations should encourage us to reject the simplistic antinomy of 'slavery' and 'freedom'. While some slaves were paid for part of their forced labour, so-called free wage labourers in former slave societies were generally subjected to various extra-economic forms of coercion and discrimination. Indeed, several mechanisms of compulsion were already operating among free labourers, white and black, during slavery.[127] While the ratio of economic and political forms of exploitation vary in chattel slavery and wage labour, in both systems the power elite utilizes whatever methods appear to promise the most effective means of labour control, and that depends, in part, upon the resistance of the exploited. Each form of exploitation, and the process of transition from one to the other, bears witness to the impact of the workers' resistance to the different forms of labour control. While methods of compulsion and exploitation varied, we should not underestimate the slaves' ability to achieve influence over their working conditions and to bargain for some remuneration, however inadequate, for their labour. The various schemes of paying cash to slaves in the Americas should be seen in this light, as part of a series of concessions made to the slaves in a further attempt to control and exploit them. Though the slaves were unable to do away with the entire exploitative system, their determined bargaining affected the specific forms and relations of their exploitation.

Though the payment of slave wages implies a conceptualization of the market value of the slave's labour power, as distinct from himself, and some acknowledgement of the slave's right to remuneration for at least a part of his labour, it did not cause the end of slavery. While slaves gained some benefits from their wages, this reward system was also a way for slave-owners to intensify their control and exploitation of slave labour. Slave-owners, by manipulating hire arrangements, continued to profit from their slaves while shifting the cost of their upkeep to others, including the slaves themselves.[128] The payment of slave wages may be seen as an attempt to further exploit slaves by pushing beyond the limits of the slave form of labour. The slave system was never entirely inflexible, but the payment of wages to slaves was evidence of a kind of flexibility that pointed towards a new form of labour. Slaves who received wages were, on the one hand, becoming more integrated into a new system of control by responding to cash incentives and rewards, but, on the other hand, they were testing and extending the bounds of the central relationship of the system itself. Just as elements of the wage system appeared within slavery, so elements of coercion persist in the system of wage labour that is formally free. There are continuities as well as contrasts between these systems of domination, and contradictions within both systems provide foci for the workers' struggle.

Former slaves, like their masters, brought a whole complex of attitudes, values, self-images, and notions of rights and entitlements out of slavery, but the meaning of freedom, which was dialectically interconnected with the system and experience of slavery, was different for ex-slaves and ex-masters.[129] What people learned while they were slaves – about strategies and techniques of organization and resistance, about self-conception and aspirations towards a free community and society – was influenced by their activities and relations as slaves. Hence, the various ways that these people behaved, whether as 'proto-peasants' or 'proto-proletarians', while they were slaves shaped their behaviour in post-emancipation society.[130] Whatever they learned about the market value of their labour power, about bargaining and negotiating with those who would hire them, became part of their repertoire as more or less free wage labourers who sought to resist domination and to shape, as best they could, a new society after their legal emancipation.

Notes

It is my pleasure to acknowledge the advice, criticism and encouragement of my friends and colleagues, Sal Cucchiari, Gad Heuman, Howard Johnson, Rod McDonald, Sid Mintz, Michael Peletz, Dale Tomich, Gary Urton and Mary Turner, who have helped improve this paper, while I retain responsibility for its remaining shortcomings.

1. M.I. Finley, *Ancient Slavery and Modern Ideology* (New York, 1980), 68–9.
2. Karl Marx, *Capital*, vol. 1, trans. Ben Fowkes (New York, 1977), 680.
3. See O. Nigel Bolland, 'Systems of Domination after Slavery: The Control of Land and Labor in

the British West Indies after 1838', *Comparative Studies in Society and History*, 23:4 (1981): 615–17.

4. Karl Marx to Pavel Vasilyevich Annenkov, 28 December 1846, in *Collected Works*, vol. 38 (London, 1982), 100.
5. Orlando Patterson, *Slavery and Social Death* (Cambridge, Mass., 1982), 5.
6. Ibid., 1.
7. Marx to Annenkov, *Collected Works*, 97.
8. Sidney W. Mintz, 'Was the Plantation Slave a Proletarian?', *Review*, 2:1 (1978): 81–98.
9. Ibid., 86.
10. Sidney W. Mintz, 'The Question of Caribbean Peasantries: A Comment', *Caribbean Studies*, 1 (1961): 31–4, and *Caribbean Transformations* (Chicago, 1974), 151–2. See also Richard Frucht, 'A Caribbean Social Type: Neither "Peasant" nor "Proletarian"', *Social and Economic Studies*, 13:3 (1967): 295–300.
11. Rebecca J. Scott, *Slave Emancipation in Cuba: The Transition to Free Labor, 1860–1899* (Princeton, 1985), 181.
12. Mintz, 'Was the Plantation Slave a Proletarian?', 87.
13. Immanuel Wallerstein, *The Modern World-System: Capitalist Agriculture and the Origins of the European World-Economy in the Sixteenth Century* (New York, 1974), 127.
14. Sidney W. Mintz, 'The So-called World System: Local Initiative and Local Response', *Dialectical Anthropology*, 2:4 (1977), 254.
15. Mintz, 'Was the Plantation Slave a Proletarian?', 97.
16. Ibid., 89.
17. Christopher Chase-Dunn, *Global Formation: Structures of the World-Economy* (Oxford, 1989), 18.
18. Ibid., 18.
19. Richard B. Morris, 'The Measure of Bondage in the Slave States', *Mississippi Valley Historical Review*, XLI (1954), 236.
20. Douglas Hall, *In Miserable Slavery: Thomas Thistlewood in Jamaica, 1750–86* (London, 1989). He generally gave them 2 bitts, but sometimes 4, a bitt being $7\frac{1}{2}$ pence Jamaica currency.
21. J. Harry Bennett, *Bondsmen and Bishops: Slavery and Apprenticeship on the Codrington Plantations of Barbados, 1710–1838* (Berkeley, 1958), 18.
22. Quoted in B.W. Higman, *Slave Populations of the British Caribbean 1807–1834* (Baltimore, 1984), 203.
23. Richard C. Wade, *Slavery in the Cities: The South, 1820–60* (London, 1964), 46.
24. Quoted in Robert S. Starobin, *Industrial Slavery in the Old South* (London, 1970), 100.
25. Stuart B. Schwartz, *Sugar Plantations in the Formation of Brazilian Society: Bahia, 1550–1835* (Cambridge, 1985), 156.
26. Roderick A. McDonald, 'Independent Economic Production by Slaves on Antebellum Louisiana Sugar Plantations', *Slavery and Abolition*, 12:1 (1991), 191.
27. Starobin, *Industrial Slavery in the Old South*, 104.
28. Ibid.
29. Mechal Sobel, *The World They Made Together: Black and White Values in Eighteenth-Century Virginia* (Princeton, 1987), 49.
30. Charles B. Dew, 'Disciplining Slave Ironworkers in the Antebellum South: Coercion, Conciliation, and Accommodation', *American Historical Review*, 79 (1974), 398.
31. Clement Eaton, 'Slave-Hiring in the Upper South: A Step toward Freedom', *Mississippi Valley Historical Review*, 46 (1960), 663.
32. Ibid., 670.
33. Morris, 'The Measure of Bondage', 233.
34. Dew, 'Disciplining Slave Ironworkers', 406.
35. John Hebron Moore, 'Simon Gray, Riverman: A Slave Who was Almost Free', *Mississippi Valley Historical Review*, XLIX (1962), 478–9.
36. Manuel Moreno Fraginals, 'Plantations in the Caribbean: Cuba, Puerto Rico, and the Dominican Republic in the Late Nineteenth Century', in M.M. Fraginals, F.M. Pons, and S.L. Engerman (eds), *Between Slavery and Free Labor: The Spanish-Speaking Caribbean in the Nineteenth Century* (Baltimore, 1985), 18.
37. William Frederick Sharp, *Slavery on the Spanish Frontier: The Colombian Choco, 1680–1810* (Norman, 1976), 50.
38. Ibid., 214.
39. Ibid., 50.
40. Ibid., 51.
41. Schwartz, *Sugar Plantations*, 321.
42. Katia M. de Queiros Mattoso, *To Be a Slave in Brazil, 1550–1888*, trans. Arthur Goldhammer (New Brunswick, 1986), 123–4.

43. Allan Kulikoff, *Tobacco and Slaves: The Development of Southern Cultures in the Chesapeake, 1680–1800* (Chapel Hill, 1986), 414.
44. Eaton, 'Slave Hiring in the Upper South', 672.
45. Wade, *Slavery in the Cities*, 49.
46. Ibid., 50.
47. Ibid., 51–2.
48. Morris, 'The Measure of Bondage', 234.
49. Ibid., 235.
50. Wade, *Slavery in the Cities*, 53.
51. Ibid., 53.
52. Barbara Jeanne Fields, *Slavery and Freedom on the Middle Ground: Maryland During the Nineteenth Century* (New Haven, 1985), 27.
53. Ibid., 49.
54. Mary Karasch, 'From Porterage to Proprietorship: African Occupations in Rio de Janeiro, 1808–1850', in *Race and Slavery in the Western Hemisphere: Quantitative Studies*, S.L. Engerman and E.D. Genovese (eds), (Princeton, 1975), 377.
55. Ibid., 385.
56. Mary Karasch, *Slave Life in Rio de Janeiro, 1808–1850* (Princeton, 1987), 200.
57. Ibid., 320.
58. Fraginals, 'Plantations in the Caribbean', 18.
59. Laird W. Bergad, *Cuban Rural Society in the Nineteenth Century: The Social and Economic History of Monoculture in Matanzas* (Princeton, 1990), 80.
60. Dale W. Tomich, *Slavery in the Circuit of Sugar: Martinique in the World Economy, 1830–1848* (Baltimore, 1990), 277–8.
61. Higman, *Slave Populations of the British Caribbean*, 203.
62. B.W. Higman, *Slave Population and Economy in Jamaica, 1807–1834* (Cambridge, 1974), 42.
63. Mary Turner, 'Chattel Slaves into Wage Slaves: A Jamaican Case Study', in Malcolm Cross and Gad Heuman (eds), *Labour in the Caribbean: From Emancipation to Independence* (London, 1988), 20.
64. See Howard Johnson's chapter in this volume.
65. Dew, 'Disciplining Slave Ironworkers', 406.
66. Starobin, *Industrial Slavery in the Old South*, 104.
67. Kulikoff, *Tobacco and Slaves*, 415.
68. Dew, 'Disciplining Slave Ironworkers', 405.
69. Charles B. Dew, 'Sam Williams, Forgeman: The Life of an Industrial Slave in the Old South', in J. Morgan Kousser and James M. McPherson (eds), *Region, Race, and Reconstruction: Essays in Honor of C. Vann Woodward* (New York, 1982), 210.
70. Dew, 'Disciplining Slave Ironworkers', 406.
71. Ibid., 410.
72. Dew, 'Sam Williams, Forgeman', 210, 219.
73. Eaton, 'Slave Hiring in the Upper South', 669.
74. Starobin, *Industrial Slavery in the Old South*, 99.
75. Eaton, 'Slave Hiring in the Upper South', 670.
76. Moore, 'Simon Gray, Riverman', 483.
77. Morris, 'The Measure of Bondage', 236.
78. Ibid., 236.
79. McDonald, 'Independent Economic Production by Slaves', 190–1.
80. Ibid., 199, 204.
81. Higman, *Slave Populations of the British Caribbean*, 203.
82. Quoted in O. Nigel Bolland, *The Formation of a Colonial Society: Belize, From Conquest to Crown Colony* (Baltimore, 1977), 69.
83. Tomich, *Slavery in the Circuit of Sugar*, 230–2.
84. Karasch, *Slave Life in Rio de Janeiro*, 206.
85. See O. Nigel Bolland, 'The Politics of Freedom in the British Caribbean', in Seymour Drescher and Frank McGlynn (eds), *The Meaning of Freedom: The Anthropology and History of Post-Slavery Societies* (Pittsburgh, in press).
86. Tomich, *Slavery in the Circuit of Sugar*, 248.
87. Eugene D. Genovese, *Roll, Jordan, Roll: The World the Slaves Made* (New York, 1974), 392.
88. Bennett, *Bondsmen and Bishops*, 126–7.
89. Turner, 'Chattel Slaves into Wage Slaves', 20.
90. Bergad, *Cuban Rural Society in the Nineteenth Century*, 237.
91. Karasch, *Slave Life in Rio de Janeiro*, 85.
92. Mattoso, *To Be a Slave in Brazil*, 124.

93. Ibid.
94. Karasch, 'From Porterage to Proprietorship', 390.
95. Eaton, 'Slave Hiring in the Upper South', 669.
96. Ibid., 678.
97. Morris, 'The Measure of Bondage', 231.
98. Peter J. Parish, *Slavery: History and Historians* (New York, 1989), 105.
99. Dew, 'Disciplining Slave Ironworkers', 404.
100. Ibid., 407.
101. Dew, 'Sam Williams, Forgeman', 224.
102. Ibid., 210.
103. Ibid.
104. Dew, 'Disciplining Slave Ironworkers', 417–18.
105. Moore, 'Simon Gray, Riverman'.
106. Morris, 'The Measure of Bondage', 239.
107. Starobin, *Industrial Slavery in the Old South*, 98–9.
108. Ibid., 102.
109. Quoted in Genovese, *Roll, Jordan, Roll*, 315.
110. Quoted in Starobin, *Industrial Slavery in the Old South*, 103.
111. Dew, 'Disciplining Slave Ironworkers', 405–6.
112. Ibid., 227.
113. Scott, *Slave Emancipation in Cuba*, 13.
114. Ira Berlin, *Slaves Without Masters: The Free Negro in the Antebellum South* (New York, 1974), 155.
115. Eaton, 'Slave Hiring in the Upper South', 678.
116. Hilary McD. Beckles, *White Servitude and Black Slavery in Barbados, 1627–1715* (Knoxville, 1989), 147.
117. Kulikoff, *Tobacco and Slaves*, 414.
118. Eaton, 'Slave Hiring in the Upper South', 670.
119. Karasch, *Slave Life in Rio de Janeiro*, 200.
120. Bergad, *Cuban Rural Society in the Nineteenth Century*, 237.
121. Ibid.
122. Ibid., 238.
123. Ibid., 340.
124. Fraginals, 'Plantations in the Caribbean', 19.
125. On the British West Indies, for example, see Bolland, 'Systems of Domination after Slavery'.
126. Dew, 'Disciplining Slave Ironworkers', 416.
127. Morris, 'The Measure of Bondage', 220.
128. Fields, *Slavery and Freedom on the Middle Ground*, 84.
129. Bolland, 'The Politics of Freedom.'
130. Whether the ex-slaves in the Americas emphasized a proletarian or a peasant strategy depended not only on their experience while slaves but also on the limited opportunities available to them within a political economy that was generally racist and alternated between periods of boom and bust. See Norman E. Whitten, Jr, *Black Frontiersmen: Afro-Hispanic Culture of Ecuador and Colombia* (Prospect Heights, 1986), 9.

7

Negotiating Freedom in Urban Suriname

1760–1830

ROSEMARY BRANA-SHUTE

For most slaves in colonial Suriname a permanent escape from slavery was never a realistic option. For some, on plantations and in town, the importance of staying with kin precluded the option of running away and joining maroons (runaway slaves) in the interior. For those who wished both to escape slavery legally and to remain near family and friends, there was manumission. When finalized by the judicial system, a manumission meant that an owner relinquished property rights over a specific slave, and that the slave's civil status was legally changed from slave to free person. In effect, a legal manumission would entail a transfer of property, as a slave came into possession of himself or herself. Manumission, however, was an exceptional occurrence: less than one per cent of the slave population was ever manumitted in any single year before 1830.[1] Despite the terrible odds against them, an increasing number of slaves in the eighteenth and nineteenth centuries both pursued and achieved manumission.

Manumission was not just a legal event. That is because manumissions evolved, rather than occurred. Long before a manumission was legal, individual slaves and owners already had agreed to a manumission. These agreements had been negotiated, with varying degrees of formality, as the owner had to acquiesce to a slave's manumission in order for it to be legal. This suggests that a manumission was possible only because over time a slave had earned and/or was allowed increasing degrees of freedom: of activity and independent mobility, of will, and of individual personality that is indicative of an arrangement or mutual understanding between slave and owner. A manumission, then, may be understood as one consequence of social relationships which developed slowly in daily life, as black and white,

148

slave and free, rich and poor came into personal contact and created relationships which allowed a slave the potential to achieve a legal and permanent escape from slavery.

In 1733, 66 years after the Dutch first acquired Suriname from the British, the Court of Policy and Criminal Justice, the most important legislative body in the colony representing the white colonists, forbade the private freeing of slaves. Thereafter, until emancipation in 1863, if a free adult in Suriname wished to manumit a slave legally, the owner was required to petition this court for its permission. These letters of petition (*requesten*) are the best sources available for the study of manumission in Suriname. There were no standardized application forms for manumission until well into the nineteenth century, so petitions were personal in style and content, improvised by notaries, scribes, owners and agents for the illiterate and those whose Dutch language skills were poor or non-existent. The only requirements of the court were that an owner who wished to manumit ask the court to legalize that decision; and that some free person(s) post a sizable cash bond (or one's word, if wealthy and a gentleman) to ensure that the manumitted person would never turn to public charity. However, petitioners filled one or many more sheets with information never requested: details, sometimes just passing comments, on the slave, on the owner, on their past relationship, on properties to be transferred to the manumitted, on promises made (and violated), on kinship (between slaves and between owners and slaves), and on patronage networks linking whites, coloureds and blacks, free and slave. Unfortunately, the data are very sparse on the occupations and ages of slaves as well as specific information on the length of servitude, contractual arrangements over wages from hiring out, sums paid owners for slaves to buy themselves, or other details. Nonetheless, based on over 2,000 petitions and supplemented by other archival data, it is possible to determine generally how slaves manipulated social, political and economic conditions in the urban environment, in particular, to negotiate their own freedom.

The period 1760–1830 is a 70-year slice cut through the 196 years when Suriname, on the north-east coast of South America, was a Dutch plantation colony based on enslaved African labour. By 1760 its export economy was at its most profitable for planters and their agents with over 500 large plantations exporting sugar, coffee, indigo, cacao, hard woods and other tropical products. Within a decade that agricultural sector began its slow but inexorable decline, the result of attacks from maroons, a decline in commodity prices, and other local and international factors. Our best rough estimates suggest that free people (of all races) constituted no more than 5 per cent in 1738 and 15 per cent in 1830 of a total population of 50–58,000 people. The British occupied Suriname in 1799 to prevent it falling into French hands and, except for a short interlude, ruled it until 1816, effectively blocking the colony's access to its traditional markets in Europe and the US. Perhaps as traumatic, in 1807 the British unilaterally outlawed the African slave trade to Suriname. The return of Dutch rule in 1816 neither reopened the slave trade nor halted the decline of export agriculture.

During the slow attrition of the plantation sector Paramaribo emerged as a handsome capital city, and by 1830 about 27 per cent of the population resided there, double its 1760 percentage.[2] The city experience of slavery was different to that on the plantations, and as a result the constraints on and opportunities for slaves to negotiate manumission also differed. The demographic patterns of the town increasingly differentiated it from the rural districts. Whereas the plantations had very few resident whites (in fact, very few free people of any colour), Paramaribo enjoyed the largest concentration of both whites and of free black and coloured[3] men and women in the colony. In the eighteenth century, the ratio of free people to slaves in plantation districts was approximately 1:65, whereas in Paramaribo the size of the free population increased as the century progressed so that by 1787 the ratio was about 2:7, and the number of free persons in the city continued to grow in the early 1800s. The overwhelming majority of free women in Suriname, of any ancestry, lived in Paramaribo.

Although in both rural and urban areas the majority of the people were enslaved, the occupations of slaves suggest important differences between the two sectors. In town many slaves were active in transporting, mostly by boat, the various plantation products destined for export and in jobs such as carpentry, tailoring, wig-making, hawking goods along the streets, taking in laundry and mending, and domestic services. A variety of jobs generally were open to the ambitious and clever slave who was willing to learn and build his or her reputation in the urban market, albeit with the owner's consent. Besides the need for workers in domestic service and in businesses in town, the government was perhaps the largest employer of slaves in the colony. It regularly hired both men and women for work in military facilities and hospitals, public buildings and parks, and on government plantations near town, supplementing its own limited slave force. When foreign trade was brisk, or during periods of heightened military and naval traffic, the influx of foreign soldiers and sailors on temporary duty increased the need for labour. Then slaves were in demand to work in boarding houses, inns and taverns, as maids and valets, and (less documented but clearly present) to provide sexual services. Captain John Stedman, who wrote the most famous account of Suriname, was a clear beneficiary of such services from his famous slave mistress Joanna.[4]

Paramaribo was a multilingual, multireligious, and multicultural city, with much more varied life than in the rural areas.[5] This is a perspective that needs stressing, as it has been customary for writers to refer to 'whites' or 'planters' as if they constituted essentially one group broadly sharing cultural and class values. On the contrary, particularly in town, the distinctions between whites must have been quite evident, as resident Europeans were divided by religious, ethnic, linguistic, religious and class differences. They spoke a number of first languages in the eighteenth century, depending on whether they were born locally, or if they had migrated from Dutch or German speaking areas, or came from territories colonized by England, France, Portugal, or from Brazil. By necessity, most probably came to speak some of the local creole, *Sranan Tongo*, the first language of slaves born and raised in the colony and the *lingua franca* of Suriname. The linguistic differences were underlined by religious divisions. The majority of urban whites before slave emancipation in 1863 were probably Sephardic and German Jews, not Christians; and the two groups of Surinamese Jews were not themselves well integrated. Christians were divided among a number of Protestant denominations and a small Roman Catholic community. The historical literature of Suriname largely ignores the sizable numbers of whites who were professionals, tradesmen, skilled and semi-skilled crafts-men, down-on-their-luck plantation employees, and former soldiers and sailors looking for a secure livelihood. Planters themselves varied widely in wealth, landholding, social prestige, and political clout. Some planters were largely resident on rural estates and some spent most of their time in town; some were heads of carefully nurtured families, whereas others were unmarried, sometimes lonely and often promiscuous. Some were cruel, some not; many appear to have been victims of economic, social and political changes in circumstances they were unable to control. In sum, although whites appeared to be a 'white' bloc of power and superiority vis-à-vis slaves and free coloureds and blacks, in practice, so long as rebellion was not involved, there were enough differences and fissures among whites to present a range of attitudes, personalities, statuses and needs that allowed some slaves room to manoeuvre and find some common grounds for negotiation.

The cultural mosaic of Paramaribo was complicated and enhanced by the fact that a majority of its population came from Africa or was of African descent; up to the early nineteenth century it was not, to any significant degree Europeanized or Christianized. Neighbourhoods were not segrega-ted by race or class, and whites, free blacks and free coloureds generally lived next to each other (although in housing that varied greatly in quality). Whites and wealthier free blacks and coloureds occupied the houses on the street front, while slaves lived in the enclosed yards behind them. The residential patterns dictated to slaves in town probably made it difficult to build a sense of a shared community separate and distinct from whites. In addition, part of the slave population was rotated regularly between town and plantations, while the white population was continually changing with the frequent arrival and departure of sailors, soldiers, and would-be plantation employees and bureaucrats.

There were trade-offs however, for slaves. The physical mobility of slaves appears to have been much greater in town than on the plantations, especially during daylight hours, providing opportunities to meet more people of African descent, both free and enslaved, away from direct supervision by owners. Close proximity meant the ways of whites could be closely scrutinized; their manners, needs and weaknesses became more evident and therefore more readily exploitable by patient and clever slaves. In town slaves and former slaves were exposed to a broader range of languages, behaviour, habits, and information than life on the plantations could offer. Town life helped to make urban slaves and free people of African descent more adept in dealing with a variety of whites and with the institutions of power established and dominated by whites: the courts and bureaucracy, the military and civil militias, and the trade and communication networks within the colony and overseas. For increasing numbers of slaves, the concentration of relatively large numbers of free people in town – coloured and black as well as white – meant more potential patrons and allies from whom slaves might garner support and learn some new survival strategies to benefit themselves or their loved ones. It is no accident that, as almost everywhere else in the Caribbean and Latin America, manumission in Suriname was largely an urban phenomenon. Most of the colony's free people – all potential manumitters – were in town, as were the bureaucrats who regulated manumissions and made the policies which affected opportunities for freedom.

A period of relative peace between whites and maroons had been inaugurated after peace treaties were signed in the 1750s. However, by the late 1760s new 'untreatied' maroon groups had emerged to attack plantation areas to the east. The subsequent two 'Boni' Maroon Wars between 1765 and 1793, named for the most famous of the rebels' leaders, were so severe that colonial officials increased the activities of the local militias and appealed to the metropole for aid in recruiting European mercenaries to track down and eliminate the slave rebels.[6] While awaiting the arrival of European soldiers, the Court of Policy and the governor very reluctantly decided to arm slaves as auxiliary troops in defence of the plantation colony. In 1772, the government requisitioned about 300 of the 'best' male slaves owned by both urban owners and plantations, providing compensation to the owners.[7] A new military unit was organized, the *Neeger Vrijcorps* (literally, Black Free Corps) or the Black Rangers; in Sranan Tongo they were known as the *Redi Moesoe*, or the Red Berets. While on active duty the government provided these soldiers with food, clothing, weapons, medical care and a small allowance. Some upward mobility within the ranks was possible, although the officer corps were white. In return for 'loyal' military service, these slave men were to receive their freedom and the use of small plots of land in a newly surveyed area on the southern edge of Paramaribo.[8]

Stedman and other sources (European, colonial and maroon) all agree that the men who accepted this option for freedom were particularly effective soldiers against the Boni rebels and in subsequent military service.[9] What no one has previously discussed is the part played by those 'best' slaves in the origin of the corps. Were they passive in the face of owners deciding who would serve? Although the option for freedom in return for military service was first offered by the white planter elite sitting on the Court of Policy, and although individual owners helped to define which of their 'best' male property would be eligible, the choice to accept or decline the opportunity was made by the slaves themselves, and they weighed their own considerations. Although there is no document recording detailed negotiations with slaves over who would serve and for what motives, apparently some men chose to let the military opportunity pass. There also are scattered archival references to individual Black Rangers who later repented of their decision to accept the offer and chose to leave military service. Their change of heart meant a return to slavery, and to their families on plantations. 'Freedom' apparently was too high a price to pay for separation from loved ones.[10]

Some of the Rangers interpreted their new status as soldiers and freedmen in terms of enhanced ability to negotiate for greater benefits and rights as freed men. A good number of the Black Rangers quickly learned the legal and bureaucratic ropes in Paramaribo and found patrons among the free coloured and free black male population and among their own officers. They used this new information to petition the Court of Policy to convert their usufruct rights to land into freehold ownership.[11] Their petitions to the Court are unequivocal in requesting an ownership that would allow them full rights to bequeath their plots using a legal testament. Less often a Ranger asked for ownership to sell the land before his death, should he wish.

This is not what the government had initially envisioned. These plots of land had not been designated for ownership, but for temporary use by Black Rangers on furlough, during convalescence, and after retirement (if they survived). This was a system that would minimize subsistence costs to government as the soldiers would be relatively self-supporting. Usufruct rights also would allow a continuous turnover in users, a perpetual resource for the government to lend one crop of recruits after another, should it remain necessary to recruit slaves for soldiering. Moreover, precluding ownership would prevent the accumulation of resources in the hands of these recruits. The Court of Policy appears to have anticipated, and perhaps preferred, that this new neighbourhood would be the new extension of the town, with the advantage that it could be patrolled and supervised by urban militias as was the rest of Paramaribo.

Now some of these same recruits were requesting, albeit in quite proper deferential form, that the original intent and contract be reconsidered. These soldiers did not have to state the obvious. They were taking great risks and suffering high casualties in the performance of their duties and the planters needed their highly praised service. The court agreed to the requests, probably recognizing the need to maintain an incentive for those men to continue to serve, and in order to more easily recruit new 'loyal' male slaves to replace the dead and wounded in the future. This is just one example of the willingness of slaves to negotiate improvements in their own living and working conditions, in this case facilitated by the need the planter class had for their military services, a need that could not be met as expeditiously or cheaply with European troops.

Over time, a number of the Black Rangers bequeathed their land to enslaved kin to be used to purchase their freedom or simply as property to be used as their inheritors (both free and slave) saw fit. Some enslaved relatives on plantations even used the military service of dead Rangers to justify petitioning the government for unusual considerations, such as pensions or guardians for orphaned slave minors. A number of the Black Rangers who survived the campaigns began relationships with free coloured and free black women, and their freehold land served as the basis of livelihood in a neighbourhood that became identified as a coloured and black residential area, still known today as Frimangron ('Free Man's Ground' in Sranan Tongo). Most of its residents remained quite poor, but their legal release from slavery and their land ownership provided some subsistence for them and their families, and the basis of an existence of some financial, physical and cultural independence from whites.[12]

Increasing military efforts against runaway slaves and maroon rebels had other effects which impinged on manumission opportunities. One was that heightened fear among whites of slave rebellion and marronage made it more difficult for slaves to run away. Once rebellions were put down and the remaining maroon forces signed treaties with the colonial government, the possibility of slaves escaping successfully narrowed, since treaty provisions included the return of runaways to their owners. It is probably no coincidence that slaves increasingly looked to legal manumission as the only way, short of death, out of slavery. By the early 1780s the number of manumission petitions began to rise very steadily, a general trend that would continue until emancipation in 1863. This trend did not change in spite of the fact that the colonial government began to tax manumissions for the first time in 1788.

Both before and after 1788 there were costs for paper, stamps and the services of a notary or lawyer to prepare the proper petition. The 1788 decree added a tax burden to the legal and bureaucratic costs. Taxes continued to increase, particularly under the British, until 1804 when they became very high indeed. For example, a slave hired out as a carpenter was paid about 1.4 florins (guilders) per day. When the manumission tax for an adult was raised to 1,000 florins, that same carpenter would have to work over 714 days just to pay the tax, not counting legal costs and cash bond. In 1811, even many white plantation directors earned under 500 florins a year, often having to cover many of their subsistence costs from their wages. The manumission tax, then, was a sizable disincentive for those who wished to free a slave as well as for slaves calculating how to cover the cost of their own legal manumissions.

The question of who exactly paid these taxes – owners or slaves – is pertinent but difficult to answer in most cases. Marginal notes penned on the petitions verify that the charges were paid, but do not indicate just whose pocket the money came from ultimately. What the contents of the petitions suggest and sometimes specify is that fees were paid by a wide variety of people: by the owners, by the slaves being freed, by one slave for another to be freed, or by free friends and patrons of the slaves. For the slaves, the worse case scenario was one in which they were required to (1) pay all the legal fees and taxes, (2) provide a large cash security or bond as a guarantee against a future need for public assistance (which would be given to a free person to post, since the slave legally was incapable of doing this), and (3) repay the owner his or her own value as property.[13] In almost every single case, negotiations had to precede payments, particularly when slaves were required to cover their own manumission costs or those of their kin. Negotiations often dealt with free time for a slave to hire out and to accumulate savings, perhaps after splitting the proceeds with the owner. Such agreements probably happened most commonly in town, although the details of how these agreements were reached were rarely documented in the manumission petitions. There was no customary or written rule regarding whether owners or slaves paid the manumission fees. As far as the government was concerned, so long as they were paid, private negotiations were private matters. What is clear is that slaves learned by examples around them that it was possible (with some owners) to make and save some extra money and in effect buy one's self from one's owner, even before approaching the Court for a legal manumission. Some owners were more open to this than others, clearly, but in all cases free time and mobility for slaves to work for their own purchase and manumission would have to be discussed and negotiated.

The consequences of high taxes on manumission resulted not only in increased revenues for the government (a result of a continuing rise in legal manumissions), but in a rise in illegal manumissions as well. Here again, owners and slaves reached accords of mutual benefit, given the constraints of the day. Illegally manumitted slaves were known in the local creole language as *piekie njan*, literally '(s)he collects food'. The *piekie njan* were considered to be free men and women by their owners who released them from their service and allowed them to fend for themselves as best they could (ergo, to go about patching their subsistence together, collecting food and income here and there). The *piekie njan* blended into the urban population, passing as legally manumitted people, finding their own berths and jobs as best they could. The owner had given up responsibilities for providing housing, food, clothing and medical care – but also had given up control over the slave's time, labour, and body. The *piekie njan* had chosen this as the best available option, perhaps because the manumission tax had become too high for owners and/or slaves to pay. In any case, one may assume that many, if not most, of the *piekie njan* preferred their independent, illegal freedom to a continued bondage under the jurisdiction and careful monitoring of an owner, no matter how kind.

The government finally recognized that this population of *piekie njan* was large, unsupervised by whites and that no one had guaranteed the illegally freed would never need government-subsidized charity.[14] Beginning in the 1820s a series of laws were passed which, by 1832, plugged all the legal loopholes which had allowed the *piekie njan* phenomenon to emerge. In effect, these new laws forced owners to either free a slave legally (by paying taxes) or risk the government expropriating the *piekie njan* slave. The new measures were effective in minimizing the number of illegal manumissions, since legal manumissions increased very dramatically when the deadline for complying with the new legislation neared. This suggests that some slaves and owners found legal freedom and high taxes preferable to the possibility of confiscation and re-enslavement of the *piekie njan* as a government slave.[15]

Economic problems with agricultural exports led to a decline of the plantation sector, but this does not appear to have increased manumissions dramatically; instead of being freed, slaves were sold or moved to more promising businesses or land holdings. Slave prices did rise sharply during the Napoleonic era, and when the slave trade was ended suddenly in 1807, slave prices increased even more, making the resale of slaves profitable for many owners. Nonetheless, even this new financial incentive for owners did not halt the rising tide of manumissions. Something other than an economic profit motive for owners needs to be advanced to explain why manumissions continued to increase in number. The explanation is complex, embedded not only in changing objective circumstances but in the characters and skills of both owners and slaves, in kinship and gender relations, in the urban life and residence patterns alluded to earlier, and a growing free coloured and free black population. I have elsewhere discussed motivations and the evolution of manumission patterns and will only briefly note some of the patterns here as they particularly illuminate the issues of labour control and negotiations for freedom.[16]

The manumission of the Black Rangers for military service should not be taken as either common or representative. Almost everything about it was uncharacteristic of manumissions before or after the creation of the Black Rangers: only males, almost all of whom were black, were freed; the government was the actual manumitter, having forced private owners to give up prime slaves; and it was a desperate measure taken by a planter elite which feared its own defeat by rebel slaves. Regular manumission patterns were characteristically very different: females were overwhelmingly favoured for freedom; being 'coloured', especially if a child, gave a slave an edge towards winning freedom; manumitted slaves themselves played very active parts in achieving their freedom; and private owners were active in helping to free slaves.

A study of the petitions submitted to the Court of Policy also suggests a prerequisite in all regular manumissions which was not crucial in the case of the Black Rangers: the 'individualization' of the slave. So long as a slave was perceived by an owner as anonymous and not a specific individual

156

with particular traits and skills, there would be no manumission. One of the values of the petitions is that they often recount how this 'individualization' occurred and suggest the nature of the interactions and negotiations that preceded most manumissions. Although owners rarely intended it, within their petitions the slaves emerge as dynamic agents in the manumission process. Slaves were not passive entities accepting freedom when and if it was bestowed by some kind owner. On the contrary, the petitions demonstrate that slaves actively worked for the manumission of themselves and their enslaved kin. It was the slaves who had the most to gain, and therefore the most incentive to find ways to bring the owner to agree to relinquish control. The characteristics which most often helped a slave become a real and important individual in the eyes of the owner were (1) personal contact on a regular and usually protracted basis, and (2) a kinship relationship between slave and owner.

Town life, where a large number of slaves were in domestic service in households of the very modest as well as the wealthy, facilitated personal contacts. Domestic workers had wide responsibilities: running entire households;[17] food preparation and storage; cleaning; care of children, the ill and the aged; gardening; running errands and marketing; and working as footboys, valets and personal servants. The more unpretentious the household, the more jobs were shared by owners and slaves alike. The more humble the owners, the more a household slave might be a co-worker or apprentice in retailing, tailoring, fishing, haulage, sewing, midwifery and a wide variety of other activities.

In all these cases, the key to manumission was the regular interaction between slave and owner. This was not a situation guaranteed to bring out the best in everyone, given the unequal status between owner and slave and the multiple daily possibilities of exacerbating tensions and hostilities. The historical literature often refers to the proclivity of owners to vent their anger on household slaves. All of this is no doubt true, and manumission was certainly never a guaranteed pay-off for slaves willing to wait patiently for years. What is true is that most of those manumitted between 1760 and 1830 had relationships with owners (not sexual in most cases) in which the owners had come to recognize important human qualities in their slaves. This had led to a willingness to see those slaves 'released from their birthright of slavery', as a few petitions phrased it. Female slaves had more success in getting owners to agree to manumissions, both for themselves and their kinsfolk. Almost 63 per cent of the manumitted were women, a finding consistent with most other studies of New World slave societies. Most domestic responsibilities were handled by female slaves, which put them in greater contact with owners.

This is not to say that manumission became a form of salary or remuneration for years of unpaid 'faithful service'. It did not. What happened over the years was that an owner sometimes became highly dependent on a particular slave's skills, presence, opinions and personality. Then, with that

157

growing dependency and some respect, if not real affection, came the possibility of a manumission. From the time that some modicum of respect and appreciation for a particular slave began, all other aspects of life, including the future, were open for discussion, negotiation and even modification: adjusting work loads; acquiring assistants to help meet responsibilities; perhaps the purchase or hiring of family members of the slave; upgrading food and clothing allowances; and expanding the amount of unsupervised mobility out of the household and into the city.

Owners who allowed themselves to become attached to, dependent on, or respectful of individual slaves were both male and female, and white, coloured and black. White widows seemed to be particularly disposed to manumit both black and coloured women. Their households were probably made up largely if not exclusively by women and children (mostly coloured and black slaves) in which the women lived in each others' constant company. They came to know each other very well over time, becoming in some cases an intimate household unit if not a family in practice. Without her dead husband to legally control her affairs and property, a widow was free to follow her own inclinations. For a good number of widows that inclination was to free the children and often the slave mothers with whom they shared their lives. Slave children were often freed by widows who claimed they did so in memory of the children's deceased mothers.

Among white men and married women who freed slaves, a dependency and regard for a specific slave was often clear in the petitions they submitted to the court. In some cases the negotiated arrangements were also detailed. For example, when one owner wanted to send her young child to Holland, she wanted a particular young man who was a slave in her household to take the boy across the Atlantic and get him settled in boarding school (presumably via Dutch relatives). It is not clear if the slave was enthusiastic about this, but he was the only one the child and the owner trusted, so the owner freed him as payment for the voyage he would then take as a free man accompanying this white child. Other slaves were freed for having fulfilled promises to owners that involved spending some years in Europe and away from their own families; one senses from the petitions that manumission was the promised payoff, if the slaves would only agree to the trip abroad. Other slaves, generally women, were freed after years of running households that owners had turned over to them in crises: raising children after the death of the mother, or caring for terminally ill, insane, or aged kin of the owner.

In Suriname there was no legal or customary framework, as in Brazil or Spanish America, which recognized or in any way encouraged self-purchase, but some of the relationships which developed between owners and slaves allowed a slave to buy him or herself free, necessitating very clear negotiations about money and time and labour. However, petitions for manumission seem to omit occupation data as if they were inconsequential to the argument that slaves would and could sustain themselves independently. Where occupations are noted, it is clear that it is the urban context that provided the added opportunities for a slave to be hired out for pay. The sparse data suggest several patterns. Owners in town often relied on their hired-out slaves to provide them with incomes; widows and single women may have been particularly so dependent.

Self-purchases by male slaves began to take place in the plantation areas only in the nineteenth century. In the eighteenth century it was frequently women with semi-skilled occupations such as laundresses, linen weavers, basket weavers and 'domestics' who purchased their own freedom and that of their kinsfolk. Contrary to expectation, highly developed skills practised only by males (such as carpentry, masonry and mill construction) were not prerequisites for self-purchase.[18] When self-purchases are acknowledged in the petitions, women doing 'women's work' bought themselves out of slavery as often, or more often, than skilled male artisans did. There are at least two reasons for this. 'Women's work' may have paid less but it was in constant demand – in homes, hospitals, inns and taverns, shops and the military (cleaning, cooking, laundering and nursing in particular). Moreover, 'women's work' put women in closer and regular proximity to potential manumitters.

There is yet another factor which helps to account for the prevalence of women among the manumitted and that is gender relations, or what contemporary European perceptions in Suriname deemed 'female character'. Females were perceived as less threatening than males, and were thought of as 'properly' relegated to childcare, food preparation, nursing the ill or aged, and managing households – the domestic sphere. However, West African and colonial traditions both accepted black and coloured women in one prominent public sphere as well – marketing.

Small-scale food and flower sales along the streets and in the open-air retail markets near the waterfront were largely the preserve of women of African descent, both slave and free. Marketing allowed for the accumulation of financial and social capital[19] and some freedom of mobility. That owners would conceive of this kind of activity as appropriate for non-white women gave these women an edge over men in negotiating personal time and space for their own activities outside the household and away from direct supervision. That the owner could also gain financially was, of course, part of the story, but marketing did not provide financial returns that could be as easily monitored, or confiscated, as could fixed daily wages for artisan slaves. The buying of fish, meat and produce by market women who then resold them was too complicated and personalized for owners to control. This left hucksters and market women more individual freedom to secretly accumulate money, gather information, and develop friendship and functional relations with potential patrons.

There are two other aspects of colonial, particularly town, life that are difficult to trace in detail, but which are worth noting, and which involved female much more than male slaves. These were the contraband trade and the hiring of female slaves to perform sexual services. Smuggling, still poorly documented, was possible largely because of the ships and sailors that frequently came to Paramaribo. Slaves and free people, including whites, would often fence stolen items in the taverns and inns of Paramaribo which were frequented by sailors who would buy them. Some of these fairly disreputable houses were run, if not owned, by free women of colour who owned or hired slaves (generally but not exclusively women) to serve clients and to cook and clean. There was money to be made in this trade, money that could buy the silence of participating slaves and allow for some accumulation of funds.

The hiring of slaves for personal service involved males as well as females, as Captain John Stedman exemplifies. His valet and personal servant was his 'true & Faithful Black boy Qwaccoo'; his maid and mistress was the mulatto slave Joanna. This is not the place to explore all the ramifications of sexual procuring by owners, but it is worth noting that Stedman manumitted the son Joanna bore him. Most white fathers did not. Those who did, according to the statements and implications in the petitions, generally did so because of very close relationships they had developed with a black or coloured slave mistress.[20] Since manumission costs could easily amount to years of wages, this would be an extraordinary price for sex. It was the ability of a few of these women and of some personal male valets, to make themselves important individuals in the emotional and domestic lives of their owners that resulted in a manumission. There was never a guarantee, however, that manumission would repay loyal service, as Joanna and Quaccoo both learned. Neither was freed by Captain Stedman.

Being female was not the only edge a slave could have; being coloured helped too, but not just because a coloured slave was favoured for somatic reasons. There is a condition related to colour that is often underestimated or overlooked: being 'coloured' is a nearly positive indication that a slave was a creole – locally born and raised. Almost 60 per cent of those manumitted were of mixed race, which means that most had been socialized locally, spoke Sranan Tongo and possibly Dutch or another European language, and knew the preferred local codes of deference together with the social and economic skills that facilitated getting positive attention from free people (of all races). In contrast, newly imported 'salt water' adult slaves would have been disadvantaged linguistically and socially in European(ized) households, especially in town, and therefore less able to initiate or sustain the personal relationships with free people that might result in a manumission. As most slaves in Suriname in the eighteenth and early nineteenth centuries were from Africa, the question of cultural orientation is important. Lighter skin may be a mark of acculturation (or creolization, a blending of a number of cultural traditions) for the coloured group as a whole, but in practice the orientation of coloured children depended on where their mothers worked and lived: in plantation slave quarters, European houses in town, or the houses and yards of free

The Palace of Justice, Paramaribo, Suriname
(P.J. Benoit, Voyage à Surinam, Brussels, 1839)

coloureds and free blacks in Paramaribo where multicultural abilities were an advantage.

Were most slave women or their children manumitted because of sex shared with white male owners, as stereotypes (and Stedman's behaviour) suggest? No, and this is particularly true as one traces manumission patterns over time. Whereas in 1760 most slaves were freed by white male owners, by 1830 they had been displaced by females of all colours and black and coloured males. A good number of these new manumitters were relatively poor, especially compared to the few wealthy planters of the mid-eighteenth century who bothered to manumit slaves; yet they were active in the expensive process of manumission. A primary reason was that they were freeing their own consanguinal and affinal relations. No wonder, then, that the manumission tax was paid by so many. Being the owner's kinsman was not only a powerful way of getting the attention of your potential manumitter, but in the nineteenth century it became an increasingly common reason for manumission, particularly if the owner was black or coloured. For free coloured and black owners, freedom for themselves meant freedom from being sold away from family members, and the freedom to try to free their kin in turn.

What if an enterprising slave was not related to his or her owner, and the owner was not the sort likely to listen sympathetically to suggestions of a future manumission? A very common situation, most likely, for which a number of nineteenth-century slaves found a very ingenious solution – they changed owners. One of the emerging trends was a very perceptible growth in the number of manumissions requested by owners who purchased slaves only to turn around and free them. The following example is one of a number of variations on this theme. A slave-owner dies suddenly and the estate, including slave property, is moved into probate with creditors and heirs pressing for a rapid disbursal of bequests. A slave who has invested a great deal of time, energy and money in getting the now dead owner to agree to the slave's use of time to accumulate money and property, is in danger of being sold to pay estate bills. The slave approaches another free person met earlier under different circumstances, a person who is known to be 'a good white'.[21] The slave gives this person the money needed to purchase the slave when the estate is auctioned, and promises to come up with the tax money for the new owner to use to legally manumit the slave thereafter. Another variation is to get a sympathetic free person to approach one's owner with an offer to buy the slave, who promises to then work to repay the new owner and also pay the manumission tax. These negotiations come to be almost routine in the early nineteenth century, and the cumulative effect of such successful agreements becoming public knowledge could only have added to the arsenal of ploys a resourceful slave had at his or (generally) her disposal.

In sum, manumissions were negotiated deals between slaves and owners. Manumission remained the exception and not the rule, in part because the conditions which could most easily foster mutually beneficial relationships were not readily transferable to an entire class of enslaved people. Manumission was highly personalized, with all the strengths and traps that implies, and it was costly. Apart from the monetary price of manumission, there were hidden costs as well. A slave had to control her or his temper and any tendency to threaten or rebel against the white-dominated social order. Accommodation within the status quo was required of those who would be free, a high cost but necessary given the unequal distribution of power. Both owners and slaves could gain from a manumission in many ways, but the costs would include some reciprocal rights and duties to each other – continuing loyalty, to some degree by both parties, but particularly by ex-slaves. This relationship was ephemeral in so far as it often ended with the lives of those who had been intimately involved in a manumission – the specific owner and the slaves freed. Goodwill that might have existed between those parties often was meaningless to their heirs.

And, finally, there was the cost of dependency. Many women who manumitted themselves, their children, and their kin were those who were most dependent on continuing employment by former owners. Free coloureds and free blacks remained for many decades a population group composed largely of females and children. Until that demographic and economic imbalance was corrected, the bulk of that community would be dependent to a large extent on domestic service. The employment which provided opportunities for freedom from chattel slavery reclaimed the ex-slaves for wage slavery.

Notes

1. The general manumission patterns discussed in this paper derive from an original systematic sample of 943 petitions within which 1,346 slaves were nominated to be freed between 1760 and 1826. Subsequent research has expanded the sample to all known manumissions between 1740 and 1832 (about 5,000), although this new database is not yet fully coded for statistical analysis. All manumission cases are being collected in order to link and trace both slaves and free people by name, where possible, over time from slavery into freedom and through subsequent generations. The names will allow an integration of manumission data with court cases, tax lists, wills and probate records. Most pre-1760 archival records are closed to researchers, although eight years between 1740 and 1759 have been added to the database. Some of the findings have appeared in Rosemary Brana-Shute, 'The Manumission of Slaves in Suriname, 1760-1830', Ph.D. Diss., University of Florida, 1985; 'Approaching Freedom: The Manumission of Slaves in Suriname, 1760-1828', *Slavery and Abolition*, 10:3 (December 1989), 40–63; and 'Legal Resistance to Slavery in Eighteenth Century Surinam', in G. Brana-Shute (ed.), *Resistance and Rebellion in Surinam: Old and New*, (Williamsburg, 1990), 119–36.

2. Paramaribo, which in the nineteenth century finally came to dominate and overshadow the plantation regions of the country, is still badly neglected in the historiography of slavery. The figures cited here are estimates made by eighteenth-century observers, accepted and repeated by historians since. They may be found summarized in Brana-Shute, dissertation, 41–94. See also B. Nelemans, 'Foto: The Capital of Suriname, Paramaribo', in C. Koeman (ed.), *Links with the Past. The History of the Cartography of Suriname, 1500-1971* (Amsterdam, 1973), 127–64, which is a brief history of Paramaribo in Dutch, English and Spanish. C.L. Temminck Groll and A.R. Tjin A Kjie's *De Architektuur van Suriname, 1667-1930* (Zutphen, 1973) is superbly and abundantly illustrated and has sections in English; the first 265 pages are on Paramaribo and the remaining hundred on the plantation districts.

3. The term coloured is used here as it was used in then Suriname (Dutch: *kleurling*; pl., *kleurlingen*): to refer to people of mixed European and African ancestry. There were other specialized terms to describe reputed admixtures of European, African, and Amerindian parentage. The general and then common term 'coloured' encompasses all other more specialized terms.

4. The best edition of the journal of Capt. John Stedman is the one transcribed from the original 1790 manuscript and introduced by Richard Price and Sally Price as *Narrative of a Five Years' Expedition Against the Revolted Negroes of Surinam* (Baltimore, 1989). It was earlier, much expurgated, versions of Stedman's account which appeared in English, Dutch, German and other languages (beginning in 1796) which established his account (and its famous illustrations) as a major interpretation of Surinamese and, by extension, West Indian slavery.

5. One European traveller who noticed this and who paid more than usual attention to city life was Albert von Sack, *A Narrative of a Voyage to Surinam* (London, 1808).

6. Captain John Stedman was one of the soldiers who served in Surinam in the 1770s.

7. The Court of Policy had a long-standing policy and custom of requiring plantations and private owners to make male slaves available to local militias on patrol, particularly in plantation areas. These slaves were requisitioned as 'required contributions' (such as weapons and food) to cover the costs of protecting the plantations and Paramaribo from attacks. Called 'commando negers', they served as porters, cooks, etc. to the white troops during militia operations. When these slaves were killed 'on commando', the Court of Policy compensated owners according to an established scale, depending on the level of skills of the deceased slave. The requisitioning of slave men for the Black Rangers was different in that these slave men would not be returned to their plantations of origin after service; they would be free men. The owners faced a permanent loss when they turned over slaves for this new corps. If a Ranger misbehaved as a soldier and was drummed out of the military, he would be returned to slavery but as property of the colonial government. Similar to 'commando' requisitions, however, was the practice of the Court determining the compensation to owners, again depending on the level of skills. A large proportion of these men in fact were considered by owners and the government to be skilled, and some owners tried to avoid turning over prime slaves. A few owners were caught trying to turn over diseased or otherwise unsatisfactory slaves, and faced condemnation and fines as a result.

8. Unlike regular manumissions, it is not clear if these recruits were considered freedmen from the time they were accepted into the Black Rangers, or if their freedom was to be conferred (formally or informally) at some later date (e.g., after mustering out of the service or after a period of service). It is almost a moot question as they would have had very little freedom of choice while on active service. Considering them to be slaves while on furlough would have necessitated some government oversight and control, and there is no evidence of this. It appears reasonable to assume that they

were considered to be similar to other inductees: men of very low status to be carefully monitored and controlled, especially to ensure their loyalty in the struggle against black rebels.

9. Among the English language sources for the Black Rangers see Wim Hoogbergen, *The Boni Maroon Wars in Suriname* (Leiden, 1990); Silvia W. de Groot, 'The Boni Maroon War 1765–1793, Surinam and French Guyana', *Boletin de Estudios Latinoamericanos y del Caribe*, 18 (1975), 30–48; and, of course, Stedman.

10. Just how much the difficulty of living and surviving as a Black Ranger affected their decisions is impossible to say, in the light of meagre sources.

11. These plots were not intended to be small farms. They were large enough for a house and side entrance on the street front, and a deep but narrow yard (Sranan: *djari*) for trees, a kitchen garden and some self-standing out-buildings and sheds.

12. Frimangron maintained a cultural identity as an Afro-Surinamese neighbourhood until the recent past when strong emigration to the Netherlands and an influx of other ethnic groups, including maroons, began to change the demographic and cultural character of the area. A number of studies in the 1970s chose Frimangron precisely because of its origin and enduring reputation as a *nengre* area. Although *nengre* translates as 'black' in Sranan Tongo, the term refers less to phenotype than to the cultural practices and beliefs of generally lower-class but definitely more traditional creoles. The *nengre* were/are generally contrasted with the *malata* (mulattos) who were more Europeanized culturally. Frimangron, then, even in modern Suriname, was known as a neighbourhood of traditional, more 'African', residents.

   The information on the Black Rangers and Frimangron is based on archival petitions. Among the English language studies of Frimangron two centuries later are Rosemary Brana-Shute, 'Women, Clubs and Politics: The Case of a Lower-Class Neighbourhood in Paramaribo, Suriname', *Urban Anthropology*, 5:2 (1976), 157–85; Gary Brana-Shute, *On the Corner: Male Social Life in a Paramaribo Creole Neighbourhood* (Assen 1979; reprinted Chicago, 1990).

13. What the slave actually paid was the lowest amount the slave could get the owner to accept. One cannot say that amount was the slave's market value, as in some cases the sum was well under what the slave auctions would have yielded, and in some cases significantly higher. In the latter case, one senses the fierceness in the determination of owners to make slaves really pay for 'the treasure of freedom'.

14. There are no population figures or estimates for the *piekie njan* population, although the very fact that a new segment of the urban population had arisen with its own new name suggests the size was large, in comparison to the number of free people and to the slave population – a new intermediate group without direct white control.

15. The court would continue to introduce new barriers to manumission until 1850, by which time general emancipation was accepted as inevitable. At that point procedures and costs for manumission were sharply reduced. The institution of slavery was ended officially in 1863.

16. See R. Brana-Shute, dissertation; 'Approaching Freedom'; and 'Legal Resistance to Slavery'.

17. In the Surinamese travel literature in particular there are references to the 'missy' or housekeeper who might also be or have been a mistress of a free male resident in the house. Some were slaves; some manumitted; some perhaps were born free. They ranged in colour although I found no reference to any who were white. They were reputed to wield great power and influence over everyone in the household. For illustrations of 'missy', see P.J. Benoit, *Voyage à Surinam; Description des possessions neerlandaises dans la Guyana* (Brussels, 1839) who visited Surinam in 1830 or 1831.

18. To some extent owners would be loath to part with skilled slaves; but some did, once a mutually beneficial and personal relationship was established. Then, negotiations over amounts and payment schedules could proceed.

19. Accumulating social capital is quite similar to what we now call finding mentors and 'networking'.

20. The important differences between sex and gender and how each affected manumission patterns were explored in R. Brana-Shute, 'Sex and Gender and the Manumission of Slaves in Suriname', unpublished paper presented at the 22nd Annual Conference of the Association of Caribbean Historians, Martinique 1990.

21. This is a daring phrase used in a petition to the Court of Policy by some free coloureds and free blacks, implying of course that some whites were bad. The court never reacted negatively to the phrase knowing, as everyone else did, that one's personal reputation was important and some whites had reputations for foul, intolerant tempers and behaviours and were to be avoided by coloureds and blacks, free or slave, if at all possible.

8

A Slow & Extended Abolition

The Case
of the Bahamas
1800–38

HOWARD D. JOHNSON

Throughout the British Caribbean, full emancipation was followed by a period of adjustment in which former slave-owners and ex-slaves negotiated the terms of their new social and economic relationship. In all colonies, this was the culmination of a process which had begun during the period of slavery.[1] In sections of plantation Jamaica, for example, slaves were successful in establishing informal contract terms for their labour which anticipated (in important respects) post-emancipation arrangements for wage labourers. As Mary Turner has demonstrated, slaves were in a position to bargain for improvements in their working conditions partly because of the labour shortage which developed in the years after the abolition of the slave trade.[2] In the non-plantation colony of the Bahamas, the restructuring of the relationship between slaves and their owners, along lines commonly associated with the post-slavery years, was more extensive than in other areas of the British Caribbean. There, the catalyst for change was not, as in Jamaica, a labour shortage but a surplus of slave labour which emerged with the collapse of cotton production in the Bahamas by 1800. This paper examines the disintegration of slavery which followed on the decline of cotton as an export staple and the evolution of new arrangements for slave labour which prefigured post-emancipation labour systems in the Bahamas.[3] These developments constituted a slow and extended abolition.

With the collapse of the cotton-based plantation system, slave-owners faced the problem of keeping their labour force productively employed. The introduction of cotton cultivation, on a commercial basis, by the American Loyalists after 1784 had led to the rapid expansion of the acreage planted in cotton and the redistribution of the slave population from the urban centre of Nassau on New Providence to the plantations of the south and south-eastern islands like Exuma, San Salvador, Crooked Island and Acklins. Between 1785 and 1788, the area under cotton cultivation increased from 2,476 to 8,000 acres.[4] By the opening years of the nineteenth century, the combined effect of soil exhaustion, the depredations of the chenille and red bugs and American competition had resulted in a sharp decline in cotton production and exports. Some planters who had resided in the Out Islands responded to this crisis by abandoning their plantations and migrating to Nassau, the American South and to other British Caribbean colonies.[5] Several slave-owners liquidated their investment by selling more than 3,000 of their slaves in the British sugar colonies between 1808 and 1825 before this inter-colonial traffic was halted.[6] These slave exports did not, however, effectively reduce the oversupply of labour on the outlying islands where the acreage which remained in agricultural production steadily contracted. No figures exist for the total acreage which was abandoned in this period. However, Daniel McKinnen's account of his visit, in 1803, to Crooked Island (where the Loyalists had established approximately 40 plantations and planted more than 2,000 acres in cotton) indicated that most of the plantations were ruinate by that date.[7] The problem of surplus labour was intensified by the high level of natural increase in the slave population and the influx of 4,851 liberated Africans between 1811 and 1838.[8]

Those landowners who remained in agricultural production turned to the cultivation of food crops and stock raising for the small local market.[9] Writing in 1812, William Wylly described the state of the agricultural sector in the Bahamas: 'We are indeed rather *Farmers and Graziers*, than *West Indian Planters* In so much that the greater part of every Plantation is generally employed as Pasture, or planted with provisions, And our Out Islands produce more corn than they consume'.[10] However, neither of those economic activities provided full employment for the slave labour force, resident on the Out Islands. Stock raising, for example, as a labour-extensive activity could absorb only a relatively small number of the steadily growing slave population. This is a conclusion supported by the evidence of Theodore George Alexander to a Select Committee of the colony's House of Assembly on a proposed general registry of slaves in 1815:

> That I verily believe from the number of Negroes now on the Islands, there is no sort of encouragement for, or advantage to be gained by the Introduction of African slaves, as in consequence of the exhausted state of the Lands, there is not enough employment for those at present upon them: Nearly whole Islands which were formerly under cultivation in Plantations of Cotton, being at present capable of little else than raising Cattle and Sheep.[11]

By the time of the abolition of slavery, no agricultural staple of comparable importance had been found to replace cotton and the Bahamian economy relied on the exploitation of the colony's marine and forest resources which had characterized the pre-Loyalist era.[12] In a colony where salt and wrecked goods were the principal exports, Governor Blayney Balfour had remarked on the extractive nature of the economy in a despatch to Lord Stanley, the Secretary of State for the Colonies, in February 1834: 'On considering then the Exports from the Colony, on which of course, our means of importing depend, you will Sir, perceive that very few are produced by the land, or the labor of the Inhabitants'. Other exports included turtles, the cascarilla bark and varieties of wood which were used either for dyes or in furniture making. Pineapples had, by that stage, emerged as a crop with export potential but cotton was 'little more than a nominal article of Export'.[13]

Slaves on the surviving plantations, without a major export staple to keep them occupied at 'maximum intensity of labour', were underemployed. On most plantations, the preferred method of organizing labour was the task system (used earlier in cotton production) which allowed slaves time to work on their provision grounds on a daily basis.[14] For the colony's Collector of Customs, writing in 1812, the task system provided evidence of 'the lightness of their [the slaves'] employment: . . . they on most of the Plantations with ease complete their task of labor for the day by three or four o'clock in the Even᷎ after which they employ themselves in their own grounds'.[15] The slaves' relatively light work regime reflected the fact that planters could, at best, make only a limited profit from the slaves' surplus labour. It was also often evidence of an agreement between slaves and their increasingly impoverished owners that, given more 'free time' outside the plantation routine, they would assume full responsibility for maintaining themselves. This was the arrangement on the Rolle plantations in Exuma where, by the mid-1820s, the slaves 'were expected to be self-sufficient as to food production and as self-sufficient as possible in other ways'.[16] It was a decision prompted by the realization that maintenance costs exceeded the income which the slaves generated. In 1828, Lord John Rolle complained that he had spent £5,000 on his slaves' maintenance over the previous decade, with a return of only £130.[17]

The practice on the Rolle plantations became widespread on estates in other Bahamian islands in the closing decades of slavery. Evidence for this development comes from an 1828 report on the 'state and condition' of the liberated Africans in the colony. Since the treatment of liberated Africans was closely patterned on that of the slaves, it is reasonable to assume that the observations of that report are also applicable to the slave population.[18] The report noted that liberated Africans (who were serving an apprenticeship) were allowed additional time to work on their provision grounds if their holders were unable to supply the weekly food allowance:

> There seems to have prevailed a sort of Understanding that six Quarts of Corn should be the weekly allowance and when this fell short one working day has been allowed to the Apprentices for himself [sic] for every Two Quarts short of their weekly allowance.

In the context of the decayed plantation system, landowners thus shifted the onus of maintenance costs decisively to the provision grounds. Some proprietors were unable to provide basic food allowances, on a regular basis, or fulfil their statutory obligation to supply 'two suits of proper and sufficient clothing' to each slave per annum.[19] As Governor Sir James Carmichael Smyth observed in 1830:

> The slaves are few; are very thinly scattered; & with the exception of those islands where there are salt ponds, are of very little value to their owners. When the owner is poor, the slave is neglected & is deprived of those comforts, and additional enjoyments, he would and does receive in better circumstances.[20]

In those circumstances, the slaves became increasingly dependent on the proceeds of the provision grounds and other independent economic activities like raising small livestock and poultry. Slaves on the Out Islands sold their surplus foodstuffs to their owners, other proprietors, passing ships and occasionally in Nassau.[21] There is also evidence that slaves sold the stock of absentee proprietors for their own benefit. In March 1805, an advertisement in the *Royal Gazette* stated:

> If the Captains of vessels stopping at the Bight Plantation St. Salvador, formerly belonging to James Hepbourn, Esq. deceased, do purchase, or allow their sailors to purchase stock of any kind from the Overseer, or Negroes on said Plantation or Plantations, belonging to the said James Hepbourn, deceased, They shall be prosecuted according to Law – John Hepbourn[22]

Slaves on the plantations in New Providence found a steady outlet for their products in the Nassau market and to incoming ships in that port town.[23] On his plantations at Clifton and Tusculum in New Providence, William Wylly claimed the right to purchase 'all hogs, pigs, poultry, and eggs, which the people may have for sale, and for which he is to pay the Nassau prices; to be fixed by the driver and two other men chosen by the seller'.[24] He also permitted his slaves to market their poultry, pigs and vegetables in Nassau on a Saturday. A notice placed by Wylly in the *Royal Gazette* of 10 February 1810 indicates that his slaves regularly bartered their produce for rum with Nassau fishermen:

> Whereas the fishermen of this port make it their practice to go on shore at the plantations situated at a distance from Nassau, under pretence of wanting wood and water, but for the real purpose of carrying on an unlawful traffic with our Negroes, and supplying them with rum, in exchange for provisions and poultry.[25]

This evidence of slave participation in the market economy (in the Out Islands and New Providence) substantiates Michael Craton's assertion that 'the transition from "proto-peasant" to true peasant . . . was probably more advanced in Exuma and similar Bahamian islands than anywhere in the British colonies'.[26]

By the time of full emancipation, two transitional forms of labour management between slavery and capitalist relations of production – labour tenancy and sharecropping – had emerged on the plantations of the Out Islands. Both labour systems (which became significant features of the post-emancipation rural economy) created a class of 'dependent cultivators' whose tenure on the land was rooted in contractual relations.[27] A system of labour tenancy was adopted on some plantations by 1828. In some instances, African apprentices divided the working week between their provision grounds and the holders' fields. The details of this arrangement were described by the apprentice Aguara who was attached to a plantation on the island of Eleuthera:

> Gets no allowance but is allowed three days in the week for the purpose of maintaining and clothing himself, which he manages to do by selling a part of what his Ground produces that he raised on it Corn [,] Yams [,] Potatoes and other things. The three other days he is employed by his Holder . . .[28]

By this system, holders of African apprentices (and slave-owners) had at their disposal the labour services of nominal dependents who were expected to maintain themselves. The voluntary agreements of the Apprenticeship between 1834 and 1838 (by which employers and praedial labourers signed contracts specifying the terms of their employment) often formalized arrangements that had already been worked out during the slavery era. This is clear from one such agreement in 1835 by which praedial apprentices were allowed to cultivate a plot of land for their 'own support and maintenance' for two and one-half days per week. On the remaining two and one-half days of the working week, they were expected to labour for their masters.[29] These post-1834 contracts reduced the working week (defined by the earlier informal contracts) from six to five days.

Unlike the system of labour tenancy, sharecropping arrangements were first introduced during the Apprenticeship years. In 1836, for example, Robert Millar, a proprietor in Eleuthera (the leading producer of provision crops and the centre of the emerging export trade in pineapples) manumitted 56 of his apprentices at Millar's Settlement and made voluntary agreements with some heads of families to remain on his estate.[30] The official report of those developments indicates that a sharecropping arrangement was involved in which Millar exploited a 'family-labour form of production':

> Voluntary agreements were . . . entered into between Mr. Millar and the heads of families, to remain on the estate and to work the same upon terms very liberal and beneficial to the people, and calculated to promote their industry, portions of land being allotted to each family, and every facility afforded them of fulfilling the contracts entered into, and comfortably maintaining themselves and children.[31]

There is no available information on the size of the holdings allocated, the crops which were grown or the division of the crop yields between landlord and tenants on Millar's plantation. However, an official report, later in 1836, described the terms of the typical agreement between proprietors and their tenants on the share system:

> There are not many settled on the lands of their former employers, when they do so, they work on shares, one third of the produce being for the land owner and the remainder for the labourer . . .[32]

There is also evidence that the sharecropping system was already being used in pineapple production. Special Justice Thomas Winder, on his visit to Eleuthera in May-June 1835, noted that 'the apprentices [were] being allowed by their masters to raise the same [pineapples]'.[33] Later that year Thomas Cash of Eleuthera was charged by his apprentice Bob 'of withholding the sum received by him for pineapples raised by said apprentice on a piece of Ground given by Mr. Cash, in addition to the land allotted by Law to apprentices'.[34]

The adoption of the systems of labour tenancy and sharecropping indicates that landed proprietors regarded a dependent tenancy as a more profitable arrangement for extracting surplus than direct production. Without a major export staple, agricultural production was not sufficiently profitable to interest some proprietors in the direct operation of their estates. However, they were able to guarantee themselves an income from a dependent and resident labour force by making land available to the direct producers rather than by denying them that resource as in capitalist economies.[35] The success of Millar's sharecropping experiment in binding his former slaves to his estate is clear from an 1837 report by Thomas Winder:

> These labourers having a distinct interest in the produce of their industry and in the protection of the property entrusted to them appear to be sensible of the advantages their own good conduct has obtained for them, and having tasted the sweets of their labour, *and not likely, in my opinion to be soon detached from the Estate* . . . [emphasis added].[36]

Bahamian slave-owners did not (like Antiguan planters) forego the transitional period of Apprenticeship. However, individual proprietors in Eleuthera shed their statutory obligations for maintaining their apprentices by manumitting them. Some of those freedmen were subsequently employed on a wage basis – an arrangement which allowed the proprietors to hire only those labourers that they needed. These developments were reported by Thomas Winder in 1835:

> Having been hospitably entertained, I left the place on Monday morning, and arrived at the settlement of J.R. Gibson, Esq. At this place there are a considerable number of Blacks, formerly belonging to the estate of Mrs. Thompson, Messrs. Wemyss, the two Mackey's and J.R. Gibson, all the apprentices belonging to which were manumitted in November and January last. Some of them are again employed by their former masters, but on terms which I fear have not bettered their condition; many of them are out of employ . . .[37]

The only major area of economic activity in the Out Islands where the relations of production remained virtually unaltered during the slavery era was the salt industry which was concentrated on Exuma, Ragged Island, Crooked Island, Rum Cay, Long Cay and Long Island. Unlike agricultural production, salt production continued to be profitable in the closing years of slavery and the demand for slave labour remained high. The labour-intensive nature of salt production can be explained by its low-level technology which relied on solar evaporation.[38] In January 1835, Governor Blayney Balfour remarked on the primitive methods which were used in the salt industry:

> As the attention of the Master and the efforts of the Labourer, are, in making Salt, only directed to supply the Ponds or Pans instantly with Salt Water as evaporation exhausts it, and, when a sufficient quantity of Saline Chrystals appear to be, by frequent evaporations, deposited, to raking and removing them from the Pond – Salt cannot with propriety be called a Manufacture . . .[39]

The arduous and unpleasant nature of the work involved in salt-raking made a system of direct supervision necessary. At the time of the abolition of slavery, the salt-producing islands were the only areas where gang labour was employed on a regular basis.[40]

The continued demand for labour in the salt industry was met primarily by those slaves who remained on the Out Island plantations and (increasingly in the years after 1811) by liberated Africans serving an indenture. Since salt-raking was a seasonal activity (restricted to the dry months), the planters temporarily reassigned their slaves to raking salt. A message to the Governor from the House of Assembly in 1823 described the round of activities in which the slaves engaged: 'A crop of cotton, or provisions being raised, or a few small cargoes of cedar or dye woods cut from the woods, the slaves are frequently sent, for the season, to rake and manufacture salt at the ponds . . .'[41] Slaves who were involved in salt-raking were provided with basic food rations. On Crooked Island, for example, the slaves (owned by James Moss) who were sent to the salt ponds were given 'Seven quarts of Corn weekly, but they were allowed to catch Fish'.[42]

In a context of agricultural stagnation, some slave-owners attempted to salvage their investment in slaves by transferring them to Nassau where they were either sold, hired out or permitted to work on the self-hire system. Slaves who were to be sold were, as William Wylly noted in 1815, usually allowed to seek out prospective masters:

> . . . Gangs of Slaves intended for Sale in these Islands are generally brought to Nassau and sold at Auction, they are however/as the Examinant believes in all instances/allowed to go about Town, previous to the day of Sale, in order to look out for Masters of their own choosing . . .[43]

The sale of slaves was an option less frequently exercised than the two systems of hiring mainly because there was a better market for their labour power than for their persons.[44] In 1815, for example, Theodore George

Alexander attributed the fall in slave prices, in part, to 'the aversion people must necessarily have to invest their money in a property that has for the most part been an unprofitable one in these Islands'.[45] Slave hiring was, moreover, a short-term relationship which was better suited to the fluctuating labour demands of most urban employers than was slave ownership.[46]

Many slave-owners who transferred their under-utilized slaves to Nassau opted for the self-hire system.[47] Under this arrangement, slaves were allowed by their masters to seek their own employment in return for periodic cash payments on which they had mutually agreed. This system involved two levels of contractual relations for the slaves, one with their masters and the other with their employers. The practice of self-hire had evolved before the arrival of the American Loyalists in a slave system where, without a major export staple, slaves were not 'occupied at all times'.[48] Slave-owners had thus commuted the labour services which they were due into cash payments. After a visit to the Bahamas in 1784, Johann David Schoepf had remarked on the existence of a self-hire system on the island of New Providence:

> Even the blacks here take part in the general contentment ... Many of them are free, or if they are slaves, by paying a small weekly sum they are left undisturbed in the enjoyment of what they earn by other work.[49]

This system survived the entry of the Loyalists and the establishment of a plantation system, with its increased demand for labour. Although they tightened controls over the slave population in general, the Loyalists recognized, in their slave codes of 1796, the long-established autonomy of slaves who operated on the self-hire system in the urban areas. Slaves were not, for example, allowed to travel around without a ticket from their owner, employer or overseer which stated the time of their departure, their destination and expected time of return to their usual place of residence. The exceptions to that ruling were those slaves engaged in economic activities from which they earned their livelihood: '. . . such only excepted as are going with Firewood, Grass [,] Fruit [,] Provisions or small stock and other Goods which they may lawfully sell to Market . . .'[50]

In the years after 1800 (when slavery ceased to be vital to the agricultural economy) the self-hire system gained even wider acceptance among both masters and slaves. For the masters, this arrangement had the advantage of providing regular cash payments without the need for supervision or the responsibility for supplying food, clothing or housing. Slaves were also enthusiastic about a system which gave them an opportunity to exercise extensive control over their lives and resources (despite their continued monetary obligations to their owners) and occupy a position somewhere between slavery and freedom. By the closing decade of slavery, slaves on the self-hire system dominated the urban labour market. Although the Slave Registration returns for 1834 referred to few cases of slaves who worked on self-hire, the qualitative evidence suggests that it was firmly established in the urban and maritime economy.[51]

In Nassau, like Rio de Janeiro, a wide range of slaves worked on the self-hire system.[52] Although skilled artisans were among the earliest participants in the system and formed a significant proportion of those who hired their own time during the slavery era, many slaves on self-hire were casual labourers who worked at a number of tasks to support themselves. As a port town and a free port, which was first opened to trade in certain enumerated commodities with Spanish and French colonies in 1787, Nassau provided employment for slaves as stevedores and porters.[53] A rare advertisement, aimed at slaves who worked on the self-hire system, appeared in the *Bahama Gazette* in June 1799:

> Wanted to Hire for 30 Days Certain Twelve active Negroes, acquainted with working on Board a Ship, at Rigging, Loading, &c – to whom Liberal Wages will be given by their applying to Wilkinson and Arnott, Nassau, June 7, 1799[54]

There was also a demand for skilled tradesmen, like ships' carpenters and sail makers, associated with the maritime economy. Slaves also worked as house carpenters, masons, joiners, blacksmiths and coopers and as labourers in stone quarrying, woodcutting and road construction. Some slaves were driven to theft in order to raise money to pay the agreed sum (commonly referred to as 'wages') to their masters. In January 1799, for example, a property owner placed an advertisement in the *Bahama Gazette* which stated:

> It having long been a Practice with Numbers of Negroes who are allowed to work out on this island, to cut Wood off Lands not the Property of their Owners, which they sell to raise money to pay their Wages; and the Subscriber having suffered much Injury from such Practice, he hereby gives this Public Warning, that he will apprehend and commit to Gaol, any Negro in future found cutting Wood on his Lands, and will seek for such further Satisfactions as the Laws will award to him.[55]

Slaves who engaged in maritime activities formed a majority of those who worked on the self-hire system.[56] They laboured as sailors on droghing vessels which linked the islands of the archipelago, on wrecking, turtling and fishing boats and on those ships which travelled to neighbouring Caribbean islands and the American coast. These slave mariners, William Wylly claimed with some degree of exaggeration, were treated no differently from their white counterparts:

> Our Black Seamen are perhaps *equal to any in the world*, our Island Vessels are principally manned by them, and many of our Droghers, Turtlers and Fishing Vessels are commanded by them; they are generally allowed certain proportions of the Profits of each Cruize or Voyage and there is no difference between their treatment and that of our White Seamen.[57]

Female slaves who worked on self-hire did so primarily as domestics and itinerant vendors. In New Providence, they found jobs as cooks, laundresses and general servants in private households. Public institutions like the hospital of the West India Regiment at Fort Charlotte also employed female slaves as nurses and washers.[58] The data on itinerant vending are not extensive but the available evidence indicates that slave women, hawking trays of merchandise around Nassau, dominated that section of the retail trade. Their trade was so well established in New Providence by 1784 that it threatened the livelihood of the newly-arrived Loyalist merchants. Owners were eventually forbidden by the 1796 Consolidated Slave Act to employ slaves to retail dry goods but this legislation proved ineffective. In 1811, members of the merchant-dominated House of Assembly complained:

> We present as a nuisance the number of baskets carried about the town by free people of colour and slaves offering dry goods and groceries for sale in violation of the Act of Assembly in that case made and provided and to the injury of shopkeepers.[59]

There were, however, no attempts to place restrictions on slave hucksters who sold prepared food, provisions and small craft items.[60] Contemporary sources hinted that itinerant vendors were often also prostitutes. In 1828, for example, the committee which investigated the 'state and condition' of the liberated Africans objected to the employment of female African apprentices as hucksters on the grounds that it would be 'palpably exposing . . . [them] to temptations and impositions of the grossest kind'.[61]

Slaves who laboured on the self-hire system were usually described as 'working out on wages'. However, that description obscures the diverse labour relations which the system involved. Although land-based slaves were usually paid money wages, slave mariners were given a share from the voyages in which they participated. In March 1830 Governor Sir James Carmichael Smyth remarked: 'The greater part of the slave population here are seafaring people. The crews in the wrecking vessels are in a great measure composed of slaves – these people are paid in shares . . .'[62] The share arrangement was one in which the individual slave had, in Steve J. Stern's phrase, 'a right of fractional appropriation in the *product* of the work performed'.[63] There are no available details on the system of payment to slaves who were employed in itinerant vending but it is likely that they were permitted to retain earnings which exceeded sales targets established by their owners.[64] Finally, there were slaves who had no steady income and resorted to 'scuffling' to earn a basic subsistence and meet the fixed payments to their masters.[65]

The pay scales for slaves on self-hire varied with their skill levels and the nature of their employment. In 1828, the committee on the 'state and condition' of the liberated Africans provided estimates of the income levels of slave mariners and other slaves who worked in Nassau. In that year, for example, the slave mechanic was paid an average daily wage of 6s 3½d sterling from which he was allowed to keep a weekly minimum of 5s 5d for his subsistence. Sailors earned an average monthly income of ten dollars but were usually provided with food while on board ship. Domestics, who were fed and clothed by their employers, were paid an average monthly wage of five dollars and unskilled labourers earned an average daily wage of $7\frac{1}{2}$d.[66] After paying 'wages' to their owners and maintaining themselves in food and clothing, some slaves probably had little disposable income. This is partly explained by the fact that there was intense competition among slaves, free coloureds and liberated Africans for casual employment in the urban labour market.[67] The 1828 report on the liberated Africans, referring to those recaptives who earned their living 'other than by agriculture', observed: 'Their occupations generally speaking are casual and multifarious, owing to the competition which there exists for the kinds of employment that they are likely to obtain'.[68] There was, however, a significant number of slaves who earned enough money (after discharging their obligations to their masters) to indulge in leisure-time activities like drinking and gambling in the urban environment. In 1804, the Grand Jurors of the Bahamas complained about the public behaviour of the slave population in Nassau:

> We present as a nuisance, the general assemblages of negroes and people of colour in the streets of Nassau, and on the parade, for the purpose of gambling, &c. particularly on Sundays, and recommend that strict attention may be paid to carrying the police act into execution.[69]

The evidence also indicates that many slaves accumulated enough money to purchase their freedom. The process of manumission was facilitated by falling slave prices in the years after 1800 and the removal of a prohibitively expensive manumission fee of £90 (imposed in 1784 when the plantation system was introduced) which was replaced by a nominal registration fee in 1827.[70] So widespread was the practice of slaves buying their freedom that Governor Sir James Carmichael Smyth, referring specifically to slave mariners, predicted in 1830 that 'if the system which at present exists is suffered to continue, they will by all degrees become free without exciting any shock or convulsion in their little community'.[71] That trend is reflected in the manumission figures for the period 1808–34. The manumissions per 1,000 slaves were 3.1 in 1808, 4.5 in 1820 and 11.4 in 1834. This was, as B.W. Higman has noted, the highest manumission rate in the British Caribbean for those years.[72]

Self-hire (like labour tenancy and sharecropping) indicates that the slave labour system was in a state of transition. In labour tenancy and self-hire, the direct exploitation of slavery had been replaced with forms of labour extraction in which slave-owners were appropriating surplus by labour rent or money payments. In the case of labour tenancy, the slave occupied land which he worked for the maintenance of himself and his family while his labour obligation to his master was limited to a fraction of his working time. Under the self-hire system, the slave-owner commuted the labour service of his slaves into cash payments.

Slaves who worked on the self-hire system in the Bahamas enjoyed a considerable degree of independence. They took the initiative in marketing their services to prospective employers and in negotiating individually the terms of their employment. For these services, many slaves earned a wage which is usually regarded as 'the very antithesis of slavery'.[73] Slave-owners showed little interest in how their slaves earned a living as long as they paid the stipulated sum regularly. Although slaves had to surrender a portion of their incomes to their owners, they made autonomous decisions about the disposal of their earnings. Slaves also made their own arrangements for accommodation, usually in the 'Negro Town' which had developed in Nassau by the late eighteenth century.[74] In these ways, slaves on self-hire established 'some distance from the conventional meanings usually conveyed by their defined status'.[75]

The extensive autonomy which slaves on self-hire had achieved by the opening decade of the nineteenth century posed problems of control for slave-owners. By that stage, there was little to distinguish them from the free non-white group into which they were gradually merging. In 1808, the colonial legislature (dominated by slave-owners) enacted a law 'for regulating the Hire of Slaves, Carts, Waggons and Drays'. This legislation stipulated that proprietors who allowed their slaves 'to hire themselves to work, either on board vessels, or on the shore, as porters or labourers' should register the names of the slaves with the police office and obtain a copper badge which each slave was required to wear on his jacket or frock 'in a conspicuous manner'. It also stated that individuals who hired slaves without such a badge would be liable to a fine of £5 for each slave employed and would have to pay double their wages to their owners. The law was intended to prevent slaves on self-hire from passing themselves off as free men to prospective employers and then evading the payment of 'wages' to their owners.[76] In this situation, slave-owners often intervened in the hiring process. An advertisement by Elisha Swain in 1794 stated:

> All persons are hereby forewarned from hiring or paying any wages to a Negro Fellow called Chatham Darre, (a Carpenter) without Leave from the Subscriber.[77]

In 1832 another slave-owner complained:

> The Subscriber again finds it necessary to forbid any person employing or paying wages to any of her Negroes, without a written order from herself, or in her absence from Henry Greenslade, Esq.
> S. A. Poitier[78]

The non-payment of 'wages' by slaves on self-hire became widespread by the 1830s. The offenders were not only those who wished to evade payment (in a bid to establish total independence of their masters) but also those slaves who (anxious to experience the freedom of action and increased earnings associated with the system) agreed to pay their masters more than they could regularly earn. Until the early 1830s slave-owners punished the slave offenders by imprisoning them in the workhouse. This was the situation which Carmichael Smyth described in 1832:

> Almost every Slave is anxious to enjoy this species of Liberty [the self-hire system] & will readily promise and undertake to pay more than, at times, he may be able to acquire. Many of them have a sort of account current with their owners; & in hopes of better times get deeper in debt every month. There are of course also some dishonest and dissolute Slaves who will spend whatever they may gain & state to their owners that they have not been able to get work. The day of reckoning is however sure to arrive at last, & I have had occasion to observe, in the weekly returns, Slaves repeatedly confined in the Work-House & punished for 'not paying wages' . . .

Carmichael Smyth took the view that the non-payment of 'wages' was a civil rather than a criminal offence and intervened to discontinue this method of disciplining slaves on self-hire. His view was endorsed by the Solicitor General who gave an opinion that 'the non-payment of wages was similar to any non-fulfillment of any agreement & was not a crime or offence which could be punished at the command of the master by a flogging'.[79] This ruling is important for it represents a further stage in the substitution of a relationship based on contract for one based on coercion.[80] The first step in this process had been the commutation of labour obligations into a money payment.

The nature of the agreement between slaves on self-hire and their owners continued to be a matter of dispute after 1832. In fact, it affected the relationship between former slave-owners and their apprentices in the years 1834 to 1838. As Special Justice Thomas Winder observed in August 1836:

> If the records of Complaints made to all Magistrates in the Colony were carefully inquired into, it would be found that nearly all of them have been made by the agents of non-resident Proprietors, or by Persons who having no profitable employment for their Apprentices at home have turned them out to seek their living in order to avoid the expence of food and clothing expecting them to pay wages although there is no agreement entered into legally requiring them to do so.[81]

Winder's statement suggests that, with the sanction of the workhouse removed many slaves on self-hire no longer paid 'wages' to their owners and operated essentially as free wage labourers even before the formal end of slavery.

In the Bahamas, full emancipation was (with the exception of the salt industry) primarily a political event which did not significantly alter the existing social relations of production. The transformation of labour relationships had been precipitated by the collapse of the cotton industry, after a brief period of prosperity, in the early years of the nineteenth century. Faced with a steadily-growing slave population which, without a profitable staple, they could keep neither productively employed nor properly maintained, the impoverished slave-owners gradually withdrew from direct production and the direct exploitation of their labour force. In the years after 1800, there was a shift in the methods of labour extraction away from slavery to methods (sometimes sanctioned by custom) in which slaves assumed responsibility for their own maintenance. The labour systems which emerged constituted alternative forms of surplus appropriation for the slave-owners in which labour obligations were converted into cash payments in the urban context and increasingly (in the last years of slavery) to a labour rent in the rural setting.

In both urban and rural settings, slaves enjoyed extensive autonomy within bondage. On the decayed plantations of the Out Islands, many slaves operated effectively as peasants, devoting a large part of the work day to their own provision grounds. By the closing years of slavery, a slave tenantry had also been established on the estates. In the town of Nassau, slaves working on the self-hire system enjoyed considerable freedom of movement and action and were, by emancipation, long accustomed to exchanging their labour power for a wage. Their ability to earn and accumulate money increased the number of slaves who were able to purchase their own freedom. By 1834 the labour relationship of slaves to their masters had also moved decisively from a coercive to a contractual one.

Notes

My thanks to Roderick A. McDonald, Mary Turner, Richart Hart and Peter Dalleo who made informed comments on the penultimate draft of this paper.

1. This view was advanced by Frank W. Pitman as early as 1921. See ch. 3 of *Slavery on the British West Indian Plantations in the Eighteenth Century* (Washington, 1926).
2. Mary Turner, 'Chattel Slaves into Wage Slaves: A Jamaican Case Study' in Malcolm Cross and Gad Heuman (eds), *Labour in the Caribbean* (London, 1988), 18–19.
3. Both Rebecca J. Scott and Barbara J. Fields have recently argued that there was 'an internal dissolution of slavery' prior to emancipation in Cuba and Maryland respectively. See Rebecca J. Scott, *Slave Emancipation in Cuba: The Transition to Free Labor 1860–1899* (Princeton, 1985) and Barbara J. Fields, *Slavery and Freedom on the Middle Ground: Maryland during the Nineteenth Century* (New Haven, 1985).
4. D. Gail Saunders, 'Slave Life, Slave Society and Cotton Production in the Bahamas', *Slavery and Abolition*, 11 (1990), 333.
5. Michael Craton, 'We Shall not be Moved: Pompey's Slave Revolt in Exuma Island, Bahamas, 1830', *New West Indian Guide*, 57 (1983), 21.
6. David Eltis, 'The Traffic in Slaves between the British West Indian Colonies, 1807–1833', *Economic History Review*, 25 (1972), 58.
7. D. Gail Saunders, 'Slave Life, Slave Society and Cotton Production in the Bahamas', 334.
8. For a discussion of the circumstances which led to the natural increase of the Bahamian slave population see Michael Craton, 'Hobbesian or Panglossian? The Two Extremes of Slave Conditions in the British Caribbean, 1783 to 1834', *William and Mary Quarterly*, 3rd series, 35 (1978) and D. Gail Saunders, *Slavery in the Bahamas 1648–1838* (Nassau, 1985). At the micro-level of the Rolle plantations on Exuma, the slave population had grown from 254 to 376 in the period 1822–34 by natural increase alone. Between 1811 and 1860, Africans captured from slavers, bound for Cuba, were settled in the Bahamas. For an extended discussion of the liberated Africans (or recaptives) in the Bahamas see Howard Johnson, 'The Liberated Africans in the Bahamas, 1811–60', *Immigrants and Minorities*, 7 (1988), 16–40.

9. Craton, 'Hobbesian or Panglossian?', 352; B.W. Higman, *Slave Populations of the British Caribbean 1807–1834* (Baltimore, 1984), 65.
10. William Wylly to Zachary Macaulay, 15 April 1812. Enclosure in Charles Cameron to Earl Bathurst, 24 Jan. 1816. C.O. 23/63. Wylly, a Loyalist, was serving as the colony's attorney general at the time of those observations. He was also a planter and slave-owner who owned three plantations at the western end of New Providence.
11. See evidence to a select committee of the House of Assembly, Dec. 1815. Enclosure in Cameron to Bathurst, 24 Jan. 1816. C.O. 23/63.
12. For a discussion of the efforts to introduce alternative crops in the Bahamas after the decline of cotton production see Thelma Peterson Peters, 'The American Loyalists and the Plantation Period in the Bahama Islands' (Ph.D. diss., University of Florida, 1960), 158–9. For a discussion of the nature of the Bahamian economy before the commercial production of cotton see Howard Johnson, 'The Emergence of a Peasantry in the Bahamas during Slavery', *Slavery and Abolition*, 10 (1989), 173.
13. Blayney Balfour to Stanley, 19 Feb. 1834, no. 78. C.O. 23/91.
14. The phrase is M.I. Finley's. M.I. Finley, *Ancient Slavery and Modern Ideology* (London, 1980), 137. The origins of the task system in the Bahamas remain obscure. However, the evidence indicates that it had been adopted before the introduction of plantation-based cotton culture. For a further discussion of this point see Johnson, 'The Emergence of a Peasantry in the Bahamas', 174–5.
15. A. Murray to the Earl of Liverpool, 18 Apr. 1812. C.O. 23/59.
16. Craton, 'Hobbesian or Panglossian?', 354.
17. Michael Craton, 'White Law and Black Custom: The Evolution of Bahamian Land Tenures' in Janet Momsen and Jean Besson (eds), *Land and Development in the Caribbean* (London, 1981), 88–114.
18. 'Report on the State and Condition of the Liberated Africans', 10 Oct. 1828. Enclosure no. 7 in Lewis Grant to Sir George Murray, 10 Oct. 1828, no. 19. C.O. 23/79. For a discussion of the treatment of the liberated Africans in relation to the slave population see Johnson, 'The Liberated Africans in the Bahamas', 29–30.
19. The Consolidated Slave Act of 1796 had specified the rations which should be given to individual slaves. Since the weekly ration was limited to one peck of unground corn, or its equivalent in other foodstuffs, Bahamian slaves had been forced to rely on their provision grounds and fishing to supplement their diet. For a discussion of slave rations in the Bahamian context see Higman, *Slave Populations of the British Caribbean*, 213–14.
20. Carmichael Smyth to Sir George Murray, 10 Apr. 1830, no. 7. C.O. 23/82.
21. Johnson, 'The Emergence of a Peasantry in the Bahamas', 175–6.
22. *Royal Gazette*, 1 Mar. 1805.
23. Johnson, 'The Emergence of a Peasantry in the Bahamas', 175–6.
24. 'Regulations for the Government of the Slaves at Clifton and Tusculum in New Providence', July 1815. C.O. 23/67.
25. Quoted in Philip Cash, Shirley Gordon and Gail Saunders (eds), *Sources of Bahamian History* (London, 1991), 38.
26. Craton, 'Hobbesian or Panglossian?', 355.
27. The phrase is Marc Bloch's. Marc Bloch, 'The Rise of Dependent Cultivation and Seignorial Institutions' in M.M. Postan (ed.), *The Cambridge Economic History of Europe* (Cambridge, 1966), i, 253.
28. 'Report on the State and Condition of the Liberated Africans'.
29. See Howard Johnson, 'Labour Systems in Post-emancipation Bahamas', *Social and Economic Studies*, 37 (1988), 182.
30. Report of Special Justice Thomas Winder, 6 July 1836. Enclosure in Joseph Hunter to Glenelg, 12 Aug. 1836, no. 51. C.O. 23/99.
31. Ibid. The term 'family-labour form of production' is David Goodman's and Michael Redclift's. See *From Peasant to Proletarian: Capitalist Development and Agrarian Transitions* (Oxford, 1981), 150.
32. Thomas Winder to William Colebrooke, 4 Nov. 1836, no. 116. C.O. 23/97.
33. Report of Special Justice Thomas Winder on his visit to the district of Eleuthera and Harbour Island, 16 May–8 June 1835. Reprinted in the *Bahama Argus*, 1 July 1835.
34. Report on proceedings in the Special Justices' Court, 1 Dec. 1835. Reprinted in *Royal Gazette*, 26 Dec. 1835.
35. V.I. Lenin, *The Development of Capitalism in Russia* (Moscow, 1977, Progess Publishers edn), 194.
36. Report of Special Justice Thomas Winder on a visit to Southern Eleuthera, 6 July 1837. Enclosure in Joseph Hunter to Glenelg, 12 Aug. 1837, no. 51. C.O. 23/99.
37. Report of Special Justice Thomas Winder on his visit to the district of Eleuthera and Harbour Island, 16 May–8 June 1835.
38. Cf. Paul E. Lovejoy, *Salt of the Desert Sun: A History of Salt Production and Trade in the Central Sudan*

(Cambridge, 1986), 92; John Edmund Stealey III, 'Slavery and the Western Virginia Salt Industry', *Journal of Negro History*, 59 (1974), 108–9.

39. Blayney Balfour to G. Spring Rice, 15 Jan. 1835, no. 39. C.O. 23/93.
40. Blayney Balfour to Stanley, 5 Aug. 1833, no. 37. C.O. 23/89.
41. Message to Governor Sir Lewis Grant from the House of Assembly, 1 Jan. 1823. *Votes of the House of Assembly of the Bahama Islands, 1821–1824*, 31–2.
42. See report of the trial of James Moss, Apr. 1815. Enclosure in William Vesey Munnings to Earl Bathurst, 10 Aug. 1818, no. 35. C.O. 23/67.
43. See statement by Wylly to a select committee of the House of Assembly on a proposal for a general registry of slaves, Dec. 1815. Enclosure in Cameron to Bathurst, 24 Jan. 1816. C.O. 23/63.
44. Cf. Fields, *Slavery and Freedom on the Middle Ground*, 48.
45. Evidence to a select committee of the House of Assembly, Dec. 1815. Enclosure in Cameron to Earl Bathurst, 24 Jan. 1816. C.O. 23/63.
46. Cf. David R. Goldfield, 'Pursuing the American Urban Dream: Cities in the Old South', in Blaine A. Brownell and David R. Goldfield (eds), *The City in Southern History: The Growth of Urban Civilization in the South* (Port Washington, NY, 1977), 65.
47. For a discussion of the self-hire system in the Bahamian context see Howard Johnson, *The Bahamas in Slavery and Freedom* (Kingston and London, 1991), 1–14. See also O. Nigel Bolland, 'Proto-Proletarians? Slave Wages in the Americas: Between Slave Labour and Wage Labour' in this volume for a comprehensive overview of slave wages in the broader New World setting.
48. The phrase is from Eugene D. Genovese who has observed: 'Slavery requires all hands to be occupied at all times'. Eugene Genovese, *The Political Economy of Slavery: Studies in the Economy and Society of the Slave South* (New York, 1965), 49. See also Ralph V. Anderson and Robert E. Gallman, 'Slaves as Fixed Capital: Slave Labor and Southern Economic Development', *Journal of American History*, 64 (1977), 24.
49. Johann David Schoepf, *Travels in the Confederation, 1783–1784* (reprint, New York, 1968), ii, 301.
50. See 'An Act to consolidate and bring into one Act the several Laws relating to Slaves . . .' in *Manuscript Laws of the Bahamas 1795–1799*, (Bahamas Public Record Office).
51. Johnson, *The Bahamas in Slavery and Freedom*, 4.
52. Cf. Mary Karasch, *Slave Life in Rio de Janeiro 1808–1850* (Princeton, 1987), 185–213; Katia M. De Queirós Mattoso, *To Be a Slave in Brazil 1550–1888* (New Brunswick, 1986), 121–3. For a valuable overview of the operation of the self-hire system in the British Caribbean see Higman, *Slave Populations of the British Caribbean*.
53. Cf. Neville Hall, 'Slavery in Three West Indian Towns: Christiansted, Fredericksted and Charlotte Amalie in the Late Eighteenth and Early Nineteenth Century' in B.W. Higman (ed.), *Trade Government and Society in Caribbean History 1700–1920* (Kingston, 1983), 19–20.
54. *Bahama Gazette*, 7 June 1799.
55. *Bahama Gazette*, 25–29 Jan. 1799.
56. Carmichael Smyth to Sir George Murray, 8 Mar. 1830, no. 30. C.O. 23/82.
57. Statement to a select committee of the House of Assembly, Dec. 1815.
58. Johnson, *The Bahamas in Slavery and Freedom*, 7.
59. Quoted in Cash, Gordon and Saunders, *Sources of Bahamian History*, 218. Cf. Neville Hall, 'Slavery in Three West Indian Towns', 21.
60. See Johnson, 'The Emergence of a Peasantry in the Bahamas', 183.
61. 'Report on the State and Condition of the Liberated Africans'. Cf. Betty Wood, ' "White Society" and the "Informal" Slave Economies of Lowcountry Georgia, c. 1763–1830', *Slavery and Abolition*, 11 (1990), 321.
62. Carmichael Smyth to Sir George Murray, 8 Mar. 1830, no. 30. C.O. 23/82.
63. Steve J. Stern, 'Feudalism, Capitalism and the World-System in the Perspective of Latin America and the Caribbean', *American Historical Review*, 93 (1988), 854.
64. Higman, *Slave Populations of the British Caribbean*, 237.
65. 'Scuffling' – a word commonly used in contemporary Jamaica – is defined by Ken Post as 'anything and everything done to make a few shillings or even pence, ranging from collecting and selling fruit to theft and prostitution'. Ken Post, *Arise Ye Starvelings: The Jamaican Labour Rebellion of 1938 and its Aftermath* (The Hague, 1978), 135.
66. 'Report on the State and Condition of the Liberated Africans'. Both sterling and dollars (Spanish in origin) were used in the Bahamas during this period, reflecting the confused situation regarding currency which persisted throughout the slavery era. Owing to the severe shortage of sterling, French, Spanish and Dutch silver and gold coins were frequently used.
67. Johnson, 'The Liberated Africans in the Bahamas', 19–20.
68. 'Report on the State and Condition of the Liberated Africans'.
69. *Royal Gazette*, 27 July 1804.

70. Michael Craton, *A History of the Bahamas* (3rd edn, Waterloo, Ontario, 1986), 187–8.
71. Carmichael Smyth to Sir George Murray, 8 Mar. 1830, no. 30. C.O. 23/82.
72. Higman, *Slave Populations of the British Caribbean*, 380.
73. Rebecca J. Scott, *Slave Emancipation in Cuba*, 181.
74. See, for example, the notice which appeared in the *Bahama Gazette*, pointing out that John Fulford or John Tall had run away. It stated: 'He formerly lived in the Negro Town, and is a Jobbing Carpenter by Trade . . .' *Bahama Gazette*, 11 Jan. to 15 Jan. 1799.
75. Sidney W. Mintz, 'Slavery and the Rise of Peasantries', *Historical Reflections*, 6 (1979), 219.
76. 'An Act for Regulating the Hire of Slaves, Carts, Waggons and Drays, and for other purposes therein mentioned', 49 Geo. III, ch. 16 (1808). Cf. Claudia Gale Goldin, *Urban Slavery in the American South, 1820–1860: A Quantitative History* (Chicago, 1976), 38; Neville Hall, 'Slavery in Three West Indian Towns', 27–8; Betty Wood, *Slavery in Colonial Georgia 1730–1775* (Athens, Georgia, 1984), 144.
77. *Bahama Gazette*, 17–21 Jan. 1794.
78. *Royal Gazette*, 27 June 1832.
79. Carmichael Smyth to Viscount Goderich, 2 Aug. 1832, no. 163. C.O. 23/86.
80. See Maurice Dobb, *Studies in the Development of Capitalism* (revised edn, New York, 1963), 51.
81. Thomas Winder to William Colebrooke, 4 Nov. 1836. Enclosure in Colebrooke to Glenelg, 15 Nov. 1836, no. 116. C.O. 23/97.

II

Counteracting Freedom

Contract
&
Coercion

9

Between Slavery & Free Labour

Early Experiments with Free Labour
& Patterns of Slave Emancipation
in Brazil & Cuba

LUCIA LAMOUNIER

In the first half of the nineteenth century the relatively diversified economies of Cuba and São Paulo were transformed to economies producing the main export staples, sugar and coffee. Large plantations based on servile labour came to characterize production in both areas – the sugar mill (*ingenio*) in Cuba and the coffee estate (*fazenda*) in Brazil. The rapid growth of plantation export production coincided with the abolition of the transatlantic slave trade, and this dictated that Cuba and Brazil consider alternative sources and forms of labour. Despite differences arising from colonial relationships, type of crop, and the form of land holding, both countries adopted similar policies on labour recruitment and control – policies which aimed to replace or supplement slave labour, as well as to effect a gradual transition from slave to free labour.

The labour supply crisis began sooner and was more acute in Cuba than in São Paulo. This reflected the fact that although Spain resisted British pressure against the slave trade, supplies were affected from the mid-1840s when the great expansion in sugar production was taking place. In São Paulo, by contrast, coffee production expanded in the 1850s when the planters were well supplied from the African and the internal slave trade. Both Cuba and São Paulo began experimenting with alternative labour supplies, however, in the mid-1840s. Later, as the last major slave-owning economies in the Americas, both countries were subjected to international pressures for abolition, and each took note of the other's efforts to manage the transition.

Cuba

Beginning in the 1790s Spanish colonial authorities, alarmed by the slave revolt in Haiti, began encouraging attempts to attract white settlers to Cuba. The Royal Economic Society (*Real Sociedad Económica de Amigos del País*) advised in 1794 that 'although for the general development of the island the introduction of slaves should be favoured, it is necessary to proceed carefully ... in order that the number of Negroes may ... be prevented from exceeding that of whites'.[1] Although Spanish immigrants were preferred, it was impossible to attract enough, and a decree on October 21, 1817, issued close to the date on which Spain and England signed a treaty to end the slave trade, permitted non-Spanish Catholic immigration. In the next two decades strategic colonies of whites were set up in various parts of the island, intended to protect coastal areas and to prevent the formation of settlements of runaway slaves (*palenques*) in the interior. Meantime a flow of other white immigrants entered the colony – a few wealthy refugees from Santo Domingo, Louisiana and Florida, and large numbers of labourers from Spain and the Canary Islands, who came to build the railways. Some 35,000 immigrants entered Cuba between 1834 and 1839.[2]

As pressure against the slave trade mounted, the fear of slave rebellions continued, but immigrants increasingly came to be seen as an alternative source of labour to slaves on the expanding plantations. In 1842 the Board for the Promotion of White Immigration was abolished and the task of encouraging the immigration of Europeans was assigned to the Council for Economic Development (*Junta de Fomento*). Prizes were offered to planters who settled white families on their land and to sugar mills employing exclusively white labour, and a contract was signed with the Domingo Goicuria company for the importation of labourers from Spain. The council agreed to pay 32 pesos towards the travel expenses of each immigrant and to furnish him with food and lodging for a month, plus 8 pesos in cash. The immigrants were to repay half of the expenses advanced and remain in Cuba for three years.[3]

Results were not encouraging. In June 1846 the council reported all these efforts had brought only 1,673 immigrants to Cuba, including 600 coolies contracted from China. The council calculated that about 20–30,000 labourers were required to supply the needs of agriculture.[4] By this time plans for the settlement of white smallholders in the island had assumed a secondary place. Smallholders, although desirable in theory, might challenge planter control of land and restrict land available for sugar production. In any case, colonies of white farmers were unlikely to help solve the labour problem on the plantations.

Further attempts to attract whites to Cuba were primarily intended to increase the supply of workers for sugar plantations. By the late 1840s and 1850s a variety of plans to promote this sort of immigration were submitted to the council by private enterprises.[5] Most schemes were similar to the plan first agreed with the Goicuria company. Most of the immigrant workers came from Spain and its possessions, some with their families. On their arrival workers stayed in 'hostels' while awaiting hire. If they did not find a job within a month they were to be employed on public works and paid 4 pesos a month. Contracts were to be for three or five years, and the council indemnified for travel expenses.

Recruitment of Spanish contract workers generally proved to be unsuccessful in providing labour on plantations. Most quickly rejected the terms of their contracts and sought employment in the cities, and a great number of conflicts between planters and workers were reported. Planters complained about non-fulfilment of contracts, demands for higher wages and desertions. Workers complained about bad treatment, non-compliance with contracts terms, low pay and difficulties in repaying debts.[6] There were also conflicts between the Council for Economic Development and the contractors. Overall, despite recurrent efforts to bring white immigrants to expand the plantation labour supply, prior to the 1880s most white immigrants came on their own initiative and engaged in non-plantation activities.

At mid-century the use of free wage labourers on the plantations was marginal. Gangs were commonly hired to clear frontier land of forest or brush. Free men were also employed in administration and supervision, or as cattle tenders (*boyeros*).[7] But field labour was the exclusive domain of slaves, who often worked also as blacksmiths, coopers, carpenters or masons. The search for an alternative source of labour was no doubt stimulated by the dramatic temporary decline in the slave trade immediately following an 1845 treaty between Spain and Britain. British Commissioners at Havana estimated that 10,000 African slaves arrived in 1844; only 1,300 were landed in 1845, 1,500 in 1846, 1,000 in 1847, and 1,500 in 1848. In 1849, however, slave imports increased to 8,700.[8]

This coincided with a rapid expansion in Cuban sugar production, which increased from 205,608 metric tons in 1846 to 462,000 metric tons in 1855.[9] The increased demand for labour meant higher prices for slaves. In 1847 slaves were sold for 500 pesos or hired for 14 pesos for a term; in 1852 it was observed: 'today the selling price is 700, and for hiring 20 pesos during the harvest [*zafra*]'.[10] With the shortage of field labour by the end of the 1840s, efforts began to be made to bring in new groups of labourers, such as Indians from Yucatan and the Chinese.

The first 175 Yucatecans arrived in March 1849, contracted by Carlos Tolmé. They were followed by another 75, all prisoners sold by the Governor of Yucatan. Purchased at 25 pesos a head, their market price in Cuba afterwards reached up to 100 pesos. According to Corbitt, some 2,000 Yucatecans were imported into Cuba during the next decade, some of whom were obtained by kidnapping. However, although it is difficult to determine the number of Yucatecans introduced in the island, they remained a tiny proportion of the population.[11]

Chinese immigration seemed to provide another source of cheap labour. In 1846 the Council for Economic Development entered into an agreement with Zulueta and Company to import into Cuba 600 Chinese under eight-year contracts. Domingo Goicuria criticized this plan on the grounds that there were economic as well as political advantages to using white immigrant workers. According to Goicuria, while the Chinese cost the council 170 pesos (70 pesos of which would be reimbursed by planters), Europeans contracted for three years cost the council only 45 pesos, half of which would be repaid by the labourer. The Committee on White Population, however, stated that work on plantations required draconian regulations that were not suited to Europeans, and argued that experience in other Caribbean islands showed Chinese or free Africans were more appropriate replacements for slaves.[12]

The first Chinese contract workers arrived in June 1847, and were divided into lots of ten and distributed to planters.[13] After this initial group arrived, international protests and other difficulties led to the discontinuance of the importation of Chinese for about six years. When the trade in 'coolies' resumed in the early 1850s, new contractors and new conditions were agreed upon by the council. Planters now were to pay 125 pesos for each Chinese worker contracted and repay the agent the expenses advanced to the worker. In addition, it was stipulated the Chinese were to be between 15–40 years of age, and that one fifth of the Chinese should be women, whom the planters were obliged to buy at the same ratio. The Chinese workers were contracted for eight years at 4 pesos a month for men and 3 pesos for women, plus food, shelter, two changes of clothing a year, and medical assistance. Wages were not to be suspended if sickness lasted less than 15 days.[14]

Just as earlier there had been concerns about the size of the black slave population, in this period Spain had reservations about the unlimited importation of Chinese workers. There was also international opposition to the continuance of the 'coolie' trade. Uprisings were reported in Shanghai against contracting Chinese for work in foreign countries, and there was virulent press opposition in Hong Kong and Macao. Investigations were made by the Chinese government into the conditions of engagement and the voyages, and incidents involving the Chinese authorities and British and Spanish consular agents occurred.[15]

Nevertheless, with new regulations and international agreements, the trade continued for more than a decade, ending only in 1874 when the Chinese Government halted further emigration of Chinese contract workers to Cuba. Between 1847 and 1874, a period coinciding with the last years of the transatlantic slave trade, some 125,000 Chinese were landed in Cuba. The majority were men, absorbed by sugar plantations in Matanzas, Cárdenas and Colón. The basic contracts remained the same throughout the period; the pay rarely varied from the norm of 4 pesos monthly, while wages for non-contracted unskilled labour in the island ranged between 17 and 25 pesos a month. Like the slaves, the Chinese were housed in huts or barracks, organized into gangs, and sent to work under armed overseers in the fields and mills.[16] The price of contracted Chinese oscillated between 340 and 425 pesos, while the price of slaves was 500 to 600 pesos.[17] The object was clearly to make contract labour as cheap as slave labour, and possibly more productive.

To enforce the contracts severe regulations were issued; the 1849 Regulation ensured 'discipline and subordination' with flogging, leg irons, shackles and stocks.[18] The Captain General explained that as blacks outnumbered the whites within the island, they required firm control; Asiatics and Yucatecans also belonged to the coloured class, and to treat them as equals of whites would cause great disruptions and disorders.[19] Regulations were softened somewhat in 1854; corporal punishment was prohibited and replaced by imprisonment and loss of wages. Marriage, the sanctity of the family, the right to acquire property, and the worker's right to redeem the debt early were protected.[20]

These regulations, though clearly favouring the interests of planters, did open a precarious space for workers to struggle against the harsh conditions. Accustomed to slavery and to a minimum of interference in plantation affairs, planters were astonished and furious when they faced official inquiries following complaints about mistreatment, non-payment of wages, excessive length of working hours, quantity and quality of food, and the like. However, the legal resources available to contract workers were minimal. Living in the countryside, prohibited from leaving the estates without permission, with a different language and culture, Chinese workers suffered constantly from injustice and corrupt practices. Corporal punishment continued to be used despite the prohibition, and the patron's influence remained paramount. The responses of the Chinese ranged from legal complaints to rebellion and flight, or to more desperate acts such as suicide or murder of overseers on the plantations. Flight was common, and it is said that the Chinese ran away five to seven times more frequently than slaves.[21]

Under yet another set of regulations (1860), Chinese workers who had completed the eight-years contract were obliged to re-contract themselves or to leave the island at their own expense.[22] The colonial office in Madrid explained that this was a mechanism 'to prevent them from constituting an independent race or class in the Island'. It was feared that the natural propensity of the Chinese was towards industry and commerce rather than agriculture, and given the freedom to do so they would abandon fieldwork, worsening the problem of rural labour shortage.[23]

Although by the 1860s a greater heterogeneity characterized the plantation labour force in Cuba, with indentured Asians, Yucatecans, and wage workers supplementing slave labour, there remained a shortage of field-hands. One possible labour source which was little used was the rapidly growing number of free persons of colour. By the 1860s the free coloured, the recently manumitted in addition to the descendants of slaves liberated generations earlier, represented 16 per cent of the total island population.[24] The majority lived in the western department, where they usually worked as artisans, domestics and day labourers in towns and cities. A great number also lived on the small farms in the east of the island producing food staples, cattle and tobacco.[25] The few employed on plantations generally performed administrative and supervisory tasks, since the Cuban elite and Spanish government were apprehensive about mixing free blacks and slaves on the plantations. The historian Pezuela wrote that it would be 'dangerous, imprudent and impolitic' to do so. More effective than prohibitions, however, may have been the reluctance of free blacks, like free Spanish workers, to work on the estates. The harsh conditions of plantation labour and its association with slavery, as well as the availability of land in frontier zones, made it unappealing.[26]

Owned or rented slaves continued to be the main labour force on Cuban plantations until the abolition of slavery, pressure for which was mounting by the 1870s. Most proposals for the abolition of slavery put forward from the 1830s to the 1860s usually recommended gradual, individual manumissions similar to the traditional method of freeing slaves in Spanish law through self-purchase (*coartación*). The gradual process of achieving freedom through self-purchase was assumed to inculcate in the slaves various characteristics such as thrift, hard work and self-discipline, and thus to prepare them for the free labour market.

When laws to dismantle slavery were passed in the 1870s, such ideas of gradual abolition linking general emancipation with individual manumissions were part of the strategy. The Moret Law, a preparatory bill for the gradual abolition of slavery, was approved by the Spanish Cortes on July 4, 1870, during the first large-scale struggle for Cuban independence, the Ten Years' War (1868–78). Although the question of slavery was not directly concerned with the independence struggle, the insurgents had declared immediate emancipation as a way of recruiting slaves into their army and seeking international support. Spain's response was the Moret Law, which freed all slaves over the age of 60 and children born to slave mothers after 1868. The free born were to be under the tutelage of the mother's master, who should provide for maintenance and assistance, and who was allowed to use their labour without remuneration up to the age of 18. The law also stipulated that a proposal for gradual, indemnified emancipation of remaining slaves was to be submitted to the Cortes, including representatives from Cuba, after the end of the war.[27] As was observed by Minister Moret, the intention of the law was to handle problems created by the insurgents while retaining the loyalty of Cuban planters. Consideration of the major issues of the transition to free labour could be discussed only when peace had been restored to the island.[28]

The Spanish government clearly was concerned to avoid any disruption of sugar production which might reduce colonial revenues. Nevertheless the provisions of the Moret Law tended to disturb the social order of slavery by making it possible for slaves to bring complaints against their masters to the authorities. Scott points out that although the law did not free significant numbers of slaves of working age, it created a lever that some slaves could use to help bring about their emancipation. It also weakened the labour discipline exercised by the planters.[29]

Thus in the 1870s young and elderly slaves were freed by decree. Others, particularly in the cities and in the east, gained freedom through litigation or self-purchase, and many slaves became free as a result of the war. Having given freedom to slaves who had served the loyalist cause, by the pact that ended the war, Spain also freed those who had fought for the insurgents.[30] The result was a sharp drop in number of slaves, from over 360,000 in 1867 to 200,000 in 1877. But sugar production remained heavily dependent on slavery.[31] According to the 1877 agricultural census about 72 per cent of the workers on the sugar plantations were still slaves owned by the planters for whom they worked. Free workers, rented slaves and Chinese made up the remainder.[32]

At the beginning of the 1880s, further pressure for another step to end slavery resulted in the establishment of the Patronship system (*Patronato*). Based on a belief in gradualism, the *patronato* represented an intermediate stage between slavery and freedom. Former slaves (*patrocinados*), still owed labour to their masters (*patronos*) but were to receive a token wage. The system envisaged the gradual liberation of slaves lasting until 1888, but in the event all *patrocinados* were freed by 1886. The law helped the *patrocinados* to achieve full freedom by various means, including mutual agreement between former slave and master, renunciation by master, self-purchase and so forth.[33]

The ending of slavery was accompanied by a transformation of the system of sugar production in Cuba. During the 1880s cane and sugar production came to be increasingly dominated by the *colonato*, the term used in Cuba to describe the system whereby large and small cane farmers, landowners and tenants, contracted sugar processing to a single mill and were paid in cash or kind.[34] This system, together with a steady stream of immigrant Spanish cane-cutters (224,000 in all in the period 1882–94, of whom about one third became resident) largely solved the labour problem.[35]

Sâo Paulo

During the first decades of the century, as was the case in Cuba, there were many attempts to attract white immigrants as smallholders to Brazil. Germans, Swiss and Azoreans were settled on crown lands in various parts of the country in official colonies (*núcleos colonias*). Colonization was designed to create a free-holding peasantry and to lessen the proportion of Africans, who were considered culturally and racially inferior, in the total population. However, aside from the difficulty of obtaining well located, fertile land on which to settle smallholders, colonization did not address the problem of the need to find workers for the plantations.[36]

In Sâo Paulo as in Cuba, the 'labour question' was triggered by the rapid growth in plantation production although, as indicated above, the chronology was different. Until nearly the middle of the century Sâo Paulo had a diversified agricultural production including cotton, manioc, corn, cattle, horses and pigs, as well as sugar. Coffee production expanded dramatically in the province only after the end of the transatlantic slave trade.[37] A difficulty faced by Sâo Paulo planters was the labour-intensive nature of all aspects of coffee production. In Cuba, with the adoption of new technology, sugar planters were able to substitute capital for labour in the mills, but this option was not available to coffee producers. With the coming of railways Sâo Paulo coffee planters were able to substitute capital for labour in the shipping of plantation products, but on the plantation itself there were few such opportunities.[38]

For a time planters in areas of expanding coffee plantations, mainly in the new frontier areas, hoped that European immigrants would replace slaves. In 1850 the Euzébio de Queiróz law suppressing the transatlantic trade and the Land Law, which controlled the sale of crown lands and attempted to regulate the acquisition of land by immigrants, were passed. These laws reveal that in official policy by this time the importation of immigrants to work on plantations already took precedence over settlement by smallholders.[39]

Some planters began experimenting with free labour in the 1840s, although retaining large numbers of slaves, while other planters were dependent exclusively on slave labour up to the 1880s. Different forms of labour often existed on individual plantations. There were slaves, domestic free labourers and immigrants all at one time or another working as field-hands or seasonal harvesters. It is therefore difficult to show a clear chronological progression in the forms of rural labour in Sâo Paulo. Although slavery remained the predominant form of plantation labour until abolition, substantial numbers of free workers were employed in areas specializing in food staples. Generally, free labour was used in the plantation sector only in clearly defined circumstances. First, free labour was invariably used for clearing virgin land. Second, free workers were responsible for administration and supervision on the estates. Third, in some plantations the semi-skilled work-force, for example carpenters, masons and blacksmiths, consisted of free labour (domestic and immigrant). Such people may also have grown crops on their own, or worked as sharecroppers. When planters became involved in projects to attract immigrant workers the nature of the schemes changed substantially over time. At least three distinct forms of organizing immigrant labour on the plantations arose between the 1840s and 1880s: sharecropping; labour-leasing (*locaçao de serviços*); and finally the Brazilian form of the *colonato*.

The first experiments with immigrant plantation labour took place in Sâo

Paulo in the late 1840s, when Nicolau Vergueiro, planter, senator and sometime minister, attempted to settle European immigrants on his land under a sharecropping system. In the early sharecropping system planters advanced an immigrant's cost of transportation from Europe, as well as funds for the purchase of tools and foodstuffs needed until the first harvest. On the plantations the sharecroppers were assigned a number of coffee bushes to tend, and were also allotted a subsistence plot on which they could grow their own food. The net profit yielded by the sale of the coffee was shared, half and half, by planter and immigrant, each also receiving half of the production of the food plots in excess of subsistence needs. Advances to the immigrants, on which interest was charged, would be re-paid out of income. The initial contracts did not specify a particular period of time, but immigrants could not legally move off the plantation until they had repaid their debts.[40]

According to Stolcke and Hall, planters adopted the sharecropping system in São Paulo because in a situation of scarce labour it was more efficient than a wage system. Since remuneration was in the form of proportion of the product this gave an incentive for the labourer to work hard and cultivate with great care, and little supervision was required. It was anticipated that sharecroppers would tend more coffee bushes than would wage labourers. Hence, fewer workers would be required and the initial investment would be lower. The immigrant families constituted a cheap labour reserve, and the assignment of subsistence plots was another way of reducing costs.[41]

In the early 1850s, the successful results obtained initially with share-cropping immigrants on Vergueiro's plantation encouraged many Paulista planters in the pioneering Western areas to follow this example. In total about 50 São Paulo coffee planters established European immigrants on their land between 1847 and 1874, and although slave labour continued to be predominant, some estates had large, free labour forces. Where free workers coexisted with slaves the tasks of each group were usually kept strictly defined and separate. Tasks which required constant supervision or were inappropriate for sharecropping continued to be performed by slaves. Such work included soil preparation, planting coffee seedlings, sowing annual crops for plantation consumption, and later, increasingly, the processing of coffee.[42]

By the 1860s the policy of setting up sharecropping colonies came to be considered a failure.[43] It took years to repay the debt to the landowner since the sharecroppers' returns from coffee cultivation turned out to be lower than expected. The money income of the immigrant was vulnerable, dependent on the productivity of the trees under his care and the prevailing world coffee prices. In addition, the system was open to mistrust and fraud, since it was the planter who controlled operations such as weighing, shipping and selling. Conflicts and discontent were therefore present from the beginning. The growing disillusionment of immigrants with their living and working conditions was expressed in various ways. For instance, in 1855 the owner of Morro Azul estate, Joaquim Franco de Camargo, dismissed 14 families for 'vagrancy', 'intrigue' and 'theft'. At the same time he reported that another eight families had departed without permission. The most serious incident occurred in December 1856, involving Swiss and German workers on Senator Vergueiro's plantation, Ibicaba. The workers complained of grave irregularities in the fulfilment of their contracts, a list of grievances was drawn up and presented to Vergueiro, and an official investigation was requested.[44] The event provoked a number of inquiries, and several European governments, including Prussia and Switzerland, prohibited emigration to Sâo Paulo.

Planters responded to this unrest at first by making minor changes to the terms of contracts. Subsequently they sought to provide greater control of productivity, increase discipline, and ensure debt repayment by demanding more severe mechanisms of coercion to oblige the workers to fulfil contractual obligations. The labour-leasing (*locaçao de serviços*) law issued in 1837 provided for punishment by imprisonment of those evading contractual obligations. But imprisonment did not solve the problem of immigrant workers' debts, nor help the shortage of labour, and the planters also saw a need for stronger methods of dealing with a collective refusal to work. However, despite planter demands for more rigorous regulations, the government was reluctant to act because of the necessity of attracting further European immigrants. When in 1879 the government did approve a severe piece of legislation on rural labour relations, it was aimed mainly at the Chinese and domestic labour force.[45]

After the 1860s, sharecropping was gradually replaced by labour-leasing contracts. Instead of receiving a share of the value of production, labourers were paid a fixed piece-rate for each measure of coffee harvested from the trees under their care. The landowner retained the right to one half of the food crops cultivated by the immigrant, reduced the size of the food plot, and sometimes charged a rent for it.[46] This was intended to discourage workers from diverting labour away from coffee to food crops, which sharecroppers had frequently done in protest at what they saw as an unfair contract. Nevertheless, although the new arrangement reduced some of the planters' risks from sharecropping, it did not solve the problem of the burden of initial debt and the recovery of the planters' investment.[47]

The problem of debt was not removed until the 1880s when the provincial and Imperial governments began to subsidize European immigration to Sâo Paulo. At this time an arrangement termed *colonato*, like the system in Cuba, became standard in western Sâo Paulo. In Brazil the *colonato* system consisted of a complex system of remuneration which combined task and piece-rates with subsistence plots. By establishing a fixed rate for the number of coffee trees cultivated, separate from the harvest piece-rate, the labourers were guaranteed some income independent of coffee yields, and encouraged to cultivate more trees. This system, which prevailed until the

1950s, guaranteed a supply of plantation labour and protected immigrants from some of the abuses of the old sharecropping system.[48]

Back in the 1850s, however, with the initial failure of schemes to attract sufficient European sharecroppers, coffee planters in southern Brazil sought to solve the problem of labour shortage by other methods. One measure adopted by many was the purchase of slaves from the decaying north-eastern sugar plantations, a practice which increased considerably over the next decades.[49] The interprovincial slave trade helped to meet the immediate needs of São Paulo coffee producers, but ultimately undermined the survival of slavery. As slaves were drained from the north-east, the political support base for slavery contracted. Brazilian planters during this period were also looking at other possible solutions to the labour problem. Importation of Chinese contract workers, following the example of experiments in Peru, Cuba and some British colonies, was one possibility. Despite numerous proposals, however, Chinese workers were imported into Brazil in relatively small numbers. Only at the end of the 1870s was a more serious initiative taken, when, despite local opposition, a mission was sent to China. However, this resulted in a fiasco, a failure accounted for mainly by international opposition.[50]

Recruitment of the large domestic free labour force was also under consideration during the whole period. In contrast to Cuba, Brazilian policy makers repeatedly suggested the use of local free white and coloured labourers as an alternative or supplement to slave labour. Whether by natural reproduction, immigration or manumission, Brazil had a large and growing free population, white and black. In most provinces of Brazil, the number of free people always outnumbered that of slaves. In São Paulo, despite the great increase in slave population demanded by the expansion of coffee production, slaves constituted no more than one third of the total population. Even in the main areas of coffee production, the free population was a majority.[51] Among the coloured population, the number who were free grew vigorously even in the new coffee regions of São Paulo and Rio de Janeiro. The proportion of free persons within the total coloured population of Brazil during the 1870s is estimated to have been between 40 and 60 per cent.[52] Some of these people were employed in coffee production. References to the employment of Brazilian free workers, white and coloured, in the export sector were frequent in the nineteenth century. Many were tenants allowed the use of marginal estate lands in return for occasional labour services (*agregados*). In addition independent workers hired for a daily wage (*camaradas*) and so forth were common in coffee estates and were usually employed during harvesting. They also grew subsistence crops for the plantation.[53]

By the 1870s the certainty that the end of slavery was coming made the use of Brazilian free workers increasingly appealing, while laws were passed to gradually transform the slaves to free workers. The 1871 Free Womb Law, while freeing the newborn (*ingênuos*), also freed other slaves (*libertos*)

195

selected by lottery under certain conditions. Planters were guaranteed the free-borns' labour until they reached the age of 21, to indemnify the planters for the cost of maintaining the free-born children of slave mothers. Others freed under the law were required to sign a seven-year contract with their former masters.[54] From this time, changes in the pattern of manumission may have also changed labour relations. Manumission had a long tradition in Brazil, but Peter Eisenberg has recently argued that the manumission pattern changed in the last decades of slavery. The number of manumissions increased and the majority of newly freed were now working-age black males, whereas the manumissions registered earlier were mostly of female, mulatto slaves, either very young or old and working in domestic service. The most common form of manumission was the granting of freedom in exchange for money (self-purchase), or services payment (a labour contract) or a combination of these. Manumission practice in Brazil remained a matter of custom rather than law until formally covered by the provisions of the Free Womb Law. After this manumission papers were issued with service obligations which resembled work contracts specifying the number of years (up to seven) as established by the law.[55]

Following the Free Womb Law another piece of legislation was issued which related strictly to free labour. This was the 1879 Labour Law (*lei de locaçao de serviços de 1879*), an attempt to regulate contracts signed by Brazilians, immigrants and freedmen engaged in agricultural work. The law established distinct conditions for each of these categories of workers. For instance the length of contracts: three years for European immigrants; five for Brazilians; and seven years for freedmen. It provided heavy punishments (prison and forced labour) for those breaking contracts and participating in collective resistance to work. This was the first anti-strike legislation in Brazil. At the same time, provisions against vagrancy and strict control over the movement of freedmen were discussed.[56]

Nevertheless, the 1880s witnessed developments which ensured the 1879 labour law was never effectively enforced and was revoked in 1890.[57] The law was abandoned with the arrival of thousands of immigrants entering the country in family groups, who were seen as a cheaper and more productive form of labour than the contract workers. Between 1884 and 1914 some 900,000 subsidized immigrants, mainly from Italy, arrived in Sâo Paulo, and most went to work on coffee plantations. The mass immigration programme promoted and subsidized by the provincial government and the *colonato* system not only helped Sâo Paulo coffee planters to finally abolish slavery in 1888, but at the same time it created the conditions for sustaining coffee production in the province.[58]

Conclusion

Although, as noted earlier, there were significant differences in the timing of changes, it is easy to draw parallels between the Cuban and Sâo Paulo experience of the transition from slavery to free labour. In both areas white immigration was first sought mainly to counteract the growing black slave population. Racial prejudice was a major motivation, and European settlers were to become industrious, independent small landholders, providing racial balance and political stability.

These considerations soon came to be outweighed in both areas by the growing problem of the scarcity of cheap labour when expansion of the plantations coincided with growing external pressures to end the trans-atlantic slave trade. In each country the planters were also quickly disillusioned with European immigrants, who were viewed as expensive and inefficient in terms of plantation requirements, although many attempts were made to use free white immigrants. The continuance of slavery in itself, along with the harsh conditions on estates, played an important role in frustrating these schemes. European workers were repelled by the association of plantation work with slavery. Moreover, land availability in frontier zones made it difficult to bind a free labourer to estates. Sugar and coffee required a large number of seasonal workers. Without mechanisms such as enforceable labour contracts and repressive legislation planters did not see how they could secure cheap, disciplined and docile labour. In Cuba, Spanish workers refused to accept harsh contract conditions and deserted the plantations. In São Paulo, immigrant sharecroppers resisted and their protests resulted in European governments proscribing emigration to São Paulo.

In both areas non-European groups such as Chinese and Africans were then turned to as sources of inexpensive labour. Racial prejudice continued to operate, enabling these workers to be seen as an alternative which permitted repressive legislation and tight contracts; these 'labour machines' were temporary expedients to ease the transition to free labour. Less pressured than their Cuban counterparts, Brazilian coffee planters turned to domestic labour while continuing to staff their plantations with slaves through the interprovincial trade. In Cuba slaves were still entering the island at a much later date than was the case for Brazil. Another main expedient in Cuba was the importation of non-European contract workers, mostly Chinese. Again, terms of service were so bad that workers rebelled and protests resulted in the Chinese government cutting off recruitment. But by this time, a considerable number of contract workers had already entered the island and helped to supplement the existing supply of plantation labour.

Gradual abolition of slavery began to be implemented in both areas in the 1870s. By this time a variety of experiments with different labour systems had led to an increasing debate over the labour question in each country, and concepts fashioned in the earlier experience with non-slave labour shaped ideas of freedom and emancipation. While the Moret Law in Cuba and the Free Womb Law in Brazil initiated the process of freeing the slaves, each established a gradual and controlled process of emancipation. By such methods as individual manumissions and long service contracts to bind former slaves to the plantations, policy makers and planters set up a framework for gradual abolition and transition to wage labour without disrupting the existing economic and political order.

In both Cuba and Sâo Paulo the abolition of slavery coincided with large-scale European immigration which eliminated the labour problem on the plantations. Abolition also entailed a considerable change in the organization of sugar production in Cuba, and to some extent also the coffee production in Sâo Paulo. However, along with these changes, it was the experiments with free labour in earlier years which led to the gradualist policies implemented in the 1870s and 1880s, and eventually helped to effect a relatively non-violent transition to free labour in each country.

Notes

The present essay resulted from a preliminary analysis of data gathered for the author's dissertation, to be submitted at London School of Economics, University of London. The author would like to thank Mary Turner and Colin Lewis for their helpful suggestions and comments. The research has been supported by the Conselho Nacional de Pesquisa e Desenvolvimento Técnico (CNPq, Brazil), the Universidad Estadual Paulista, and the Central Research Fund, University of London.

1. Duvon C. Corbitt, 'Immigration in Cuba', *Hispanic American Historical Review*, 22 (May 1942): 284.
2. Arthur F. Corwin, *Spain and the Abolition of Slavery in Cuba, 1817–1886* (Austin, 1967), 33; Corbitt, 'Immigration', 294.
3. Corbitt, 'Immigration', 298; Julio LeRiverend, *Historia Económica de Cuba*, 4th edn (La Habana, 1985), 329; Archivo Nacional de Cuba (ANC), Fondo Real Consulado y Junta de Fomento, leg. 194 contains copies of various Goincuria's contracts. See for instance n. 8679 and n. 8688.
4. Informe Junta de Fomento de Agricultura y Comercio, June 18, 1846. Archivo Historico Nacional (AHN), Madrid, Ultramar, leg. 91, n. 1, exp. 8.
5. See for instance the Goicuria's project to import Germans and Scots submitted to the Junta's Committee on White Population, in ANC, Fondo Real Consulado y Junta de Fomento, leg. 195, n. 8729; and Feijóo Sotomayor to import Galicians. Urbano Feijóo Sotomayor, *Isla de Cuba* (Madrid, 1855).
6. See for instance, ANC, Fondo Real Consulado, leg. 197, n. 8856 and n. 8864.
7. Laird W. Bergad, *Cuban Rural Society in the Nineteenth Century. The Social and Economic History of Monoculture in Matanzas* (Princeton, 1990), 245–6.
8. David R. Murray, *Odious Commerce, Britain, Spain and the Abolition of the Cuban Slave Trade* (Cambridge, 1980), 244, table 9.
9. Rebecca J. Scott, *Slave Emancipation in Cuba. The Transition to Free Labor, 1860–1899* (Princeton, 1985), 36, table 8.
10. Fiscal Olivares, Habana, February 29, 1852, AHN, Ultramar, leg. 85, n. 1, exp. 6.
11. Scott, *Slave Emancipation*, 7, table 1; LeRiverend, *Historia*, 344; Corbitt, 'Immigration', 302.
12. ANC, Fondo Real Consulado, leg. 195, n. 8706.
13. Corbitt, *A Study of the Chinese in Cuba 1847–1947* (Wilmore, 1971), 4. The contracts bound the workers for eight years, at a wage of 4 pesos a month plus daily maintenance and clothing. The cost of transportation from China was to be repaid by the worker through a deduction of 1 peso a month from his wage. Juan Perez de la Riva, *Para la historia de las gentes sin historia* (Barcelona, 1976), 112–13. On the experience of Asian workers in Peru see Michael J. Gonzales' essay in this volume.
14. AHN, Ultramar, leg. 185, no. 1, exp. 1. The profitability of the trade of importing workers to the island is revealed by the number of plans submitted to the Council for Economic Development. Between 1852 and 1858 the council received at least 30 petitions to import Chinese, and in 1860 there were 40. Corbitt, *A Study of the Chinese*, 15, 18.
15. See reports of the Consul General de España in Macao to Ministro de Guerra y Ultramar, May 7, 1859 and September 9, 1859, AHN, Ultramar, leg. 85, no. 6, exp. 6 and 7.
16. Scott, *Slave Emancipation*, 29.

17. Juan Pérez de La Riva, *El Barracón: Esclavitud y Capitalismo en Cuba* (Barcelona: 1978), 109.
18. 1849 Reglamento, reproduced in Corbitt, *A Study of the Chinese*, 67-9.
19. AHN, Ultramar, leg. 91, no. 1, exp. 8.
20. 1854 Regulation, reproduced in Juan Jimenez Pastrana, *Los Chinos en las luchas por la liberación Cubana, 1847-1930* (La Habana, 1963), 130-40.
21. Pérez de La Riva, *El Barracón*, 121.
22. 1860 Regulation, reproduced in Jimenez Pastrana, *Los Chinos*, 140-52.
23. AHN, Ultramar, leg. 85, no. 7.
24. Franklin Knight, 'Cuba' in David W. Cohen and Jack P. Greene (eds), *Neither Slave nor Free. The Freedmen of African Descent in the Slave Societies of the New World* (Baltimore and London, 1972), 284, table 9.1.
25. Scott, *Slave Emancipation*, 8.
26. Jacobo de la Pezuela, *Necesidades de Cuba* (Madrid, 1865), 114-15. According to Fé Iglesias García the population residing on sugar mills in 1862 was 79 per cent slaves and liberated Africans (*emancipados*), 19 per cent Whites and Asians, and only 2 per cent free blacks, 'The Development of Capitalism in Cuban Sugar Production: 1860-1900' in M.M. Fraginals, Frank Moya Pons and Stanley L. Engerman, *Between Slavery and Free Labour: the Spanish Speaking Caribbean in the Nineteenth Century* (Baltimore and London, 1985), 58.
27. The Moret Law is reproduced in Hortensia Pichardo (ed.), *Documentos para la Historia de Cuba* (Havana, 1965), 394-7.
28. *Diario de las sesiones de las Cortes Constituyentes*, Tomo XIII, June 10, 1870, 8768 and May 28, 1870, Apendice Primero al num. 292, 8417.
29. Scott, *Slave Emancipation*, 73.
30. R. Scott, 'Gradual Abolition and the Dynamics of Slave Emancipation in Cuba, 1868-86', *Hispanic American Historical Review*, 63, 3 (1983): 456.
31. Scott, *Slave Emancipation*, 87, table 10.
32. Scott, 'Gradual Abolition', 456.
33. See Scott, *Slave Emancipation*, Part Two, for a detailed examination of the *patronato*, the interaction between *patronos* and *patrocinados* and its results.
34. *Colonato* was a system of land use; *colono* was the individual recruited by the landowner. *Colono* was the term originally applied both to immigrant settlers and to Chinese and Spanish contract workers. In the 1880s however *colono* referred to a sugar-cane grower in the *colonato* system. Cuban *colonos* in the later usage did not comprise a social class; it included both former slaves who rented or owned small plots and large estate owners. Bergad, *Cuban Rural Society*, ch. 15; Scott, *Slave Emancipation*, 208-13.
35. Corbitt, 'Immigration', 304; Scott, *Slave Emancipation*, 217.
36. On attempts to settle colonies on crown lands see Emilia V. da Costa, *The Brazilian Empire, Myths and Histories* (Chicago, 1985), 94-100.
37. See data in Affonso E. Taunay, *História do Café no Brasil* (Rio de Janeiro, 1939), v. III, t. I, 156, 212-15.
38. The impact of railways for São Paulo coffee production is commented on in Taunay, *Historia do Café*, v. IV, t. II, 223; Colin M. Lewis, *Public Policy and Private Initiative. Railway Building in Sao Paulo, 1860-1899* (London, 1991) 19-20; its impact on labour in da Costa, *The Brazilian Empire*, 113-18. For Cuba see M.M. Fraginals, *El Ingenio*, v. I, ch. 4.
39. Robert Conrad, *The Destruction of Brazilian Slavery: 1850-1888* (University of California, 1972), chap 2; da Costa, *The Brazilian Empire*, 78-93.
40. 'Contracto' in T. Davatz, *Memórias de um colono no Brasil*, 2nd edn, (São Paulo, 1951), 223-37; J.J. von Tschudi, *Viagem às Províncias de Rio de Janeiro e São Paulo*, trans. Eduardo de Lima Castro (São Paulo, 1953), 137.
41. Verena Stolcke and Michael M. Hall, 'The Introduction of Free Labour on São Paulo Coffee Plantations', *Journal of Peasant Studies*, 10:2 (1983): 174.
42. Most sharecropping colonists were imported by a firm set up by Vergueiro, an ex-slave-trader. By 1855 about 3,500 immigrants of various origins were located in the province working on 30 plantations. Stolcke and Hall, 'The Introduction of Free Labour on São Paulo Coffee Plantations', 172. Tschudi, *Viagem*, 131, observed that only colonists from Portugal and Azores would consent to work alongside slaves.
43. For explanations of the failure of sharecropping experiments see S. Buarque de Holanda, 'Prefácio' in T. Davatz, *Memórias*; da Costa, *The Brazilian Empire*, 94-100; Warren Dean, *Rio Claro. A Brazilian Plantation System, 1820-1920* (Stanford, 1976), ch. 4; and Stolcke and Hall, 'The Introduction of Free Labour', 170-6.
44. Davatz, *Memórias*, contains a detailed account of the events.
45. M.L. Lamounier, *Da escravidão ao trabalho livre. A lei de locação de serviços de 1879* (São Paulo, 1988), ch. 3.

46. Stolcke and Hall, 'The Introduction of Free Labour', 177. For instance, land leasing on Joaquim Bonifácio do Amaral's contracts stipulated plots of 1,000 *braças quadradas (braça quadrada* = 4,8384 square metres) at $2,000 *réis*. Families were allowed to take up to four plots depending on family size and prices of plots decreased accordingly (four plots of 1,000 *braças quadradas* at $6,000 *réis),* in *Contracto entre o Comendador Joaquim Bonifácio do Amaral e os colonos da sua fazenda de Sete Quedas, no município de Campinas, 186(4),* MSS, Biblioteca Nacional, Rio de Janeiro, II–35, 21, 56 n4. Conflicts over size and price of rents on subsistence plots are reported in *Relatório da Commissao encarregada de examinar as colônias Martyrios e S. Lourenço na Província de S. Paulo* (Rio de Janeiro, Typ. Nacional, 1874), 9–10.
47. Stolcke and Hall, 'The Introduction of Free Labour', 177–80.
48. The term *colono* was first used to describe settlers, then agricultural labourers and in some instances also sharecroppers. Stolcke and Hall, 'The Introduction of Free Labour', 179–86.
49. Conrad, *The Destruction,* Tables 8, 9 and 10.
50. Robert Conrad, 'The Planter Class and the Debate over Chinese Immigration to Brazil, 1850–1893', in *International Migration Review,* 9 (Spring 1975), 41–55; Lamounier, *Da escravidâo,* 128–145.
51. Peter Eisenberg, 'O homem esquecido: o trabalhador livre nacional no seculo XIX: sugestôes para uma pesquisa' in *Homens Esquecidos. Escravos e Trabalhadores Livres no Brasil. Séculos XVIII e XIX* (Campinas, 1989), 224. In São Paulo the percentage of slaves in the population was about 36 per cent in 1837 and about 20 per cent in 1874. Daniel P. Müller. *Ensaio d'un Quadro Estatístico da Província de São Paulo, ordenado pelas leis provinciais de 11 de abril de 1836 e 10 de março de 1837* (São Paulo, 1838) table 5; Conrad, *The Destruction,* table 2. The free coloured in São Paulo corresponded to about 28 per cent of the total free population by mid-1830s and about 32 per cent in 1872. Herbert S. Klein, 'Nineteenth-Century Brazil' in Cohen and Greene, *Neither Slave nor Free,* table 10, 314.
52. As Klein observes this figure is unusually high, particularly if contrasted with the Cuban and US during the period of slavery where the proportions were about 36 per cent and 11 per cent respectively. Natural reproduction as well as a steady process of emancipation might have explained the rapid expansion of free coloured in Brazil. Klein, 'Nineteenth-Century Brazil', 315–17.
53. See Dean, *Rio Claro,* 19–20; Costa, *Da Senzala a Colônia,* 13; Maria Sylvia de Carvalho Franco, *Homens livres na ordem escravocrata,* 2nd edn (São Paulo, 1976) discuss aspects of these relations. In 1854 the work-force of the 2,618 coffee estates existing in the province of Saô Paulo consisted of 55,834 slaves, 4,223 *agregados,* and 2,159 *colonos,* cf. 'Quadro estatístico de alguns establecimentos rurais da provîncia de São Paulo, organizado pelo Brigadeiro José Joaquim Machado de Oliveira', cited in Taunay, *Historia do Café,* v. III, t. I, 134. In one of the major coffee districts, Rio Claro, in 1872 there about 1,700 free persons were employees or tenants on plantations and small farms, compared to 2,753 slaves. In 1876 although 45 plantations in Rio Claro employed some free as well as slave labour there were still 22 other plantations with no free hands. (Dean, *Rio Claro,* 122.) At the end of the 1870s in the Barâo de Souza Queiroz's coffee plantations São Jerônimo and Cresciúmal there were 688 free workers, including 339 Brazilians; in Queiroz's Santa Bárbara colony of 304 free workers, 250 were Brazilians. *Relatórios do Ministerio da Agricultura, Comércio e Obras Públicas* (Rio de Janeiro, 1879), 74–5.
54. Law 2040, September 28, 1871, reproduced in Conrad, *The Destruction,* Appendix 2 and discussed in chap 7; see also Ademir Gebara, *O mercado de trabalho livre no Brasil* (Sâo Paulo, 1986).
55. Peter L. Eisenberg, 'Ficando livre: as alforrias em Campinas no século XIX', *Estudos Economicos,* 17 (2): maio/agosto, 1987, 177, 196, 201–2 and table 9. This study was based on analysis of 2,093 manumission papers (*cartas de alforria*) freeing 2,277 slaves in one of the major coffee districts in São Paulo, during the period 1798 to 1888.
56. Decree 2827, March 15, 1879, *Colleçâo das Leis do Imperio do Brasil, 1879,* 11–20; on the law see Lamounier, *Da escravidâo,* chs 3 and 4.
57. Decree of February 22, 1890, *Decisôes do Governo Provisório.*
58. Stolcke and Hall, 'The Introduction of Free Labour', 182.

10

Resistance Among Asian Plantation Workers in Peru

1870–1920

MICHAEL J. GONZALES

Historians have identified several causes for the destruction of African slavery in the Americas during the nineteenth century. Chief among them are Britain's successful campaign to terminate the slave trade, the unrelenting political pressure of abolitionists and the growing resistance of slaves to their own bondage. The effectiveness of resistance has been demonstrated, in part, by broadening its definition to go beyond obvious acts of defiance, such as armed rebellion and flight, to include destruction of slave owners' property, refusal to work and other actions that undermined the profitability of slavery.[1]

The destruction of slavery was, of course, only the first step toward equality and justice for blacks. Emancipation did not (with the exception of Haiti) destroy the plantation economy or necessarily undermine the political authority of the planter elite. Nor did it result in significant economic rewards or empowerment for former slaves. For planters, the key economic challenge of abolition was to find alternative sources of cheap labour, or to compel blacks to remain on the estates as sharecroppers or poorly paid wage labourers. Planters in the southern United States and on some of the smaller Caribbean islands succeeded in transforming their former slaves into impoverished labourers. Growers elsewhere in the British Caribbean employed a different strategy and imported hundreds of thousands of Indian indentured servants, while their counterparts in Peru and Cuba brought in tens of thousands of Chinese indentured servants. In the case of Peru, planters also imported some 20,000 Japanese contract labourers during the early twentieth century. The arrival of Asian indentured servants helped to maintain the prosperity of plantation economies in these regions, but it also meant that blacks and Asians competed for scarce economic resources. This sometimes resulted in bitter conflicts between the two groups, all to the benefit of planters.

This chapter concerns the experiences of Chinese and Japanese plantation labourers in Peru during the period of transition between indentured and free labour. It focuses on the forms of resistance they employed to combat the planters' system of economic and social control. During the second half of the nineteenth century, planters subjected the Chinese to the same methods of control they had employed with African slaves, such as corporal punishment, imprisonment and execution. Similarly, the Chinese resorted to methods of resistance employed by Africans, such as rebellion, armed assault, feigning illness, refusing to work and running away. Their most extreme individual act of resistance was suicide, which was relatively commonplace. These acts of defiance, combined with the end to the coolie trade and the growing unproductivity of the Chinese, forced planters to seek alternative sources of labour.

The situation of Japanese contract labourers, who partially replaced the Chinese, was significantly different. They were contracted by Japanese emigration companies who maintained agents in Lima and on the estates, and they received some protection from the Japanese government. However, it should also be stressed that planters did not depend exclusively on Japanese labour. They simultaneously recruited Peruvian labourers from nearby peasant communities, which gave them access to a larger labour market and permitted them greater flexibility in social control. They no longer believed, as they did with the Chinese, that they had to resort to violence to hold on to a finite number of labourers. They never completely abandoned the use of these tactics, but they resorted to them less frequently.

The most serious and common dispute involving Japanese labourers occurred when planters, in violation of the standard contract, stopped paying daily wages in favour of paying by piece-work (*tarea*). This, in effect, reduced wages because the Japanese typically were unable to complete their daily assignments. The Japanese protested by complaining to their representatives, threatening to strike and, in some cases, walking out. On those estates that depended most heavily on Japanese labour, these actions earned labourers some temporary rewards.

Resistance and the Decline of African Slavery

There were several reasons why slavery declined in Peru during the nineteenth century. The most important cause was Britain's successful closure of the slave trade by 1810, followed (in no particular order) by very low birth-rates among slaves, self-manumission of artisan-slaves in Lima, and impressment of slaves into both royalist and rebel forces during the wars for independence from Spain (1821–24). It should also be stressed that slaves played a key role in securing their own freedom by running away in large numbers.[2]

When manumission came in 1854, slavery was already a dying institution. The number of slaves had declined from 40,337 in 1792 to 25,505 in 1854, and planters had already begun to import Chinese indentured servants on a large scale. President Ramón Castilla, the slaves' liberator, actually helped planters by granting them a generous indemnification of 300 pesos for each slave freed. Since this exceeded a slave's market value, it gave planters the necessary capital to increase importation of indentured servants.[3]

The absence of estate records and other internal documentation for this period makes it impossible to know all the ways in which Afro-Peruvians resisted slavery. There is abundant evidence in public records and newspapers, however, to show that large numbers of slaves ran away from coastal estates; this undoubtedly undermined the institution of slavery, contributed to the decline of plantation agriculture and hastened the importation of the Chinese. Moreover, many runaways joined the growing number of bandit gangs that terrorized travellers on the roads outside of Lima. The logic of the situation was clear: runaways had already broken the law, there did not exist a 'free zone' to escape to (as in the United States), and banditry was one of the few ways in which runaways could support themselves.

The large-scale flight of slaves began during the wars of independence as opposing armies recruited Afro-Peruvians and the conflict created opportunities for other slaves to run away. This began a pattern that was difficult to break in the decades ahead. Several sugar plantations in the Lima area reported these massive losses of slaves: Villa (80 per cent), Santa Beatriz (45 per cent), Chacra Cerro (54.8 per cent), La Menacho (76 per cent), Infantas (74 per cent), Armendaris (50 per cent), and Monterrico (86 per cent).[4] Moreover, tithe records from the Surco Valley reported 24 of 36 farms had been abandoned,[5] and José María Pando, a knowledgeable contemporary, complained that runaways had caused a general decline of coastal agriculture.[6] For the sugar industry, the result was falling production and reduced capacity to compete for overseas markets in northern South America and the Rio de la Plata.[7]

Court records provide the best available evidence for slaves' motivations for fleeing. In trials involving recaptured slaves, testimony revealed that many fled to escape frequent beatings, over-work, or to reunite with family members. According to Carlos Aguirre, runaways believed that flight was justified to escape masters who had violated mutually understood codes of behaviour. Some of them even believed that they would be vindicated in court and turned over to more benevolent masters. These individuals clearly had some knowledge of Peru's mildly paternalistic laws that theoretically gave slaves some protection against abusive masters. Some runaways were also probably influenced by the ideas of 'liberty' and 'democracy' emanating from the wars of independence. [8]

Court records show that many runaways, especially those from rural areas, joined the numerous bandit gangs that terrorized travellers on coastal highways. Highway robbery was, in fact, predominately a black endeavour, as a full 90 per cent of apprehended bandits were Afro-Peruvian (*zambos*, Negroes, or mulattos). Of these, 40 per cent were escaped slaves and 56.4 per cent had last worked in agriculture. Slaves who had run away from plantations would have been familiar with roads and possible hiding places, while urban runaways had more opportunities to merge into the large free black population in cities and to make a living in petty commerce or crime.[9]

Banditry flourished during the chaos of the early nineteenth century when political authority was undermined by almost constant civil conflict. Bandits proved elusive as they moved hideouts, maintained contacts with plantation slaves (with whom they sometimes traded stolen goods), and blended into the free black population. Frequently operating in gangs of 20 to 40 men, highwaymen also proved difficult to defeat when they were found by public officials.[10]

The most frequent victims of bandits were, according to court records, landlords, merchants, public officials and travellers. However tempting it might be, there is no evidence to suggest that blacks targeted these people for social or political vengeance. Rather, they were simply the most likely persons to be carrying money and other valuables. On the other hand, bandits did invade haciendas and attack landlords, foremen and administrators, sometimes killing those with a reputation for being especially cruel to slaves. This not only settled old accounts but eliminated those most likely to pursue runaways.[11]

Dramatic raids on haciendas in the Lima area significantly damaged plantation agriculture during the 1840s and 1850s. According to Aguirre, violent confrontations in 1854 influenced Castilla's decision to free the slaves.[12] Although this is difficult to prove, banditry undoubtedly frustrated political and business leaders otherwise euphoric over prospects for development and graft arising from the guano boom. The timing seemed especially right to alleviate the problem of banditry through whatever means necessary, including the abolition of slavery. This was especially true if emancipation with indemnification would actually benefit planters by giving them more capital, facilitating the recruitment of a more reliable source of labour. The spectacular profits realized by the Peruvian government and the merchant community from guano would be invested in the 1850s and 1860s in railroad development, modernization of sugar cane plantations and importation of Chinese indentured servants. [13]

Resistance and the Decline of Chinese Servile Labour, 1870–90

China suddenly emerged as an important labour source for the West as a result of a series of domestic tragedies, culminating in the Taiping Rebellion in which perhaps as many as 30 million people lost their lives and millions more became refugees. This situation was then exploited by Chinese warlords, local labour contractors and Portuguese merchants to funnel the desperate into labour markets abroad. The so-called coolie trade lasted for nearly 30 years, from 1847 to 1874, and involved over one million men.[14] Of this total, over 90,000 were transported to Peru.[15]

The coolie trade ended in 1874 primarily as a result of British and Chinese Imperial initiatives. The Imperial Chinese government had always opposed the recruitment and shipment of indentured servants, but chaotic political conditions had prevented it from taking decisive action. By the 1870s, the government was stable enough to begin executing labour contractors and enforcing a blockade of Macao. The British government, which had extensive interests in China, incorporated the coolie trade into its long campaign to halt the slave trade to the West. London forbade merchants in Hong Kong to participate in the trade, instructed the Royal Navy to seize coolie ships on the high seas, and pressured Portugal, a traditional ally, to close down Macao as the principal way-station. When Lisbon finally agreed to the last demand, it became impossible to continue shipping indentured servants abroad.[16]

British efforts to end the coolie trade, however, should not be attributed to humanitarian objections to indentured servitude. British merchants were simultaneously transporting hundreds of thousands of Indian indentured servants to British colonies in the Caribbean, South America, South Africa and elsewhere,[17] and they later shipped some 63,000 Chinese indentured servants to South Africa between 1904 and 1907.[18] When British economic interests were directly served, the policy was to encourage wholesale exploitation of indentured labour.

The end to the coolie trade presented Peruvian planters with another major crisis in labour supply. This time, however, they were also hurt by the end to the guano boom, the global depression of 1873, and Peru's invasion and defeat at the hands of Chile during the War of the Pacific (1879–83). Those who survived the chaotic 1870s and 1880s did so largely through the exploitation of Chinese labourers, who were subjected to a harsh regime of social control patterned after slavery times. Planters limited labourers' mobility through debt peonage, shackling and imprisonment, and intimidated them through the use of corporal punishment. Moreover, the Peruvian state helped planters by forcing the Chinese to register with local authorities and to carry a letter from their employers stating that they had completed their work contracts.[19] The state's effectiveness, however, was severely limited by the chaotic military and political situation. Planters received more effective assistance from Chinese labour contractors who emerged during the war as major suppliers of Chinese labour.

By the mid-1870s the vast majority of Chinese labourers had completed their indentureships and were free to leave the plantations. However, most of them remained as contracted labourers and free wage labourers (*chinos libres*) either through coercion or lack of viable alternatives.[20] The situation of contracted workers resembled that of 'classic' debt peons. By definition, the length of their work contract was determined by the amount of their debt. Thus, if they were advanced the equivalent of one year's wage, then their work contract ran for one year. If they received additional loans during the year, additional time was added to their contract. Work missed because of illness or any other cause was also added onto their contracts. While under contract, the Chinese were not permitted to leave estates without the special permission of planters.[21]

Contracted labourers complained to authorities that planters illegally extended their contracts and forged their signatures onto new contracts. In most cases, however, the planters' account books were too unclear to prove malfeasance. Only in a few cases were authorities sufficiently satisfied with the evidence to release workers from their contracts. Free wage labourers earned a substantially higher wage than contracted workers and were less likely to be trapped in the web of debt peonage. However, they sometimes expressed legitimate complaints about withheld wages and other abuses.[22]

During the War of the Pacific, the Chilean army invaded Peru, put several plantations to the torch, and demanded tribute from those that remained standing. Thousands of Chinese labourers took advantage of the chaos to flee from the estates into nearby towns and cities. Within months, however, many of them had been mobilized into work gangs by Chinese contractors and returned to the plantations. An indication of how this was done comes from a representative of the Chinese community in Lima, Cheng Isao Ju, who accused ten Chinese contractors of 'kidnapping' between 3,000 and 4,000 Chinese labourers during 1881 and 1882 and bringing them to the plantations. During 1883 and 1884, he claimed, many more were forced to work on plantations to recover debts owed to contractors.[23] Planters paid Chinese contractors a percentage of the wages earned by their labourers, and allowed them to operate stores on the plantations. In return, *hacendados* received large allotments of labourers during a period of severe labour shortages.[24]

All Chinese workers, regardless of their contractual status, laboured under a harsh regime of social control. Evidence from plantation records and official reports shows that coastal estates typically maintained private jails where they imprisoned Chinese workers accused of crimes or disruptive behaviour. Common offences included running away, fighting, stealing, destruction of plantation property and failure to work, all of which also suggest a pattern of resistance. Both planters and officials considered private jails a necessity for effective control, despite the fact that their existence transferred some judicial authority to the private sector. An extreme case of worker imprisonment was discovered in 1893 on the La Viñita estate in the Chicama Valley. The owner, Jesús García y García, had imprisoned one Chinese labourer for 15 years and three others for nine years. García argued he was free to discipline his own workers and he would not release them from jail. Formal charges were brought against him, but the outcome of the case is unknown.[25] In addition to putting workers in jails, planters routinely shackled and beat them for unruly behaviour or running away.

Sometimes, offending labourers were first placed in stocks and then forced to work in chains.[26] In 1877 the Aspíllagas, owners of both sugar and cotton estates, instructed administrators to whip workers for 'grave offences', such as 'lack of respect', 'running away', or 'fighting'.[27]

The planters' most extreme act of private justice came when they ordered executions as punishment for murder. Homicides occurred with some regularity on coastal estates, and were indicative of oppressive working and living conditions as well as the lack of effective public authority. Murders most commonly occurred among the Chinese themselves. We know of two cases where Chinese labourers murdered Chinese foremen. One foreman was decapitated with a machete after he had unfairly ordered a field re-worked, and another was stabbed repeatedly by two men who had been paid by 11 Chinese workers to commit the crime. The hated foreman had beaten them during the day and sold them goods at inflated prices during the evening.[28]

Corporal punishment and imprisonment were the most visible methods of social control on coastal plantations. However, planters also controlled Chinese workers through the use of opium. The British cultivated opium poppies on plantations in India and supplied huge quantities of the drug to China.[29] British merchants, who had strong commercial ties with South America, soon realized that the opium market could be expanded to include the Chinese in Peru.[30]

The Peruvian government established an official monopoly over opium imports and sales. Merchants supplied public bids to the Minister of Trade and Commerce who accepted the most attractive offer. The amount of opium imported was limited to 50,000 kilograms, which was sold to retailers at 10 per cent profit. Retailers were licensed by the government, and they were required to keep an accurate accounting of sales. Most retailers were planters or Chinese merchants. In addition to official imports, there was also a lively contraband trade in opium.[31]

The planters used opium to facilitate debt peonage among the Chinese, and to reward and punish addicted workers for job performance. I have already published a detailed calculation showing that the Chinese could not have paid for opium with their meagre wages.[32] Instead, they had to borrow money from either planters or contractors to maintain their habit, and their indebtedness bound them to the estate. Planters also used the drug to reward and punish addicted workers. For example, on Palto estate near Pisco managers threatened to withhold distribution of opium unless the Chinese completed their work. Thus, planters helped turn these men into drug addicts and then controlled them through supplying or denying them drugs.[33] It is, however, ironic that planters did not see the correlation between opium consumption and falling worker productivity and absenteeism, which were major preoccupations. It seems likely that planters were primarily concerned with having workers securely bound to estates, regardless of their physical condition.

Considering the harshness of planters' methods of control, it seems unlikely that the Chinese could have mounted an effective resistance to total domination. However, the Chinese did resist and their defiance contributed to falling production and to the transition to alternative forms of labour.

Resistance took many forms, some of which have already been alluded to. Available evidence suggests that resistance was more effective on smaller, less carefully managed estates, in comparison with the large sugar-cane plantations that had large administrative staffs and Chinese contractors.[34] The most desperate act of resistance was suicide, usually done by ingesting large amounts of opium. There were six recorded suicides on the sugar-cane plantation Cayaltí during the 1870s, and it seems likely that there were more on this estate.[35] We know that the 'final straw' came for one man after a whipping and for another because of his debts.[36] Suicides also occurred on sugar estates in the Pativilca Valley[37] and on the guano islands. Living and working on huge mounds of bird manure was especially conducive to suicide as, over a two-year period, 60 Chinese workers took their lives out of a work-force of approximately 500.[38] High as these figures for Peru were, however, Juan Pérez de la Riva claims that the frequency of suicide among the Chinese in Cuba gave the Caribbean island the highest suicide rate in the world.[39]

A common form of resistance on Peruvian plantations was flight. In the most extreme case known, the plantation Lurifico claimed that over 270 Chinese workers had fled over the years.[40] More typical were the experiences of the estates Cayaltí and Palto, sugar and cotton plantations respectively, for which we have detailed documentation. Between 1875 and 1882 there were 45 recorded runaways from Cayaltí, of whom only 14 were captured and returned to the estate.[41] Most runaways were contracted workers who were poorly paid and heavily indebted. A majority sought refuge in the Chinese community in nearby Chiclayo, although one fled to Lima and three others to Pisco. On other occasions, planters believed that runaways ended up working, either through choice or coercion, on neighbouring sugar-cane plantations.[42]

On the hacienda Palto, which had a work-force about one-tenth the size of Cayaltí's, there were six recorded escapes from 1876 to 1881.[43] We know some details about two of these cases. One worker owed 20 *soles* to fellow Chinese who were pressuring him to pay up. He had requested an advance of 10 *soles* from the administrator in return for renewing his contract and, when this was denied, he fled to avoid punishment at the hands of his creditors.[44] Another case involved a determined worker named Silvestre. Within six months of his arrival at Palto he had run away. Nevertheless, he was captured and forced to work in chains for eight years. At the end of his contract, he signed on again in return for 64 *soles*,[45] only to run off to Iquique with a female friend.[46]

Those Chinese workers who did not escape from plantations still found ways of resisting the social order. At Palto and Cayaltí several fires and thefts resulted in serious losses for the plantations' owners, the Aspíllagas. In the absence of testimony by the Chinese themselves it is difficult to know their motivations. Fires may have been accidents, but they were also a traditional form of protest by sugar workers. Thefts seemed designed to hurt planters as well as to make money. On the other hand, there is no indication that thievery was meant to extract additional income because planters had failed to comply with some reciprocal obligation.

There were two major fires at Cayaltí caused by Chinese workers. In 1878 the Aspíllagas blamed 15 Chinese for burning approximately 1,000 acres of sugar cane. This cost them a considerable amount of money in potential sugar sales and in the cost of clearing and re-planting. These workers were forced to repay these losses with their labour.[47] Ten years later, a fire destroyed some 55,000 pounds of sugar worth approximately £320 on the London market. The Aspíllagas blamed a Chinese watchman for the blaze, and he was imprisoned for an indefinite period of time.[48]

Fire and thefts at Palto were more clearly attacks on the estate. In 1876 a Chinese man was seen running from a fire that did considerable damage to the building where machinery was stored.[49] The following year a Chinese worker stole all of the estate's chickens and, in the process, destroyed the chicken coop. This man was captured, placed in chains and imprisoned.[50] Four years later some Chinese workers disassembled a cotton gin and stole several key parts. The administrator offered workers a reward of 200 *soles* for naming the thieves, but they refused. Management strongly suspected some contracted Chinese labourers but they were never able to recover the lost machinery.[51] The Aspíllagas had difficulty replacing the parts and efforts to keep the gin running through special rigging proved disappointing.[52]

Additional forms of resistance occurred on coastal estates. Managers at Palto frequently accused Chinese workers of feigning illness in order to avoid work, which could be considered a form of resistance. The difficulty comes in differentiating between the truly ill and the resisters. Health conditions all along the coast were bad and the Chinese periodically fell seriously ill with malaria, influenza, typhus, typhoid, dysentery and other diseases. Planters recognized this and took steps to prevent epidemics that could halt production. Especially noteworthy were the hiring of physicians and the distribution of medicines (notably quinine).[53] In addition to the truly ill, managers at Palto were convinced that Chinese workers were clever fakers and, in fact, there was an unusually high percentage of sick at Palto in comparison with Cayaltí. For example, during 1876–7 an average of 20 of the 150 Chinese at Palto were sick, compared with 20 of the 420 Chinese at Cayaltí.[54]

Palto's managers attempted to solve this problem with force. In 1877 the administrator took 24 suspected malingerers to Pisco where a doctor judged nine of them to be healthy. They were placed in the custody of the subprefect who put them to work in the barracks.[55] Moreover, on at least two other occasions suspected fakers were either beaten or forced to spend the night in jail.[56] These tactics had proved ineffective and management continued to complain about malingerers.[57]

Some credence is given to managements' claims by the general tendency of the Chinese at Palto to resist total domination. For example, managers repeatedly complained that the Chinese were disobedient and talked back.[58] On one occasion a Chinese worker stole six sacks of cotton and, when caught, explained that he was only 'completing his *tarea* in harvesting'. The manager had him whipped and chained, and placed a 24-hour guard on harvested cotton.[59] More significantly, the Chinese acted collectively to protect individuals and to protest against low wages and excessive physical abuse. On six occasions during the 1880s they stopped work and demanded higher wages.[60] Moreover, in 1876, 10 to 12 Chinese rioted after the administrator severely punished a Chinese worker for insolence. Firearms were used to force the rioters back into their dormitory and behind locked doors.[61] The following year the administrator severely bludgeoned a Chinese worker who had run away for three days, and two others for malingering. The beatings occurred before the assembled work-force and were meant as a lesson for all. Instead, they produced a 'great disturbance' that forced the manager to retreat to the *casa hacienda*. He barricaded himself in the dining room and grabbed a rifle while the *mayordomos* (foremen) gradually calmed down the workers. The Aspíllagas were sufficiently concerned to make a special trip to the estate. They admonished the Chinese to respect their *patrones* and threatened to send 60 soldiers to Palto to enforce order.[62]

Other forms of violence also occurred on the plantations. We have already mentioned that two *mayordomos* were killed by Chinese workers. *Mayordomos* were frequently hated by the Chinese. The foreman's job was to push workers as hard as possible, and some of them were especially brutal. At Cayaltí, a *mayordomo* once administered 100 lashes to a Chinese worker simply because he did not like the man,[63] and at Palto a foreman named Gutiérrez was so violent that his mere presence made it difficult to recruit workers.[64] According to the knowledgeable contemporary J.B.H. Martinet, black *mayordomos* were particularly cruel to the Chinese:

> Black mayordomos, the majority reared under the lash of slavery, enjoy administering the blows that before had caressed [*acariciado*] their backs to others, like the Chinese, who are under their orders and who they view with supreme contempt [*soberano desprecio*].[65]

There is, of course, an important psychological dimension to this contentious relationship which lies beyond the scope of this paper.

The most significant homicide committed by the Chinese was the murder of the owner of Pucalá, a large sugar-cane plantation in Lambayeque. The contemporary British traveller George R. Fitz-Roy Cole described the incident:

The father of one of the writer's companions in this expedition [José María Izaga] was killed by his own Chinamen in an outburst of vindictive passion, when the coolies conspired together to revenge the harsh treatment they had received, and breaking into the house, beat their master to death with their farm tools. This was after long endurance; for one of the punishments this man had imposed on any coolie whom he had caught in the act of escaping was to hobble him with an iron chain, forcing him to work as usual with this heavy weight added, until he considered his punishment sufficient. For lighter offenses he used to beat them unmercifully, and curtail their rations to the starvation point. This went on till even the long-suffering Chinaman's patience was exhausted, and, rousing himself one morning, he avenged himself in the summary fashion already related.[66]

On two occasions the Chinese rose en masse and severely tested local authority. The first uprising occurred in 1870 when 1,200–1,500 overran the Pativilca Valley and attacked urban areas. The revolt began on the hacienda Araya where they killed the estate administrator, his family and all *mayordomos*. Rebels successfully overran several valley estates, killing administrators and *mayordomos* and sacking stores and houses. In the meantime, surviving property owners regrouped to defend the town of San Ildefonso de Barranca, and President José Balta sent troops from Lima under the command of Colonel Antonio Rodríguez Ramírez. The Peruvians defending Barranca were well armed and managed to repulse the Chinese, who had very few firearms. The rebels dispersed with the main group falling back on the plantation Upaca, which had been occupied by armed Peruvians from Supe. The Chinese suffered over 100 casualties at Upaca and the rebellion was crushed.[67]

When troops arrived from Lima they hunted down the Chinese and shot many on sight. The survivors were subsequently rounded up and distributed to planters. Three important growers were appointed governors of local districts and Lima was asked to establish a rural police station. Local notables blamed the rebellion on *chinos libres*, who were considered agitators, and the Chinese workers' lust for opium. However, they presented no evidence to substantiate their interpretation[68]. *Chinos libres* were disliked because they demanded higher wages and were harder to control. Moreover, the Chinese did not have to steal to buy opium, they could buy it on credit from planters. The rebellion is best explained as a primitive outburst of anger directed at planters and *mayordomos*.

The Chilean invasion of Peru in 1880 was the second occasion for the Chinese to rebel. The war caused the temporary collapse of the oligarchic state and ushered in a period of political, military and class conflict. The Chileans, led by General Patricio Lynch, 'the red prince', burned plantations, demanded ransom from survivors and occupied Lima.[69] Many Chinese saw the Chilean invasion as an opportunity to avenge years of abuse by planters. In Pacasmayo 600–800 Chinese workers helped the Chileans sack sugar estates and *casas haciendas*, and this scene was repeated in the Chicama, Lambayeque and Cañete Valleys.[70] The Chinese also fought alongside the Chileans during the battles of San Juan and Miraflores,[71] and there was also rioting and looting by non-Chinese workers in coastal cities. As Heraclio Bonilla has observed, oligarchs soon came to fear the popular classes more than the Chileans, and this was an important reason why they sued for peace.[72]

Unfortunately for the Chinese, the Chilean invasion did not result in their liberation. Following the devastating defeats of the Peruvian army on the outskirts of the capital, the troops fell back on Lima and began looting the city. Among the victims were 70–80 Chinese merchants who lost their lives as well as their businesses.[73] For their part, the Chileans sent many Chinese to work in the occupied guano and nitrate fields and forced 2,000 more to bury fallen soldiers.[74] The Chinese in the Cañete Valley even fell victim to a massacre by black peasants in 1881. According to the British consul, anywhere from 700 to 1,500 Chinese workers were killed.[75] Pedro Paz-Soldán y Unanue, writing shortly after the slaughter, has left us with a graphic description that depicts the deeply scarred hatred that divided the two marginalized ethnic groups:

> The mob of armed and mounted blacks and cholos, with nobody to resist them – since they had always made up the entire population of the valley – went round one hacienda after another. The Chinese, taken by surprise, lacking any defence and sure of their innocence, were killed with clubs, knives, stones, machetes, in a thousand ways. Some subaltern estate dependents – the only men in charge of the abandoned properties at the time – locked the labourers into their quarters. The attackers burned these down, or broke down the doors to reach and kill the innocents within.
>
> Some sought safety in the sewers; but the blacks waited for them at the outlets and killed them as they came out. Other unfortunates, who still believed in what was traditionally sacred, sought asylum in the Casagrande school . . . There, they were also killed by the renegades, bent on vengeance and rapine. As they stormed through, they smashed furniture, windows, doors, destroying everything and making bonfires in the very heart of the homes of their former and apparently 'dear masters'.
>
> The corpses of the Chinese were dragged out into the courtyards of the masters' houses. There, before being left to be torn to pieces by the birds, they were the subjects of savage profanation, as in some Bacchic carnival, by the women and the boys. The very black women who had once been the paid concubines of their victims, now mutilated their bodies, cutting off their bleeding and palpitating organs and placing them into their open mouths, as with a cigar. 'Leave this one for me!', the black women screamed, quarrelling over the victims, drunk with blood like the women who tore Pentheus limb for limb . . .[76]

The deep-seated animosity that divided blacks and Chinese obviously hindered the ability of both groups to resist domination by the Peruvian bourgeoisie. The ability of the Chinese to rebel during the war was also hurt by the eagerness of the Chileans to exploit their labour. Class divisions among the Chinese themselves also undermined their ability to resist, and helped planters enormously. No group contributed more to planters' survival of the war than Chinese contractors who rounded up thousands of their countrymen and brought them back to the plantations. Contractors were members of an emerging Chinese petty bourgeoisie that also included merchants and landowners. Like Peruvian planters, they all profited from the labour of Chinese workers.

Chinese contractors had found an avenue of social mobility within a racially divided and repressive society. By the late 1880s, a few had even become planters, and others had become established merchants. More commonly, however, they became petty capitalists in coastal towns and cities where they established small stores, restaurants, vegetable stands and artisanal trades.[77]

Despite their success, these individuals were still vulnerable to abuse by Peruvians, as witnessed by the sacking of Chinese stores during the War of the Pacific. For the majority of Chinese these years were spent labouring on the plantations. Their productivity allowed several planters to survive the crisis of the period and to develop their estates in the 1890s. The Aspíllagas acknowledged that they treated the Chinese as virtual slaves, but explained that it was common practice as well as necessary for their economic survival and glorious future:

> It is not necessary to think of slavery since it exists for but short periods of time, besides we are not the only ones, although they say that to follow the bad example of several is to take the advice of fools, but some need others and this brings us forward as heroes who search for a sure death in order to live eternally in the pages of history.[78]

The Aspíllagas also believed that the Chinese were racially inferior and therefore undeserving of better treatment. This was a common belief among Peruvians who were generally ignorant of Asian culture and history. The Aspíllagas frequently characterized Chinese workers as perverse, lazy, degenerate and vice-ridden. They concluded that these characteristics stemmed primarily from opium consumption and gambling. This analysis was not altogether flattering to the Aspíllagas, however, because they were opium retailers and racehorse owners. The inherent contradiction in the Aspíllagas' view of the Chinese is perhaps captured best in this statement:

> The Chinese not only trouble us as racial degenerates, but also because they can create with time very serious social problems, since they, be it because of their intelligence, or their habits, are absorbing all wholesale and retail businesses, even haciendas. They do so without leaving any permanent benefit for the country, since they, although they could be over eighty years old, once they have money they take it to their country.[79]

Despite Chinese success in the business world, the Aspíllagas insisted on viewing them as racial degenerates. These views were certainly common-place elsewhere in the Americas, including the United States, where the Chinese also endured racial and ethnic prejudice. There is common ground here with the experience of Africans in the New World. Westerners justified slavery and indentured servitude on assumptions of racial inferiority, economic need, historical precedent and other spurious arguments. Peruvian planters were aware of the legal distinctions between slavery, indentured servitude and contract labour. However, they took advantage of their superior social, economic and political position to fashion regimes of social control with glaring similarities to slavery. It should not be surprising that the Chinese resorted to acts of resistance similar to those employed by African slaves.

Resistance Among Japanese Labourers

Through the exploitation of Chinese labour several planters survived the crisis of the 1870s and 1880s. During the 1890s, the economy and polity of Peru stabilized and newly arrived entrepreneurs, many of them merchants, also acquired sugar-cane plantations. Planters succeeded in securing large loans from British import-export houses, which also marketed their sugar, and this capital was used to modernize estates.[80]

The growers' most vexing problem was to find a new source of labour to replace the Chinese. *Hacendados* looked once again to the Orient because Japan had emerged as a promising source of cheap contract labour. The importation of Japanese workers to Peru coincided with a second wave of Asian emigration to the New World.[81] This time, however, emigration was not the result of internal disorder in the East but of carefully arranged agreements between Japanese emigration companies, chiefly the Morioka Emigration Company, and Peruvian planters. Most of the Japanese who came to Peru were poor farmers and labourers from Okinawa. Work contracts stipulated that they be physically fit, of good character, and between 20 and 45 years of age. Monthly wages ranged from £2. 10s. for men to £1. 10s. for women. Planters agreed to pay for the cost of the voyage to Peru, and emigration companies for the return trip. For each 50 workers delivered, emigration companies supplied a Japanese supervisor conversant in Spanish, who would be paid by the plantation. For their services, the companies received £2. 10s. for each contracted worker supplied. Workers, for their part, agreed to remain for a period of four years, or forfeit a bond posted in Japan with the emigration company.[82] Between 1898 and 1923, 17,764 Japanese were imported into Peru, 14,829 by Morioka alone.[83]

Simultaneously however, planters also recruited tens of thousands of Peruvian peasants from nearby highland communities to work on the plantations. Over time, Peruvians replaced the Japanese and the transition to wage labour was complete.[84] Planters preferred Peruvians over Japanese for several reasons. In brief, natives could be recruited more easily and in larger numbers; they adjusted more rapidly to the harsh living and working conditions on coastal plantations; they produced more for lower wages; they were considered less contentious; and they did not enjoy the support of third parties.

The Japanese were considered 'contentious' because they were willing to fight for their rights. Conflict most commonly arose when planters, in violation of the standard contract, changed the method of payment from a daily wage to payment by piecework (*tarea*). Planters did this because Peruvians were paid by *tarea* and they produced significantly more than the Japanese. In other words, growers were paying the Japanese more for less work, which was uneconomical and likely to result in protests from the Peruvians. When the Japanese began receiving payment by *tarea*, their income declined and they protested. Labourers sought support both from emigration company officials, who were obliged to respond, and from the Japanese government. Although the final results favoured planters, the willingness of the Japanese to resist cost the planters time and money and hastened the transition to wage labour.

Conflicts between Japanese labourers and Peruvian planters over wages and other issues began with the first wave of immigrants. Their experience was particularly disappointing as a large number quickly fell ill and died and dozens more returned to Japan without having earned a *centavo*. As previously mentioned, the Peruvian coast was (and still is) an insalubrious place with a wide variety of contagious diseases constantly threatening the lives of workers. The Japanese, like the Chinese before them, were also unaccustomed to the torrid climate and arduous work routine. The results are shown below.

Status of Japanese Immigrants to Peru, 1898–1909[85]

Died	Returned to Japan	Migrated out of Peru	Remained
481	414	242	5,158

In addition to complaints over wages, the Japanese voiced grievances over the imperious manner of planters, the language barrier, and planters' attempts to force them to buy goods at plantation stores. The following quote from Teikichi Tanaka, chief representative of Morioka Emigration Company in Peru, explains how these issues caused a major disturbance at the San Nicolás sugar-cane plantation in the Pativilca Valley.

On April 25 I received a message saying that a strike was being called at San Nicolás and went immediately to investigate on the spot. The cause of the difficulty was that the plantation officials tried to prevent the immigrants from dealing with Chinese stores so that they could monopolize their business through the *tambo* [company-owned store]. The immigrants wanted to buy their necessities from Chinese stores with cash rather than from the *tambo* with coupons, and they requested wage advances.

Because of language difficulty, suspicions were aroused on both sides. If voices were raised a little, it was immediately thought that there was a fight. If a few persons gathered around and talked, it was immediately feared that a mass uprising was taking place. It was rumoured that the Morioka Company had brought 800 soldiers disguised as farmers who were planning to start a fight at an opportune time. Evidently believing these rumours, Mr. Pomar, company manager, had been on guard. Thinking that serious trouble had started, plantation officials armed themselves, and natives closed their doors. It is no wonder that the immigrants, who had no intention of doing the things of which they were suspected, were puzzled.

At the telegraphic request of the plantation manager, an officer and 12 soldiers were sent. Fearing a clash, the immigrants requested that the soldiers be withdrawn and explained that they had no intention of staging an uprising. The manager declared that the Japanese get angry about little things, are lazy, do not obey regulations and orders and regard Japanese supervisors and plantation officials as dogs and horses. He also said that approaching supervisors in a group constitutes an uprising and would set a bad precedent for the natives, unless punished. He wanted to get rid of 25 persons whom he considered instigators.

Seeing that it was entirely a case of misunderstanding, I explained things and cautioned all immigrants as to their future conduct. In the end, five persons from Hawaii who had been troublesome were expelled.[86]

Problems over wages were less easily resolved. Sugar-cane plantations along the coast had ordered shipments of workers ranging in number from 50 to 450. However, *hacendados* exhibited little patience with the new recruits, and they quickly complained to Morioka that labourers were not earning their wages. Most estates forced the Japanese to work by *tarea* and, when this resulted in lower wages, many refused to work and asked Morioka to intervene. Some Japanese workers reluctantly agreed to payment by piece-work, but others left and ended up working on coffee estates in the Bolivian selva, on plantations in Mexico, or returning to Japan. On the northern coast, the principal area of sugar production, only a few Japanese labourers remained after 1910.[87]

Large numbers remained, however, on the sugar estates on the south-central coast. There are several reasons for this. Planters in this region had initially exhibited the most enthusiasm for immigration, and they were supported by the president of Peru, Augusto B. Leguía, who had formerly worked for British sugar interests in the area and had married into a British planter family. Moreover, estates in this region apparently had more reservations about the wholesale recruitment of Peruvian wage labour.

The persistence of Japanese labourers on the south-central coast, however, did not signal an end to labour disputes. Conflicts continued over wages, particularly during the First World War when inflationary pressures placed an extra burden on workers. The Japanese were also inspired by Peruvian workers who, in both urban areas and on north coast sugar-cane plantations, launched a working-class movement seeking an eight-hour day, the right to unionize, and higher wages. The following history of labour conflicts involving the Japanese are taken from the British Sugar Company in the Cañete Valley, for which we have a detailed record.[88]

The first dispute involving Japanese workers centred on management's attempt to lower wages paid to women. Japanese women received 1 *sol* to 1 *sol* 20 *centavos* per day, while Peruvian men earned 1 *sol*. The problem was that the women had significant domestic responsibilities and completed only about 25 per cent as much as Peruvian males. The situation was further aggravated by the estate's decision to provide the Japanese with superior housing and other amenities. In the words of the estate manager: '. . . there is certain to be trouble, the more especially when one considers the good houses, baths, schools and other facilities offered to the Japanese, while, it must be admitted, that the *serrano* [highlander] gets what is left over.'[89]

When management lowered the Japanese women's wages to 80 *centavos*, the Japanese called a mass meeting that lasted through the night. The emigration company's representative, Takei, promised that women's wages would rise to 1 *sol* 20 *centavos* once the price of sugar rose on the world market. This pledge, however, had not been authorized by management, which threatened to dismiss Takei. Several months later the women accepted the lower wage, but the issue of low wages surfaced again the following year.[90]

This time the Japanese were demanding higher wages to offset rising food prices. When management refused, the Japanese government threatened to suspend future shipments of workers to the estate, and eventually cancelled a shipment of 150 workers. This caused management considerable concern, but it would only agree to lower the price of rice, the basic staple of the Japanese diet. Management counted on Takei and other emigration company officials to avert a threatened strike by disgruntled workers.[91]

On this and on other occasions, divisions among the Japanese themselves undermined efforts to secure higher wages. Emigration company officials worked with planters to prevent labour conflict, and they did not always have the workers' best interests in mind. For example, in 1913 an official of the Yokohama Specie Bank accused Morioka of embezzling funds from Japanese labourers in the Cañete Valley.[92] Moreover, as with the Chinese, a small group of Japanese had become established as shopkeepers, small landowners and merchants in coastal towns and plantations. Most of their customers were Japanese plantation workers and they opposed pressuring planters by delaying shipments of more of their countrymen to Peru. There were also important divisions among the workers. For example, in 1917 a strike was averted primarily because the older workers convinced the younger ones that wages would increase once the grinding season started up again.[93]

These conflicts were a prelude to more serious disturbances in 1919. The troubles coincided with massive demonstrations in Lima-Callao for an eight-hour day, which the President was forced to concede, and by a dockworkers' strike in the nearby port. The eight-hour day was extended to factory workers on plantations (Japanese and Peruvian alike), but ignored fieldworkers. Several canefields were set ablaze in Cañete and suspects included both plantation workers and dockworkers. Feeling the pressure, the British Sugar Company agreed to a raise of 10 *centavos* per ton of harvested cane, which the Japanese accepted.[94]

From management's perspective, the experienced Japanese workers and the local shopkeepers and merchants were more likely to stir up trouble than those who had recently arrived.

I hope when the new Japs arrive there will be less chance of strikes. What has happened is that there have been no arrivals of new blood for some time and the old lot have been winnowed and sifted down, till we have the Peruvianized Japs left and owners of *tambos*, *peluqueros*, etc. who appear to me to be the ones who make most of the noise. I think that it will be convenient to cut down the Jap *fondos*, etc. by giving them a few months notice and then gradually oust them all except the two or three good ones who would be quite able to attend to the needs of the colony.[95]

From the onset of immigration, the Japanese had demonstrated a willingness to complain about low wages. However, it makes sense that those who had been in Peru the longest would have greater familiarity with local culture, language, and politics and could protest more effectively.

Five months after these disturbances, the company suffered a major strike involving both Peruvian and Japanese workers. The union of the Japanese and Peruvians particularly alarmed management. In the past, vast cultural and contractual differences had kept the two groups of workers apart and prevented them from forming a united front. This allowed management to pay Peruvians less, and to use Peruvians' higher productivity as a rationale for lowering Japanese wages. Both groups had been working on plantations for over 20 years and were more knowledgeable of the system of production and of effective methods of protest. Moreover, many of the Japanese had completed their contracts and were now working as free wage labourers. The strikers' catalyst was the rampant inflation of the war years coupled with the working-class movement in nearby cities and harbours.

Once again, the key grievance was over wages. Management agreed to increases, but insisted on different pay-scales for Peruvians and Japanese. Their objective was to keep the two groups apart by offering the Peruvians higher wages on paper, but secretly giving the Japanese a non-publicized bonus which gave them a slighter higher wage. Thus, Peruvians would have the illusion of higher wages and would not be tempted to strike, while the Japanese would be pleased with their *de facto* higher wages.[96] The success of the ruse was, of course, based on the assumption that sufficient divisions persisted among the two groups to prevent them from sharing information about wages.

In 1923 the Peruvian and Japanese governments agreed to end Japanese emigration to Peru. From the perspective of the planters, Japanese labourers were no longer needed because tens of thousands of Peruvian peasants had become transformed into plantation workers. Moreover, the Japanese, who had always protested over low wages, were now joining forces with Peruvians to put more effective pressure on planters. Previously, growers had successfully lowered the wages of Japanese contract workers, who did not receive effective support from either emigration companies or their government. Now Japanese free wage earners and veteran contracted workers were forming alliances and winning some wage increases. Their success made them less desirable. Finally, the Japanese became expendable because many planters on the south-central coast began switching from sugar cane to cotton production during the First World War. Cotton cultivation required fewer hands and could be done most economically and effectively with tenants and sharecroppers.[97]

Conclusion

Peruvian plantation agriculture, always a mainstay of the national economy, depended on the importation of servile labour until the 1920s. African slavery had persisted until the mid-nineteenth century when the Peruvian government, under the liberal reformer General Ramón Castilla, freed the bondsmen with a generous indemnification to slave-owners. Resistance played a part in slavery's demise primarily through the flight of hundreds of Africans who, in many cases, terrorized well-to-do travellers on the roads outside of Lima.

Emancipation with indemnification allowed planters to import nearly 100,000 Chinese indentured servants, whose experience resembled that of slaves. Subjected to corporal punishment, imprisonment, drug addiction and debt peonage, the Chinese resisted through physical attack, flight, refusal to work, feigning illness, suicide and other tactics. Still, the rest of society seemed stacked against them. Even their countrymen, Chinese labour contractors and merchants, contributed to their plight by delivering them to planters and selling them goods at inflated prices. The invading Chileans, rather than coming to their rescue, forced them to do menial labour and treated them as badly as the Peruvians. Nevertheless, the resistance of Chinese labourers cut into planters' profit margins and contributed to the necessity for identifying alternative sources of labour.

The Chinese were replaced with Japanese contract labourers, supplied by Japanese emigration companies, and with Peruvian peasants. The Japanese protested against attempts by planters to lower their wages, against the provisions of their contracts, and later joined ranks with Peruvians to strike for higher wages. Initially, the Japanese efforts at resistance met with failure and many of them suffered loss of income or were relocated to Bolivia, Mexico or Japan. By the First World War, however, the Japanese had accumulated considerable experience and, in a general atmosphere of conflict between labour and capital, formed a united front with other workers to win modest wage increases.

Notes

1. A recent work on resistance is Gary Y. Okihiro (ed.), *In Resistance: Studies in African, Caribbean, and Afro-American History* (Amherst, 1986).
2. Christine Hunefeldt, 'Relaciones rural-urbanas de los esclavos de Lima 1790–1854', paper presented at meeting of the Andean Studies Committee, American Historical Association, New York City, December, 1990; Carlos Aguirre, 'Cimarronaje, Bandolerismo y Desintegración

Michael J. Gonzales

Esclavista. Lima, 1821-1854', in Carlos Aguirre and Charles Walker (eds), *Bandoleros, Abigeos y Montoneros. Criminalidad y Violencia en el Perú, Siglos XVIII-XX* (Lima, 1990); and Nils P. Jacobsen, 'The Development of Peru's Slave Population and its Significance for Coastal Agriculture, 1792-1854' (unpublished MS, 1974).

3. Michael J. Gonzales, *Plantation Agriculture and Social Control in Northern Peru, 1875-1933* (Austin, 1985), 22.
4. Aguirre, 144-5.
5. Manuel Burga, 'El Perú Central, 1770-1860: disparidades regionales y la primera crisis agrícola republicana', *Revista Peruana de Ciencias Sociales*, no. 1, 1987.
6. Aguirre, 146.
7. Manuel Burga, *De la encomienda a la hacienda capitalista: El valle de Jequetepeque del siglo XVI al XX* (Lima, 1976); and Susan E. Ramírez, *Provincial Patriarchs: Land Tenure and the Economics of Power in Colonial Peru* (Albuquerque, 1986).
8. Aguirre, 147-8, 154.
9. Ibid., 157-8.
10. Ibid., 164-5.
11. Ibid., 167-8.
12. Ibid., 170.
13. On the guano boom see, W.M. Mathew, *The House of Gibbs and the Peruvian Guano Monopoly* (London, 1981); and Heraclio Bonilla, *Guano y burguesía en el Perú* (Lima, 1974). On railroad development see, Watt Stewart, *Henry Meiggs Yankee Pizarro* (Durham, 1946); and on investments in coastal agriculture and the importation of Chinese indentured servants see Watt Stewart, *Chinese Bondage in Peru* (Durham, 1951); Pablo Macera, *Las plantaciones azucareras en el Perú, 1821-1875* (Lima, 1974); and Gonzales, *Plantation Agriculture*, chs 1, 2, and 5.
14. Arnold J. Meagher, 'The Introduction of Chinese Laborers to Latin America: The "Coolie" Trade, 1847-1874', Ph.D. Diss. (University of California, Davis, 1975), 50-5.
15. J.B.H. Martinet, *L'agriculture au Pérou. Résumé du mémoire présenté au Congrès International de l'agriculture* (Paris, 1878), 32.
16. Ibid., 307-10, 324-6, 331; Robert L. Irick, *Ch'ing Policy toward the Coolie Trade, 1847-1878* (Taipei, 1982); Stewart, *Chinese Bondage*, chs 6 and 7.
17. Hugh Tinker, *A New System of Slavery* (London, 1974).
18. Peter Richardson, 'Coolies, Peasants, and Proletarians: The Origins of Chinese Indenture Labour in South Africa, 1904-1907', in Shula Marks and Peter Richardson, eds, *International Labour Migration: Historical Perspectives* (London, 1984), 167-86.
19. 'Expediente sobre el reclamo formulado por varios asiáticos en los pueblos de Supe, Chancay y Barranca', Supe, 26 May 1886, Biblioteca Nacional, Lima, D5534. Francisco Pérez Céspedes to Señores Aspíllaga Hermanos, 27 May 1877, Palto to Lima, Archivo del Fuero Agrario, Lima. Much of the information for this paper comes from the Aspíllaga family's private correspondence, which is now housed in the Archivo del Fuero Agrario in Lima. The names of the principal correspondents are referred to in the notes by their initials, except in those cases where they simply signed the title of the family firm, Aspíllaga Hermanos. The following is a list of all correspondents and titles that are abbreviated: Antero Aspíllaga Barrera (AAB) Ismael Aspíllaga Barrera (IAB) Ramón Aspíllaga Barrera (RAB) Aspíllaga Hermanos (AH) Baldomero Aspíllaga Barrera (BAB) Archivo del Fuero Agrario (AFA).
20. Gonzales, *Plantation Agriculture*, ch. 15.
21. 'Oficio del Prefecto del Departamento de Lima al Director de Gobierno remitiéndole los cuadros y las actas de los acuerdos realizados por la comisión encargada de visitar los fundos donde existen asiáticos contratados', Ica, 15 June 1888, Biblioteca Nacional, Lima, D5347.
22. 'Expediente sobre la averiguación practicada por la comisión china, asesorada por funcionarios del gobierno, respecto a la situación de sus connacionales que prestan sus servicios en las haciendas', Lima, 9 December 1887, Biblioteca Nacional, Lima, D11416. (Hereinafter cited as Chinese Commission Report, 1887, BN.)
23. In Heraclio Bonilla, 'The War of the Pacific and the National and Colonial Problem in Peru', *Past and Present*, no. 81 (Nov. 1978), 110.
24. Michael J. Gonzales, 'Chinese Plantation Workers and Social Conflict in Peru in the late nineteenth century', *Journal of Latin American Studies*, no. 1 (Oct. 1989), 403-6.
25. *Informe*, Chinese consul Ten Ayan, subprefect of Trujillo Lizardo Lavalle, interpreter P.A. Ponky, Biblioteca Nacional; Jesus García y García to el ministro de gobierno, 21 Aug. 1893, Biblioteca Nacional.
26. José Pérez y Albela to AH, 1 Nov. 1878, Palto to Lima, AFA; José Pérez y Albela to AH, 9 Aug. 1878, Palto to Lima, AFA; Francisco Pérez Céspedes to AH, 30 Oct. 1877, Palto to Cayaltí, AFA; E. Augusto to Geraldo Pérez, 12 March 1876, Palto to Cayaltí, AFA; Francisco Pérez Céspedes

to AH, 21 July 1877, Palto to Lima, AFA; José Pérez y Albela to AH, 11 Oct. 1878, Palto to Lima, AFA.

27. AAB to Aspíllaga Hermanos, 30 April 1877, Palto to Lima, AFA; E. Augusto to AH, 7 March 1876, Palto to Lima, AFA; Francisco Pérez Céspedes to AH, 19 June 1877, Palto to Lima, AFA; José Pérez y Albela to AH, 11 Oct. 1878, Palto to Lima, AFA.

28. Gonzales, 'Chinese Plantation Workers', 409-11.

29. Jonathan Spence, 'Opium Smoking in Ch'ing China', in Frederick Wakeman, Jr and Caroline Grant, eds, *Conflict and Control in Late Imperial China* (Berkeley, 1975).

30. According to Pablo Macera, between 1852 and 1879, 767,401 pounds of opium were sold to Peru by Britain. See Macera, *Las plantaciones azucareras*, cxviii.

31. 'Estanco del opio', *El Comercio*, 10 Jan. 1888; *El Comercio*, 27 Feb. 1888; *El Peruano*, 27 Sept. 1887; AH to AH, 19 May 1891, Cayaltí to Lima, AFA.

32. Gonzales, *Plantation Agriculture*, 32, 102-3.

33. José Pérez y Albela to AH, 4 April 1879, Palto to Lima, AFA; José Pérez y Albela to AH, 21 March 1879, Palto to Lima, AFA.

34. Gonzales, 'Chinese Plantation Workers', 413-22.

35. AH to AH, 8 May 1876, Cayaltí to Lima, AFA; AH to AH, 12 May 1876, Cayaltí to Lima, AFA; AH to AH, 18 July 1876, Cayaltí to Lima, AFA; RAB to AAB, 4 Jan. 1876, Cayaltí to Lima, AFA; RAB to AAB, 25 Jan. 1876, Cayaltí to Lima, AFA; AH to AH, 4 June 1878, Cayaltí to Lima, AFA. This was also the most common way for Chinese to commit suicide in Cuba: Juan Pérez de la Riva, *El barracón: Esclavitud y capitalismo en Cuba* (Barcelona, 1975), 70.

36. AH to AH, 8 May 1876, Cayaltí to Lima, AFA; RAB to AAB, 4 Jan. 1876, Cayaltí to Lima, AFA.

37. Humberto Rodríguez Pastor, *La Rebelión de los Rostros Pintados* (Huancayo, Peru, 1979), 34.

38. Cecilia Méndez, 'La otra historia del guano: Perú 1840-1879', *Revista Andina*, ano 5, num. 1 (ler semestre 1987), 13, 45.

39. Pérez de la Riva, *El barracón*, 67.

40. Chinese Commission Report, 1887, BN.

41. RAB to AAB, 21 Sept. 1875, Cayaltí to Lima, AFA; RAB to AAB, 5 Oct. 1875, Cayaltí to Lima, AFA; RAB to AAB, 8 Oct. 1875, Cayaltí to Lima, AFA; AH to AH, 21 May 1876, Cayaltí to Lima, AFA; AH to AH, 21 Feb. 1877, Cayaltí to Lima, AFA; AH to AH, 2 June 1877, Cayaltí to Lima, AFA; AH to AH, 6 July 1877, Cayaltí to Lima, AFA; AH to AH, 16 July 1878, Cayalti to Lima, AFA; AH to AH, 11 Sept. 1877, Cayaltí to Lima, AFA; AH to AH, 14 Sept. 1877, Cayaltí to Lima, AFA; AH to AH, 16 Oct. 1880, Cayaltí to Lima, AFA; AAB to IAB, 3 May 1881, Cayaltí to Lima, AFA; unsigned letter dated 8 June 1882, Cayaltí to Lima, AFA.

42. AH to AH, 18 July 1876, Cayaltí to Lima, AFA; AH to AH, 14 Sept. 1887, Cayaltí to Lima, AFA; RAB to IAB, 26 July 1881, Cayaltí to Lima, AFA; RAB to AAB, 5 Oct. 1875, Cayaltí to Lima, AFA.

43. José Pérez y Albela to AH, 19 July 1878, Palto to Lima, AFA; AH to AH, 10 Sept. 1880, Lima to Palto, AFA; José Pérez y Albela to AH, 24 July 1878, Palto to Lima, AFA; Francisco Pérez Céspedes to AH, 17 April 1877, Palto to Lima, AFA; E. Augusto to AH, 31 March 1876, Palto to Lima, AFA; Francisco Pérez Céspedes to AH, 27 July 1877, Palto to Lima, AFA.

44. Francisco Pérez Céspedes to AH, 17 April 1877, Palto to Lima, AFA.

45. Rodríguez Pastor, 'Biografías de Chinos', 14.

46. E. Augusto to AH, 31 March 1876, Palto to Lima, AFA.

47. AH to AH, 19 Nov. 1878, Cayaltí to Lima, AFA; AH to AH, 25 Nov. 1878, Cayaltí to Lima, AFA.

48. AH to AH, 10 Oct. 1888, Cayaltí to Lima, AFA; AH to AH, 7 Nov. 1888, Cayaltí to Lima, AFA.

49. E. Augusto to AH, 31 March 1876, Palto to Lima, AFA.

50. Francisco Pérez Céspedes to AH, 30 Oct. 1877, Palto to Lima, AFA.

51. Manuel J. Brihuego to Señores Prevost & Co., 30 June 1881, Palto to Lima, AFA; Manuel J. Brihuego to Señores Prevost & Co., 7 July 1882, Palto to Lima, AFA.

52. Manuel J. Brihuego to Señores Prevost & Co., 9 May 1882, Palto to Lima, AFA.

53. See Gonzales, *Plantation Agriculture*, 103-6, for a discussion of health conditions at Cayaltí and along the coast. For Palto see Humberto Rodríguez Pastor, 'Salud y muerte en los trabajadores chinos de una hacienda costena', in Humberto Rodríguez Pastor (ed.), *Chinos culies: bibliografía y fuentes, documentos y ensayos* (Lima, 1984), 150-75.

54. Rodríguez Pastor, 'Salud y muerte', 166. Rodríguez puts the number of Chinese at Cayaltí at 800, but the true number is closer to 400.

55. Francisco Pérez Céspedes to AH, 21 Sept. 1877, Palto to Lima, AFA.

56. AAB to AH, 30 April 1877, Palto to Lima, AFA; José Pérez y Albela to AH, 11 April 1879, Palto to Lima, AFA.

57. For example, '*Peones libres* [Peruvians] have been employed in weeding because the contracted

workers left over from ploughing all take turns going to the hospital. There are always 5 or 6 even 7, this game is played among them, because the truly ill the past two weeks are no more than Matos and Atac flaco'. Manuel J. Brihuego to Muy Señores Mios, 30 June 1881, Palto to Lima, AFA.

58. José Pérez y Albela to AH, 11 Oct. 1878, Palto to Lima, AFA.

59. José Pérez y Albela to AH, 5 April 1878, Palto to Lima, AFA.

60. Manuel J. Brihuego to Muy Señores Mios, 9 June 1881, Palto to Lima, AFA; Manuel J. Brihuego to Señores Prevost y Co., 16 Aug. 1881, Palto to Lima, AFA; Manuel J. Brihuego to Señores Prevost y Co., 9 May 1882, Palto to Lima, AFA; Manuel J. Brihuego to Señores Prevost y Co., 24 Aug. 1884, Palto to Lima, AFA.

61. E. Augusto to AH, 7 March 1876, Palto to Lima, AFA.

62. AAB to AH, 30 April 1877, Palto to Lima, AFA.

63. Aspíllaga y Cia. to Señores Zaracóndegui y Cia., 6 Sept. 1865, Cayaltí to Lima, AFA.

64. Manuel J. Brihuego to Señores Prevost Co., 11 July 1882, Palto to Lima, AFA.

65. Quoted in Macera, *Las plantaciones azucareras*, cxxi.

66. George R. Fitz-Roy Cole, *The Peruvians at Home* (London, 1884), 139–40, 200.

67. Rodríguez Pastor, *La Rebelión*.

68. Ibid., 72–9.

69. Jorge Basadre, *Historia de la República del Perú*, 4th edn, 2 vols (Lima, 1949), vol. 2, 225; Gonzales, *Plantation Agriculture*, 31–2; Bonilla, 'The War of the Pacific', 92–119.

70. Bonilla, 'The War of the Pacific', 107–8.

71. Rodriguez Pastor, *La rebelión*, 95.

72. Bonilla, 'The War of the Pacific'.

73. Ibid.

74. Ibid., 107.

75. Ibid., 109.

76. Juan de Arona [Pedro Paz-Soldán y Unanue], *La inmigración en el Perú: Monografía histórico-crítica*, 2nd edn (Lima, 1947), 99–102. Also quoted in Bonilla, 109–10. Translation by Eric J. Hobsbawm.

77. Gonzales, 'Chinese Plantation Workers', 422–3.

78. AH to AH, 28 May 1878, Cayaltí to Lima, AFA.

79. AH to AH, 24 Jan. 1893, Cayaltí to Lima, AFA.

80. Gonzales, *Plantation Agriculture*, chs 2 and 3.

81. This included some 15,000 Chinese immigrants to Peru who, however, did not work on sugar-cane plantations. See Peter Blanchard, 'Asian Immigrants in Peru, 1899–1923', *North/South: Canadian Journal of Latin American Studies*, 9 (1979), 60–75.

82. Standard contract, AFA (xeroxed copy in my possession); BAB to Muy Queridos Hermanos, 6 May 1899, AFA.

83. Toraje Irie, 'History of Japanese Migration to Peru', trans. William Himel, *Hispanic American Historical Review*, 21, part 2 (November 1951), 648–723.

84. Michael J. Gonzales, 'Capitalist Agriculture and Labour Contracting in Northern Peru, 1880–1905', *Journal of Latin American Studies*, 12, part 2 (Nov. 1980), 291–315; and Gonzales, *Plantation Agriculture*, ch. 7.

85. Irie, part II, 652.

86. Quoted in Toraji Irie, 'History of Japanese Migration to Peru', trans. William Himel, *Hispanic American Historical Review*, 21, part I (Aug. 1951), 446.

87. Gonzales, *Plantation Agriculture*, 119–20; Amelia Morimoto, *Los inmigrantes japoneses en el Perú* (Lima, 1979); Irie, parts I and II.

88. Bill Albert, *An Essay on the Peruvian Sugar Industry 1880–1920*, and the *Letters of Ronald Gordon, Administrator of the British Sugar Company in Cañete, 1914–20* (Norwich, 1976). All Gordon correspondence cited is in Albert.

89. Ronald Gordon to Edward L. Houghton, Esq. 22 December 1915, Cañete to Lima.

90. Ronald Gordon to Edward L. Houghton, Esq., 11 January 1916, Cañete to Lima; Ronald Gordon to Edward L. Houghton, Esq., 4 March 1916, Cañete to Lima; Ronald Gordon to Edward L. Houghton, Esq., 7 June 1916, Cañete to Lima.

91. Ronald Gordon to Edward L. Houghton, Esq., 31 May 1917, Cañete to Lima; Ronald Gordon to Edward L. Houghton, Esq., 11 June 1917, Cañete to Lima; Ronald Gordon to Edward L. Houghton, Esq., 26 July 1917, Cañete to Lima.

92. Irie, part II, 660. The following is from the Yokohama Specie Bank report:
    1. When the immigrants made remittances, the officials of the Morioka branch office took advantage of their ignorance, entered smaller amounts on the books and pocketed the difference.
    2. Similarly taking advantage of this ignorance, the company appropriated a large part of the remittances for its own use, claiming that the money was deducted by the bank because of the rate of exchange.

3. When the branch office did not have enough expense money, it diverted remittances to that purpose. It deposited the money in its current account in a Lima bank, increasing its bank credit and, at the same time, drawing interest.

4. When the main office in Tokyo was in need of money it frequently telegraphed its Lima branch to wire remittances instead of sending cash. As soon as the money was received it was diverted to company expenses. The money would finally be sent from Tokyo by postal money order after repeated inquiries from relatives.

93. Ronald Gordon to Edward L. Houghton, Esq., 23 February 1918, Cañete to Lima; Ronald Gordon to Edward L. Houghton, Esq., 7 July 1918, Cañete to Lima; Ronald Gordon to Edward L. Houghton, Esq., 25 September 1918, Cañete to Lima. On the central and southern coasts there was a grinding season. However, on the northern coast, which experienced longer hours of intense sunlight, cane was grown, harvested and processed throughout the year.

94. Ronald Gordon to Edward L. Houghton, Esq., 7 February 1919, Cañete to Lima; Ronald Gordon to Edward L. Houghton, Esq., 13 February 1919, Cañete to Lima.

95. Ronald Gordon to Edward L. Houghton, Esq., 13 February 1919, Cañete to Lima.

96. Ronald Gordon to Edward L. Houghton, Esq., 8 July 1919, Cañete to Liverpool.

97. Bill Albert, '*Yanaconaje* and Cotton Production on the Peruvian Coast: Sharecropping in the Cañete Valley during World War I', *Bulletin of Latin American Research*, vol. 2, no. 2 (May 1983), 107-16; Michael J. Gonzales, 'The Rise of Cotton Tenant Farming in Peru, 1890-1920: The Condor Valley', *Agricultural History*, vol. 65, no. 1 (Winter 1991), 51-71.

11

The Worker & the Wage in a Plantation Economy

Trinidad in the Late Nineteenth Century

KUSHA HARAKSINGH

The encounter between labourer and paymaster at the wage table of Caribbean sugar plantations in the late nineteenth century might have appeared to the casual observer to be a fairly ordinary event. After all, it took place with some regularity and the rules of the game seemingly were well understood by the participants. However, the workers' expectation of the interval between successive dealings was always liable to be upset as pay-day could be and often was postponed by the employer; moreover, understanding the rules was certainly no guarantee that they had been accepted. Thus it was that in the transaction the perceptive observer would have discerned at the very least a slightly concealed irritation which occasionally flared into open resentment – on all sides.[1] This was only to be expected as the apparently mundane task of handing over the wage in fact encapsulated an essential dilemma of that conflict-ridden society, exposing as it did the divergent attitudes held by the various groups not only on the ideology of the work-place but also on the proper role of those who sold their labour. In an attempt to make this clearer, this paper will look at the idea of the wage in late nineteenth-century Trinidad.

From one point of view, it is possible to see the dilemma as residing in the capture of the contending parties in the thraldom of plantation agriculture. To speak of capture is hardly to exaggerate the point, for as we have become accustomed to notice the debilitating effect of slavery on the slave-owner himself, so too the position of planters, attorneys and managers caught in a boom and bust over which they had little control needs to be appreciated. This position can be summarized as one of practical vulnerability, the occasion for which was not hard to discover. The sugar plant had a long growing season, and also held out the promise of ratoons to

Pay table, Perseverance estate, Cedros, Trinidad
(Photographic Album of late Nineteenth-century Trinidad,
University of the West Indies Library, Trinidad)

come, so it was not as if significant changes could be made at short notice, either to take advantage of some prospective windfall or alternatively to limit actual or comparative loss. The weather posed its own hazards and set limits on what was possible, while the disruption of the manufacturing process was all too easy to activate; but quite apart from the possibility of industrial sabotage, milling machinery in particular was notoriously prone to break-down and collapse. And in the canefields, a single lighted match was a real source of terror, as is reflected in the symbolism of even the most touristic versions of the Camboulay dance.

The planters' only hope of maintaining or improving profit margins lay in commanding cheap productive labour. This was always the case in the sugar industry though its importance has been obscured by the persistent claim that in the immediate post-emancipation period labour shortage was the most important problem facing the planters of Trinidad.[2] It is time to abandon that idea which, quite simply, mistakes the symptom for the disease. The real concern was always with cost of production, and the planters and their managers naturally focused firmly on the only cost com-ponent over which they could exert any degree of effective control. Indeed, their relative impotence at the level of international market prices, bounties, duties, subsidies and also freight and insurance costs merely served to persuade them to redouble their efforts with respect to wage determination. Labour was the first and most enduring target as capital sought to accom-modate itself to the pressures of the trading world, and the worker at the bottom of the heap was made to bear the brunt of any burden of adjustment.

The certainty that such adjustments would generate resentment and pro-test stimulated a search for additional equipment to buttress the apparatus of existing power relations. The planters had recourse to legal coercion, both in relation to free workers and also to contract workers who from the 1840s supplemented the work-force. The former were eventually covered by the Masters and Servants Ordinance of 1846 and the bulk of the latter, comprising indentured workers from India, by various Immigration Ordinances which were consolidated in 1899. The Masters and Servants Ordinance was designed, in the opinion of those who thought that the planters were never reconciled to the loss of slave labour, to return the workers to a situation as close to that of chattel slavery as was politically and otherwise feasible in all the circumstances. It is to be surmised that from the point of view of the employer the Ordinance worked well, not only in the substance of its various provisions but also in what was left unsaid, for there were no serious attempts to tamper with it and it did remain in its undiluted form on the statute books well into the twentieth century.[3] Case law, moreover, except for the brief and ultimately unsuccessful inter-vention of the Chief Justice[4] in the period 1889–92, simply ran in tandem with official design. Though many of the provisions of the Ordinance were so drafted as to endow the Magistrates with discretionary power, usually without any guide-lines as to the factors to be considered when exercising such power, it is clear from the general drift of the cases that the framers of the legislation had not misplaced their confidence in its power to protect them.[5] The Immigration Ordinances, though, were subjected to several amendments, some more far-reaching than others, often attributable to the prompting of officials in India[6] and also to Colonial Office sensitivity to the recurring charge of indenture as a new version of slavery. But the provisions of the Immigration Ordinances were interpreted by the same Magistrates who administered the Masters and Servants Ordinance, and generally with the same results as far as workers were concerned.

It is of course possible to identify some of the clauses of both pieces of legislation which, theoretically at least, provided some safeguard for workers' interests. For example, the Masters and Servants Ordinance allowed the worker to resign from his contract 'in consequence of ill-usage by his employer'; and the Immigration Ordinances stipulated the rations payable to the workers and limited the hours of work. But in the field of employment relations the interpretation of statutory intent was greatly influenced by developments in the common law of contract which in the latter half of the nineteenth century indicated an increasing momentum in the direction of 'freedom of contract'.[7] This was part of the general ideology of laissez-faire and was viewed by businessmen as crucial in removing obstacles to their progress. They welcomed the idea that two parties, possessed of the required competence as defined by law, should be permitted to make, again within the wide limits allowed by the law, whatever agreement they wished, and which the courts, should it come to that, would not hesitate to enforce.[8] Real freedom perhaps was present when the parties were dealing with each other from an equal footing, but was merely illusory when they were separated by status, wealth and power; and more than illusory where the bargain was in the nature of 'take it or leave it' and where there was little chance that leaving it was a genuine alternative. This was precisely the situation of plantation workers in Trinidad, many of whom could not afford to spurn the terms of employment which were offered to them because they were already in debt, or living in estate accommodation, or because alternative means of earning a livelihood had been successfully foreclosed. But the notion of economic duress, or of inequality of bargaining power as capable in some circumstances of vitiating a contract was then hardly conceived of; indeed, freedom of contract was designed to allow one party to take advantage of the straitened circumstances of the other, and to permit the shark to swallow the sardines.

In the plantation economy of Trinidad in the nineteenth century, that was precisely what was happening. This might not have been predictable before 1838 when Trinidad, compared to its neighbours, was relatively new and underdeveloped. By mid-century, despite an influx of immigrants mostly from the smaller colonies to the north, the island was still undermanned and its resources largely untapped; its population density in 1851 stood at only 28.4 per square mile, compared to 137 (St Lucia), 246

(Grenada), 304 (Antigua), and 817 (Barbados). But while some of the older islands had long passed their golden age of sugar, Trinidad had large areas of untouched land awaiting the plough, and some of its sugar plantations, comparatively young by Caribbean standards, still had a long way to go before room for expansion could have become a problem or declining soil fertility a matter of concern. As a field for investment, then, Trinidad held rich promise.

By the 1870s it was clear that indentured labour and those ex-indentureds who seemed inclined to remain in Trinidad were something of a guarantee to the planters who were willing to invest the large sums required for the modernizing of their operations. In the nature of things, however, it was only the larger plantations with access to capital which could go this route and take advantage of the new manufacturing equipment which had become available – more efficient mills, vacuum pans, improved centrifuges – and which could spend money on railways to upgrade methods of cane transportation from the field and so inaugurate the new world of central factories.[9] Technology and innovation began to separate the dwarfs from the giants, and the former, unable to lower their production costs and maintain a competitive edge were steadily swallowed up by the larger concerns. Thus, whereas in the late 1860s there were 153 sugar estates in the island, by 1897 that figure had fallen to 90, and the number of owners had been reduced from 60 to 22, with the largest six firms controlling 78 per cent of sugar production.

As we shall see below, the larger business concerns, like the Ste Madeline Sugar Company Limited, set the tone in employment practices and demonstrated real versatility in approaching the wage question. They exploited to the limit the propaganda value of seemingly attractive wages and in the determination of wage levels they employed strategies which anticipated those of modern personnel departments; the mechanisms they put in place for doing this, however, were vintage nineteenth-century. At the same time they spared no effort to ensure that as much as possible of the money which they had disbursed as wages was, in one way or another, recovered. So thorough were they in their approaches to the remuneration of their employees that cane farming by smallholders, like metayage in the neighbouring island of Tobago, though ostensibly an alternative arrangement to wage labour, was reduced at the bottom to the same operation.[10]

The propaganda effect of wage figures was not something which the large sugar companies had discovered. In the post-emancipation epoch, labourers from the more populated colonies were attracted to Trinidad by the promise of higher wages. Many workers from Barbados, for example, were persuaded to come to Trinidad in much the same way as a later generation would be influenced by stories of the money to be made working on the Panama Canal. The technique was perfected, however, by the steadily expanding firms in the second half of the nineteenth century, especially in relation to indentured labourers from India. Their agents and recruiters made the most of wage figures, which, given the arcane mysteries of the exchange rate, would have made little sense to their potential catch in the Indian countryside without further embellishment. In any case the migrants would have had little notion of the purchasing power in Trinidad of the wages which were being quoted to them in India. The Government of India did wake up eventually to this use of wage figures, after persistent complaints from returning workers, and expressed its alarm over the deliberate chasm between the wages quoted and real earnings.[11] Its strictures, however, seemed informed by its recognition that some of the workers had done better than they could have hoped to do if they had remained in India, and more so by the view that, in the language of contract, the recruiter's promise was mere sales pitch and no more than an invitation to treat; the attitude seemed to be that if the migrants were gullible enough to believe everything they were told, then they had only themselves to blame.

The Government of India, however, did from time to time take steps to protect its subjects from such exploitation, as, for example, in the classification issue which is discussed later. But it was never able successfully to penetrate the smoke screen which covered the issue of wages. At the grass roots level, all the estates in Trinidad which employed Indian workers, both indentured and free, were required to keep pay books but the entries in these, like *patwari* records in village India itself, often were decipherable only by the persons who had made them. Local officials charged with looking after the welfare of Indian workers were stumped when they tried to examine these books, a task which was part of their official duties, and deputations sent out from India fared little better. It is difficult to escape the conclusion that obfuscation was the deliberate goal, and this was reinforced by the kind of testimony which was offered to official commissions of enquiry. For example, Henry Daniel Higgins, a magistrate of long standing in Trinidad, was able to supply the Sanderson Committee of 1909 with details of mendicants and charity, nutrition levels and coroners' inquests, and the lack of 'constancy' of Indian women, but when asked whether wages had fallen could only say: 'That is not easy to answer; that requires a knowledge of statistics.' When pressed on the point, he added that he was not 'aware' of any fall.[12] The Sanderson Committee had so many different figures quoted to it – some mentioning $0.25 per task, others $0.35 and still others $0.35 to 0.45 – that it appears to have given up in frustration its attempt to make sense of earnings levels. The committee persisted in its efforts to compare indentured with free wages, which was part of its brief since statutory provisions enjoined employers to pay indentured workers not less than the prevailing free rates for the same description of work. However, since the bases of comparison had eluded the committee it had no greater success here.

The obfuscation was carried further by the planters in their use of questionable evidence to make statements about the satisfactory nature of arrangements on the plantations in general, and about the good prospects for indentured labour in particular. Every year, the Protector of Immigrants, the official charged with responsibility for looking after the welfare of the migrants, produced statistics relating to money which the workers had remitted to India through the Government Savings Bank or which they had carried back with them on their return voyage. These were global figures, and did not reveal how the money in question had been earned, whether by ordinary labourers, or by returnees who had served as leaders of work gangs, or who had set up shops or gone into other trades after indenture. Nor did the figures disclose that some of the money represented family and not individual savings and had been accumulated from the earnings of friends and relatives who were no longer alive.[13] Moreover, the averages constructed from the figures were presented without any evidence of distribution. But planters and their spokesmen caught on very early to the propaganda potential of the tables, though paradoxically when they wished to argue for greater concessions from the Imperial Government they were not reluctant to indicate that, no matter what tale they had made the figures tell, they had really reduced the wage levels as far as they could go.

By the end of the nineteenth century that was no idle boast; the West India Royal Commission of 1897 were certainly convinced that that was so,[14] which indicated how efficiently the employers had addressed themselves to the issue of wage determination. Their approach revealed three prongs – classification of workers, compartmentalizing of work units, and the avoidance of comparability. In all three areas they showed great creativity in their regard, or lack of regard, for the relevant ordinances and regulations. In this, they were assisted by prevailing notions of the employer's right to a suitable discretion, made more secure in the colonies by the general sentiment that only men with a real stake in terms of wealth and property had any entitlement to the perquisites of decision-making. More importantly, they were aided by their control of work-place information, and their ability to thwart the efforts of those who sought to pry too closely into their affairs. In any case, even those investigators who were most sympathetic to the interests of the workers were themselves suitably schooled into an awareness of the equivalent nineteenth-century version of what is today called management prerogative.

The grading and classification of workers were largely left, consequently, to individual managers and overseers. Several categories were identifiable, but it is by no means certain that they meant the same thing from estate to estate, or from one year to the next. Even the relatively neutral designations of 'skilled' and 'unskilled' were fairly amorphous in practice, while one can only guess at the substance of more esoteric descriptions such as 'able-bodied' and 'non able-bodied'. On estates employing indentured labour there was a special list of 'invalid' workers; they were excluded from even the scant protection provided by minimum earnings clauses which were construed as relating only to the able-bodied. Consequently, one can speculate to what purposes this classification was put, and whether it was not fortuitously expanded to include those who were in fact able-bodied. By the letter of the ordinances, indentured labourers were also guaranteed payment for days on which no work was offered by the estates (excluding Sundays and holidays), provided that the managers deemed them to be 'willing and able' to work. This open-ended description was enough to ensure that nobody who remained idle due to the unavailability of work was actually paid.

Classification was a Caribbean-wide practice; in Jamaica, for example, planters dealing with indentured Africans divided them, among other groupings, into 'first-class African worker', or 'farm and domestic' or 'cook and washer'.[15] Some of these descriptions did convey an indication of the actual work function, but in the case of indentured Indians in Trinidad the classifications represented arbitrary decisions by the planters aimed at side-stepping provisions in the indenture contract for guaranteed minimum wages and for wages comparable to those offered to free workers. The workers themselves were alive to this ruse, but mostly after the event. Some complained that on entering into the contract in India they had been designated as 'able-bodied' only to be downgraded on being allotted to the estates in Trinidad. The Government of India was disturbed that in this way the planters could at a stroke escape from some of their contractual obligations, but there seemed to be no easy way to tackle the problem. It was recognized that the long voyage from India often had an adverse effect on the health of the migrants and that therefore the demotion in some circumstances could be explained if not justified. In neighbouring British Guiana where the same problem was encountered, some suggestions were floated about instituting a trial period after the arrival of the migrants during which no alteration in classification would be permitted, and about making it mandatory for the opinion of a medical officer to be taken, but in the end the planters' discretion was left undisturbed.

There was one classification (apart of course from that determined by sex) with respect to which employers on the face of it had no discretion – that of adult and child. The threshold age was 15, after which a higher wage was payable. Trinidad planters and their allies in the local legislature mounted a spirited campaign to postpone the entry of minors into the adult work-force until they were 16, but these efforts ultimately failed. Part of the reason was that the Government of India was aware that it entailed serious ramifications, as the furious controversy which erupted in India over the Age of Consent Bill of 1891 revealed. The government's reading of the situation proved correct, and the planters consequently were destined to lose this particular battle.[16]

If manpower was classified, then so was work itself. The descriptions were deliberately designed to frustrate attempts at comparison. There were two aspects to this: firstly, the separation of jobs by functions, and secondly, the compartmentalizing of work units. Official reports tended to collapse categories but the clever manager, as in a modern firm, knew the value of detailed job descriptions. Grievances were more easily deflected when the complaining worker, pointing to his fellow who was on a higher rate (assuming in the first place that he could come by that information), could be told that his job was not quite the same. It could be made to appear different either by reference to some variation in the actual work function or by highlighting some difference in the work load itself. This was a basic ploy, and its execution was facilitated by the task system in place on Caribbean sugar estates. In the nature of things, no two tasks or work units were ever quite the same, even when they involved the same physical activity. A task in the digging of trenches, for example, was not just a matter of the distance to be covered (and that too was not as routine as it seemed, for there were ways of making measurement a complicated affair) but could be made to involve the nature of the field, whether new or old land, hilly or flat, the type of soil, the distance from the barracks, or even the weather on the particular day in question. There were highly variable aspects of the work, not only from one work site to the other, but also from one day to the next. As might be expected, the differences in tasks which were stressed by managers and overseers often were not accorded the same weight in the calculations of the workers, and this variation of emphasis resided at the heart of many controversies at the work-place which were recorded as wage disputes.

Obviously, there was a deliberate attempt to avoid the setting of work-place norms. The result from the workers' point of view was that the amount of work required from them was unpredictable; but from the employers' point of view, the more undefined the situation, the greater the room for management prerogative. The Masters and Servants Ordinance did not lay down any guide-lines about the size or nature of a task, leaving such matters to be settled in bargaining between employer and individual employee; it was intended to promote individual contracts rather than a collective bargain. The Immigration Ordinance (1875) specifically defined a task as a unit of work which the able-bodied male worker could complete in seven and a half hours 'without extraordinary exertion'. This reads like the proverbial hole in the wording of a statute through which a coach-and-four could be driven. Judging from the spate of entries in the pay lists labelled 'N F', for 'not finished', it seems that the legislation allowed the employers to set impossible limits, or units measured by the performance of only the most energetic and physically fit worker. Thus effort was turned on its head; the busy bee ran the risk of undermining worker morale as a whole. For the workers knew that any easy completion of their tasks was liable to earn them the reward the next day of larger work units, since the management consistently operated at the highest common denominator in terms of the productivity demanded.

With fluid work norms any attempt by workers to control the definition of the task was bound to meet with major difficulties, and the 'protective' legislation was hardly worth the paper on which it was written. Minimum wage provisions were rendered largely ineffective in practice, as were clauses in the 1870 Immigration Ordinance which sought to equalize free and indentured rates. This law suffered from the drafting pitfalls which have become all too familiar in equal pay legislation, and which can be summarized generally as an inability to define a workable comparator. As drafted, the legislation required planters to pay indentured workers 'not less than that ordinarily paid for the same description of work' to free labourers on the same plantation. If there were no such free workers, then the applicable rate was that paid to free workers on 'neighbouring plantations', and if that did not apply, then the payment was to be not less 'than that ordinarily paid for the same description of work to indentured labourers upon neighbouring plantations'. An easy way around this was simply to avoid having free and indentured labourers engaged in the same work, and consequently to leave indentured rates to reinforce themselves. But employers did not always need to go this far, for as we have seen, it was not difficult to frustrate attempts to establish work-load equivalences on the estates.

Fluid standards at the work-place also resulted in an enlarged field for the exercise of judicial discretion which was grounded in both the Masters and Servants Ordinance and the Immigration Ordinances. Indeed, the overall approach of the statutory disputes procedure was to enlist the opinion of the magistrate. This was not easily done, for the magistrates were not always on the spot; and in any case, for some kinds of disputes, for example, whether work had been satisfactorily done, some of the evidence would no longer be available by the time the investigation could be held. To stop work and await the magistrate would mean a loss of earnings, irrespective of the outcome of the particular dispute, while to continue working even under protest could be construed as worker acceptance of the situation. In the case of indentured workers, immigration agents sometimes tried to get in on the act, but they were generally warned against acquiring the 'odium of deciding for the master' and reminded that their proper role was limited to assisting workers in putting forward their cases. If the case was taken to court it could be attended with delays and adjournments which cost the workers money so that, even if the particular dispute was resolved in their favour, the price at the end of the day might still be an overall loss in their earnings.

In fact, it was always unlikely that the workers would prevail at court. The individual contracts under the Masters and Servants Ordinance were almost always oral in form, and in a contest between the word of the employer and that of the employee the former was accorded much greater weight. This has usually been explained by social affinity between employers and the magistrates, but in addition, preferring the employer's word conformed to prevailing attitudes towards the interpretation of contractual terms. And of course, language difficulties placed the worker at a further disadvantage, particularly the indentured Indian. Moreover, since the sanctions for breach of contract under both the Masters and Servants Ordinances and the Immigration Ordinances were penal in nature, the judicial hearing carried all the hallmarks of a criminal trial between prosecutor and defendant, with the usual biases which marked that kind of procedure in the nineteenth century.

Theoretically, the mandatory requirement to keep pay lists could have helped indentured workers when they needed to make a case, but as we have seen these were under the control of the managers. Some estates kept wage accounts on loose sheets of paper, others in books which contained puzzling notations. An investigation in the 1890s revealed that rows and columns did not add up, that many spaces were left blank, that erasures and crossings out were common, and that managers could sometimes give no explanation for inconsistencies. As the report of that investigation noted, where sums were scratched out, the inference was that the money was earned but not paid.[17] Some estates entered in the pay book the value of the task when it was assigned, others when it was half-completed, and others still when the work was fully executed; the result was that the pay book was 'no longer a record of work done or wages earned' as was required by statute. No help for the worker could come therefore from that quarter.

From the foregoing it emerges that for the employees wage rates were certainly not to be confused with real earnings; at the most they represented a kind of goal to which one might aspire. This was even more clearly revealed in the interpretation which was sometimes given by the planters to the minimum earnings clause of the 1872 Immigration Ordinance. The rate of $0.25 per task which the ordinance specified was, it was argued, merely 'available'. In practice of course, even if that argument was not used, the task could simply be expanded with the money held constant. The employers clearly did not view wages as an incentive to work, certainly not in the ordinary sense. They appeared constantly to be monitoring the situation to see they paid an amount of money which would suffice to meet the minimum needs of the workers and no more. They felt that once those needs were met, any additional payments would cause them to lose that command of the work-force which the practical vulnerability of the workers' situation provided. There was to be no margin for comfort.

The employers' urge to constantly refine the wage level is revealed in arrangements, some of them extra-legal and some of only dubious legality, to recover money paid out as wages. The area most fraught with the potential for dispute concerned the due performance of the contract, and what the payment should be if in the management's opinion there was less than full performance. It is perhaps just as well to notice in this connection that there could be no standard definition of 'bad work', 'unfinished work' or what the Masters and Servants Ordinance termed refusal to 'fulfil' the contract. The common law distinguished between 'entire' and 'severable' contracts; in the former case, nothing was earned unless there was complete performance. The inclination of the employers was to treat all contracts as entire, and the result was that the worker had completely to satisfy the management, or forfeit his wages. Some estates also resorted to the 'long task' which often led to the replacement, before its completion, of one worker by another. In some cases, the first worker was given a chit representing the value of his contribution to the task which he was able to redeem at pay-day out of the wages of the second worker; but in other cases the first worker earned nothing for his efforts.

Short payment and worse – the complete withholding of wages (entered in the books as 'stop payment') – were frequently encountered, especially in relation to the years 1884 and 1894, the depression years of the sugar industry. Sometimes the employer was simply taking steps to manage his cash flow, and sometimes he was testing the waters. In some cases, given the meagre earnings of the labourers, finding enough small change was a problem.[18] In these instances, as well as on a more general scale, payment was effected by chits or tokens which could be exchanged at a premium at estate shops or other establishments in the vicinity of the estates where overseers and the leaders of work gangs had an interest. Overseers and shopkeepers sometimes colluded to deduct money at the pay table from the wages of customers to satisfy shop accounts.[19] Deductions were also made to set off the expense of work-place accidents, like that resulting from a broken shovel, or to cover the cost of providing new migrants with field implements and rations. One calculation was that it could take five years to pay off one year's rations.[20] The rations and other accounts could become a bone of contention, to reveal once more how control of information operated to the workers' disadvantage.

The most obvious extra-legal method of recovering wages was the imposition of fines for small offences in the adjudication of which the employer was both complainant and judge. It is difficult to explain why this practice became so widespread, or why it was tolerated by the authorities for so long. What the legislation permitted, apart from imprisonment, was the imposition of monetary penalties determined by the magistrate and recoverable from wages. It is possible that the workers, convinced of the affinity of interests between employer and magistrate, considered that summary punishment by the former was just as good as by the latter, or even better since the worker could not be imprisoned by the employer and would be spared the trouble and expense of attending court. The employers abrogated to themselves jurisdiction over a wide range of offences – trespass, late-coming, sleeping, incomplete work, damage to property, responsibility for straying animals. Some of these, by their very nature, disclose the expanse of employer discretion. They disclose too the absolute determination of management that no expense, even if purely accidental or unavoidable, should be laid at their door until all other avenues of defraying it had been explored. Most estates seemed to keep a fines book, and on those where no separate accounts were maintained the fines were shown as credits in the pay lists. In any case, the estates routinely operated the practice of a 'trust week' whereby one week's wages were withheld as a guarantee of satis-factory performance in the ensuing week; as a consequence, the workers in turn had to buy on trust or credit at the local shop.

The sustained campaign by Trinidad planters to whittle down the migrants' right to a return passage to India and so to reduce their own liability in this regard also represented an attempt to recover money which had been disbursed as wages. Their argument focused not only on the loss of 'seasoned' workers occasioned by the entitlement to the return passage, but also remarkably on the signs of affluence which they noted among the workers in the women's fondness for jewellery and in the community's unrestrained celebration of religious and cultural occasions. This campaign eventually bore fruit; the migrants were called upon to bear an increasing proportion of the cost of the return voyage, and ultimately in the twentieth century were made to stand the full cost.

The final device related to the recovering of money disbursed as wages, however, was not something for which the planters as employers were responsible but was related to the operation of the law of intestacy. A large proportion of the children born in the colony from the union of migrant parents were at law illegitimate, for marriages under the migrants' religious or customary law were not validated unless registered by the civil author-ities. In the absence of a valid will, which was the rule rather than the exception, illegitimate offspring did not succeed to their parent's estate, and tracing relatives in India was next to impossible, for, as one report put it: 'the names of persons and places have, under the system of transliteration in vogue and in the colonies, become completely disguised'.[21] The ultimate beneficiary, then, was the Administrator-General of Estates and the coffers of the colony.

Thus both the employer and the state felt competent to delve into the workers' pay packets, usually before they were paid. Admittedly, this was the only way, since the workers found it difficult to accumulate any savings, from which fines or penalties, or debts of one kind or another, could be satisfied. But the impunity with which wages could be tampered with crystallized general attitudes towards labour. Given these attitudes, the terms of indenture and measurements based on wages were set on drifting sand. The 1899 consolidation of the Immigration Ordinances provided, for example, that indenture was terminated when a worker had earned a total of $350. The duration of indenture was thus related to wages. But, at a working year of 280 days and with a wage rate of $0.25 per task, which was generally the going rate, that sum could not be earned before five years, which was the length of indenture anyway. Again, when it became clear that minimum wage provisions were not being adhered to, and that the Government of India was becoming increasingly restive on this account, it was provided that no estate on which more than 15 per cent of the adult male indentured workers had failed to earn an average of $0.12 per day during the previous calendar year would receive a further allotment of migrants. Here was an attempt to judge the condition of the labourers by the transaction at the pay table, but the operation of this particular clause was repeatedly suspended. Indeed, it had to be, for to adhere to it would have resulted in the termination of indentured immigration. In arguing that the clause should not be implemented, the employers insisted that the workers had access to other means apart from their earnings on the estates, and that wages did not tell the whole story. In that they were more correct than they would have cared to admit, but so blithely did they make the point that it seems fairly clear that they were, partially at least, the victims of their own propaganda, especially in their estimation of what made a man work. Whether they believed it to be the case or not, they certainly did not operate on the assumption that increasing the wage was the lever to obtain a desirable labour response.

The level of wages in late nineteenth-century Trinidad bore less relation to the labour market than has usually been assumed and more to the structure of power in the society. Thus, convincing as it sounds, it is by no means certain that it was indenture which kept down wages on the plantations. It is debatable, too, how much the workers themselves internalized some of the employers' views about the fruits of their labour. One fairly pessimistic account notes that when protest action on the plantations did come, it was usually prompted by managerial withdrawal of some benefit or condition rather than by the workers' attempt to secure a new demand,[22] but it is possible that that view gives too much weight to the planters' ability to extract advantage from the fluid work norms which we have noted.

The very imprecision of working arrangements presented opportunities for bargaining and negotiation, and the heavy incidence of strike and protest action in the last quarter of the nineteenth century provides ample testimony that the workers were indeed able to exploit those openings.[23] Both sides strove to claim the edge of advantage in the day-to-day encounters which marked the employment relationship; the planters' aim was to seek to compel labour to perform, the workers' aim to turn that compulsion on its head. In this regard the unplanned cane fire which produced a situation which required the almost instant harvesting of the crop was a major strategy of the workers. Yet, despite unrest and strike, it seems clear that the workers were unable to force the planters to accept the idea of the wage as their property, legitimately won by their exertions at the work-place. That victory would have to await a changed political climate and the more formalized bargaining between employer and trade union not available in Trinidad until the 1930s.

Notes

1. The exceedingly stylized posturing of the illustration on p. 225 'Pay Table, Perseverance estate, Cedros' gives the story away. The female labourers squat in the front row with the males standing behind them; in the foreground the overseer and the headman sit, a money bag between them, at a small square table which has just enough space underneath to accommodate a reclining dog; to the extreme right two groomsmen wait, almost impatiently, with the manager's horse. From the *Photographic Album of Late 19th Century Trinidad* in the Collection of the Main Library, UWI, St Augustine.
2. Most recently repeated in Roy D. Thomas, *The Development of Labour Law in Trinidad and Tobago* (Wellesley, Mass., 1989), 2.
3. It was ultimately replaced by a new Ordinance bearing the same name in December 1938 following serious labour disturbances. See *Laws of Trinidad and Tobago 1950*, ch. 22, no. 5.
4. Bridget M. Brereton, 'Sir John Gorrie: A Radical Chief Justice of Trinidad and Tobago 1886-1892', *Journal of Caribbean History*, 13 (1980).
5. The role of the planters in securing the passage of the Masters and Servants Ordinance in 1846, and the trend in the nineteenth century of committals for breach of contract under the Ordinance (and under the immigration laws) are discussed in David Trotman, *Crime in Trinidad. Conflict and Control in a Plantation Society, 1838–1900* (Knoxville, 1986), 188–96.
6. Argued in Basdeo Mangru, *Benevolent Neutrality. Indian Government Policy and Labour Migration to British Guiana 1854–1894* (London, 1987).
7. Discussed in Morton J. Horowitz, *The Transformation of American Law, 1780–1860* (Cambridge, Mass., 1977).
8. See P.S. Atiyah, *The Rise and Fall of Freedom of Contract* (Oxford, 1979).
9. Some of the relevant technological change is discussed in J.H. Galloway, *The Sugar Cane Industry. An Historical Geography of its Origins to 1914* (Cambridge, 1989).
10. The private cane farmer, in his more optimistic moments, might think that he was working for himself, but there was nothing that he could do with his crop except sell it to company-owned mills; the pricing arrangements ensured that if the farmer was to take into account the cost of his own labour he would be operating at a loss. See D. Maharaj, 'Cane Farming in the Trinidad Sugar Industry' (Ph.D. thesis, Edinburgh, 1966).
11. Mangru, *Benevolent Neutrality*, 194.
12. Sanderson Report, Cmd. 5194 (1910), 314.
13. Mangru *Benevolent Neutrality*, 147–8.
14. The Report of the Royal West India Commission, Cmd. 6359 (1897), vol. 8, 15.
15. M. Schuler, *Alas, Alas, Kongo. A Social History of Indentured African Migration into Jamacia 1841–1865* (Baltimore, 1980), 54–5.
16. See D. Engels, 'The Age of Consent Act 1891: Colonial Ideology in Bengal', *South Asia Research*, 3, 2 (1983). In the late nineteenth century in India the government remained cautious about introducing any law which appeared to infringe local custom, especially when the custom in question, like early marriage, could claim some religious sanction. This approach did not commend itself to the planters of Trinidad.
17. D.V.D. Comins, *Note on Emigration from India to the Colonies* (Calcutta, 1893), 32.
18. Republic Bank of Trinidad and Tobago, Ltd, *From Colonial to Republic - 150 Years of Banking and Business in Trinidad and Tobago 1837-1987*, 49.
19. H. Johnson, 'The Chinese in Trinidad in the Late Nineteenth Century', *Ethnic and Racial Studies*, 10, 1 (1987).
20. Comins, *Note on Emigration*, 20.
21. Ibid., 38.
22. See H. Tinker, *A New System of Slavery. The Export of Indian Labour Overseas 1830-1920* (London, 1974).
23. I have discussed this in 'Control and Resistance among Indian Workers, a Study of Labour on the Sugar Plantations of Trinidad 1875-1917' in D. Dabydeen and B. Samaroo, eds, *India in the Caribbean* (London, 1987), 61–80.

III

Achieving Rights
for Labour

Confrontation
&
Collective Bargaining

12

Contested Terrains

Houses, Provision Grounds
& the Reconstitution of Labour in
Post-Emancipation Martinique

DALE TOMICH

The history of slave emancipation in the French West Indian colony of Martinique suggests the complexity of social forces and political projects involved in the abolition of slavery.[1] To speak schematically, a 'revolution from above' converged with a 'revolution from below'. The Revolution of 1848 brought anti-slavery forces to power in France. Most notably, Victor Schoelcher, the most vigorous and uncompromising advocate of immediate emancipation and the symbol of French anti-slavery, became Under-secretary of State for the Colonies and was later elected Deputy to the National Assembly for Martinique and Guadeloupe. Under his tutelage, one of the first acts of the provisional government (4 March, 1848) was to declare its intention to abolish slavery immediately. A commission was appointed under Schoelcher's direction to organize the transition to freedom, and emancipation was decreed on 27 April, 1848. Ironically, the arrival in Martinique of the news of the fall of the July Monarchy provoked a local slave uprising (22–3 May, 1848) which compelled authorities in the colony to declare slavery abolished before word of emancipation arrived from France.

The slave uprising appears to have been an episodic flash and little overt resistance followed the May events. Nonetheless, in the aftermath of emancipation, metropolitan authorities, colonial planters and the freed population engaged in a struggle over the political and social organization of labour and property and, consequently, the nature and content of the new freedom. Central to this confrontation was the disposition of houses, provision grounds and other resources to which the labouring population had established customary rights while still enslaved. Slaves in nineteenth-century Martinique engaged in extensive provision ground

241

cultivation, fishing, food gathering and handicraft production both for their own consumption and for sale in local markets. By developing such proto-peasant activities, they not only improved the material quality of their lives, but also established customary rights to property and to free time. They thus fashioned a sphere of independent activity, at once within and against the slave relation, that allowed them to assert their own needs, purposes and cultural forms.[2] With the end of slavery, the labouring population consolidated and expanded these practices in an effort to redefine the character and purposes of plantation labour and its place in social life.

Sidney Mintz has emphasized the importance of house and yard, provision ground, and internal markets for understanding the subtle yet significant processes of adaptation and resistance through which Afro-Caribbean slaves sought to shape their material and social environment during slavery and after.[3] His approach suggests the links between slavery and post-emancipation developments as well as the originality and the diversity of Caribbean peasantries and, indeed, of Caribbean history.

This perspective has properly drawn the attention of scholars to the movement of freed populations off the estates; the acquisition of land by squatting, purchase or rental; and the diverse ways in which subsistence and market production combined with plantation labour in the peasant households. However, the historical experience of emancipation in Martinique calls attention to another dimension of the interrelation of proto-peasant practices and the formation of a plantation labour force. Rather than deserting the plantation, the freed population of Martinique sought to redefine the character of plantation labour while remaining resident on the estate. House and yard, provision ground, and the activities associated with them emerged as strategic terrains of contention in the attempts to fashion the post-emancipation labour regime. They provided the former slaves with a means of controlling the conditions of their labour and resisting the reimposition of work routines and labour discipline even as they were being incorporated into the internal organization of the plantation.

This chapter investigates the reconstruction of labour relations in Martinique during the first nine months of the Second Republic. It is particularly concerned with the ways in which housing and provision grounds were implicated in the struggles to reconstitute a labour force and maintain sugar production after emancipation. It draws primarily on the correspondence of François-Auguste Perrinon, Commissioner General of the Republic and member of the Schoelcher Commission, between his arrival in Martinique in June, 1848 and his departure in October of that same year. Perrinon undertook a series of tours of the rural districts to implement the emancipation decrees and organize labour. His correspondence documents not only the ways in which workers sought to subordinate the rhythm and organization of work to their individual and collective needs in the first moments after emancipation, but also the attempts of the Republican regime to regulate labour and property.[4]

Martinique's plantation system was in crisis even before emancipation. Although sugar cane had been cultivated there since the mid-seventeenth century, the island's sugar industry underwent intensive development during the first half of the nineteenth century after the Haitian Revolution deprived France of its wealthiest colony. New plantations were established and old ones increased their output. More land and labour were devoted to sugar at the expense of other crops. By 1847 there were 498 sugar plantations in Martinique. Cane was cultivated on 19,735 hectares and 32,093 metric tons of sugar were produced.[5] The largest and most productive plantations were in the series of fertile valleys running along the northeast coast and on the broad alluvial plain of Lamentin. Plantations in the arid south were smaller and less productive. Despite the rapid growth of sugar monoculture during the first part of the nineteenth century, the end of the slave trade and the re-emergence of the beet sugar industry in France after 1830 dramatically altered the conditions of production. Unable to renew their labour supply, colonial planters were forced to compete with a dynamic and technically more efficient rival within the French market. As the price of sugar steadily declined, they were unable to either expand on to new land or to modify the social and technical organization of the plantation to reduce costs. Instead, they were compelled to intensify production and increase output within the existing framework. Even as they produced more sugar, they became increasingly impoverished and indebted.[6]

With the coming of freedom, some former slaves abandoned life on the plantations and went to settle in the towns. Others occupied land in the mountainous interior of the island or on abandoned estates by either squatting or purchase, and engaged in producing various combinations of subsistence and market crops. If and when members of either group required additional income, they could provide a source of casual labour for the plantations. However, despite the planters' fears that slaves would abandon the plantations after emancipation, the great majority of the rural population remained resident on the estates and engaged in sugar production. Of the 40,429 slaves employed in the production of sugar in 1847, 27,006 or about two-thirds, remained as free workers in 1848.[7] Upon his arrival in the colony in June, 1848, Perrinon reported that there were few sugar plantations on the island where the present harvest or future harvests were compromised by the inaction of the newly freed (*nouveaux affranchis*), and that in the districts (*quartiers*) of François, Gros-Morne and Lamentin cultivation had been resumed by the work gangs (*ateliers*) with all the old intensity.[8] Perrinon was favourably impressed with the capacity of the former slaves to adapt to the rights and duties of freedmen, and was enthusiastic about the possibility of maintaining production. He noted that the great majority of workers were well disposed, and thought that their remarkable sense of order, dignity, propriety and hope for the future would have a favourable impact on the island's production. [9]

In contrast, the planters were demoralized and had lost political initiative. Deprived of slavery as a source of labour and means of social control, they were faced with unrest and uncertainty at home and their adversaries in power in the metropolis. 'The obstacles', Perrinon observed, 'do not always emanate from the cultivators, but rather from the proprietors'.[10] Some former slaveholders, afraid of a general insurrection, or perhaps of their creditors, abandoned their properties and fled the countryside or even the island, often taking their liquid assets with them. (The Emancipation Decree of 27 April 1848 for the first time permitted sugar plantations to be seized for debt.) Others broke their estates into small plots and rented them to freedmen. Still others sold their property or lost it to their creditors.[11] Although Perrinon encountered some local disorders, he reported that their origins were less in the insubordination of the freed population than in 'the impudence of the former masters, some of whom have taken refuge in Saint Pierre leaving their plantations vacant and refusing to send representatives to negotiate with the labourers'. He cautioned that the inactivity of these plantations could become a bad example for the colony.[12]

However, since emancipation came during the harvest season, there was great pressure to bring in the standing crop and manufacture sugar. Under these conditions, most planters, at times aided by municipal administrations, spontaneously reorganized work and improvised new forms of labour relations in conjunction with the workers. In order to maintain an adequate and regular labour force, planters allowed the former slaves to keep their cabins and provision grounds and, as during slavery, free Saturdays to grow and market their own crops. Wage labour was uncommon. Except on the larger and more prosperous plantations in the northern part of the island, few planters had sufficient cash with which to pay wages, especially in the absence of an indemnity for their 'lost property'.[13] Even where wages were paid, this often meant the simple allocation of money and/or goods in kind that the proprietors and the workers arranged among themselves. More common were various sharecropping arrangements (*contrats d'association*). Workers received a portion of the proceeds from the sugar crop, generally either a half or a third, in return for their services. Depending upon how the crop was divided, the costs of production fell upon the proprietors alone or were shared jointly with the workers.[14]

The income from sugar production, whether as wages, shares or profits, whether in money or kind, may have represented an important economic resource for the labouring population. Indeed, Perrinon reports a number of estates where workers themselves organized cane production under the direction of the former slave drivers after the planter or overseer deserted the property. Beyond purely economic considerations, Perrinon emphasized the attachment of most new citizens to their birthplace: 'Leaving the plantation on which they had previously been employed is generally repugnant to them'. Because of this sentiment, emigration and changes of occupation were rare. In his view, such a disposition, which he sharply contrasted to the situation following emancipation in the British West Indies, assured public order, the success of agriculture and the interests of the proprietors of the soil.[15]

Yet, despite Perrinon's optimism about the attitude of labour, he encountered a stubborn refusal to submit to conditions that recalled slavery. Thus in Trou-au-Chat, Perrinon reports that:

> The attitude is good, but there as almost everywhere else, exactitude of labour is lacking. The associated workers do not completely give the days and hours agreed upon. Subordination to an overseer is repugnant to them as is submitting to roll-call. They see in these formalities reminders of slavery.[16]

Similarly, in Vauclin, a prosperous commune during slavery, Perrinon describes the labourers as docile and intelligent. Nonetheless, the commune is distinguished by the difficult and insubordinate attitude of its workers.

> They believe themselves exempt from coming to work at fixed hours or at any time other than at their own convenience, from receiving direction from the proprietor or the overseer, and finally from keeping the commitments that they find too demanding or too analogous to the obligations of slavery.[17]

The newly freed workers responded to emancipation not by open resistance, but by a persistent refusal to submit to supervision and regular hours of work. They utilized the threat of unrest, the fear of a labour shortage, and the need to harvest the current sugar crop to assert their control over houses, provision grounds and petty marketing activities and to thereby contest the conditions of life and labour on the sugar estates.

Attachment to their houses and provision grounds was a fundamental factor in keeping the former slaves resident on the plantations.[18] During slavery, house, yard and provision ground were sources of shelter, a more adequate and varied diet, and perhaps marketable produce. They formed 'niches' within the slave system that allowed slave families to improve the quantity and quality of goods available to them, and permitted individual and collective self-expression. They were thus interwoven in a multiplicity of ways with the formation of proto-peasant activities, slave community and Afro-Caribbean culture. With the coming of emancipation, the freed population treated such property as their own. Reasserting customary rights established under slavery, they refused to abandon their houses and provision grounds or to compensate the planters for their use. According to Perrinon:

> There generally exists among the workers a very pronounced pretension regarding the possession of houses and gardens. Persuaded of their right to property, they refuse to abandon their customary premises and believe that they should be able to continue to enjoy them without having to make arrangements with the real proprietor.[19]

Not only did the attempt of the workers to consolidate their hold on houses and provision grounds engender conflict with planters and the colonial state over property rights, by asserting control over these resources workers were able to expand individual and collective resistance to the imposition of work routines and labour discipline, and even to subordinate the plantation to their domestic economy.

According to Perrinon, wage labour enjoyed great prestige in the eyes of the newly emancipated workers, and they greatly preferred it to share-cropping (*association*). However, while workers asserted their claims to houses and provision grounds, they frequently refused to labour on the estate where they lived. They would either work on another plantation or, if they possessed sufficient resources, live off the income of their garden plot or other subsidiary occupations. In Lamentin, a major sugar district, Perrinon reported a number of plantations where few of the former slaves who remained resident on the property worked there. They preferred instead to hire themselves out elsewhere for a franc a day. Thus, on the Volmenier estate, 35 individuals were employed, but only eight were former slaves on the plantation. The workers constantly rejected sharecropping. Production was instead carried on with the assistance of day labourers from outside the property at a wage of a franc a day.[20] Similarly, the new citizens on the nearby Prix Garnier estate all kept their houses and gardens against the wishes of the proprietor and hired themselves out as day labourers on the neighbouring plantations.[21]

If pervasive efforts by workers to separate the places of work and residence reduced their dependence on the planter and increased their space for manoeuvre, from the perspective of the landowner such initiatives subverted labour discipline and undermined the effectiveness of wage labour.[22] For many planters, even for those who could afford to pay wages, labour by the day or week was unsuitable. It resulted in an unstable and irregular labour force that was not subject to discipline. In the words of one planter, wage labour demoralized the Negro and maintained 'all of his habits of insubordination and capricious idleness'. He complained that it was impossible to force the Blacks to perform the amount of work agreed upon for a day or week and that controls could not be established to verify that work was done properly. They arrived late, put down their tools, returned to their homes, or followed any other whim – but the proprietor still had to pay them their wage. Irregular and undependable labour resulted in growing losses. Extensive fields were left uncultivated. Slow and careless manufacture reduced the quantity and quality of the sugar. Production declined to the point of ruining the planter. Recourse to the local magistrates provided no relief. It was so difficult for planters to obtain labourers that they did not dare to take their complaints to the authorities for fear that the workers would abandon the plantation.[23]

In the absence of generalized wage labour, the majority of rural labourers worked on the plantations where they resided. However, although share-cropping gave them a stake in sugar production, the former slaves were not profit-maximizers. Instead, they utilized their control over houses and provision grounds to define their labour around a variety of activities that included not only cane cultivation and manufacture, but also the production and marketing of crops from their provision grounds, fishing, pottery-making and charcoal-burning. They not only rejected regular hours of work and the supervision of overseers but appropriated the labour time of the estate and sought to subordinate sharecropping to their own purposes. Thus, for example, in the commune of Sainte Anne Perrinon reported:

> The associated workers whether on half or on third shares, all take Friday to cultivate their gardens, to fish, to make pottery or other objects of personal interest. On the four days that they do work, none of them furnish the hours due to the society.[24]

Similarly, in Ste Luce and Diamant, where sharecropping by half shares prevailed, almost the entire former population remained in occupation of its houses. Workers combined fishing with agriculture. Perrinon reported that estate labour was weak and irregular. 'Work is deserted on Fridays and irregularly done on the other days. Management is not recognized. Property rights to houses and gardens are contested'.[25] There was widespread resistance to his efforts to regularize labour in these districts. Perrinon reported similar appropriations of labour time elsewhere in the south. The population of neighbouring Trois-Ilets was described as insubordinate, inexact in the hours of work, and disposed to desert work altogether on Fridays.[26] Even in Rivière Pilote, where Perrinon recorded that sharecropping was operating reasonably well, he nonetheless had to demonstrate to the labourers 'the necessity and the advantages of regular daily labour five days a week'.[27]

Although some of the arrangements between planters and workers for wage labour or sharecropping had been legalized by the competent municipal authorities and had the status of contracts even before Perrinon's arrival, the majority were provisory. In general, the parties waited for the Commissioner General's arrival in order to regularize these relationships by registering them as legally valid contracts.[28] Perrinon was faced with the problem of reconciling Republican political principles and the idea of liberty with the necessity of maintaining a viable labour force and social order in the colony.[29] While an uncompromising enemy of slavery and partisan of immediate and general emancipation, he saw the maintenance of the sugar industry as the only alternative for the colonial economy.[30] He sought to secure labour, but without coercion. In his view,

> ... all compulsion ... would be incompatible with the principles of liberty. Furthermore, it would be impolitic and would become a source of danger for the colonies because the freed population would only see the continuation of servitude in every attempt of that nature.

Instead, he defined the goal of his mission as ensuring equitable arrangements for a prompt return to labour and educating former masters and slaves in their new rights and duties.[31]

For Perrinon, the problems arising from the arrangements that had been made between planters and workers were minor ones that would be resolved when the new basis of freedom was established. The very existence of these acts, the good faith and ease with which they were made, were, for him, proof that the abolition of slavery was not the abolition of labour. In his view: 'The principal difficulty in the present situation resides uniquely in the mode of remuneration applicable to labour. The urgency of this latter problem is generally recognized'.[32]

While there were some successful examples of plantations operating with wage labour, Perrinon was persuaded that the extreme poverty of the colony precluded wage labour as a viable option and that sharecropping was more suited to the conditions prevailing in Martinique.[33] The benefits, in his view, were social, moral and economic. It provided the best way to educate the labouring classes, create habits of order, and re-establish mutual trust between proprietors and workers. It would thereby revive and perfect agricultural labour, increase production and bring the country to its fullest prosperity. He was, in fact, so convinced of its utility that he envisioned converting to it even those plantations where wage labour was successful.[34]

By modifying the experience of several successful planters, Perrinon formulated a standardized sharecropping contract (*contrat d'association*) and propagated it throughout the colony. 'This document', he wrote, 'seems to me to satisfy the needs of the moment and equitably assure the rights of workers and proprietors'.[35] With it, he sought to create model plantations that would educate former masters and former slaves to the new conditions of production.

The contract formed an annually renewable association between the owner and the worker for the exploitation of the estate. The proprietor provided land, animals, machinery and buildings (except the owner's house). These became the property of the association. The associated workers had to provide for their own food, clothing and care when sick. They had the right to enjoy the use of houses and gardens on the property. Saturdays were set aside for the cultivation of their provision grounds and the sale of its produce. The contract prohibited workers from keeping animals other than pigs and fowl.[36]

The work day was set at nine hours a day. The labourers were to divide themselves into work groups and designate one of their number to act as chief. The latter was to work alongside the others. In exchange for their labour, the workers received a portion of the crop. There were two ways of sharing the product of the association. In the first, the product was divided into three equal parts: one for the owner; one for the expenses of the society; and one for the workers. In the second, after having deducted the expenses of the society, the remaining product was divided in half between owner and workers. Division among the workers was to be made either after the manufacture or after sale of the produce. Each associate was to receive a part proportional to the number of working days he or she furnished to the society.[37]

Further, the workers elected from among their ranks a council of five members who were to resolve any difficulties that might arise among them. They presided over the division of shares among the workers and served as the intermediary between the workers and the proprietor or the administrator. In addition, the council determined the size and location of provision grounds, assigned responsibility for collective tasks like watching animals or collecting fodder for them. Finally, the council had the right to exclude workers from the association for misconduct or laziness.[38]

This contract demonstrates Perrinon's attempt not only to subordinate proto-peasant activities to sugar cultivation, but to transform them into mechanisms of labour discipline and social control. On the one hand, the use of housing and provision grounds was made conditional upon labour for the estate. On the other hand, the owners' property rights to land, buildings and other assets were secured and used to constrain the activities of the labourers. In addition, aspects of worker self-organization were incorporated into the operation of the estate, and the half- or third-share of the crop due to the associated workers promised greater reward than did the wage. The workers' direct stake in the success of the plantation was to replace the coercion of slavery with self-interest. In this way, Perrinon attempted to reconcile freedom, labour and property; to balance the interests of planters and workers; and to create a stable and disciplined labour force bound to the estate.

Perrinon initiated a series of tours of the colony's rural districts in order to 'organize agricultural labour and, at the same time, enlighten the new citizens about their true interests as well as their duties'.[39] In order to establish his model contract, Perrinon urged severe measures in order to chase off those 'idlers' who attempted to keep their houses and their gardens without making arrangements with the proprietors. He commented: 'Many of them seem to ignore the limits of their rights in this respect and insist on wanting to remain in possession of their houses and gardens without any compensation for the proprietor'.[40] Thus, he exhorted the labourers to form associations, but used the clause regarding vagrancy in the 27 April emancipation decree to expel from the property any workers who failed to do so. (However, it should also be noted that he often delayed evictions until the crops in the provision grounds were harvested.)[41] Of such expulsions, Perrinon remarked: 'But what are these petty inconveniences in the presence of such evident hope that emerges from them for the organization of agricultural labour with free labourers, for the future of the country'.[42]

For Perrinon, such evictions were not intended simply to expel unsubmissive workers and secure order and discipline, but also to provide the new citizens with a moral lesson regarding the relation of liberty and property in the new order. Thus, on La Trompeuse estate in Lamentin, where some of the labourers worked on shares but the remainder kept possession of their cabins and gardens while refusing to do so, Perrinon reported:

> I congratulated the associates on their laudable conduct, I prompted several admissions to the society, and finally, I made the recalcitrant ones understand that though they are entirely free in the legal limit of their behaviour and their will, they cannot restrict the liberty nor violate the property of another by remaining against his wishes in possession of his things. These individuals will leave in a week if they have not enrolled in the society by that time.[43]

For Perrinon, the changes of place, of habits, and of supervision resulting from eviction were among the most important elements in the success of his undertaking.

> Such workers, demanding and insubordinate with their former master in the place where they live with the memories and habits of slavery, are the most docile and hard-working when a change of residence makes them understand that it is at the price of their labour that they acquire the enjoyment of house and garden as well as the benefits [*bénéfices*] that provide them with the means of existence.[44]

Perrinon also moved vigorously to suppress what he viewed as excessive involvement in secondary activities and to subordinate them to plantation labour and sugar cultivation. He not only sought to delimit the extent of provision grounds, but to restrict other practices such as fishing and charcoal-burning.[45] The unrestrained development of these activities infringed upon the property rights of the owner, disrupted discipline and reduced the labour time available for estate agriculture. Thus, in Vauclin, he prohibited charcoal making and fishing during the hours of work due to the association. From Marin, he reported:

> My exhortations have attempted to . . . have the cultivators give all the time that they owe to the society and to make them understand that they cannot, without the formal consent of the proprietor dispose of the wood in order to make charcoal for their individual profit.[46]

Similarly, while in Case Pilote, he recommended restrictions on the unauthorized production of charcoal made in the proprietors' forest, arguing that this activity not only violated property rights, but greatly harmed cultivation.[47]

Beyond asserting property rights, social order and labour discipline, Perrinon's restrictions were intended to provide workers with a lesson in self-interest and comparative advantage. He urged workers to maximize the return to their labour by devoting their efforts to the more profitable sugar production instead of provision ground cultivation. (He also made a similar argument about the advantages of sharecropping over wage labour.) Thus, in Saint Anne, he instructed the workers, 'about the damage they cause to themselves by deserting cane cultivation (*grande culture*) for less profitable work for which unlimited competition depreciates the price'.[48]

Successful implementation of sharecropping contracts required not only that Perrinon discipline the labourers, but that he strengthen the resolve of the proprietors as well. The majority of planters feared that if they tried to impose control over the workers, they would lose their cultivators and not be able to easily recruit others.[49] Perrinon had to encourage them to adopt a more rigorous attitude toward their workers and show them that the power of the state was behind them. Thus, he reported that in Rivière Pilote, the planters lacked initiative and abandoned themselves entirely to the mercy of their labourers. They did not dare limit the extent of their labourers' gardens, the large number of animals they kept, or punish them for their absence from the agreed upon hours and days of work. This situation was aggravated by the inaction of the Mayor. Perrinon encouraged the planters to exert themselves, to set up sharecropping contracts, and take control. He left behind the Inspector of Police who restored labour and discipline after arresting several vagabonds who had been sheltered by the proprietors themselves.[50] Ironically, the very success of sharecropping later compelled Perrinon to remind planters that they had contractual obligations. Once cultivation resumed, some proprietors manifested

> ... pretensions that they were far from having a few months ago when the authorities had to intervene to limit their concessions. Seduced by the good appearance of their crops and immoderate in their claims for exorbitant revenues, they want to cancel the contracts of association on the strength of which their workers have redoubled their efforts. Six or eight persons have been pointed out to me as having this intention.[51]

Perrinon was well-received during his tours of the island. He spoke before gatherings of labourers in every rural neighbourhood and at each significant plantation in the colony, extolling the nobility of agricultural labour, and urging the new citizens to return to work. At each meeting, he spent several hours explaining the new legislation and the advantages of sharecropping contracts.[52] There were a few instances of resistance. For example, on La Jambette estate in Lamentin, sharecropping by half-shares was agreed upon, but the workers drew back from a contract, which they felt would bind them too tightly. Perrinon persuaded them that the formality of a contract was as much in their interest as in the interest of their proprietor. While waiting to formalize a contract, the workers processed all the cane that was ready to harvest averaging a daily wage of one franc and working with the assistance of labourers from the vicinity.[53] In the Robert district, Perrinon encountered many gangs composed of African-born ex-slaves (*noirs de traite*). He described them as 'ignorant and defiant, confounding subordination with slavery, doubting the advantages of sharecropping which they willingly sacrificed for the simple, positive immediate regularity of a daily salary'. Many favoured working at a fixed price; they harvested and manufactured sugar for 35 francs per barrel, and Perrinon wrote: 'I made them understand by comparative calculations that such a mode was disadvantageous for their interests. I had to rudely advise these workers of the privileges and obligations of their new social position'.[54] However, as a rule, Perrinon's encounters with the new citizens generated enthusiasm and good-will, and in most instances agreements were immediately made on the basis of the model contract.[55]

After seeing first-hand the conditions in the countryside, Perrinon reappraised the impact of emancipation on Martinique. Even though the freed population did not leave the plantations, two months of labour in the middle of the harvest season, from May to July, 1848, had in fact been lost. This interruption caused immense damage to the current harvest and prejudiced future ones.[56] Nonetheless, on the eve of his departure from the colony in October, 1848, Perrinon felt that his efforts had been successful. In his final report, he wrote that labour was reorganized throughout the colony. On a few elite plantations the new organization gave results superior to those obtained under slavery. On almost all the others, it promised to maintain the equilibrium even at the price of diminished labour time. Finally, those plantations that did not function at all were the exceptions. On these latter, he asserted, it was only a matter of the proprietors acting within their rights and expelling those workers who refused to completely fulfil their obligations. He added: 'I have not ceased to advise them to act thus in case of prolonged disagreement; I have not failed to inform them that recourse to public force is assured to them for the realization of rigorous measures'.[57]

Sharecropping contracts achieved some outstanding results, and Perrinon reported some exemplary plantations. The Joyau plantation in Robert district was a model of order, cooperation and prosperity. Regulations were simple and strictly obeyed. Work was performed promptly and regularly under the supervision of an elected council. The associated workers received half-shares and enjoyed the added advantage of having the crop processed at the neighbouring central refinery, Usine Laguigneraye. Similarly, Perrinon reported that the Berté Saint-Auge plantation in Gros Morne was exceptionally well kept. Its owner directed operations and kept the accounts of the society with care. Its 36 associated workers produced more than before emancipation. During the harvest, they stayed in the refinery until two each morning on their own initiative and produced up to 15 hogsheads of sugar a week.[58]

Perrinon observed that the best labour gangs were those that had been well treated by their masters during slavery.[59] Yet, benevolent, generous and enlightened administration was not by itself sufficient to secure order and cooperation. Perrinon cited the Ithier estate in suburban Saint-Pierre as a model for the district. Yet, on the contiguous Morne l'Etoile planta-tion belonging to the same owner, not one-tenth of the workers were assiduous in the performance of the their work. Perrinon reprimanded them strongly, and recommended that the proprietor promptly expel the uncooperative workers, though he noted that Citizen Ithier was too indulgent to do this.[60]

However, despite the enthusiasm with which the workers greeted Perrinon and embraced sharecropping, and the numerous examples of successful plantations, irregularity of labour and the persistence of proto-peasant activities remained pervasive problems throughout the colony. In Lamentin, one of the largest sugar districts, for example, Perrinon found that order had been maintained and production reorganized due in large measure to the vigorous activity of the local administration. Sharecropping contracts had been concluded throughout the district. Nonetheless, they were executed with a certain defiance and indolence which all efforts had failed to eliminate.[61] After his visit to Diamant he warned that vigorous action was necessary in order to restore labour:

> It is insufficiently supplied despite my efforts. Absence on Friday, incxactitudc in hours of work, refusal of supervision, pretension to ownership of cabins are the vices I have fought in Diamant. I have not sufficiently extirpated them.[62]

Indeed, in his final report, Perrinon cautioned that the failure of workers to perform punctually and regularly during the agreed upon hours and days was a general vice. With the exception of a few elite workers, the normal amount of labour was not given but, he reassured his superiors, it was generally recognized that six or six and a half hours of labour under freedom are more productive than nine hours under slavery.[63]

Perrinon remained optimistic about the productivity of the association, and declared that free labour gave results superior to those of slave labour. Indeed, while the number of workers employed in sugar declined by a third in the first year after emancipation, the amount of sugar produced fell by only a bit more than 20 per cent (from 23,668 to 18,736 metric tons).[64] Nonetheless, the absolute decline in production was sufficient to put hard-pressed planters in jeopardy. Emile Thomas, the organizer of the national workshops (*ateliers nationaux*) in Paris who had been sent to Martinique to report on labour conditions, remarked that the ruin of the planters there was complete.[65] One prominent planter complained:

> Rural labour has not recovered. The continuity, the regularity which alone produce results do not exist anywhere. The efforts of the Commissioner-General, [those] of the proprietors are to no avail. The present harvest, the next harvest are lost. A plantation that ordinarily produces 15 thousand kilograms of sugar per week, now only makes 500.

He urged the government of the colony to form disciplinary labour gangs and severely enforce the laws against vagrancy. Only then could labour be reconstituted on a basis that was adequate for the future.[66]

After inspection of plantations in a number of districts, Emile Thomas confirmed these judgements. In a confidential report to metropolitan authorities, he wrote: 'Everywhere that sharecropping exists, work is illusory. Where a regular wage is established, work begins to merit the name'. He estimated that in the richest districts of the island more than half the able workers were engaged in regular labour on the plantations, but the average working day was not more than five hours. The coming harvest would be only one-third of the normal one, that of 1849 only one-half, and it was difficult to see where such a decline would lead by 1850. In order to resolve the crisis, he also recommended the establishment of disciplinary labour gangs as the only remedy for growing vagrancy and urged planters to return to their properties and resume an active role in their direction.[67]

The sharecropping contract indicates the complexity of the historical processes forming the labour regime in post-emancipation Martinique. It developed as a response to the efforts of the working population to shape the plantation regime according to their needs and perspectives. It played an important role in maintaining the continuity of labour and assuring the survival of the sugar industry. But it was an inadequate form of social and economic organization. It did not provide the sugar plantation with labour in sufficient quantity and quality. Instead, house, yard and provision ground remained important terrains of conflict through which workers sought to assert a peasant economy of small-scale production and exchange within the processes of reorganization of the plantation and reconstitution of the labour force. Persistent resistance by the workers would call forth more repressive labour codes under Perrinon's successors, Bruat and, especially, Gueydon. But repression alone was an insufficient response to resistance. In the words of Bruat, labour was 'the regenerative element of the colonies, the source of their strength and of their prosperity'.[68] For both Bruat and Thomas, wage labour appeared as the only means to contain the initiatives of the working population and secure an adequate and regular supply of labour. Yet, the impoverishment of the planters would present a continuing obstacle to the implementation of such a programme. Only through the restructuring of the colonial economy could labour be effectively subordinated and the survival of the sugar industry be guaranteed.

Notes

1. Slavery was first abolished in the French colonies in 1792 by the government of the First Republic only to be restored by Napoleon in 1802. In 1830, the government of the July Monarchy committed itself in principle to slave emancipation but, after 18 years of debate, was unable to reach agreement on the proper formula for emancipation. The final abolition of slavery accompanied the Revolution of 1848 and the establishment of the Second Republic in France.

2. See my *Slavery in the Circuit of Sugar: Martinique and the World Economy, 1830–1848* (Baltimore, 1990), esp. 259–80.

3. Sidney W. Mintz, *Caribbean Transformations* (Chicago, 1974); 'Descrying the Peasantry', *Review*, VI, 2 (Fall, 1982), 209–25; 'Slavery and the Rise of Peasantries', *Historical Reflections*, VI, (Summer, 1979), 213–42; 'Currency Problems in Eighteenth Century Jamaica and Gresham's Law', in Robert A. Manners (ed.), *Process and Pattern in Culture* (Chicago, 1964), 248–65; Sidney W. Mintz and Douglas Hall, *The Origins of the Jamaican Internal Marketing System* (New Haven, 1960).

4. The majority of this material is in France. Archives Nationales – Section d'Outre Mer (hereafter ANSOM), *Martinique*, Carton 56, Dossier 464. Unless otherwise specified, all further citations of Perrinon's correspondence refer to this source.

5. ANSOM, *Martinique*, Etat des cultures.

6. Tomich, *Slavery in the Circuit of Sugar*.

7. ANSOM, *Martinique*, Etat des cultures; ANSOM, *Martinique*, Carton 11, Dossier 109, Bruat à Ministre de la Marine et des Colonies, Fort-de-France, 9 novembre 1848.

8. Perrinon à Ministre de la Marine et des Colonies, St Pierre, 29 juin 1848.

9. ANSOM, *Martinique*, Carton 11, Dossier 108, Perrinon à Ministre de la Marine et des Colonies, Fort-de-France, 8 Octobre 1848.

10. Perrinon à Ministre de la Marine et des Colonies, St Pierre, 29 juin 1848.

11. Raymond Renard, *La Martinique de 1848 à 1870*, (Pointe-à-Pitre, Guadeloupe, 1973), 41–2.

12. Perrinon à Ministre de la Marine et des Colonies, St Pierre, 29 juin 1848.

13. Perrinon à Ministre de la Marine et des Colonies, Macouba, 10 juillet 1848.

14. Perrinon à Ministre de la Marine et des Colonies, St Pierre, 29 juin 1848.

15. Perrinon à Ministre de la Marine et des Colonies, Macouba, 10 juillet 1848. Perrinon à Ministre de la Marine et des Colonies, St Pierre, 29 juin 1848. Perrinon à Ministre de la Marine et des Colonies, Fort-de-France, 21 octobre 1848.

16. Perrinon à Ministre de la Marine et des Colonies, Fort-de-France, 21 octobre 1848.

17. Ibid.

18. All slaves stayed in housing furnished by the master. There were, in general, three types of slave houses in Martinique: those made of stone or masonry with tile roofs; those made of boards with straw roofs; and those made of bamboo laths plastered with mud, also with straw roofs. Some houses, particularly those of stone or masonry, were well built, but much of the housing was poorly built and maintained. The cabin, whichever the type, was generally 16 to 20 feet long and 12 feet wide. A partition divided it into a kitchen and a sleeping room. There was no chimney, and the only light came through the door, which was never more than four feet high. The house belonged to the master, and there is little evidence of slaves trying to improve their houses or using their free time to build one. Perrinon found only a single worker who furnished the material for the construction of his house at his own expense during the slave regime. But whatever the condition of the houses, it was a private space, a place where slaves could escape the surveillance of the master. They jealously guarded this privacy. Schoelcher writes that the slaves did not like whites to enter their homes, and some masters only showed him the slave quarters with great discretion. France, Ministère de la Marine et des Colonies, *Exposé général des résultats du patronage des esclaves dans les colonies françaises* (Paris, 1844), 267–81; Victor Schoelcher, *Des colonies françaises. Abolition immédiate de l'esclavage* (Paris, 1842), 2–4; Perrinon à Ministre de la Marine et des Colonies, Fort-de-France, 21 octobre 1848.

19. Perrinon à Ministre de la Marine et des Colonies, Fort-de-France, 19 août 1848. Perrinon à Ministre de la Marine et des Colonies, Fort-de-France, 21 octobre 1848.

20. Perrinon à Ministre de la Marine et des Colonies, Fort-de-France, 21 octobre 1848. Perrinon à Ministre de la Marine et des Colonies, Fort-de-France, 19 août 1848.

21. Perrinon à Ministre de la Marine et des Colonies, Fort-de-France, 19 août 1848.

22. For a comparison with Jamaica see Douglas Hall, 'The Flight from the Plantations Reconsidered: The British West Indies, 1834–1842', *Journal of Caribbean History*, 10–11 (1978), 7–23.

23. A. Charroppin, *Du travail libre dans les colonies françaises* (Bordeaux, 1848), 9–10.

24. Perrinon à Ministre de la Marine et des Colonies, Trou-au-Chat, 9 octobre 1848.

25. Perrinon à Ministre de la Marine et des Colonies, Fort-de-France, 21 octobre 1848. Perrinon à Ministre de la Marine et des Colonies, Trou-au-Chat, 9 octobre 1848.

26. Perrinon à Ministre de la Marine et des Colonies, Fort-de-France, 21 octobre 1848.

27. Perrinon à Ministre de la Marine et des Colonies, Trou-au-Chat, 9 octobre 1848.

28. Perrinon à Ministre de la Marine et des Colonies, St Pierre, 29 juin 1848.

29. Perrinon à Ministre de la Marine et des Colonies, Fort-de-France, 21 octobre 1848.

30. See Victor Schoelcher, *Histoire de l'esclavage pendant les deux dernières années* (Paris, 1847), II, 373–80.

31. Cited in Renard, *Martinique*, 74.

32. Perrinon à Ministre de la Marine et des Colonies, St Pierre, 29 juin 1848.

33. Perrinon à Ministre de la Marine et des Colonies, Fort-de-France, 21 octobre 1848.
34. Perrinon speculated that wages ought to provide a transition to *association*. 'I have the conviction that substantial sums of money circulated in the colony would be an immense benefit for agriculture, by giving the proprietors the means of preparing the workers for sharecropping and of leading them there bit by bit provisionally from the wage, the most efficacious means of establishing confidence among the parties'. Perrinon à Ministre de la Marine et des Colonies, Fort-de-France, 19 août 1848; Perrinon à Ministre de la Marine et des Colonies, Fort-de-France, 21 october 1848; Perrinon à Ministre de la Marine et des Colonies, Macouba, 10 juillet 1848; Renard, *Martinique*, 74.
35. Perrinon à Ministre de la Marine et des Colonies, Macouba, 10 juillet 1848.
36. ANSOM, *Martinique*, Carton 56, Dossier 464. *Projet d'Association Formulé sous l'Approbation du Commissaire Général, pour l'Exploitation des Usines à Sucre de la Colonie, soit Tiers Brut, soit à la Moitié Nette.*
37. Ibid.
38. Ibid.
39. ANSOM, *Martinique*, Carton 11, Dossier 108; Perrinon à Ministre de la Marine et des Colonies, Fort-de-France, 8 octobre 1848; Perrinon à Ministre de la Marine et des Colonies, Macouba, 10 juillet 1848.
40. Perrinon à Ministre de la Marine et des Colonies, Fort-de-France, 19 août 1848.
41. During the deliberations of the Schoelcher Commission, Citizen Chéry, a member of the delegation of blacks and mulattos, claimed that since the slave generally built his own cabin, it belonged to him. However, in response to Perrinon's question, he conceded that, although the slaves built the houses, the land belonged to the master and that the latter had the right to compel the *affranchis* to leave . . . During this exchange, Schoelcher stated that the cabin could not be treated as the slave's property as it was constructed with materials furnished by the master and during work time belonging to him. ANSOM, *Généralités*, Carton 43, Dossier 350, Procès-Verbaux des déliberations de la Commission Schoelcher, 45–6. Perrinon à Ministre de la Marine et des Colonies, Fort-de-France, 21 octobre 1848. Perrinon reported from his tour, 'I have only found a single worker who has furnished the material for the construction of his house at his own expense during the slave regime. At my suggestion, the proprietor consented to indemnify him although he was not obliged to do so by the law'. Perrinon à Ministre de la Marine et des Colonies, Fort-de-France, 21 octobre 1848. Perrinon à Ministre de la Marine et des Colonies, Fort-de-France, 19 août 1848.
42. Perrinon à Ministre de la Marine et des Colonies, Fort-de-France, 21 octobre 1848.
43. Ibid., 19 août 1848.
44. Ibid., 21 octobre 1848.
45. Perrinon à Ministre de la Marine et des Colonies, Trou-au-Chat, 9 octobre 1848.
46. Ibid.
47. Perrinon à Ministre de la Marine et des Colonies, Fort-de-France, 21 octobre 1848.
48. Perrinon à Ministre de la Marine et des Colonies, Trou-au-Chat, 9 octobre 1848.
49. Perrinon à Ministre de la Marine et des Colonies, Fort-de-France, 21 octobre 1848; Perrinon à Ministre de la Marine et des Colonies, Trou-au-Chat, 9 octobre 1848.
50. ANSOM, *Martinique*, Carton 7, Dossier 83, Bruat à Ministre de la Marine et des Colonies, Fort-de-France, 23 novembre 1850. Such eviction could take place on a substantial scale. Perrinon wrote from Diamant: 'Citizen Telliam Maillet the largest proprietor in the commune, has just asked me to expel 50 unsubmissive workers from his property. I complied immediately'. Perrinon à Ministre de la Marine et des Colonies, Fort-de-France, 21 octobre 1848.
51. Perrinon à Ministre de la Marine et des Colonies, Fort-de-France, 21 octobre 1848.
52. Ibid., 9 août 1848.
53. Ibid., 19 août 1848.
54. Ibid., 9 août 1848.
55. Ibid.
56. Perrinon à Ministre de la Marine et des Colonies, St Esprit, 25 septembre 1848.
57. Perrinon à Ministre de la Marine et des Colonies, Fort-de-France, 21 octobre 1848.
58. Perrinon à Ministre de la Marine et des Colonies, St Esprit, 25 septembre 1848.
59. Perrinon à Ministre de la Marine et des Colonies, Macouba, 10 juillet 1848.
60. Perrinon à Ministre de la Marine et des Colonies, Macouba, 9 septembre 1848.
61. Perrinon à Ministre de la Marine et des Colonies, Fort-de-France, 9 août 1848.
62. Perrinon à Ministre de la Marine et des Colonies, Fort-de-France, 21 octobre 1848; Perrinon à Ministre de la Marine et des Colonies, Trou-au-Chat, 9 octobre 1848; Perrinon à Ministre de la Marine et des Colonies, St Esprit, 25 septembre 1848.
63. Perrinon à Ministre de la Marine et des Colonies, Trou-au-Chat, 9 octobre 1848.
64. ANSOM, *Martinique*, Etat des Cultures.

65. ANSOM, *Martinique*, Carton 11, Dossier 109, Emile Thomas à Ministre de la Marine et des Colonies, Fort-de-France, 9 novembre 1848.
66. ANSOM, *Martinique*, Carton 56, Dossier 464, A. Joyau à Ministre de la Marine et des Colonies, St Pierre, 29 août 1848.
67. ANSOM, *Martinique*, Carton 11, Dossier 109, Emile Thomas à Ministre de la Marine et des Colonies, Fort-de-France, 28 septembre 1848.
68. ANSOM, *Martinique*, Carton 11, Dossier 109, Extrait des Procès-Verbaux des déliberations de la session ordinaire du mois de Novembre 1848, Séance de 7, Conseil Privé.

13

Post-Emancipation Protest in Jamaica

The Morant Bay Rebellion
1865

GAD HEUMAN

The Morant Bay Rebellion was a landmark in Jamaican and Caribbean history. It broke out in October 1865, approximately 30 years after slavery had been abolished, and resulted in the death of over 400 blacks. The rebellion led to the political transformation of the colony and much of the British Caribbean, from a representative system of government, with locally elected Assemblies, to direct rule from London. The case became a *cause célèbre* in Britain, as liberals such as John Stuart Mill sought to try the Governor of the colony, Edward Eyre, for high crimes in violently putting down the rebellion. However, this account will concentrate on the events at Morant Bay itself on the first day of the outbreak. It will also suggest some of the wider causes for the rebellion.

The Outbreak

On 11 October, 1865, several hundred blacks marched into the town of Morant Bay, the capital of the predominantly sugar-growing parish of St Thomas in the East. As one observer put it, they went into the town 'like a mob, dancing and blowing horns'.[1] They carried a red flag, and were in at least two groups emanating primarily from a village known as Stony Gut about four miles away, in the hills above the town. On this day the vestry, the political body which administered the parish of St Thomas in the East, was holding one of its regular meetings.

The crowd was unlike any other which had made its way to Morant Bay. Vestrymen were familiar with crowds which 'used to come down there sometimes on Vestry days and kick up a row – make a noise'. But this gathering was different: the people were armed and 'came in with some intention'.[2] Only a small number had guns but most of the others had either sharpened sticks or cutlasses. The crowd was also highly organized. As one observer noted, they 'came in rows ... they were well packed together close behind each other, but not at all straggling; they advanced slowly and deliberately'. Though dressed in ordinary labourers' clothes, they looked more like troops than an irregular mob.[3]

From the point of view of the authorities, there were other worrying aspects about this crowd. Although the majority were from Stony Gut and neighbouring villages in the area, many were not. A manager of the Jamaica Cotton Company's estate in St Thomas in the East, Arthur Warmington, who was also travelling to Morant Bay, found large numbers of people on the road from Manchioneal going to Bath and then toward Morant Bay, a total distance of over 30 miles. He was surprised to see a great number of people with cutlasses – 'it was not usual for them to walk up the public road ... like that except when they are near the estates'. One group, from a more nearby settlement known as John's Town, had a good deal of encouragement from women along the road. About two or three miles from Morant Bay, Warmington heard women crying out, 'Flog them John's Town'. He also saw a large number of men and women assembling near a river about a mile from Morant Bay.[4]

Even more menacing were the utterances of leading members of the crowd. As they passed by the druggist's shop on the way into town, they knelt down, tasted some dirt and swore, 'we will kill every white and Mulatto man in the Bay, and when we finish, we will return and go to the estates'.[5]

The crowd's first objective in Morant Bay was the police station. There were only two or three policemen inside or near the station, one of whom, Henry Good, hastened to block the crowd from entering, but was knocked down, stabbed and beaten. A second policeman, George Fuller Osborne, tried to escape but was caught by Paul Bogle, the leader of the rebellion. Bogle released Osborne after ordering the policeman to remove his police jacket.[6] Inside the station, the crowd also attacked another policeman, William Lake. According to Lake, one of the men in the crowd raised a cutlass to kill him, but another man prevented it, saying 'it is your colour; don't kill him. You are not to kill your colour'.[7] The crowd then took down all the swords, guns and pistols and demanded ammunition. But the police had none; moreover, none of the guns had any flints, rendering them useless. Having determined that there were no more weapons in the station, the crowd marched resolutely with their drum and fife playing toward the court house, where the parish vestry meeting was taking place.[8]

The head of the parish, Custos Baron von Ketelhodt, had anticipated trouble. A German who had married an Englishwoman and settled in Jamaica, Ketelhodt, as the principal magistrate of the parish, chaired the vestry meetings, He had called up the volunteer militia to guard the vestry that day and written to the Governor requesting troops. His despatch expressed concern that the forces at his command would be insufficient to uphold the law. The custos warned, 'the shells are at this moment blowing to collect men all through the Blue Mountain Valley . . .'[9]

The immediate cause of the difficulty had arisen from a court case four days previously, on 7 October. According to Custos Ketelhodt, over 150 men had come into Morant Bay that Saturday 'armed with sticks and preceded by a band of music', with the intention of rescuing a man who was to be tried in court, if he was found guilty. During the proceedings, a boy was convicted of assault and ordered to pay a fine of 4s. and costs of 12s. 6d. Another man, James Geoghegan, interrupted the court, arguing that the boy should not pay any costs. Geoghegan was ordered out of the court, but he continued to make a noise while he was leaving. When a justice on the bench ordered him to be arrested, the crowd prevented it. The police apparently grabbed Geoghegan in the square, but the mob pulled him away. According to the clerk of the parish, some '40 or 50 people with sticks [were] licking at the police. The rioters were drawing away a man through the market, and the police trying to prevent them taking him away'. Fearing that the policemen would be injured by such a menacing crowd, the magistrates called them back into the court house. In the process, one of the policemen suffered a broken finger and at least one other was beaten. Paul Bogle was among the people involved in this scuffle.[10]

The next case was the one the crowd had come to witness. It concerned a trespass on Middleton, land bordering Bogle's village of Stony Gut. Middleton was owned by Wellwood Maxwell Anderson, a white planter who had become the Inspector-General of Immigration for Jamaica. He had leased the land to James Williams in April, 1865, who in turn rented it to small settlers. However, some of the settlers refused to pay rent on the grounds that 'the land was free'. One settler claimed that he had 'been to the Record Office, and found that the land was given to them free, some years ago'. The settler warned Williams to reduce the rent; otherwise he 'would not get any at all'.[11]

In this atmosphere, it was likely that legal difficulties would arise between Williams and his tenants, although the court case that Saturday concerned a trespass rather than non-payment of rent. One of the settlers, Lewis Miller, had apparently allowed his horse to stray on Williams's land. Miller was found guilty of the offence and fined 20s. Paul Bogle, Miller's cousin, advised him to appeal against the fine and acted as Miller's surety. While this case was being tried, the court house had filled with people involved in the skirmish with the police. One justice reported that the 'bearing of the people . . . was most threatening and insolent, and calculated to intimidate us'. The justices felt it was therefore impossible to make any arrests that day.[12]

The following Monday, the justices issued warrants against 28 people for the assault on the police at the court house. On the Tuesday, the police proceeded to Stony Gut, Bogle's village, to execute the warrants. They found Bogle in his yard, read him the warrant, and sought to arrest him. But Bogle refused to go and shouted for help. As one of the policemen reported it, as soon as Bogle appealed for help, 'the shell blew, and the drums rolled at the same time', and the police were surrounded. Immediately, upwards of 300 men armed with cutlasses and sticks appeared out of the nearby canefields and from the chapel in the village. Although the police tried to escape, several were caught.[13] They were handcuffed, threatened with death, and eventually forced to swear an oath of loyalty. According to one of the policemen, he had to kiss the Bible and say, 'So help me God after this day I must cleave from the whites and cleave to the blacks'.[14] While at Stony Gut, the policemen also witnessed other men taking the oath. 'Paul Bogle spoke to the men in a language I did not understand. The men then took the oath, they kissed a large book, the bible. Paul Bogle gave each of them a dram of rum and gunpowder which they drank'.[15] Bogle ordered three of his lieutenants, Colonel Buie, James Davies and his own brother Moses Bogle, to drill three gangs of men. The men carried sticks, cutlasses and lances and practised marching a short distance away from Bogle's house.[16] Before being freed, the police learned that Bogle would be coming to Morant Bay with his men the following day.

Bogle confirmed his intentions in a petition to the Governor, probably written while the police were still being held. In it, Bogle and his allies complained that 'an outrageous assault was committed upon us by the policemen of this parish, by order of the Justices, which occasion an outbreaking for which warrants have been issued against innocent person, of which we were compelled to resist'. The petition continued:

> We, therefore, call upon your Excellency for protection, seeing we are Her Majesty's loyal subjects, which protection if refused to will be compelled to put our shoulders to the wheel, as we have been imposed upon for a period of 27 years with due obeisance to the laws of our Queen and country, and we can longer endure the same . . .[17]

When the police were eventually released from Stony Gut later that day, they immediately reported what had happened and warned the parish officials of Bogle's plans.[18] The custos was thus enabled to call on the small group of volunteer militia to protect the meeting of the vestry.

The volunteer militia, made up mostly of whites and browns, was composed primarily of bookkeepers and overseers, that is, lower-level members of the plantation hierarchy. They were not professional soldiers. The largest group available for duty on 11 October was the Number 1 Company of Volunteers from Bath. Approximately 20 of them came into Morant Bay that morning, led by Captain Edward Hitchins.[19] The sergeant-major of the corps, E.N. Harrison, indicated how untrained many of them were for their duties. On the way into town, a few rounds of ammunition were handed out to the men, and they were shown, apparently for the first time, how to load with ball cartridges. When the volunteers marched into Morant Bay, they found everything 'quiet, a few women only dancing before us to the music of our drum corps'. They were probably relieved to hear that the Stony Gut people were not planning to come into town. Instead, the members of the militia believed that the people of Stony Gut were armed, but waiting in the village to resist any attempts to take Bogle and the others to town. While the meeting of the vestry was taking place in the court house, the members of the militia had lunch and were resting or strolling around the parade.[20]

Suddenly, around 3 o'clock in the afternoon, a man galloped into the parade (the central part of the town facing the court house) shouting, 'the negroes are coming'. The volunteer bugle was sounded, and Hitchins ordered his men to their posts. The corps now also included up to ten volunteers from the Number 2 Company at Morant Bay, but it should have been a much larger contingent than that. Many members of the militia from the town had clearly not reported for duty. About ten minutes later, they saw a crowd of about 400 people approaching them.[21]

The crowd had come together from different roads leading in to the parade. They appear to have entered Morant Bay together but had taken alternative routes which joined at the parade. These moves seemed well orchestrated. As the crowd began to march toward the court house, one of the volunteers observed an African with a pistol in front of the mob and reported that the crowd was advancing 'with a blowing of shells or horns, and a beating of drums'.[22]

By this time, the members of the vestry had come onto the balcony of the court house. From his vantage point, one of the vestrymen reported seeing the armed crowd marching in what he termed 'regular soldier style'. Another vestryman saw people in the crowd brandishing the arms they had taken from the police station and heard them cry 'Colour for colour!' and 'War, war!' As the mob surged forward, Baron von Ketelhodt cried out, 'Peace!' and other officials called out 'Peace in Her Majesty's Name!' But the people responded 'No Peace! Hell today!'[23]

Ketelhodt then asked for a copy of the Riot Act and began reading it. But he was so alarmed by what was happening that he had difficulty getting through it. He had not progressed very far when the crowd began throwing stones at the militia. A volunteer observed a woman he knew named Geoghegan throwing the first stone, followed by a hail of stones from other women in the crowd. The crowd was hurling glass bottles as well as stones, and some of these proved effective. Several of the volunteers were hit and some injured, including the captain.[24]

The crowd was now so close that some of them began to attack the volunteers. Members of the mob managed to get between the volunteers and the court house and struck them from behind. Several volunteers were badly beaten and had their guns taken away from them.[25] In the face of this onslaught, either the custos or the captain gave the order to fire. Several members of the crowd were killed, possibly as many as seven, and others were wounded. The crowd briefly retreated, but then charged the volunteers before they could reload. Rev. Stephen Cooke, the Anglican curate from Morant Bay who formed part of the vestry, later suggested that a more effective militia or even a military commander could have dispersed the crowd. But the failure of the volunteers to fire in succession gave the crowd their opening. They rushed at the militia, forcing them as well as the vestrymen to retreat back into the court house.[26]

Once inside the building, the militia and vestrymen barricaded the doors. Shooting continued. The crowd had scattered behind nearby buildings, but continued to throw stones and shoot at the court house, and their fire was returned by the troops. At one point the custos sent out an old black man with a white handkerchief seeking peace; however, he disappeared and never returned. Later in the afternoon, probably around 5 o'clock, Ketelhodt tied a handkerchief to the end of an umbrella and hung it out a window. When the mob was told that it meant peace, they replied that they had come for war, not peace. Ketelhodt even volunteered to give himself up to the crowd, if they would spare the others in the court house. But at least two or three voices cried out that they wanted him and every white and mulatto man there.[27]

The situation was quite desperate, yet some people managed to escape from the court house. After about an hour and a half inside the court house, Baron Ketelhodt's son-in-law jumped out of one of the windows. He was shot at, but managed to get away. At least one person managed to get into and then out of the court house. Seeing the shooting and then the 'white flag' from the court house, Mrs Cooke, the wife of Rev. Cooke, sent a servant to 'see if Mr. Cooke wanted anything'. Although the servant did not find Rev. Cooke, the Baron and the Inspector of Police gave him letters to carry directly to the Governor.[28]

After about two hours, members of the crowd decided that the best method of attack was to burn down the court house and force the volunteers and vestrymen to come out. It is likely that women were responsible for this plan. One witness claimed that a woman from the Stony Gut area, Rosanna Finlayson, 'said they must go and get a fire stick and trash, and set the school-room on fire. She said the white people were locked up in the court house, and if they set fire to the school room the whole people would be burnt up alive'. Five minutes later, the school house was on fire. It was adjacent to the court house and it was not long before that building began to burn as well.[29]

Women were also instrumental in encouraging the men in the crowd to continue their attack on the court house. After the volunteers had fired at the crowd, some of the men had withdrawn. But women on one of the roads leading into the town reportedly told the men: 'Now, you men, this is not what you said in the mountain. You said you would come to the Bay and do so and so, and now you leave all this work to the women; go to the Parade and see what the Volunteers do to the men there.'[30]

Once the court house was on fire, the volunteers and vestrymen could no longer remain there. They had a number of quick discussions about what to do; several decided to jump out of a back window while others removed the barricades and ran down the front stairs of the court house. Some made their way to the neighbouring home of Charles Price, a black builder who was also sitting on the vestry that day, escaping the collapse of the court house roof by a matter of a few minutes. In the process, several of the parish officials and militiamen were either wounded or killed. Price's home then also began burning.[31]

The situation was hopeless. One of the members of the volunteer corps, Lieutenant Hall, was killed in Price's house and another was badly wounded. Several of the vestrymen were also hit. At one point, the men inside the building thought they saw a steamer coming to the rescue, but that proved to be a mirage. As they were surrounded and the building was on fire, they all seemed doomed. Rev. Victor Herschell, the Anglican minister in Bath, offered a prayer, and a vestryman, Arthur Warmington, shook hands with two others in the building and made them promise to send his wife and baby to England if they survived and he did not. They then all sought other hiding places.[32]

By this time, it was dark. Some of the officials and militiamen were able to hide in the penguins, thick prickly bushes near the court house. Others were caught by the mob, badly beaten, and sometimes mistakenly left for dead. Many others were killed by the crowd.

The custos was unable to escape. One volunteer heard Ketelhodt asking, 'What are you beating me for? What have I done to you?' as he was dragged along by the crowd and beaten to death.[33] Charles Price, the prominent black whose house had been a temporary refuge, was also attacked by the crowd, but there was a debate about what to do about him, largely because of his colour. A policeman reported the following exchange:

'Price, don't you know that you are a black nigger and married to a nigger?' They said, 'Don't you know, because you got into the Vestry, you don't count yourself a nigger'. He said, 'Yes, I am a nigger'. They said, 'Take a looking glass and look on your black face'. And Price said, 'Yes, I am a nigger'.[34]

A vestryman who was also hiding nearby heard a member of the crowd warn that they had 'orders to kill no black; only white and brown'. Another replied, 'But he has got a black skin and a white heart'.[35] The crowd decided to keep guard on Price, but then the women said: 'We work for him on the road and he not pay us, and we burn bricks for the church at Morant Bay, and he not pay us. You need not keep him till before day'. Price was then beaten to death, despite offering £200 for his life.[36] Rev.

Herschell also offered his attackers money – £300 – to save his life, but to no avail. 'Damn the parsons: kill him', was the crowd's response.[37]

Several of the volunteers and vestrymen were badly beaten and left for dead. The volunteer, R.G. Harrison, was one of them. He and his brother were attacked, the brother killed and Harrison left for dead. Members of the crowd came to examine him two or three times, but he remained still, despite their pulling off his trousers and boots and later, when things were quiet, he hid in a bush near the sea until daylight.[38]

Another volunteer, M.N. Wolfe, was severely wounded by men wielding cutlasses. When he pretended to be dead, the crowd stripped him of his uniform and underwear and left him naked. Wolfe recounted what happened next:

> Two other rebels came to me when I was lying on the ground, and they said, 'This is one of the Volunteers; he is dead, the d – d son of a bitch'. As he said so, the other one said, ' Come let us see', and they came and turned me over on my back; then they came and searched if I was dead. They came and felt my chest to see if it was blowing, and they felt my nose. I stopped my breath as well as I could, and when they found no breath was coming, they believed I was dead, and they moved off about the distance of four or five yards. One of them returned with a cutlass, and said to the other, 'Come let us cut off his head', and he immediately came and placed his knees down upon my chest, with one hand extended, and he pointed the cutlass at my throat.

But his companion advised against it and suggested they search for others who were still alive.[39]

Some of the volunteers were caught trying to conceal themselves in the bushes. One of them, W. Mitchell, was hiding there, and heard men in the crowd expressing a desire to go to their homes because they feared that the soldiers were coming. But the women said, 'No, search the bush, plenty more in the bush'. The men responded, 'No more', but the women insisted, 'Plenty more'. They rigged up a light on a long bamboo pole and found Mitchell in a bush. He was pulled out, beaten and robbed but eventually taken to his employer, a shopkeeper in Morant Bay. Members of the crowd then demanded Mitchell's salary for saving his life.[40]

A planter and vestryman, William Payne Georges, lay undiscovered in the penguins. He was wounded while the court house and then Price's home were under siege, but successfully avoided detection. At about 1 a.m. the next morning, Georges decided to head toward the rectory. He was surrounded by a dozen people, and one of them wanted to know: 'Who is that?' He said, 'A friend'. They immediately sung out, 'No friend – white man, chop him down'. A man lifted his cutlass, but Georges had a pistol and fired at him. The others ran away, and Georges proceeded to the rectory. He wrote a despatch to the Custos of Kingston, Lewis Q. Bowerbank at 6 a.m. that morning, informing him that he 'was about the last of the few whites who are left to tell the mournful tale'.[41]

The crowd did not only consist of people anxious to kill the vestrymen or the volunteers. Many actively aided some of the injured men. James Moore Ross was a volunteer who, although wounded, was trying to escape to the wharf. A woman was helping him when Bogle appeared and threatened to kill him. The woman shouted to Bogle, 'Don't kill him; he is nearly dead already'. Ross managed to get to the wharf and onto a boat to safety.[42] Francis Bowen, a magistrate and a planter who sat on the vestry, had a similar experience. He escaped from the court house just after the militia had fired its volley into the crowd. Bowen was followed by a man and stoned but managed to get to the road leading to the wharf. There he saw men beating the sub-collector of customs, Brooks Cooke. As he ran past this affray,

> a man with a gun and fixed bayonet stopped me, and putting the bayonet against my side said, 'Which side you belong to?' [he was a black man]. I said, 'For God's sake don't put that into me'. Immediately then a black man called Thompson bawled out from the wharf, 'For God's sake don't do that, it's Mr. Bowen from Coley, he is a good man'.

Bowen lunged toward Thompson and pleaded for a place to hide. Thompson told Bowen to run onto the wharf, where the boat, *The Eleanor* was in port. Bowen hid in an outhouse, while some other men hailed the boat for him. Fortunately for Bowen, the captain was able to rescue him.[43]

These were not isolated incidents. For instance, another volunteer, W.W. McGowan, had been badly hurt and left for dead. The crowd had removed his boots, shirt and money. He remained on the ground until the next morning, when a member of the mob came across him, realized he was not dead, and threatened to behead him. A woman whom McGowan did not know offered him a glass of water, but the man threatening the volunteer knocked it out of her hand. She then offered 4s. for McGowan and another wounded volunteer, saying that McGowan was her brother. According to McGowan, her action and the timely arrival of British troops saved his life.[44]

Before leaving Morant Bay, the crowd marched to the district prison. Again, they proceeded in a military fashion, headed by Paul Bogle. One of the officers in charge of the prison reported that as the mob entered the jail, Bogle ordered a sentry to be put at the gate. The crowd liberated the 51 prisoners in the jail, but Bogle insisted that the prisoners 'must get their own clothes, for he would not like to rebel against the Queen, and he would not strike as a rebel against the Queen, and so they wanted their own clothing'. The prison officer had to break open the chest where the personal clothes of the prisoners were kept and hand them out. Bogle also had the prison officers swear on a Bible that they would no longer serve as public officers; in addition, the officers 'must go home and work for [themselves]'. Bogle then formed the prisoners into a line and marched them out of the prison.[45]

The events at the Morant Bay jail illustrated the significant degree of organization of the crowd. It was clear that there were specific gangs, with captains in charge of each. One volunteer, Joseph Williams, had been beaten by several of these gangs as he sought to escape. He reported that the captains included McLaren, Ennis Napier and Scipio Courle. A resident of Morant Bay, Cecilia Gordon, had heard captains ordering men to march and to stand guard in various locations in the town. She identified two of the captains as Grant and Stewart. Yet it was Bogle who was clearly in charge. Whether it was a question of the treatment of a captive or one of tactics, Bogle was generally giving orders and was referred to as 'General Bogle'.[46]

The organized nature of the crowd may explain the lack of pillaging or looting in the town. Apart from the burned-out buildings, there was little other destruction in Morant Bay. The crowd demanded gunpowder from Mrs Lundie's shop, took bread from the bakery, and a range of items, including tobacco, fish, candles and soap, from Marshalleck's store. But even there, they left the rum and other spirits.[47] Bogle and his men had come to attack the vestry, but were not intent on destroying the town. When they returned to Stony Gut, Bogle offered a prayer in his chapel to 'thank God, that he went to do his work and God succeeded him in his work'.[48]

The events at the court house, at the prison, and in the town occurred before any troops could arrive. When they did land the next morning, 12 October, the troops found the dead and many of the wounded in the area around the court house. In all, 18 of the officials and the militia were dead, and 31 others wounded. Seven members of the crowd had been killed. The reprisals by the troops began almost immediately and, in the next month, more than 400 blacks would be shot and hanged, 600 flogged, often brutally, and at least 1,000 homes would be destroyed. Although it is not possible here to examine the suppression of the outbreak or the subsequent actions of the rebels, there follow some suggestions about why the rebellion occurred at all.

Causes

In assessing the outbreak, it may be useful to consider the immediate origins of the rebellion as well as more long-term reasons for it. It is therefore important to examine the developments in St Thomas in the East, especially the considerable tension during the 1860s. In part, this centred around the figure of a coloured politician, George William Gordon. Apart from serving as a representative of St Thomas in the East in the House of Assembly, Gordon was a church-warden on the local vestry until expelled by Custos Ketelhodt on the grounds that he was not an Anglican. In reality, it was Gordon's radical politics which had alienated him from Ketelhodt and the more powerful parish officials. Gordon contested his expulsion in court but lost twice and was in the process of a further appeal at the time of the rebellion. To make matters worse, in September 1865, parish officials engineered the transfer out of the parish of the stipendiary magistrate, T. Witter Jackson, who was the only neutral magistrate on the bench. Like Gordon, Jackson was a brown man and was popular among the blacks. Both of these acts created a marked degree of hostility toward the custos and the other parish officials.[49]

Yet it was not politics alone which created bitter feelings among the populace of the parish. Many people also believed that it was impossible to obtain justice in the local courts. Since almost the entire magistracy was dominated by planters, it was often the case that employers were judging the cases of their employees. High court fees also made it very difficult for labourers and small settlers to pursue cases in court. One of the grievances of the crowd at Morant Bay was the lack of justice in the parish. For example, when asked the reason for the rebellion the day after the events at Morant Bay, one of the members of the crowd at Bath claimed it had broken out 'because the poor black had no justice in St Thomas in the East ... there was no other way to get satisfaction in St Thomas in the East, only what they had done'.[50]

For the blacks in the parish, there was at least one other alternative that some of them had tried. In several areas, blacks had organized their own courts. These people's courts were held in districts not far from Morant Bay where offences were punished by fines and by flogging. Such alternative courts seem to have existed in other parts of the island as well and were further evidence of the dissatisfaction of the people with the administration of justice.[51]

Another source of difficulty for the people of St Thomas in the East was the issue of wages. The problem was over low as well as irregular wages on the sugar estates. Two of the prominent figures killed at Morant Bay, Custos Ketelhodt and Rev. Herschell, had experienced problems with their labourers over this issue. At Oxford, Ketelhodt's estate in the parish, there were complaints about low pay for the workers. Many of the people who worked on the estate came from Stony Gut and the surrounding villages. Herschell also had an estate, an abandoned sugar plantation near Bath known as Potosi. There was a dispute between him and some of the settlers who had occupied the land before he purchased it, and a court case was pending.[52] On the morning of the rebellion, Henry Lawrence, Gordon's overseer on his estate, predicted that 'the negroes know who fit for retribution' and that 'the Baron and Mr. Herschell will be dead'. Lawrence proved to be correct.[53]

There were also serious complaints about the irregularity of payment. A missionary reported that his parishioners believed that they were 'not paid regularly on some of the estates, that their money was docked, [and] their tasks were heavy ...'[54] Given the lack of redress in the courts, the concern about wages figured prominently among the grievances of the crowd at Morant Bay.

In addition to these issues, there was also the problem of land. More specifically, there was a belief that the provision grounds away from the estates – the land which peasants and labourers used to grow their own crops – belonged to the people and not to the estates. As previously stated, the people's view was that they should have this land without paying rent. It is likely that one of the planters killed in the days following the outbreak at Morant Bay, Augustus Hire, was a target of the crowd because of his stance on this issue.

Hire was the planting attorney for Amity Hall, an estate in the Plantain Garden River district of the parish. Acting for the owners of Amity Hall over some nearby property, Hire had authorized a survey on the land known as Rowland's Field. He had been unable to collect rent from people he believed were squatting on the land. However, when the surveyor, along with Hire, began work in July, 1865, they were surrounded by an armed crowd of over 100 blacks. The crowd seized the surveyor's chain, broke it, and became 'very violent'. Despite having the ringleaders arrested, Hire and his surveyor met considerable resistance when they tried again the following day. Hire recorded the precise words of one man, Henry Doyley, who grabbed the surveyor's chain; when Hire asked him what right he had to the land, Doyley responded, 'What God Almighty make land for? You have plenty; we have none'. The surveyor also reported that the crowd told him, 'if we wanted war, we should have war'.[55] Hire's recourse was to try the people involved in the scuffle in the Circuit Court; the case was scheduled to take place the week after Hire's murder.[56]

These problems over land, justice and wages in St Thomas in the East should be seen in light of the wider problems affecting Jamaica as a whole. One of the significant aspects of Jamaica's history has been the large number of rebellions and conspiracies, especially during the slave period. The most important of these occurred in 1831 and was instrumental in the emancipation of the slaves. Slaves in the 1831 rebellion made use of the structure of the missionary churches and chapels to organize the out-break. After the abolition of slavery, the tradition of protest persisted. Riots continued in the post-emancipation period – one in 1848, for example, because of a rumour that slavery was to be reimposed.[57]

The economic problems which Jamaica was suffering in this period, especially in the 1860s, also contributed to the rebellion. Sugar was the economic mainstay of the island's economy, but it underwent a steep decline in the decades after emancipation. Partly because of the loss of a protected market in Britain in the 1840s and partly because of the relatively high cost of producing sugar in Jamaica, many estates disappeared. By 1865, at least half of the sugar plantations which had operated in the 1830s no longer existed.[58]

In the 1860s, Jamaica's economic situation worsened considerably. The American Civil War had the effect of dramatically increasing prices for imported goods, including foodstuffs. A series of prolonged droughts devastated the peasants' provision grounds, further adding to the cost of food. The output of sugar was also reduced, and work on the dwindling number of estates was harder to find.[59]

The 1860s also witnessed significant developments in the religious life of many Jamaican freedmen. In the wake of emancipation, many ex-slaves regarded the European dissenting missionaries in the island as their allies. The number of members in the Baptist and Methodist Churches was particularly high. In the decades after emancipation, however, the influence of the missionaries began to wane. The people turned increasingly to native churches which practised more African and Afro-Caribbean forms of worship. The Great Revival, an evangelical movement which swept Jamaica in 1861, was symptomatic of this shift toward Afro-Caribbean religions.[60]

Among the most important of these native religions were the Native Baptists. They were particularly strong in the eastern part of the island and in St Thomas in the East. Their message was political as well as religious: according to a white Methodist missionary, the native preachers emphasized the oppression of blacks and the need to defend themselves. The missionary reported the works of one black preacher: 'You are black and I am black, and you ought to support your own color. The blacks are seven to one of the others, and they ought to have the Island'.[61]

The leader of the Morant Bay Rebellion, Paul Bogle, was a Native Baptist preacher. Moreover, Bogle served as the election agent for the man who was regarded by the local administration as responsible for the outbreak, George William Gordon. During the 1860s, Gordon saw himself increasingly as the spokesman for the ex-slaves; at the same time, he was shifting his religious allegiance from the Established Church to the Native Baptists. One student of post-emancipation religion in Jamaica has argued that Gordon appropriated religion to politics and used it as a basis of protest.[62]

Jamaica's problems in 1865 were highlighted by a letter from Edward Underhill, the Secretary of the Baptist Missionary Society in England to the British Secretary of State for the Colonies. In the letter, Underhill complained about the dire situation in Jamaica and pointed especially to the starving condition of the peasantry. For Underhill, there was no doubt about 'the extreme poverty of the people' which was evidenced 'by the ragged and even naked condition of vast numbers of them'. As there was less work on the estates and since the drought had caused a general failure of the provision grounds, the people either had to 'steal or starve. And this is their present condition'. Underhill believed that the Jamaican Legislature was partly responsible for the state of the colony and predicted that unless 'employment can be given to [Jamaica's] starving people, I see no other result than the entire failure of the island'.[63]

The Colonial Office forwarded the letter to Jamaica, where it was widely circulated; in addition, meetings were held all over the island to discuss the letter. These meetings were heavily attended by blacks, and

A view of Morant Bay, Jamaica. The burning court house is to the left
(Illustrated London News, *1865*)

often dominated by members of the opposition to the local administration. One group, some of whom were connected to the Native Baptist movement, organized what became known as the Underhill Convention to support Underhill's claims. At the Underhill meeting in Kingston, for example, the chair was taken by George William Gordon, the most prominent opponent of Governor Eyre. Those who submitted resolutions included local preachers, some of whom were attached to the 'Tabernacle', a Native Baptist chapel Gordon had helped to establish in Kingston. There were also black politicians and other independent clergymen involved in the gathering.[64]

The resolutions of the Kingston meeting provided strong support for Underhill as well as a radical critique of the Government and the ruling class in Jamaica. One resolution complained about the 'class legislation' of the island and suggested that 'the time has arrived when the masses

271

of this country must speak out their woes, labouring as they do under many wrongs and disabilities . . .' Those attending the meeting were also opposed to the enormous expenditure used to import labour and pointed to 'the systematic abnegation of every principle involving the Education of the Masses and other measures of a preventative and ameliorating character'. However, what may have worried the authorities most was the meeting's call

> upon all the descendants of Africa in every Parish throughout the Island, to form themselves into Societies and hold Public Meetings, and cooperate for the purpose of setting forth their grievances, especially now, when our philanthropic friends in England are leading the way.[65]

The Underhill meetings were held all through the island in the spring and summer of 1865. Dissidents such as Gordon travelled from parish to parish, speaking at these gatherings and pointing to the oppression of the population. Some of the language he was reported to have used worried the authorities. In one parish, Gordon was alleged to have encouraged the people to follow the example of Haiti: in effect, to institute their own Haitian Revolution.[66]

Signs of tension were evident in the summer of 1865. Rumours of a conspiracy in western Jamaica began circulating in late July. It was reported that the people believed that the Queen had sent them money in response to their appeals for help, but that the Governor and the planters had withheld it from them. Fearing an outbreak, the Governor sent a warship to the western part of the island; in the event, nothing happened.[67]

But in St Thomas in the East, Paul Bogle and other leaders of the rebellion were organizing meetings at which the people of the parish expressed their grievances, especially over the issues of land, justice and wages. At these meetings, oaths were administered on a Bible to willing adherents. All those who refused to swear the oath were not allowed into the meetings. One interpretation of the oath, which was secret, was that the people 'wanted the back lands without paying rent and they were to kill the Buckra [the whites]'.[68] These oaths tallied with the cries of the mob at Morant Bay and elsewhere: 'Colour for colour; skin for skin; cleave to the black'. There was a clear anti-white and anti-brown feeling among the crowd at Morant Bay, although the people agreed to save any black or brown person who joined them.[69] There were also many subsequent reports of men being drilled militarily and preparing for what they called, 'War'.

Faced with an unyielding Government and ruling class, Paul Bogle and his allies saw no solution to their grievances. They were concerned about the lack of justice in the parish as well as the problem of access to land and to work. They were supported by an African-oriented religion, they believed they had allies in Britain and in Kingston, and the atmosphere was rife with arguments about white oppression of the blacks. Fearful that they might even be re-enslaved, the people marched into Morant Bay.

Notes

I am grateful to Mary Turner for her comments on this paper. The research was supported by the British Academy and the University of Warwick.

1. *British Parliamentary Papers*, 1866, [3682], XXX, Papers Laid before the Royal Commission of Inquiry by Governor Eyre (hereafter Papers), 355.
2. *British Parliamentary Papers*, 1866, [3683-1], XXX, Report of the Jamaica Royal Commission, Part II, Minutes of Evidence and Appendix (hereafter JRC), Evidence of Brookes Cooke, 52-3.
3. JRC, Evidence of Edward William Major, 28.
4. JRC, Evidence of Arthur Warmington, 57-8.
5. JRC, Evidence of William Alvarenga, 136.
6. JRC, Evidence of Henry Good, 30; Evidence of George Fuller Osborne, 32.
7. JRC, Evidence of William Lake, 79.
8. Papers, In the Court held under Special Commission, January 1866; The Queen v. Bogle and Others, Copy evidence, Robert Evan Jones, 442.
9. JRC, Evidence of Edward J. Eyre: Custos of St Thomas in the East to the Governor's Secretary, 10 October 1865, 84.
10. JRC, 83; Papers, 389. See also the description of the disturbance in PRO 30/48/44, Cardwell Papers, 'Jamaica', by Lewis Q. Bowerbank, 17.
11. JRC, Evidence of James Williams, 184.
12. Ibid.; Papers, 396.
13. JRC, Evidence of William Fuller, 80.
14. Colonial Office (hereafter C O) 137/140, Storks to Cardwell, 19 February 1866, no. 28, Enclosure: Statement of William Fuller, Policeman, 5 January 1866.
15. Ibid., Statement of James Foster, rural constable, 5 January 1866.
16. JRC, Evidence of James Foster, 135.
17. JRC, 14.
18. JRC, Evidence of John Burnett, 229.
19. JRC, Evidence of Edward Norman Harrison, 15.
20. Papers, Statement of Edward Norman Harrison, Sergeant-Major, St Thomas in the East Volunteers, 6 January 1866, 24.
21. JRC, Evidence of Wallace Wood M'Gowen, 115-16; Evidence of H.J. Cowie, 473; Evidence of Edward Norman Harrison, 15.
22. Papers, In the Court held under Special Commission, January, 1866: The Queen v. Bogle and Others, Copy evidence for Mr Attorney General, McGowan, 387.
23. Papers, 396; JRC: Evidence of Arthur Warmington, 58; Evidence of James Britt, 178.
24. Papers, 150; Ibid., In the Special Commission, 5 March 1866: The Queen v. Bogle, Henry Theophilus and others for Felonious Riot, Evidence of Stephen Cooke, 352: JRC, Evidence of James Britt, 178.
25. JRC, Evidence of Edward Norman Harrison, 17; Papers, R.G. Harrison, Volunteer, to J.S. Williams, 78.
26. Papers, Statement of Edward William Major, 28; JRC, Evidence of Rev. Stephen Cooke, 37.
27. Papers, Statement of Moses Nathaniel Elolfe, 391; JRC: Evidence of Brooks Cooke, 53; Evidence of Arthur Warmington, 58; Evidence of Stephen Cooke, 36.
28. JRC, Evidence of Baron Alfred Ketelhodt, 5; Papers, Statement of Robert Milne, 114.
29. Papers, In the Special Commission, 7 March 1866: The Queen v. Bogle, Henry Theophilus and others for Felonious Riot, evidence of Charlotte Carter, 360.
30. JRC, Evidence of Cecilia Gordon, 180.
31. Papers, Statement of Edward William Major, 28-9.
32. Papers, Statement of Arthur Warmington, 168.
33. Papers, Statement of Edward Norman Harrison, 26.
34. JRC, Evidence of Henry Good, 30.
35. JRC, Evidence of William Payne Georges, 4.
36. JRC, Evidence of Henry Good, 30.
37. Papers, Statement of Arthur Warmington, 168.
38. Papers, R.G. Harrison, Volunteer, to Mr J.S. Williams, 3 January 1966, 78-9.
39. JRC, Evidence of M.N. Wolfe, 234.
40. JRC, Evidence of W. Mitchell, 142.
41. JRC, Evidence of William Payne Georges, 4; C.O. 884/2, Confidential Print, no. 2: Papers

Relating to the Insurrection in Jamaica, October, 1865, Printed for the Use of the Cabinet, December 1865, 15, The Hon. W.P. Georges to the Hon. L.Q. Bowerbank, 12 October 1865, 6 a.m. – Morant Bay.

42. Papers, In the Court held under Special Commision, January, 1866: The Queen v. Bogle and Others, Copy evidence, James Moore Ross, 444.
43. Papers, Statement of Francis Bowen, 396–7.
44. JRC, Evidence of W. W. M'Gowen, 117.
45. JRC: Evidence of Sligo Campbell, 140; Evidence of W. Cuthbert, 139.
46. Papers, In the Special Commission, 7 March 1866: The Queen v. Bogle, Henry Theophilus and others for Felonious Riot, Evidence of Joseph Hardy Williams, 358; JRC: Evidence of Cecilia Gordon, 180; Evidence of Edward William Major, 28; Papers, Statement of Robert M. Whittle, 150.
47. Papers, Statement of Robert Evans Jones, Sworn: 3 January 1866, 33; JRC: Evidence of Mary Ann Thomas, 191; Evidence of Daniel Marshalleck, 42–3.
48. JRC, Evidence of Joseph Muir, 797.
49. Papers, 154; C.O. 137/393, Eyre to Cardwell, 4 September 1865, no. 220.
50. JRC, Evidence of Henry Silvera, 484.
51. JRC, Evidence of William Codner Miller, 919–20. See also Noelle Chutkin, ' The Administration of Justice in Jamaica as a Contributing Factor in the Morant Bay Rebellion of 1865', *Savacou* 11/12 (1975): 78–85.
52. JRC: Evidence of James Taylor, 450; Evidence of the Hon. A. Heslop, 331.
53. C.O. 137/400, Stocks to Cardwell, 19 February 1866, no. 28, Enclosure: Eyre to Cardwell, January, 1866.
54. JRC, Evidence of Rev. William Copeland Harty, 409.
55. JRC: Evidence of His Excellency Edward J. Eyre, Hire to Myers, July, 1865, 988; Evidence of Roger Swire, 951.
56. JRC, Evidence of The Hon. Alexander Heslop, 330–1.
57. Mary Turner, *Slaves and Missionaries: The Disintegration of Jamaican Slave Society, 1787–1834* (Urbana, 1982); Lorna Elaine Simmonds, ' "The Spirit of Disaffection": Civil Disturbances in Jamaica, 1838–1865' (MA diss., U. of Waterloo, 1982).
58. Philip D. Curtin, *Two Jamaicas: The Role of Ideas in a Tropical Colony, 1830–1865* (Cambridge, Mass., 1955), 104–7.
59. Douglas Hall, *Free Jamaica, 1838–1865: An Economic History* (New Haven, 1959), 240–2.
60. Curtin, *Two Jamaicas*, 170–1; Robert J. Stewart, *Religion and Society in Post-Emancipation Jamaica* (Knoxville, 1992), 145.
61. Stewart, *Religion and Society in Post-Emancipation Jamaica*, 167.
62. Ibid., 161.
63. *The Morning Journal*, 20 March 1865.
64. Gad Heuman, '1865: Prologue to the Morant Bay Rebellion in Jamaica', *Nieuwe West-Indische Gids/New West Indian Guide*, 65, (1991), 114–16.
65. *The Colonial Standard*, 6 May 1865.
66. Heuman, '1865', 122.
67. Ibid., 118–20.
68. C.O. 137/400, Storks to Cardwell, 19 February 1866, no. 208, Enclosure: Eyre to Cardwell, January, 1866.
69. Papers, 116.

14

The Pursuit of 'Higher Wages' & 'Perfect Personal Freedom'

St Kitts-Nevis
1836–1956

GLEN RICHARDS

The islands of St Kitts and Nevis form part of the island grouping known as the Leeward Islands, the north-eastern arc of the Caribbean archipelago.[1] A volcanic island, 68 square miles in size, St Kitts is endowed with rich, sandy loam soils which allow unimpeded natural drainage and are easily worked. This, along with abundant rainfall in the central and western coastal regions, made the island eminently suitable for sugar-cane agriculture.[2] The neighbouring island of Nevis is a mere 30 square miles in size and is not as well favoured, since its soils have a high clay content, and the low-lying coastal lands are strewn with large rocks making cultivation highly labour intensive. Despite these unfavourable conditions, sugar cultivation also prospered in Nevis during the period of slavery. Sugar still dominated the economic landscape of both islands on the eve of slave emancipation although there had been a marked decline in output. Like their counterparts elsewhere in the British West Indies, the planters of St Kitts and Nevis insisted upon a period of compulsory labour service from their former slaves in partial compensation for their loss of property. Under the apprenticeship system introduced by the British government, the ex-slaves were compelled to work 40 hours per week on the estates of their former masters.[3]

This system of involuntary labour was explained as a period of adjustment which would prepare the former slaves for the new regime of wage labour. To the sugar planters and the British Colonial Office the great problem of slave emancipation was, in the words of the Under Secretary of State for the Colonies, Henry George Grey, 'how to devise some mode of inducing them [the ex-slaves], when relieved from the fear of the Driver and his whip, to undergo the regular continuous labour which is indispensable in carrying on the production of sugar'.[4] A disciplined labour force was needed which would work 'for wages, not uncertainly and capriciously, but steadily and continuously, at the times when their labour is wanted, and for so long as it is wanted'.[5] The greatest fear of the Colonial Office officials was that the newly-freed labouring population would descend 'into a barbarous indolence' sending the plantations into 'ruin'.[6]

In fact the former slaves needed no preparation for a wage labour system. By the late-eighteenth century, the working conditions of West Indian slaves had begun to assume an increasingly proletarian character.[7] They were completely divorced from ownership of means of production and had long been participating in the wage labour market. In her study of two Jamaican sugar plantations, Mary Turner found that slaves sometimes earned money working for other slaves or for the masters.[8] Urban slaves throughout the British West Indies had even greater access to opportunities for wage labour.[9] In addition, some urban slaves engaged in independent artisanal and commercial activities. Elsa Goveia points to several examples of slaves who were permitted to live apart from their owners, plying their trade in the towns and 'paying the master a weekly rate . . . for the privilege'.[10]

Not only were West Indian slaves engaging in wage labour, they had also adopted proletarian-like strategies in their labour disputes with their owners. Mary Turner shows that slaves employed the weapon of collective strikes, and engaged in collective bargaining with their masters over their conditions of work and in support of demands for an extension of their customary rights.[11] The Jamaican slave rebellion of 1831 included a general strike with the slaves refusing to carry out their tasks on the plantations. Even more remarkable was the slaves' demand that wages be paid for all labour performed on the plantations. The rebels, led by Sam Sharpe, declared their readiness to end the strike if 'Buckra would pay them'.[12] This demand for wages indicates that slavery had formed the plantation slaves into a semi-proletariat willing to earn a major portion of their income through wage labour.

When slave abolition was being planned in the Colonial Office, no commissions of inquiry were sent out to the islands to enquire what the slaves expected of freedom, yet the slaves had a clear concept of what a free society should be, as was revealed in their actions after emancipation. They were not opposed to plantation labour in itself. Many of them had gained a sense of pride and achievement by excelling at certain plantation tasks.[13] They wanted ample free time to meet their domestic requirements and to undertake their own agricultural activities. A related but subordinate demand was the right to carry out their jobs in human dignity and with as little interference as possible from plantation staff and proprietors. What they were opposed to was being compelled to work without remuneration under servile and inhumane conditions. The main demand of West Indian slaves was for personal liberty and fair wages for work done.

The readiness of former slaves to remain on the plantations, the site of their enslavement, has been demonstrated by Douglas Hall. He argued conclusively that had the ex-slaves been permitted to remain in secure possession of their houses, their gardens and their provision grounds, and allowed to choose their own employers without reference to their place of abode, there would have been no movement from the estates.[14] The problem was that the ex-slaves were willing to work 'only six hours a day, four days a week, and an unreliable number of weeks a year'.[15] To work beyond these limits, they wanted a level of remuneration which the planters were unwilling to pay. It was the attempts of planters to tie workers to the estates and force them to work steadily and continuously by charging rents on the ex-slaves' houses and provision grounds, which prompted the flight from the estates and consequent labour shortages. In testimonial after testimonial, ex-slaves declared their willingness to continue to work on the estates 'providing in we getting what is right'.[16]

The interpretation of freedom held by the ex-slaves stood in direct opposition to that definition which the West Indian planters and the Colonial Office shared and sought to impose. For the planters, freedom meant the final discharge of their uneconomic customary obligations to their former slaves. They intended to use their 'own emancipation', as Douglas Hall so aptly puts it, 'to dispose of superfluous or unproductive people and to rid ... (themselves) of the responsibility for their maintenance'.[17] But while the planters sought to remain free of any compulsion to employ labourers, they wanted to be in a position to compel labourers to work in such quantities and at such times as was needed. Further, they wanted labour at a price that would permit the realization of a profit in an industry in which the price of the commodity produced often fell below the cost of production. The planters thus were unwilling to leave the price and availability of labour to be determined by the unregulated mechanism of the labour market. They looked to the intervention of the colonial state to secure a steady supply of labour at prices which they were willing to pay.[18] And the emancipation plan formulated by the Colonial Office was not intended to undermine the planters' control over the labour of their former slaves.[19]

Given these conflicting ideas on the character of freedom, the immediate post-emancipation period was a period of contention throughout the British West Indies.[20] St Kitts was no exception. When informed by the governor, at a public gathering, of the legal compulsion to labour without payment on the estates under the apprenticeship system, the ex-slaves of St Kitts vociferously declared their opposition. They were reported as saying: 'Me free, no bind, no work'. James Cox, a Wesleyan minister who observed these protests, commented that what the ex-slaves wanted was 'perfect personal freedom and wages'. The former slaves in St Kitts refused to carry out the involuntary labour required under the apprenticeship system and many deposited 'their hoes and bills near the dwelling of their respective [estate] managers, thus expressing their determination not to use them'.[21]

In response to what rapidly became a general strike, the colonial authorities declared martial law. This prompted a significant number of the
ex-slave population, including women and children, to desert the estates and
flee into the central mountain range, where some of them, under the leadership of a runaway known as 'Marcus of the Woods', violently resisted
all attempts to dislodge them. Only a military assault by a regiment from
Barbados which had been landed from a British warship, assisted by troops
from the local garrison, broke the resistance of the ex-slaves who were forced
back to the estates.[22]

The events in St Kitts indicate that while the ex-slave population was
ready for a wage labour system, it was the planters and the colonial
authorities who were not ready for freedom and all it implied. The absence
of alternatives to plantation labour meant the St Kitts ex-slaves had, in fact,
been proletarianized to a greater degree than the ex-slaves of the other
British West Indian colonies like Jamaica and Trinidad. The St Kitts
workers' objective was not to become independent peasant cultivators but
to proletarianize their conditions of work, that is, to end the personal
domination of the planters over their daily lives.[23] But the immediate
post-emancipation period saw concerted attempts by planters to restore
the levels of labour control which they had attained during slavery. In
particular, a contest emerged on the hours of work under the new labour
regime. Some estates required nine hours a day, over five days, leaving
Saturdays free. Other estates established a seven-and-a-half-hour working
day, over six days, robbing labourers of their Saturdays to go to market
or to work in their provision grounds. This practice was the cause of
frequent disputes on the estates where it was instituted. The most frequent
and intractable conflicts arose, however, around the ex-slaves' insistence
on dealing with their employers on a basis of equality. John Nixon,
Lt Governor of St Kitts, reported that there was 'a jealousy between some
of the managers or overseers on estates and the work people, the former
not recollecting that slavery no longer exists, and the latter forgetting
themselves, and behaving in a very insolent and provoking manner towards
their superiors'.[24]

The planters in St Kitts were in a much more favourable position to
control their labour force than most of their West Indian counterparts. In
St Kitts, there were no reserves of Crown land which could be occupied by
the former slaves. The little vacant land that existed was in the central
mountain range, where cultivation had been prohibited in an attempt at soil
conservation. During slavery almost all cultivable lands had fallen under the
ownership of the sugar estates and their monopoly of arable land did not
diminish with emancipation.[25]

This land monopoly became the main instrument of labour control in the
hands of the planters who refused to sell land to their labourers, who were
dependent on the estates for access to land not only for cultivation, but also
for housing. This provided one method for binding labour to individual

estates. One planter in St Kitts testified that employers provided labourers with a house and mountain land free, or rented at 'pepper corn rates' on condition that they performed regular labour year-round on the estates.[26] Such estate land was occupied without any security of tenure and at the pleasure of the proprietor. Labourers in Nevis complained in a 1903 petition to the Secretary of State for the Colonies, Joseph Chamberlain, that at the 'slightest displeasure, whim or caprice' of the estate management, land occupied by labourers could be repossessed and their crops sold or destroyed. Livestock pastured by labourers on estate land could be impounded and were only redeemable upon payment of an impounding fee to the estate.[27]

Even more basic to the existence of workers were the houses and house plots which they received from the estates. Because of the estates' monopoly of land no 'free village' system such as existed in Jamaica, Guyana, and even in nearby Antigua, emerged in St Kitts. As late as 1930 up to 70 per cent of rural workers in that island continued to live in estate housing. Workers who lived in estate housing were seen as 'contract labourers' and, as one planter observed in 1898, if they 'will not work can be turned out'.[28] The threat of eviction proved a most powerful instrument for securing a pliable work-force. Land monopoly was supported by other mechanisms of labour control including the manipulation of credit advanced to workers for house building, and the widespread practice of black-listing recalcitrant workers.[29]

Through land control and other mechanisms, the planters of St Kitts-Nevis were able to re-establish their control over plantation labour and to impose the wage rates which they were able or willing to pay. Wages were often set by open collusion between planters particularly during periods of economic depression brought on by falls in world sugar prices. For example, after the end of apprenticeship there was a steady rise in agricultural wages, with the daily rate for men increasing from 6d in 1838 to one shilling by 1846. The precipitous fall in the price received for their sugar following on the passage of the Sugar Duties Act, from 35s. to 15s. per cwt, induced the St Kitts planters to reduce their outlays by cutting wage costs. At a public meeting, the planting body unanimously agreed to reduce the standard rate for male agricultural labourer from 1s. to 10d per day.[30] In a slight variation later in the century, during the economic depression in 1885 a public meeting of planters decided to reduce labour costs by the expediency of increasing tasks rather than cutting wage rates. However, the rate for cutting cane was reduced from 8d to 7d per ton. In 1895 the cane cutting rates were further reduced to 6d per ton by another combination of planters responding to a sharp fall in sugar prices.[31]

The most important instrument of control which the planters had at their disposal was their continued influence over the colonial government. After 1871, with the introduction of Crown Colony rule in the Leeward Islands, the planters were able to exert sway over the presidential adminis-tration through the legislative and executive councils. The members of both councils were either officials or drawn from among the leading planters and merchants, thus guaranteeing that the interests of the upper class would be decisive in the political and economic life of the presidency. One Leeward Islands governor observed as late as 1936, that 'the unofficial representatives for the island [of St Kitts] on the Presidential Legislative Council consisted wholly of European planters and heads of commercial firms'. This meant, he continued, that 'their control ... of such things as taxation, customs, etc., was almost paramount'.[32]

This decisive influence over the presidential councils also meant that the employers were able to determine unilaterally the shape of labour relations in the presidency of St Kitts and Nevis. They were able to buttress the informal control over labour which they had secured through their monopoly of arable land with legal mechanisms for labour compulsion. This mainly took the form of the Masters and Servants Act, which was passed by the planter-dominated legislature of St Kitts in 1849 and remained in force until 1922, when it was replaced by an ordinance which was not repealed until 1938.[33] This legislation entrenched in law the inequality between workers and employers by making a breach of contract by a worker a criminal offence, while an employer who broke his contract with his employee was only liable to civil action for damages or wages due. Under the Act, employees who withdrew their labour before the termination of a signed or unsigned contract would suffer forfeiture of any wages due, and could be sentenced to a fine of up to 50s., or to imprisonment for one month's hard labour. A labour contract was deemed to last one month in the case of non-agricultural workers and one week in the case of agricultural workers.[34] The one-week duration of a praedial contract ensured that the estate worker could not respond immediately to any real or perceived injustices and would have to serve out the contract despite any grievances which might have appeared during its timespan.

The colonial state, in Robert Miles's phrase, 'constituted in law the unfree relations of production' thereby subjugating the workers to the needs of their employers.[35] The West Indian masters and servants legislation became the model for similar colonial legislation in South Africa. But, unlike South African law, the West Indian legislation did not aim at creating a labour force willing to leave their independent economic activities and work for wages. Such a labour force already existed in the West Indies. The West Indian legislation sought instead to subject West Indian workers to the sugar plantations' need for regular and continuous labour at wage levels which could permit planters to maintain profitability.[36] As Daphne Simon observed, the masters and servants legislation of England and, by extension, the British colonies was 'the tail-end of the penal labour laws which were essential to the early growth of capitalism' and 'were meant to secure the disciplining and subordination of the worker'.[37] Planters in St Kitts and Nevis, and in the West Indies as a whole, refused to dispense with the traditions of domination and command which they had established during slavery. Robert Miles has noted the structural similarity between the West Indian slave codes and the masters and servants legislation which succeeded them after emancipation. Both were instruments through which the subjugation of plantation workers to the labour requirements of the plantations was enforced.[38]

Their control of land and their influence over the colonial state thus enabled the planters to determine almost unilaterally the meaning of freedom, but there were working-class attempts to resist domination. Although at a great disadvantage when compared to their fellows in the other islands, the ex-slaves of St Kitts and Nevis sought nonetheless to insist on the expected benefits of freedom. The success of planters in maintaining the social traditions of authority and command elaborated under slavery forced the ex-slaves to resort to strategies of bargaining and protest similar to those evolved during the slavery period. Yet the legal status of freedom allowed the labouring population to carry out certain challenges to the authority of the planters within the framework of the law. The illegal slave practice of running away and marronage was transformed into the legal strategy of mass working-class emigration.

In the immediate post-emancipation period workers from St Kitts and Nevis began an annual migration to Trinidad in search of the higher wages paid on estates there during the sugar harvest. This migration was seasonal in character as most of the workers returned at the end of the crop.[39] Emigration began to accelerate after 1846, following the wage reductions of that year. The male population of St Kitts declined from 10,523 in 1844 to 9,525 in 1855.[40] The female population also declined but at a more moderate rate. In the late nineteenth and early twentieth centuries a wider range of destinations were added, including Costa Rica, Colombia, Panama and Bermuda. Then, as the twentieth century began, the major destinations became the Spanish islands of Cuba, Santo Domingo, and Puerto Rico where US dollar employment was available on the relatively high-waged American-owned sugar plantations.

The planting community of St Kitts and Nevis initially adopted a benign attitude towards working-class emigration. During the long period of economic depression initiated by the Sugar Duties Act, and intensified under the pressure of beet sugar competition during the period 1885 to 1905, the sugar estates of St Kitts were unable to employ all available labour. In 1897 one planter member of the presidential legislature argued that 'the labour problem of St Kitts was not one of scarcity but of over-supply'. He advocated the introduction of assisted emigration for agricultural labourers in order to 'relieve the island of its surplus population'.[41] Between 1904 and 1909 St Kitts-Nevis was the only Leeward Islands presidency to permit the Isthmian Canal Commission to recruit workers directly for work on the Panama Canal.[42]

A sharp rise in working-class emigration during the second decade of the twentieth century coincided with a rise in sugar prices, which led to a change in planter attitudes and growing concern about the possibility of labour scarcity. The St Kitts Agricultural and Commercial Society, the representative body of the island's planting and mercantile interests, submitted a resolution to the executive council early in 1910 complaining of the 'large scale exodus of the labouring people to Costa Rica', and calling for the introduction of legislation to control working-class emigration. The following year, the Emigration Regulations Ordinance was passed into law, prohibiting the recruiting of workers by any person other than licensed recruiting agents. Such agents were required to make a deposit of 5s. per worker as security for their repatriation.[43]

The ordinance failed to slow the departure of workers for higher paying employment elsewhere in the Caribbean and in Central America. Between 1891 and 1921 the total population of St Kitts fell from 30,876 to 22,415 while that of Nevis declined from 13,087 to 11,569. The decline in the male population was even more pronounced, falling from 14,410 to 9,115 in the case of St Kitts, and from 5,945 to 4,678 in the case of Nevis.[44] Mass emigration had become the most widely employed and the most successful strategy used by the working class in their confrontation with their employers. Emigration was a survival strategy enabling workers to increase their income and, through remittances, improve the living conditions of their families.[45] The decision to leave family and countrymen behind and migrate to new and unknown territories required both initiative and courage. It was a choice which many chose not to take. Those who left, primarily young males, departed in search of higher paying employment and working conditions which were free of the socially degrading and humiliating circumstances which typified employment on the sugar estates of St Kitts-Nevis. There were other responses, usually illegal, available to those who remained, and these also had parallels in slave practices.

The most potent weapon which the disgruntled estate labourer had at his command was fire. Arson, as George Rudé observed, is a 'well-established weapon in agrarian disputes', and cane burning was a bargaining tactic widely utilized by slaves in the British Caribbean during disputes with their masters.[46] The combustibility of sugar cane and the rapidity with which the juice lost its sucrose content made fire an especially devastating tool in the hands of sugar estate workers. As Quintin Hogg, a nineteenth-century planter in British Guiana, commented: 'The negro, when he wants work, burns your cane fields. When your cane fields are once burnt, you must grind immediately and he knows that as well as the planters.'[47] Cane burning could be employed by the solitary worker to pursue an individual grievance.[48] Incendiarism, however, was most often a collective expression of discontent with reductions in wage rates or dissatisfaction with working conditions. After the general wage cuts of 1846 disaffected workers in St Kitts were accused of setting cane fires.[49] In 1896, when labour disturbances affected both islands, 402 acres of ripe canes were destroyed by fire in St Kitts.[50] Cane burning was more likely during periods of general unrest, and cane fires always preceded the commencement of the sugar crop during periods of worker dissatisfaction with wages or conditions of work. Indeed, arson could be seen as the workers' opening statement in their attempt to bargain for higher wages. At times it precluded the need for negotiations as the wise planter would concede an increase in wages before further working-class protests became necessary.

One form of legal protest open to workers was petitioning the Crown or its local representative for redress of perceived wrongs. These legal channels were used with relative frequency by workers in St Kitts-Nevis and throughout the British Caribbean. It can be seen as a continuation of the slave practice of appealing over the heads of overseers with whom they were in dispute to visiting absentee owners or to masters and magistrates on neighbouring plantations. The appeals to the higher authority of absentee owners were now replaced by petitions to the government. Petitions were often undertaken in response to planter combinations to reduce wage rates or to cuts in the labour force. In 1896, after presidency-wide wage reductions had been implemented by the planters, 12 workers representing the '[estate] labourers, porters and boatmen' of Nevis delivered a petition to the governor. The petition called on the governor for an increase in wages which should 'be paid at such an hour on payday, as to enable us to procure our daily necessaries'. It also called on the government to increase the tariff of the porters and boatmen and to fix a schedule which the merchants would be obliged to honour.[51]

In 1905 the workers of St Kitts at the commencement of the sugar crop sent a letter to a local newspaper stating their demands regarding wages and conditions of work. Workers on individual estates sent delegations to negotiate with their respective employers, and a joint deputation of estate workers met with the administrator to represent their case.[52] The peaceful representations failed, however, and far from increasing wages the estate proprietors, pointing to lower sugar prices, decided collectively on a 25 per cent reduction in wages.

These peaceful petitions were sometimes combined with more overt forms of working-class protest. In both 1896 and 1905 the workers' peaceful representations to estate proprietors and the local administration led to the outbreak of general strikes and, in the former case, rioting. When legal channels of protest failed the workers' final resort at times was violent protests, although these were infrequent, occurring only during times of great economic distress or in response to some grave social injustice. General strikes occurred in St Kitts-Nevis in 1896, 1905, and again in 1935. In the first and last years, the general strikes were accompanied by widespread disturbances and rioting. The cause of all three was the same: collective wage reductions imposed by the planters in response to falling sugar prices.[53]

The 1896 general strike began after workers, having received reports of increases in sugar prices, asked planters for an increase in wages at the beginning of the sugar crop and were refused. The strike and the labour disturbances which followed revealed in compelling manner the mechanics of what E.P. Thompson described as the 'moral economy of the poor'.[54] The workers saw their protest as a legitimate action in defence of established norms of fairness and their precarious living standards. The planters had justified their original wage reductions by pointing to the sharp fall in sugar prices. With the recovery in sugar prices workers expected a commensurate increase in their wages and protested violently when planters refused to concede to their demands. A newspaper account of the 1896 riot reported workers as saying, 'The managers won't tell us when sugar prices rise, but we know that sugar prices rise and our money must rise too'.[55] The spontaneous general strike affected nearly every estate in St Kitts, as gangs of workers, armed with heavy sticks and lighted torches, paraded the country roads from estate to estate to enforce the strike. The marching bands of workers were accompanied by musicians playing various instruments and blowing on conch shells. Proprietors and managers, on estate after estate, readily conceded wage increases when confronted by these vocal and determined gangs of workers. On 17 February, the workers' protest moved to the streets of the capital, Basseterre, after the waterfront workers joined the strike and began a peaceful demonstration through the streets of the town. They were joined by gangs of the unemployed and, later in the day, striking estate workers who had marched in from the countryside.

The demonstrations ended in an outbreak of rioting after a party of marines, landed from a British warship which had been sitting in the Basseterre harbour throughout the entire day of protest, attempted to disperse the angry crowd. It is notable that the riots only began after the striking workers were confronted by armed marines and defence force volunteers drawn mainly from the upper class of planters and merchants.[56] The armed marines were used to quell labour protests in the countryside and the planters took advantage of their presence to retract the wage increases that had already been conceded.

The general strike of 1905 took a much more peaceful course. Only two cane fires, both on the same estate, were recorded. The strike, started by estate workers, affected the entire island of St Kitts and quickly spread to include waterfront workers. The administrator attributed the absence of rioting during the 1905 general strike to the prompt action of the district magistrate who threatened to jail any striker who was brought before him for breach of contract. For his outstanding service to the Crown, and to the planters of St Kitts, the magistrate was made a Commander of the Imperial Service Order in the following year.[57]

It is notable how plantation workers, during slavery and freedom, pursued strategies of collective bargaining usually identified with trade unionism on their own and without formal organization. The 1905 protest had been conducted in an entirely legal manner and was marked by the attempt of workers to represent their demands to, and negotiate with, both their employers and the government. This strategy was also employed in the earlier protest of 1896. After those disturbances one planter suggested that wages be set annually by a meeting between delegates chosen by the workers and representatives of the planters. His proposal won little support from his fellow planters and the idea was abandoned.[58] But trade unionism when it came to St Kitts-Nevis helped to institutionalise traditions of working-class protest which were already long established.[59]

There were no attempts to form trade unions in the presidency before 1916.[60] In that year a small group of men from the black lower middle class, led by a shopkeeper named Joseph Nathan, decided to form a trade union.[61] The decision to form a trade union came at a time of growing discontent among the labouring population of the presidency.[62] The dramatic rise in sugar prices which followed the outbreak of World War I had seen no commensurate increase in wages, although consumer prices rose. After two years of waiting for an improvement in their wage rates while their living standards declined, the workers had become increasingly restless. This discontent was accompanied by the rising racial consciousness which had become evident throughout the British West Indies during the war years.[63] The vast majority of black men in St Kitts and Nevis who volunteered for service in the British West India Regiment were rejected on the basis of illiteracy by the planter-dominated selection committees. This, combined with the open discrimination practised by the colonial administration in their selection of non-commissioned officers, became a source of growing racial antagonism. Thus the growth of working-class militancy was fuelled by a deepening sense of racial solidarity among the workers.

Shortly before the commencement of the 1916 sugar crop a petition organized by Joseph Nathan was submitted to the executive council which called for a uniform schedule of wage rates for agricultural workers and for government regulation of conditions and hours of work. The sending in of the petition was followed by several cane fires. Upon the advice of the governor, the planters decided to grant a substantial wage increase and the average rate for male agricultural workers rose from 1s. to 1s. 6d per day. This success encouraged Nathan and his fellow labour activists to form the union early in November 1916. The legislative council, composed entirely of European planters and merchants, urged the governor to intervene, and before the end of November the Trade and Labour Unions (Prohibition) Ordinance was passed, making the formation of trade unions illegal and providing for a sentence of six months' imprisonment or a fine of £50 for any individual involved in forming unions, or printing or distributing literature about unions.[64]

Forced to abandon their project Nathan and his colleagues formed the Universal Benevolent Association. This society was described by one Colonial Office official as one of several West Indian examples of 'disguised trade unionism and nurseries of colour agitators'.[65] The leaders themselves acknowledged their real aims telling a working-class audience at a public meeting that the only difference between the 'Labour Union' and the benevolent society was that 'with the Labour Union we could fix the price of labour for you, but under the heading of this Society, we cannot fix the price but you ought to know how much to ask for your labour and to see that you get it'.[66]

The discontent among the labouring population continued into 1917. A report from the Chief Inspector of Police warned that strikes and possible disturbances were likely at the commencement of the new crop if no concessions were made. On the personal intervention of the governor, the planters agreed to increase wages by a further 25 per cent, hiking the average daily wage rate to 2s. for male estate workers and to 1s. for women.[67] Despite these increases there were a few outbreaks of cane burning and isolated strikes, most of which appear to have been spontaneous actions with no direct involvement by the benevolent society, although the society had launched a programme of recruitment among sugar workers. In October 1917 workers on two adjoining estates began a strike which was believed to be engineered by the 'Benevolent Association'. Nineteen workers were prosecuted under the Masters and Servants Act for breach of contract and sentenced to a fine of 8s. or ten days' imprisonment by the magistrate. On the urging of the society the workers refused to pay the fine and were imprisoned, thereafter being styled locally as 'the St. Pauls martyrs' in commemoration of their heroism. At the end of the 1917 crop the presidential administrator privately admitted the role of the society's agitation in bringing about the wage concessions.[68]

The society was also active among the factory workers of the Basseterre Sugar Factory, the only central sugar factory in St Kitts. In August 1917 there was unrest at the factory which, according to the manager's report, 'was fomented by the union leaders'. The workers had demanded a 100 per cent wage increase in addition to the 50 per cent increase which had been granted at the start of the crop. The manager fired the three 'ringleaders' of the protest bringing to a halt the workers' plans for a strike. A subsequent report from the factory manager observed that the workers had 'settled down' and 'were working willingly after their little indiscretion'.

The organizational efforts of the society enjoyed lasting success only among the waterfront workers in Basseterre. In September 1917 the society organized a one-day strike among the porters and boatmen at the port. The strike failed in its immediate aim of securing an increase in the tariff, but the society was able to pay a strike benefit of 1d to each worker who participated. An active branch of the society was established at the waterfront among the boatmen. One of the society's leading activists, Anthony Harris, a licensed boatman, had his licence suspended soon after the strike for alleged insolence. He was accused of making speeches at public meetings of the society 'containing attacks on the police and foul abuse of white people'.

Despite subsequent petitions submitted by the 'Passenger Boatmen' on behalf of Harris, who continued his organizational work at the waterfront, his licence was not renewed.

In 1918 and 1920 the waterfront workers, advised by the benevolent society, successfully petitioned the government for an increase in the tariff. The success of these petitions helped to cement the society's support among the waterfront workers. These workers were among the most militant in the presidency and their internal solidarity, along with their long-established tradition of collective action in support of their claims for tariff increases, made them more amenable to union organization.

Aside from the waterfront workers, the society's attempts to enroll members proved largely unsuccessful. The refusal of employers to recognize the society as a representative body for workers and the victimization of those who openly supported the society were deterrents to the growth of support. The leaders were harassed by the police who regularly interfered with their attempts to meet and address workers at the work-place.

While it was the activities of the benevolent society which pushed the colonial administration and the presidency's employers to make the substantial wage concessions, it was the high level of working-class emigration and the consequent labour shortage which sustained the relatively high wage rates of this period. Mass emigration continued despite the attempts of the planter-dominated legislative council to control or end it. In 1917, the Agricultural and Commercial Society called for, but failed to convince the executive council of the need to prohibit workers from emigrating to Santo Domingo, their main destination. Between 1916 and 1921 emigration rates averaged over 4,300 annually, or 11 per cent of both islands' combined 1911 population of 39,228.[69] Under this pressure average daily wage rates, which in 1913 ranged from 8d to 10d for men and 3d to 4d for women, by 1920 had increased to 2s. for male labourers and 1s. for females. There was a corresponding increase in the cane cutting rate from 6d per ton in 1916 to slightly over 1s. per ton by the mid-1920s.[70] These wage increases failed to stop the flood of emigrants which was brought to an end only by the Great Depression of 1929 and the subsequent repatriation of West Indian migrant workers by governments in the Spanish Caribbean. This mass emigration helped keep wages up during the 1920s, but it also robbed the benevolent society of potential members, especially among young workers. Even the society's leadership was affected by emigration when George Wilkes, the treasurer, migrated to the United States in the late 1930s.

Despite the failure to organize the labouring population, the benevolent society was able to widen the scope and objectives of working-class protest. It added a political dimension to working-class demands and introduced new strategies and methods of agitation. In September 1917 the society launched a public campaign calling for the repeal of the Masters and Servants Act which it condemned as 'purely a class legislation'. The Colonial Office initially advised that 'legislation undertaken in St Kitts alone might be thought to have been passed as a result of agitation in that island', and the Act's replacement by a Masters and Servants Ordinance, which kept intact its main features, was finally carried out in 1922 as part of a general revision of labour legislation in the West Indies.

The society also successfully established a newspaper, the *Union Messenger*, in 1921. Originally established as a weekly, the paper was turned into a daily within a year. The newspaper provided workers with a public medium of expression for the first time. The newspaper sought to inform and educate the workers by publishing news on the movement of sugar prices and other information of interest to workers. It reprinted articles from Garvey's *Negro World* and from the *Crusader*, the Harlem newspaper edited by the Nevis-born Communist, Cyril Briggs. In its editorials and columns, the *Union Messenger* attacked the 'system of land monopoly', calling on the government to acquire an estate for use in a land settlement scheme. An editorial of 1929 urged the British government to nationalize the Basseterre Sugar Factory and redirect its huge profits to the development of the presidency. The paper also fiercely denounced the system of Crown Colony government and the domination of the presidency by a 'round table oligarchy'. In a public meeting held in September 1917, Frederick Solomon, the president of the society, declared that 'it won't be very far off when we [black people] must rule'. Through the pages of the *Messenger*, and in public meetings, the leaders of the society constantly reaffirmed their desire for an end to Crown Colony government and for 'black man rule'.

The political impact of the society can best be judged by the panicky reaction of the colonial administration. Starting with the Trade and Labour Unions (Prohibition) Ordinance, the government introduced an entire battery of repressive laws aimed at curbing the society and restricting its ability to organize among workers. Some of these sought to impose limits on already existing channels of working-class protest like the Petitions and Appeals Ordinance of 1918 which restricted the rights of individuals to sign or submit petitions on behalf of other persons. The Friendly Societies (Amendment) Act of 1919 aimed to give the 'governor control over the political activities of such societies and to prevent their funds being applied to purposes not authorised by the rules'. A law introduced in the following year, the Undesirable Persons Expulsion Act, was, in the words of the governor, directed at 'British subjects who set on foot an agitation among the labouring classes'. Even before the passage of the law an Antiguan labourer named Martin, who was probably associated with the benevolent society, was deported from St Kitts for making mischievous public utterances. The main repressive legislation directed at the society itself was the Newspaper Surety (Amendment) Ordinance of 1919 which required the publishers of any newspaper to post a bond of £200. Anyone publishing a newspaper not registered under this law would be guilty of a criminal offence punishable by a fine of £50 or six months' imprisonment. The law was introduced only after the plans of the society to commence publication of a newspaper had come to light. The executive council unanimously expressed the view that 'steps should be taken to prevent the publication of any paper by this seditious organisation'. The law, however, failed to accomplish its design as the publishers of the *Union Messenger* successfully raised the required bond.

However, government intimidation and legal repression, as well as emigration had affected the ability of the benevolent society to widen its influence among workers. Its failure to win recognition from employers and its inability to recruit new members led to a sharp fall in numbers. The membership declined from a high of 1,500 soon after its formation in 1917, to 124 by 1934. By the latter year the society's influence among the labouring population had almost entirely disappeared, just as new opportunities were emerging.

The 1935 labour disturbances in St Kitts were the first in a series of workers' riots and protests which shook the British Caribbean during the late 1930s and set these colonial societies upon the path of social and con-stitutional reform. The 1935 labour unrest was strikingly similar, both in cause and form, to that of 1896. The labour protests in both years followed a period of sharp wage reductions on the sugar estates and mass lay-offs of agricultural workers. Estate wages were reduced by 25 per cent in 1932 with the rate for cutting cane falling from its post-First World War high of 1s. to a low of 8d per ton, the same as the prevailing rate in 1884. In July 1930 1,130 estate workers, or 16.5 per cent of the 6,847 estate workers recorded in the 1921 census, were reported as unemployed. The decline in wages was accompanied by a sharp fall in remittances from the United States and Canada from a combined total of £6,085 in 1931 to £1,694 in 1933.[71] The sharp fall in working-class incomes was further compounded by the high number of destitute workers, many of whom had been away for over ten years, who were being repatriated by the governments of Cuba and Santo Domingo. In 1930 the chief medical officer reported a marked rise in the total number of deaths which he attributed to 'drought and poverty'. The deterioration in working-class living standards continued and, in November 1934, the senior district magistrate wrote to the adminis-trator observing that 'year after year, the number of poor and destitute in Basseterre have increased, and most markedly so this present year'.[72]

At the commencement of the 1935 crop, the Basseterre Sugar Factory increased the price paid for canes purchased from the estates and this encouraged the growing hope that workers' wages would also be increased. Through the pages of the *Union Messenger*, the now moribund benevolent society renewed its appeal to estate workers to join the society which would then represent their claims to the estate proprietors. However, the society advised that the planters would be in no position to increase wages for the 1935 crop and urged workers to remain calm. The labour protests began when workers on Buckleys estate, on the outskirts of the capital Basseterre, approached the manager with a demand for a return of the cane cutting rate to the pre-1932 level of 1s. per ton. Upon his refusal the estate gang of male and female workers, using the same tactics as in 1896, began a march around the island, parading the countryside armed with long sticks, clubs and pieces of iron piping. They were accompanied by a musical band equipped with drums, fifes and conch shells. These gangs marched from estate to estate calling out their fellow workers and disabling the cattle-drawn carts of the estates in an attempt to prevent the commencement of the crop. The workers' march took place over two days with the demon-strators reversing their direction on the second day. During the disturbances in St Kitts fires were started on several estates, but they were not as wide-spread as in 1896.[73]

As in 1896, the protest ended violently. The armed power of the colonial state was unleashed on an angry crowd of estate workers which had gathered in an attempt to prevent the management of Buckleys estate starting the crop with the help of strikebreakers. Two rioters were killed and seven others seriously wounded before order was restored. The colonial govern-ment employed identical repressive measures as those used in 1896 and in 1834. A party of marines, landed from a British warship which arrived after the riot, was despatched to the countryside to intimidate the workers, restore order and ensure the commencement of the crop.[74]

The 1935 labour disturbances served to eliminate, once and for all, the leadership aspirations of the black lower-middle-class leaders of the benevolent society who had advised caution and offered to negotiate with the estate proprietors on the workers' behalf. Ironically, the main benefi-ciaries of the workers' protest were the coloured upper-middle-class leaders of a rival organization, the Workers' League, which had been established in 1932. The League was formed as a protective association which sought to advance the interests of the entire community, and those of the impove-rished workers in particular. Its members were motivated by a paternalistic interest in the welfare of workers whose impoverishment had begun to affect the incomes of these middle-class merchants and businessmen. Many of them were also dedicated to the attainment of representative government and sought to play a greater role in the politics of the presidency.

Outstanding among the leadership of the League were Thomas Manchester, a coloured small estate owner and businessman whose family had long played a role in presidential politics, and his cousin, Edgar Challenger, whose family had formerly been small estate owners, but by the 1930s were engaged solely in commerce.[75] The League came to prominence during the 1935 protest after Manchester established his claim to working-class leadership by persuading half of the protesters gathered outside of Buckleys estate to leave the site before the outbreak of rioting. After listening to a public address some of the crowd, primarily shop clerks and better-paid workers, had peaceably dispersed to their homes.

Despite the League's success in urging a peaceful course upon a signi-ficant number of workers, it was the spontaneous working-class protests of 1935 which paved the way for constitutional reform in St Kitts-Nevis. In 1936, under pressure from the imperial government, the presidential constitution was changed to allow for elections to the presidential legislature. Three years later trade unions were legalized under the Trade Union Act of 1939. The Act gave trade unions protection from actions in tort, guaranteed the right of peaceful picketing and established regulations governing the registration and legal operations of trade unions. In the following year, the St Kitts Trades and Labour Union was established under the leadership of the middle-class members of the Workers' League. Edgar Challenger became the union's first president while the treasurer of the League, John Harney, the coloured manager of a Portuguese-owned commercial establishment, was elected union treasurer.

The success of the middle-class leaders in establishing a lasting trade union organization contrasts sharply with the earlier failures of working-class and lower-middle-class leaders like Nathan, Wilkes and Solomon. Middle-class leaders were able to benefit from the change in imperial policy from one of open antagonism to labour organizations to the encouragement of 'responsible trade unionism'. The authorities hoped to ensure that newly-formed labour organizations did not, in the words of Lord Passfield, Secretary of State for the Colonies, 'fall under the domination of disaffected persons by which their activities may be diverted to improper and mischievous ends'.[76] British colonial labour policy sought to deter militant, working-class union leadership by promoting the leadership of middle-class individuals who shared the proper respect for property rights and legally constituted authority.[77] The imperial government's promotion of 'responsible' middle-class trade unionists was accompanied by the studious neglect or systematic harassment of working-class leaders who sought to develop autonomous and internally directed trade union organizations. In 1939 Joseph Nathan appealed as secretary of the benevolent society for £300 to assist in the development of trade unions in St Kitts, but received no reply. In the same year, Walter Citrine, with the blessing of the presidential administration, delivered an address on trade union methods to a public meeting organized by Thomas Manchester and Edgar Challenger. The discreet encouragement given the middle-class leaders by the colonial administration ensured, for a time, the hegemony of middle-class notions of constitutionality within the labour movement.[78]

The middle-class leaders of the trade union were responsible for the adoption of one new method of struggle: the direct representation of working-class interests in the legislature. This form of representation was not available to workers until the constitutional reform of 1936 which introduced elections for a minority of seats on the legislature under a restricted franchise. With eligibility for membership of the legislature limited to property owners, workers were able to gain legislative representation only because these sympathetic middle-class leaders had chosen to participate in the labour movement. Challenger and Manchester were elected to the reconstituted legislature in 1937 by a combination of middle-class voters and the upper echelons of the working class, including skilled factory workers, artisans, head cutters on estates, junior civil servants and head teachers, who were able to meet the income qualification of £30 per annum, or who made annual payments of 15s. in direct taxes. The middle-class labour leaders were able to use their position to push through legislation aimed at improving the living and working conditions of the working class.

The constitutional strategies of the new union failed to supplant the old methods of working-class resistance including strikes and demonstrations. Even before the registration of the union, the new trade union leaders were called on to represent workers at the central sugar factory who had spontaneously gone on strike to pressure the management for an increase in wages. Edgar Challenger successfully persuaded the workers to call off their strike, even though several of their leaders had been summarily dismissed by the factory management, and led the union in the adoption of a no-strike resolution.

Growing working-class discontent with such policies led to the replacement of the middle-class executive by working-class leaders in the early 1940s. The union's general secretary, Joseph France, who had been the assistant editor of the *Union Messenger*, organized another strike of the sugar factory workers in 1940, with the support of new working-class leaders like Robert Bradshaw, a factory mechanic who was fired for his role in the strike. The success of this strike, which was opposed by Challenger and the more moderate leaders, undermined Challenger's leadership and he was forced to resign along with other middle-class leaders. This led to the rescinding of the no-strike resolution and the increasing use of the strike weapon, and transformed the union into a militant mass working-class organization.

Under the leadership of Bradshaw and France, the union frequently resorted to general strikes and demonstrations as a means of mass mobilization. The union organized a major strike almost every year between 1944 and 1949 and two successive general strikes in 1947 and 1948. Widespread incendiarism also figured as an important part of trade union strategy. Although it may not have been ordered by the trade union leadership it was carried out by persons who were almost certainly trade union members. During the 13 weeks long general strike of 1948, 1,500 acres of ripe cane were burnt between January and July. The estates lost 45,000 tons of cane, but since the canes were insured the owners experienced no financial loss.[79]

The St Kitts Trades and Labour Union had the same basic objectives as unorganized workers in the pre-trade union period, the setting of fair wages commensurate with the workers' effort. Labour organization introduced one new element into working-class protest. The spontaneity of traditional working-class protest was replaced by the orderly pursuit of trade union objectives through the official medium of direct negotiations between the union leadership and the employers' representatives. The absence of rioting in 1948 was due largely to the existence of the union which had turned its working-class members into a disciplined force. The trade union leaders had been able to assert their command over their working-class followers and were able to call the workers out and disperse them at will.[80] This power proved even more threatening to the colonial state and the plantocracy than the indiscriminate violence and wanton destruction experienced in earlier labour disturbances. The constant mobilization of workers and the threat or the actual implementation of general strikes forced the estate owners to meet their demands. Under the pressure of annual general strikes called by the union the planters were compelled to increase the rate for cutting cane from 16 cents per ton in 1939 to 60 cents per ton by 1948. Between 1945 and 1949 an annual increase in wages became a fixed feature of the collective agreements concluded between the union and the sugar employers at the start of each crop.

However, the most important strategic innovation of the trade union era was the direct involvement of the labouring population in colonial politics. This was the political legacy of the period of middle-class leadership of the trade union movement, and it seems unlikely that the union could have acquired its political authority as quickly as it did without the early involvement of middle-class leaders. But the actual mass mobilization of the labouring population around political demands occurred under working-class leadership. It was the trade union leaders who spearheaded the nationalist struggle for self-government at the same time as they were securing the objectives of higher wages and industrial and political equality between the workers and their employers. With the winning of trade union recognition and the accomplishment of the other industrial objectives of the trade union, including closed shop agreements in the sugar industry and at the waterfront as well as regular wage increases, the leadership turned its attention to political demands such as the nationalization of the sugar factory, universal adult suffrage, and self-government for St Kitts-Nevis. In 1943 the union's electoral candidates defeated an electoral alliance of merchants and planters put up by the Agricultural and Commercial Society. The planters' control over the presidential legislative council was broken, and the laws of the presidency could no longer be used as an instrument for subordinating the plantation workers.

Again in 1950 the union's candidates defeated, by an even wider margin, the pro-employer St Kitts Democratic Party, which was formed the previous year during the third of the consecutive general strikes which the union had organized every year since 1947. The introduction of universal adult suffrage in 1951 allowed the union and its allies to win all the elective seats in the presidential legislature and cemented its dominance in the politics of the presidency. In 1953 the British government incorporated the trade union leaders in the legislature into the administration of the presidency by giving them direct responsibility for certain government activities. When internal self-government was finally conceded by the British in 1956, the trade union majority in the legislative council formed a government and union president Robert Bradshaw, the former factory mechanic, became the presidency's first chief minister.

The formation of a trade union government, while seeming to finally establish industrial and political equality between workers and employers, soon led to the transformation of the union itself into an instrument for the disciplining of plantation labour to the needs of the sugar industry. This was possible because the organization of plantation workers, by stifling the independent activity of workers, made them less able to defend their own interests independent of the union leadership. The organizational discipline of the union had ensured united action and had helped win many victories, but at the same time it had undermined working-class self-organization, since decision-making power within the labour movement became centred in the hands of a small union executive. As government ministers, the union leaders now had responsibility for the prosperity of the sugar industry and they sought increasingly to subordinate the special interests of workers to the general needs of the industry.

The abolition of the Masters and Servants Act in 1938 had laid the ground for the progressive whittling away of the estates' control over their workers' labour time. It was to the union that the employers now turned for assistance in obtaining regular labour from their workers. One of the duties of a joint union/sugar industry committee set up in 1955 was to reduce absenteeism among workers, especially on Sundays and Mondays. The transformation in industrial relations had proceeded too far, however, and the union proved unable to restore the command over labour which the estate proprietors had once enjoyed. The new opportunities for emigration, particularly to the United Kingdom, which appeared in the 1950s broke, once and for all, the planters' control over estate labour.

But it is not surprising that workers began to resort to some of their traditional strategies of protest during the period of trade union government, particularly to the use of arson. The total tonnage of cane lost through arson increased from 2,000 tons in 1950 to 70,000 tons in 1961.[81] The widespread use of arson by the workers was a direct challenge to the trade union leaders themselves. In 1951 the union and the planters had established a joint cane fire committee which was responsible for carrying out a propaganda campaign against incendiarism and encouraging workers to 'regard the extinction of fires as a permanent duty'. The union's urgings were either disregarded or misunderstood by workers for, in the following year, 3,275 acres of cane were destroyed by arson.[82]

Despite the changing role of the trade union and its leadership, and their changed relationship to the union's working-class followers, one cannot ignore the fundamental accomplishments of the union in achieving a marked increase in working-class income. The annual increase in wages after 1941 made sugar cane cutters among the best paid workers in the island. However, the most important accomplishment of the union was in

WORKERS WEEKLY

"FOR THE GOOD THAT WE CAN DO" —:— 1 cent per copy; 50 cents per year, postage 1/- extra

No. 83   Basseterre, St. Kitts   Saturday, 14th August 1943

The Future Of The Working Class

Unite, Workers, Unite

THE eyes of the working class are turned towards the future. Their minds are rightly occupied with the important question what will the position be next year, next five years, next generation?

The island wide estate workers strike of last month has shown the labouring population what great things can be done when workers make up their minds to stick together. From now onward there should be a firmer determination to remain together and go forward together. Whether a worker toils by hand or by brain, in field factory, store or office in rags or in smart cut suit and white collar, he should join an organisation for his own protection and to promote his future welfare.

Seeking increase of wages and calling strikes when necessary are only a part of trade union objects. The Labour Programme is a big one. It covers from the welfare of children yet unborn to the care of the poor and destitute and of people too old to work. The workers League has mapped out a "Programme for progress" for the people of St. Kitts. Nevis and Anguilla as a part of a united and self governing West Indian nation in the British Empire. The back ground of this programme is to remove the many evils which have caused much suffering and human misery among some of the people of these fair islands. The local government and the Colonial Office in London have shown some sympathy for the aims and organised efforts of the people, but the people would be making a serious mistake if they attempt to sit back and expect that the fight for better conditions will be carried on entirely in official quarters instead of continuing the struggle themselves with renewed strength.

There are other matters just as important to the welfare of the common man as his weekly pay. There is the matter of poor schooling of children. There is the ignorance among grown up people evidenced in filthy language and crime and the trooping to the magistrate's court over simple differences which can be settled among themselves in a peaceful way. These should be stopped. The working class have to turn over a new leaf and show a better spirit towards one another. Workers unite and prepare to face the future. Take your brother by the hand and go forward

together all for one and one for all. Cut out petty feelings and face the world as men and women with stiff backbones, hearts and deep fellowship feeling. If you have these things and are in the right, you should fear not even the powers of hell!

Factory Workers Meeing

Last Sunday evening a special meeting of Sugar Factory Workers was held at the M I S hall. The object of the meeting was to reorganise that section of the union. The acting President of the union presided. In his opening address he pointed out the need for factory workers to get together to promote their common interests. The question of bringing the section back on its feet was thrown open for discusion. Among the speakers were members of the Executive Committee. The speeches direct and moving. The keynote throughout the meeting was a genuine desire to restore to factory workmen that high union spirit which was so marked in the early part of 1940. The regular monthly meeting of this section will take place on Sunday 22nd instant.

SHORT TIPS

Estate Workers in Basseterre are reminded of the regular meeting of Estate Workers section of the union to be held at 8 o'clock at the M I S hall on Sunday evening 15th instant, at this meeting a section committee will be elected.

The Daily Chronicle of British Guiana says the Georgetown City Council in May last fixed a minimum wages for labourers of 3/4 per day for men and 2/6 per day for women. The Council meeting the Mayor said the principle was that the men should work for no less than 3/4 per day whether he was a watchman, road worker or else. Persons whose wages were below the minimum would receive back pay as from January 1st, 1943.

From 1st April last civil servants in British Guiana will receive an increase of two thirds on their present war bonus rates of 15 percent on the first $240 per year, 10 per cent on the next $240 per year & 5 percent on the next $240 per year.

'The Future of the Working Class', from The Workers Weekly, *St Kitts, 1943*
(Trade Union Congress Library)

the field of labour relations. Employers could no longer physically abuse or insult their workers for fear that such action would result in an immediate loss of labour, if not direct government intervention. Workers now faced their employers as equals. No longer were conditions of employment and wage rates laid down unilaterally by the employer. They had to be negotiated through the recognized channels of collective bargaining between the workers' and the employers' representatives. The equality between workers and employers was, perhaps, best symbolized in the person of Robert Bradshaw, who, as chief minister, had ministerial responsibility for the sugar industry. The president of the trade union and the workers' elected representative had acquired a direct and official voice in the future on the sugar industry and neither he nor the other union leaders could be treated in a dismissive or condescending manner by estate proprietors.

This paper has emphasized the continuities in the strategies of protest and resistance adopted by plantation workers of St Kitts-Nevis during slavery and freedom. It does not argue that such continuities were the result of some consciously-held tradition of resistance maintained by the plantation workers over a 300-year period from slavery to the formation of a trade union government. The continuities in working-class strategies and objectives reflected the structural continuities in the plantation system. During and after slavery the estate proprietors sought to maintain control over the plantation workers, who responded by evolving strategies of labour bargaining and protest to challenge the system of planter domination over their labour and their persons. It was ultimately the trade union which was the instrument for attaining those objectives which the plantation workers of St Kitts-Nevis pursued during slavery and freedom. Foremost among these were fair wages and an end to the arbitrary authority exercised over their persons by their masters and employers. The trade union movement had successfully transformed the relations of workers to employers in the process of production from one of personal subordination to one of industrial equality. In the wider sphere of colonial life, the formerly powerless and disenfranchised workers had acquired a dominant role in the politics of the presidency. The need to ensure the loyalty of workers to the trade union leadership also meant that employers in the sugar industry were compelled to concede to the workers' demand for an improved standard of living. Through the instrumentality of the trade union, the plantation workers of St Kitts and Nevis could be said to have attained their goals of 'perfect personal freedom' and 'higher wages'.

Notes

This was a paper originally delivered in a seminar series organized by the Post-emancipation Societies Project of the Centre for Afro-American and African Studies, University of Michigan. I am indebted to Mary Turner, Howard Johnson, Verene Shepherd, Rebecca Scott, Thomas Holt and Edward Cox whose detailed comments and suggestions have assisted me in the preparation of this article.

'Higher Wages' & 'Perfect Personal Freedom'

1. The islands of St Kitts and Nevis were separate British colonies until they were merged into a single Leeward Islands colony in 1871 along with Antigua, Dominica, Montserrat and the British Virgin Islands. In 1882, St Kitts and Nevis were merged into a single administrative unit or presidency. For a full account of the constitutional development of St Kitts and Nevis see C.A. Kelsick, 'The Constitutional History of the Leewards', *Caribbean Quarterly*, 6 (1960), 177-209.

2. By the end of the eighteenth century St Kitts, in proportion to its extent, had become the single richest colony in the British empire. Richard Sheridan, *Sugar and Slavery* (Eagle Hall, Barbados, 1974), 160.

3. Only the Antiguan planters, in an island subject to recurrent droughts, were convinced of their ability to retain control of their estate labour force without this coercive system. One planter calculated that he could cultivate his estate 'at least one third cheaper by free labor than by slave labor'. Douglas Hall, *Five of the Leewards*, (St Laurence, Barbados, 1971), 23.

4. Henry George Grey (later Lord Howick), memo 1832, quoted in Lloyd Best, 'Biography of Labour' in George Beckford (ed.), *Caribbean Economy* (Kingston, 1975), 153.

5. Quoted in Hall, *Free Jamaica: 1838-1865* (New Haven, 1959), 245.

6. Thomas Holt, *The Problem of Freedom: Race, Labor and Politics in Jamaica and Britain, 1832-1938* (Baltimore and London, 1992), 45.

7. Sidney Mintz, in answer to his own question 'Was the plantation slave a proletarian?', concludes only that 'it is not analytically most useful to define either "proletarian" or "slave" in isolation, since these two vast categories of toiler were actually linked intimately by the world economy that had, as it were, given birth to them both, in their modern form.' Sidney Mintz, 'Was the Plantation Slave a Proletarian?', *Review 2* (1978), 97. C.L.R. James, in much less equivocal terms, declares, 'Working and living together in gangs of hundreds on the North Plain [of St Dominigue], they [the slaves] were closer to a modern proletariat than any group of workers in existence at the time'. C.L.R. James, *Black Jacobins* (New York, 1963), 85-6.

8. Slaves working on the provision grounds of other slaves could earn 1s. 8d plus breakfast, and for working in the estate attorney's garden could earn up to 2s. 11d plus breakfast. Mary Turner, 'Chattel Slaves into Wage Slaves: A Jamaican Case Study,' in Malcolm Cross and Gad Heuman (eds). *Labour in the Caribbean* (London and Basingstoke, 1988), 20.

9. Slave porters in Antigua were able to hire themselves out provided they had received from their owners a badge and a ticket signifying the owner's consent. An Antiguan Act of 1757 was introduced 'permitting Slaves to go about the Towns and Country to hire themselves out, or take their own Liberty and pay their Masters and Mistresses for their time'. Elsa Goveia, *Slave Society in the British Leeward Islands at the End of the Eighteenth Century* (New Haven and London, 1965), 159. Barry Higman also provides detailed accounts of the independent wage earning activities of urban and rural slaves in his *Slave Populations of the British Caribbean, 1807-1834* (Baltimore and London, 1984), 203-4, 244-7. Slaves in the United States South also engaged in wage labour on their own account. In the 1850s, one slave, skilled in ironwork, earned an average income of $50 to $100 per year from paid 'overtime' work. Peter Parish, *Slavery: History and Historians* (New York, 1989), 102.

10. Goveia gives the example of one, John Corey, a tailor by trade, who worked at his trade by day, paying his master a dollar a week, and preached in the town at night. The Pinney estate in Nevis allowed its slaves to hire themselves at fixed rates and expected an annual income of £250 from the practice. See Goveia, *Slave Society in the British Leeward Islands*, 141.

11. See Turner, 'Chattel Slaves into Wage Slaves: A Jamaican Case Study', 18-26; Mary Turner, 'Slave Workers, Subsistence and Labour Bargaining: Amity Hall, Jamaica, 1805-1832', in Ira Berlin and Philip D. Morgan (eds) *The Slaves' Economy, Independent Production by Slaves in the Americas* (London, 1991).

12. Michael Craton, *Testing the Chains: Resistance to Slavery in the British West Indies* (Ithaca and London, 1982), 300.

13. The willingness of the slaves at Mesopotamia estate during the Jamaican slave rebellion of 1831-2 to start up the sugar works and bring off the sugar on their own in the very midst of widespread unrest reveals a certain proprietorial attachment to their work. See Richard Dunn, ' "Dreadfull Idlers in the Cane Fields": The Slave Labour Pattern on a Jamaican Sugar Estate, 1762-1831' in Barbara Solow and Stanley Engerman, eds, *British Capitalism and Caribbean Slavery* (Cambridge, 1987), 189.

14. Douglas Hall, 'The Flight from the Estates Reconsidered: The British West Indies, 1838-42', *The Journal of Caribbean History*, 10 and 11 (1978), 23.

15. Holt, *The Problem of Labour*, 148.

16. Ibid., 12.

17. Hall, *Five of the Leewards*, 21.

18. As Robert Miles points out, the 'capitalist requires that the labour market "produces" labour power at a price which permits the realization of surplus value'. See Miles, *Capitalism and Unfree*

297

Labour: Anomaly or Necessity (London, 1987), 33. Karl Marx observes that the 'bourgeoisie, at its rise, wants and uses the power of the state to "regulate" wages, i.e. to force them within the limits suitable for surplus-value making . . .' Marx, *Capital*, vol. 1 (London, 1983), 689.

19. William Green describes the emancipation strategy of the Colonial Office as seeking to 'preserve traditional property rights and utilize existing resources without imposing excessive restraints on freedmen'. While he may not consider the imposition of five and a half days of continuous and unremunerated labour on the ex-slaves as constituting 'excessive restraints on freedmen', the ex-slaves themselves wanted the right to determine how to employ their labour and it was this right which the Colonial Office sought to deny. See William Green, 'The Perils of Comparative History: Belize and the British Sugar Colonies after Slavery', *Comparative Studies in Society and History*, 26 (1984), 117.

20. Woodville Marshall writes of the post-emancipation period in the West Indies: 'Strikes, sometimes lasting as long as two or three weeks occurred in most islands; many ex-slaves refused to surrender their provision grounds and some resisted violently; and nearly all of them objected to the wage rates'. See Marshall, 'Commentary', 247.

21. Richard Frucht, 'Emancipation and Revolt in the West Indies: St Kitts, 1834' *Science and Society*, 39 (1975), 206. The labourers' response to apprenticeship in Jamaica was described in very similar terms. One planter in Ocho Rios reported that apprentices on estates in that region 'displayed a determination not to work and flung down their hoes and bills'. See Swithin Wilmot, 'Not "Full Free": The Ex-Slaves and the Apprenticeship System in Jamaica, 1834–8', *Jamaica Journal*, 17 (1984), 4.

22. Richard Frucht, 'Emancipation and Revolt in the West Indies: St Kitts, 1834', 203–12. See also R. Frucht, 'From Slavery to Unfreedom in the Plantation Society of St Kitts, W.I.' in Vera Rubin and Arthur Tuden (eds), *Comparative Perspectives on Slavery in New World Plantation Societies* (New York, 1977), 377–88.

23. The role which Marx and Engels ascribe to the bourgeoisie is here being performed by the plantation workers themselves, seeking to replace the 'ties that bound man to his "natural superiors" ' with an equitable relationship based upon the 'nexus of cash payment'. See K. Marx and F. Engels, *Manifesto of the Communist Party* (Moscow, 1975), 44.

24. Frucht, 'From Slavery to Unfreedom', 386.

25. Land returns submitted to the West Indian Royal Commission of 1897 showed that the estates occupied 77 per cent of the total land area of St Kitts and 62 per cent of Nevis. Uncultivable land made up 30 per cent and 25 per cent respectively of each island's land area. *West India Royal Commission*, 1897, Memorial of statistics, 211.

26. *West India Royal Commission*, 1897, Evidence by E.G. Todd, 209–10.

27. C.O. 152/279, Petition from James Clarke Taylor and Nevis Labourers, Enc., Strickland to Chamberlain, 30 May 1903.

28. C.O. 152/243, Davis to Griffith, 6 September 1898, Enc., Fleming to Chamberlain, 11 February 1899.

29. For an example of the extensive use of credit as a mechanism for labour coercion in the Bahamas see Howard Johnson, ' "A Modified Form of Slavery": The Credit and Truck Systems in the Bahamas in the Nineteenth and Early Twentieth Centuries', *Comparative Studies in Society and History*, 28 (1986), 729 – 53.

30. *West India Royal Commission*, 1897, Evidence of Solomon Shelford, 242–3.

31. See Glen Richards, 'Masters and Servants: The Growth of the Labour Movement in St. Christopher Nevis, 1896 to 1956' (Ph.D. Diss., Cambridge, 1989), 98.

32. Secret memo: Federation of the British colonies in the Caribbean area comments on Secretary of State's letter of 26 July 1944, and on draft despatch, by Sir Gordon Lethem, n.d., Oxford, Rhodes House, papers of Sir Gordon Lethem, MSS Brit. Emp. 5276.

33. The Act was modelled upon contemporary English legislation which regulated relations between employers and workers, particularly the statute of 1823, 4 Geo. iv c. 34. For a detailed account of the evolution of masters and servants legislation in England see Daphne Simon, 'Master and Servant' in John Saville (ed.), *Democracy and the Labour Movement* (London, 1954) 160–200.

34. C.O. 240/20, Masters and Servants Act, no. 84 of 1849.

35. Miles, *Capitalism and Unfree Labour*, 182.

36. David Trotman points out that by 1854, in Trinidad, combined committals for breach of contract under the Masters and Servants Ordinance of 1846 and offences against the Immigration Ordinance of 1850 were greater than committals for all other offences combined. Trotman, *Crime in Trinidad: Conflict and Control in a Plantation Society, 1838–1900* (Knoxville, 1986), 65.

37. Simon, 'Master and Servant', 198.

38. Miles, *Capitalism and Unfree Labour*, 182.

39. Hall, *Five of the Leewards*, 40–1.

40. Bonham Richardson, *Caribbean Migrants: Environmental and Human Survival on St. Kitts and Nevis*, (Knoxville, 1983), Table 5, 93.
41. *West India Royal Commission*, 1897, Memorandum submitted in evidence by Hon. Andrew Munro, 242.
42. Velma Newton, *The Silver Men: West Indian Labour Migration to Panama, 1850–1914* (Kingston, 1984), 72.
43. C.O. 241/47, Minutes of the St Kitts Nevis Executive Council, 20 October 1910; C.O. 240/24, Emigration Regulation Ordinance, no. 2 of 1911.
44. Richardson, *Caribbean Migrants*, Table 5, 93.
45. Bonham Richardson observes that for the peoples of small Caribbean islands like St Kitts and Nevis, 'oscillating migration has always been a basic economic strategy'. See Richardson, *Caribbean Migrants*, 172.
46. George Rudé, *The Crowd in History: A Study of Popular Disturbance in France and England, 1730–1898*, (London, 1981), 241. For the use of arson as a bargaining tactic by slaves see Mary Turner, 'Slave Workers, Subsistence and Labour Bargaining: Amity Hall, Jamaica, 1805-1832', 101-2.
47. *West India Royal Commission, 1897*, Evidence of Quintin Hogg, 29.
48. One estate manager in a letter written to the absentee proprietor expressed his delight at the apprehension and prosecution of a worker who had set fire to a cane piece on the estate and his hope that the 'ruffian would be made an example of'. Solomon Shelford to H.W. Estridge, 19 March 1895, Reading Berkshire Record Office, Estridge Letter Book, D/EM Z17.
49. Hall, *Five of the Leewards*, 113.
50. A smaller acreage was lost in Nevis with most of the damage confined to Pinney's and Paradise estates, two of the largest estates in that island. The planters responded to the widespread incendiarism of 1896 by insuring their canes collectively.
51. C.O. 152/203, Petition of Labourers, Boatmen and Porters, 21 February 1896, Enc. Fleming to Chamberlain, 16 March 1896. The workers' call for the payment of wages to be made by mid-day on Saturdays directly challenged one of the mechanisms employed by planters to secure steady labour from their labour force. The delay in wage payments sought to ensure that workers completed their tasks during their half-day of Saturday work.
52. *St Christopher Advertiser and Weekly Intelligencer*, 24 January 1905; *St. Christopher Gazette and Caribbean Courier*, 23 January 1905.
53. It is notable, as Bonham Richardson points out, that they all occurred at a time when workers were forced to remain at home because of a temporary halt in emigration due to external conditions. Richardson, *Caribbean Migrants*, 181.
54. E.P. Thompson, 'The Moral Economy of the English Crowd of the Eighteenth Century', *Past and Present*, 50 (1971), 78-9.
55. *The St. Christopher Advertiser and Weekly Intelligencer*, 11 February 1896.
56. See Richards, 'Masters and Servants: The Growth of the Labour Movement in St. Christopher-Nevis, 1896 to 1956', ch. 3.
57. C.O. 152/286, Bromley to Knollys, 1 March 1905, Enc. Knollys to Lyttleton, 8 March 1905.
58. C.O. 152/202, Minutes of a Meeting of Planters held by invitation of the Governor, 22 February 1896, Statement of F.A. Hall, Enc. Fleming to Chamberlain, 28 February 1896.
59. This trade union impulse of workers in the British Caribbean goes back even before emancipation, with attempts of slaves to negotiate with their masters through chosen delegates. One observer has contrasted this 'parliamentary' impulse of West Indian workers with the practices of workers in colonial Africa who insisted on meeting with representatives of their employers en masse rather than selecting delegates who they believed would then be open to victimization. This is an example of how the captive African populations of the Americas have learned and integrated the social behaviour and mores of their captors and have sought to use them to win improvements in their life conditions. Interview with Marjorie Nicholson (former secretary of the Fabian Colonial Bureau), St Albans, England, 14 April 1987.
60. There were no specific laws against combination in St Kitts-Nevis, in contrast to the legal situation in Jamaica where Law 15 of 1839 prohibited 'all combinations for fixing the wages of labour'. See Richard Hart, 'Origin and Development of the Working Class in the English-speaking Caribbean area 1897-1937' in Cross and Heuman, *Labour in the Caribbean*, 72-3.
61. In addition to Nathan they included Frederick Solomon, an undertaker who had become one of the leading building contractors in the island, and George Wilkes, a barber. They were joined in this venture by two members of the coloured middle class, William Seaton, a senior clerk in a Portuguese-owned commercial establishment, and A. St Clair Podd, who was a member of a well-to-do coloured family of Nevisian merchants. The source of material in this section, unless otherwise stated, is Glen Richards, 'Masters and Servants: The Growth of the Labour Movement in St. Christopher Nevis, 1896 to 1956' (Ph.D. Diss., Cambridge, 1989), ch. 4.

62. The immediate inspiration for the labour leaders in St Kitts-Nevis was probably the success of Hamilton Jackson, a labour agitator and trade unionist in St Croix, who in 1915 successfully won wage increases for sugar workers in that island. In December 1915 the presidential administrator reported that Jackson was allegedly on his way to St Kitts and that he had instructed the harbour master to keep an eye out for him. However, Jackson was arrested in St Croix and failed to make it to St Kitts. Administrator Roger to Governor Bell, 8 December 1915, Basseterre, St Kitts Archives, Despatches to the Governor, 1915, 395/557/15. Another labour activist, a Barbadian named 'Professor' Arlington Newton, did visit St Kitts in May 1916 where he attempted, according to the governor, 'to imitate the lucrative agitation of the man Jackson in Santa Cruz'. The attempt to form a trade union in St Kitts followed Newton's visit by a little over four months. CO 152/358, Best to Long, 28 March 1918.

63. For an account of the rise of black nationalist ideas in the British West Indies during and after World War I see W.F. Elkins, *Black Power in the Caribbean: The Beginnings of the Modern Nationalist Movement*, (New York, 1971).

64. Joseph Nathan, who had migrated to the United States shortly after the 1896 labour disturbances and returned to establish his retail business in 1913, was the leading figure in the attempt to create the union. There is no information on Nathan's activities while in the United States, but it seems likely that he had developed contacts with the American Federation of Labor. Immediately after the passage of the Trade and Labour Unions (Prohibition) Ordinance, Nathan smuggled a letter to Samuel Gompers of the AFL enclosing a copy of the Ordinance and calling upon Gompers as 'head of the most powerful organization of labour in the world' to use his influence in support of the workers of the presidency and bring the issue to the attention of the British 'Federation of Labour' and the Secretary of State for the Colonies. Gompers informed C.W. Bowerman, secretary of both the British TUC and the Labour Party parliamentary committee, who raised a question concerning the Ordinance in parliament. See C.O. 152/357, Solomon, Nathan, Wilkes to Gompers, 22 January 1917, Enc. Long to Appleton (General Secretary, General Federation of Trade Unions, UK), 7 March 1917; *Report of Proceedings at the Forty-Ninth Annual Trades Union Congress*, 3–8 September 1917, 135.

65. C.O. 152/360, Minute by C.R. Darnley, 15 November 1918 in Mahaffy to Long, 3 October 1918. Friendly Societies in England had long been regarded as 'disguised trade unions'. Sidney Webb (later Lord Passfield) deplored the tendency of workers to establish a friendly society 'which invariably proceeds to discuss the rate of wages offered by the employer, and insensibly passes into a Trade Union with friendly benefits'. Sidney and Beatrice Webb, *The History of Trade Unionism* (London, 1894) 24.

66. C.O. 152/356, Public Address by Frederick Solomon, 4 February 1917, Enc. Best to Long, 24 August 1917.

67. As a precautionary measure, a French warship, the *Jeanne D'Arc*, was invited to anchor in the Basseterre harbour until the New Year celebrations were over. The islands remained quiet, however, and the governor observed that, while there was never any real 'danger of riot', the presence of the warship calmed the fears of the upper-class inhabitants.

68. In a letter to the governor, the presidential administrator requested that the section of his report for the Leeward Islands Blue Books dealing with wages not be published. For, he warned, 'the St. Kitts agitators cannot fail to be fortified by a reference to their achievements in a government publication'. C.O. 152/356, Quoted in Best to Long, 30 October 1917.

69. Ibid.

70. Richards, 'Masters and Servants', Table 3, 105.

71. See Richards, 'Masters and Servants', 262–3.

72. Magistrate Semper to Administrator Stewart, 28 November 1934, Enc., Stewart to St Johnston, 24 December 1934, Basseterre, St Kitts Archives, Despatches to the Governor 1930, 457/225/30.

73. There were no cane fires in Nevis, which was unaffected by the labour unrest. Workers' knowledge of the planters' collective insurance of their canes may partly explain the decreased employment of cane burning by estate workers in 1935. See Richards, 'Masters and Servants', 143–9.

74. For a full description of the 1935 labour disturbances see Richards, 'Masters and Servants', ch. 5.

75. Other leaders included V.P. John, a pharmacist and drug store owner, and the ubiquitous William Seaton, one of the founders of the 1916 union.

76. Quoted in Jeffrey Harrod, *Trade Union Foreign Policy: A Study of British and American Trade Union Activities in Jamaica* (London, 1972), 208.

77. The shift in imperial labour policy facilitated the rise of members of the professional and mercantile class to leading positions in the trade union movement. Throughout the West Indies, the newly-formed trade unions fell under the domination of coloured professionals and businessmen like Edgar Challenger, Alexander Bustamante, Norman Manley, Grantley Adams or the Indian lawyer, Adrian Cola Rienzi. Through their middle-class protégés in the West Indies, the imperial

government, with the willing assistance of organized labour in Britain, was able to determine the ideological orientation and organizational shape of the West Indian trade union movement.

78. Richards, 'Masters and Servants', 326. Working-class leaders like Uriah 'Buzz' Butler of Trinidad were constantly harassed by the colonial authorities. The colonial government of Kenya harassed the militant and independent African Workers Federation, deporting its leader Chege Kibachia, thus paving the way for more conciliatory leaders like Tom Mboya. See Frederick Cooper, *On the African Waterfront: Urban Disorder and the Transformation of Work in Colonial Mombasa* (New Haven and London, 1987), 108.

79. See Richards, 'Masters and Servants', ch. 6.

80. The union's vice president boasted that their working-class supporters were 'accustomed to receiving and obeying snap commands from their leaders'. See Paul Southwell, *The Truth about 'Operation Blackburne'*, (Basseterre, 1951), 11.

81. Nathaniel Raymond, 'Cane Fires on a British West Indian Island', *Social and Economic Studies*, 16 (1967), 284.

82. Richards, 'Masters and Servants', 413-14.

Index

Index

Index

Index

Index

DATE DUE

Janet Momsen, Jan Brown
& Indiana University Press

BARBARA BUSH
Slave Women
in Caribbean Society
1650–1838

OLIVE SENIOR
Working Miracles
Women of the
English-Speaking Caribbean

Edited by
JANET MOMSEN
Women & Change
in the Caribbean